Foundations
of Psychological
Testing

Foundations of Psychological Testing

Sandra A. McIntire

Rollins College

Leslie A. Miller

Wilson Learning Worldwide

Boston   Burr Ridge, IL   Dubuque, IA   Madison, WI   New York   San Francisco   St. Louis
Bangkok   Bogotá   Caracas   Lisbon   London   Madrid
Mexico City   Milan   New Delhi   Seoul   Singapore   Sydney   Taipei   Toronto

McGraw-Hill Higher Education

A Division of The McGraw-Hill Companies

FOUNDATIONS OF PSYCHOLOGICAL TESTING

This book is printed on acid-free paper.

1 2 3 4 5 6 7 8 9 0 QPF/QPF 0 9 8 7 6 5 4 3 2 1 0

ISBN 0-07-045100-1

Editorial director: *Jane E. Vaicunas*
Executive editor: *Joseph Terry*
Editorial coordinator: *Lai Moy*
Developmental editor: *Susan Kunchandy*
Senior marketing manager: *James Rozsa*
Project manager: *Susan J. Brusch*
Production supervisor: *Enboge Chong*
Coordinator of freelance design: *Rick Noel*
Senior photo research coordinator: *Carrie K. Burger*
Senior supplement coordinator: *Candy M. Kuster*
Compositor: *ElectraGraphics, Inc.*
Typeface: *10/12 Times Roman*
Printer: *Quebecor Printing Book Group/Fairfield, PA*

Cover design: *Welch Design Group, Inc.*
Interior design: *Kathy Theis*
Cover image: *SuperStock, Inc.-Mad Rush by Diana Ong*

The credits section for this book begins on page 393 and is considered an extension of the copyright page.

Library of Congress Cataloging-in-Publication Data

McIntire, Sandra A., 1944-
  Foundations of psychological testing / Sandra A. McIntire, Leslie
A. Miller. — 1st ed.
      p.   cm.
  Includes index.
  ISBN 0-07-045100-1
  1. Psychological test.   I. Miller, Leslie A.   II. Title.
BF176.M38   2000
150′.28′7—dc21

99–29129
CIP

www.mhhe.com

Dedication

We would like to dedicate this book to our children,
Jonathan McIntire Hart, Zachary Kenneth Miller,
and Kia Anne Miller.

Leslie Miller would further like
to dedicate this book to her
husband, Robert Miller.

Acknowledgments

We could not have written this book without the assistance of various individuals. First, we wish to thank a former student of ours, Bernice Lupo, who, during the early stages of our writing, spent a significant amount of her time gathering information and reviewing our chapters for their readability. We would also like to recognize the contributions of our reviewers whose suggestions have resulted in improvements to the organization and content of this textbook. These reviewers include Jeffrey M. Adams at High Point University, Barbara Fritzsche at The University of Central Florida, Perry N. Halkitis at New York University, Douglas J. Herrmann at Indiana State University, Michael J. Lambert at Brigham Young University, Howard B. Lee at California State University (Northridge), Dennis R. Musselman at Humboldt State University, Bradley C. Olson at Northern Michigan University, Donald J. Polzella at University of Dayton, and Mary L. Wandrei at Marquette University. Finally, we would like to express our thanks to Lai Moy and Susan Brusch at McGraw Hill and Wendy Nelson who have been particularly helpful during the editing and production of this textbook.

Brief Contents

ix

Section Three
DEVELOPING AND PILOTING PSYCHOLOGICAL
TESTS AND SURVEYS

Secion Four
USING TESTS IN DIFFERENT SETTINGS

Contents

Section Two
PSYCHOMETRIC PRINCIPLES

Section Three
DEVELOPING AND PILOTING PSYCHOLOGICAL
TESTS AND SURVEYS

Section Four
USING TESTS IN DIFFERENT SETTINGS

Preface

Approximately 20 million Americans take standardized tests each year (Hunt, 1993). As a result, people are using psychological tests more than ever to make important decisions. For example, educators are using psychological tests to help determine who will be admitted to college, who will participate in special school programs (for example, gifted or remedial), and who will receive high and low grades. Clinicians are using psychological tests to help diagnose psychological disorders and plan treatment programs. Industrial/ organizational psychologists are using psychological tests to help select people for jobs, measure individual's job performance, and evaluate the effectiveness of training programs. Students are using psychological tests to gain greater insight into their personal interests, what major they should select, and to which graduate or professional schools they might apply.

In spite of their widespread use, psychological tests continue to be misunderstood and improperly used. At one extreme, these misunderstandings and misuses have led many people to believe psychological tests are useless and extremely harmful. At the other extreme, a substantial portion of the population believes that psychological tests are ideal and extremely precise instruments of measurement. More commonly, these misunderstandings and misuses have led to the misconceptions that psychological testing is synonymous with diagnosing mental disorders, that psychological tests can and should be used as a sole means for making decisions, and that anyone can administer and interpret a psychological test.

OUR MISSION

We have written *Foundations of Psychological Testing* in response to the growing need for an introductory textbook for undergraduate students. Specifically, we have written a text for undergraduate students new to the field of psychological testing and to the concepts of statistics and psychometrics that support its practice. Over the years, many of our students have lamented that textbooks do not always explain materials as clearly as a professor would during a class lecture. We have designed this text with those students' comments in mind.

Foundations of Psychological Testing provides a fresh look at the field of assessment and is written in a style that we believe will encourage student learning and enthusiasm. We focus on the basics of assessment and relate those concepts to practical situations that students can recognize. Although current texts on psychological testing are moving in this direction, we believe that some texts—especially at the introductory level—are written at a level too complex for undergraduates and contain more detailed discussion of certain technical issues than is necessary.

Students must understand the proper application of psychological tests in order to appreciate how to maximize their usefulness. The prevalent use of these tests in the decision-making process necessitates a vital understanding of their capabilities and weaknesses. One way we, as educators, can stress the importance of this understanding is by promoting the inclusion of psychological testing courses in the undergraduate curriculum of all colleges and universities and to encourage students to enroll in these courses. Many positive changes have occurred since the first college courses and textbooks on psychological testing appeared. Courses and texts now stress the applied nature of psychological testing and focus more attention on the relevance of this topic to all individuals. Clarifying the concepts associated with psychological testing in the effort to increase understanding and to dispel all related myths and misconceptions has become a primary goal for many instructors.

Our primary objective in writing *Foundations of Psychological Testing* is to prepare students to be informed consumers as test users or test takers—not to teach students to administer or interpret individual psychological tests. Therefore, we have taken care to provide information on the basic concepts, issues, and tools used in psychological testing and their relevance to daily life. We conclude our text with an overview of how tests are used in educational, clinical, and organizational settings.

Foundations of Psychological Testing concentrates on the essentials of psychological testing at an introductory level; instructors can supplement these basic concepts with specific types of tests. We have divided the book into four sections. The first section of this text consists of four chapters that provide an overview of the basics of psychological testing. It discusses, among other things, what a psychological test is, where to find information about psychological tests, who uses psychological tests and for what reason, the history of psychological tests, some concerns our society has about the use of psychological tests, and the ethical and proper use of psychological tests.

Section Two consists of five chapters that cover psychometric principles. These chapters discuss the procedures we use to interpret test scores, the concepts of reliability and validity, and the methods for estimating reliability and validity. Section Three consists of three chapters in which we describe the process of designing and pilot testing a psychological test and how to construct, administer, and use surveys. The fourth, and final, section of the text consists of three chapters that discuss how tests are used in three important settings: education, clinical practice, and organizations.

In our experience, students learn best when information is not only presented at a comfortable reading level and in a conversational format, but when information is previewed, discussed, reviewed, and reinforced in multiple ways. Our text reflects these learning strategies and contains a number of learning tools at both the section level and the chapter level.

- **Preview.** Each section opens with a preview of the chapters in that section and a concept map that pictorially displays the material covered in those chapters. Concept maps make information meaningful through displaying relationships. They are multipurposeful in that they can be used to outline lecture notes, to represent materials graphically for papers or presentations, and to reinforce conceptual comprehension. We intend these previews to provide two tools that appeal to two very different learning styles—visual and verbal—and to prepare students to receive the material to be covered.

- **Chapter-opening vignettes.** Each chapter opens with anecdotes that pertain to the chapter topic. These anecdotes provide students with means to identify with the material by relating them to their own experiences.
- **Key words and concepts.** Within each chapter, we have taken care to alert students to key words and concepts that are important for them to master. Key words are in boldface in the text and are defined within a logical structure to promote ease of comprehension. Key concepts are listed at the end of each chapter and again in the glossary at the back of the book.
- **Instruction through conversation.** In response to our students' cries of "Why couldn't the text have said it that way?" we have written each chapter the way our students best understand the information—at as simple a reading level as possible, and in most cases, in conversational style.
- **True to life.** The concepts in each chapter are illustrated by real-life examples drawn from the testing literature and from the authors' own experiences.
- **Boxes.** Each chapter contains the following boxes:
  - *For Your Information* boxes present relevant and interesting information about a particular topic.
  - *In Greater Depth* boxes provide more detailed information and calculations relevant to a particular topic.
  - *Summary Boxes* appear at varying intervals. These boxes summarize important, and often misunderstood, information discussed in the chapter.
- **Learning activities.** Activities for groups and individuals appear at the end of each chapter and can be assigned as in-class activities or homework.

We hope you will find this text to be an informative, interesting, and appropriate undergraduate introduction to the field of psychological testing. We encourage you to communicate with us. We look forward to your comments and suggestions for improvements to *Foundations of Psychological Testing.*

Sandra A. McIntire, Ph.D
smcintire@rollins.edu

Leslie A. Miller, Ph.D
leslie_miller@wlcmail.com

Overview of Psychological Testing

The first section of this text consists of four chapters that introduce psychological testing.

- **CHAPTER 1—Categorizing Psychological Tests**   In Chapter 1 we discuss what a psychological test is and the three defining characteristics of psychological tests. We identify the assumptions we must make when using psychological tests and the various ways we can classify psychological tests. We distinguish four concepts that students often confuse: psychological assessment, psychological tests, psychological measurement, and surveys. We also tell about the various resources including the World Wide Web that are available for locating information about psychological tests.

- **CHAPTER 2—Learning About Psychological Tests**   In Chapter 2 we discuss the importance of psychological testing and who uses psychological tests for what reasons. We review the history of psychological testing. We also examine some of the concerns our society has about the use of psychological tests.

- **CHAPTER 3—Using Tests Ethically and Properly**   In Chapter 3 we discuss the ethical use of psychological tests, including issues of privacy, anonymity, and informed consent. We introduce proper test use—focusing first on the responsibilities of test publishers, then on the responsibilities of test users. We then define the different types of test users and list the knowledge, skills, abilities, and other characteristics vital to proper test use.

- **CHAPTER 4—Testing With Computers and Testing Special Populations**   In Chapter 4 we discuss three important topics: computer-based testing, testing persons who are physically and mentally challenged, and testing college students with learning disabilities.

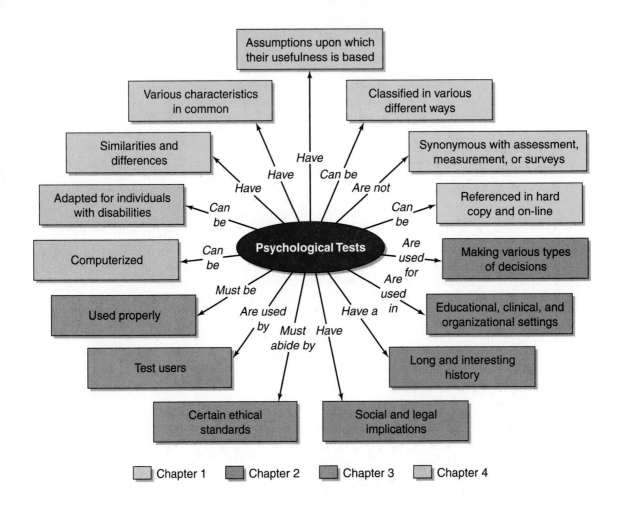

Categorizing Psychological Tests

"When I was in the second grade, my teacher recommended that I be put in the gifted program. The school psychologist interviewed me and had me take an intelligence test."

"Last semester I took a class in abnormal psychology. The professor had all the students take several personality tests, including the Minnesota Multiphasic Personality Inventory (MMPI). It was really neat! We learned about the different types of psychological disorders that the MMPI can detect."

"I had to take two college entrance exams this year because some of the colleges I applied to required that I submit SAT (Scholastic Assessment Test) scores with my application and some required that I submit ACT (American Collegiate Test) scores."

"How did you do on your psychology midterm? I thought it was easy. I was the first one done. Can you believe I only got a C?"

"This year I applied for a summer job with a local bank. They made me participate in a structured interview and an assessment center."

"Yesterday I took my driving test—both the written and the road test. I couldn't believe everything they made me do. I had to show the examiner where all of the gauges were in the car. I had to parallel park. I had to switch lanes and make both right and left turns."

If your professor were to ask whether you have ever taken a psychological test, like most students you would probably report the intelligence test you took as an elementary school student or the personality test you took in your abnormal psychology class. If your professor asked what the purpose of psychological testing is, you would probably say its purpose is to determine whether someone is gifted, psychologically disturbed, or mentally retarded. Intelligence tests and personality tests are psychological tests—and psychological tests are used to help identify giftedness and to diagnose psychological disorders and mental retardation. However, this is only a snapshot of what psychological testing is all about. There are many types of psychological tests, and they have many purposes.

In this chapter, we discuss what a psychological test is. We discuss the three defining characteristics of psychological tests and the assumptions we must make when using psychological tests. We also discuss the various ways of classifying tests. We tell you about the various resources (including the World Wide Web) that are available for locating information about psychological tests. We also distinguish four concepts that students often confuse: psychological assessment, psychological tests, psychological measurement, and surveys.

WHAT ARE PSYCHOLOGICAL TESTS?

Each anecdote at the beginning of this chapter involves the use of psychological tests. Intelligence tests, personality tests, interest and vocational inventories, college entrance exams, classroom tests, structured interviews, assessment centers, and driving tests are all psychological tests. Even the self-scored tests that you find in magazines such as *Glamour* and *Seventeen* (the tests that supposedly tell you how you feel about your friends, stress, love, and more) can be considered psychological tests. Although some are more typical, all meet the definition of a psychological test. Together, they convey the very different purposes of psychological tests. Figure 1.1 displays a continuum of some of the most and least familiar psychological tests. The terms in this figure will be defined for you throughout this text.

Similarities Among Psychological Tests

Psychological testing can be defined as "the process of administering, scoring, and interpreting psychological tests" (Maloney & Ward, 1976, p. 9). But what is a psychological test? All **psychological tests** require the performance of some **behavior**—an observable and measurable action (e.g., answering a question, putting together a puzzle). The behavior is used to measure some personal attribute, trait, or characteristic, such as intelligence, that is thought to be important in describing or understanding behavior. The behavior is also sometimes used to make a prediction about some outcome, like success on the job.

Differences Among Psychological Tests

Although all psychological tests require that you perform some behavior in order to measure personal attributes or predict outcomes, psychological tests differ in various ways. They differ in terms of the behavior they require you to perform, the attribute they measure, their content, their format, how they are administered, how they are scored and interpreted, and their *psychometric* quality (**psychometrics** is the quantitative and technical aspect of mental measurement). Much of this text will prepare you to evaluate the psychometric quality of psychological tests.

Behavior Performed

The behaviors the test taker is asked to perform vary by test. For example, a popular intelligence test, the Wechsler Adult Intelligence Scale–Revised (WAIS-R), requires test takers to, among other things, define words, repeat lists of digits, explain what is missing from pictures, and arrange blocks to duplicate geometric card designs.

The Thematic Apperception Test (TAT), a personality test, requires test takers to look at pictures and tell stories about each picture. The Graduate Record Exam

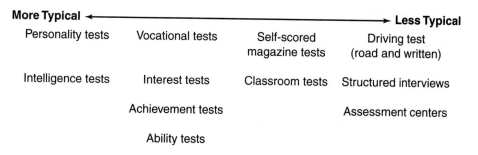

FIGURE 1.1. A continuum of psychological tests

(GRE), a graduate school admissions test, requires test takers to answer multiple-choice questions, as do many self-scored magazine tests and classroom tests. The "road portion" of an auto driving test typically requires test takers to start a car, drive in traffic, properly use turn signals, and parallel park. Assessment centers require job applicants to participate in simulated job-related activities, such as confrontational meetings with disgruntled employees, in-basket exercises, and manager briefings.

Attribute Measured and Outcome Predicted

The behaviors mentioned above are used to measure various personal attributes or traits that help us describe and understand behavior. For example, the WAIS-R asks respondents to repeat lists of digits to measure memory. This information is used to estimate respondent's intelligence. The TAT has you tell stories about a picture and uses that information to measure your personality. A driving test has you use turn signals and parallel park to measure your driving ability. These different behaviors are also sometimes used to predict an outcome. The SAT is used to predict success in college. The GRE is used to predict success in graduate school. Assessment centers are often used to predict success on the job. Some of the attributes commonly measured by tests are these:

- Personality
- Intelligence
- Motivation
- Mechanical ability
- Vocational preference
- Spatial ability
- Anxiety

Some of the outcomes tests, are commonly used to make predictions about, are these:

- Success in college
- Worker productivity
- Who will benefit from specialized services

Content

Two tests that measure the same attribute can consist of significantly different questions. Sometimes this is due to how the test developers define the attribute. For example, one test author might define intelligence as the ability to reason, whereas another might define it in terms of **emotional intelligence**—one's ability to understand one's own feelings and the feelings of others and to manage one's emotions (Gibbs, 1995). The difference in content could also be due to the theoretical orientation of the test. We will talk more about theoretical orientation and its relation to test content in Chapter 9.

Format

Tests can also differ in terms of their format: how they are administered and the style of questions they contain. A test can be administered in paper-and-pencil format (individually or in a group setting), on a computer, verbally, or in some other form. Similarly, a test can consist of multiple-choice items, agree/disagree items, true/false items, open-ended questions, a rating scale, or some mix of these.

There are also tests that ask respondents to perform some behavior, such as sorting cards or playing a role.

Scoring and Interpretation

Tests can also differ in how they are scored and interpreted. Some tests are completed on scannable sheets and are computer scored, some are scored by the person administering the test, and others are scored by the test takers themselves. Some tests generate results that can be interpreted easily by the test taker; the results of other tests can be interpreted only by a knowledgeable professional.

Psychometric Quality

Last, but extemely important, tests can differ in terms of their psychometric quality. For now, let us just say this: There are a lot of really good tests out there that measure what they say they measure and do so consistently, but there are also a lot of really poor tests out there that do not measure what they say they measure. A good test measures what it claims to measure (i.e., it is what we call *valid*); it consistently measures whatever it measures (i.e., it is what we call *reliable*); and, if appropriate, it includes an adequate group of scores to which a single test score can be compared (i.e., it has what we call *norms*). The concepts of reliability and validity are covered in Section II. Norms are covered in Chapter 5.

Summary Box 1.1
The Similarities and Differences Among Psychological Tests

SIMILARITIES	DIFFERENCES
• All psychological tests require an individual to perform a behavior (e.g., answering a question, sorting cards, making a right turn).	Psychological tests can differ in terms of
• The behavior performed is used to measure some personal attribute, trait, or characteristic (e.g., intelligence).	• the behavior they require the test taker to perform • the attribute they measure • their content
• This personal attribute, trait, or characteristic is thought to be important in describing or understanding behavior.	• how they are administered and their format • how they are scored and interpreted • their psychometric quality
• The behavior performed might also be used to make predictions (e.g., regarding job success).	

THE DEFINING CHARACTERISTICS OF PSYCHOLOGICAL TESTS

All psychological tests have three primary characteristics in common: They assess a representative sample of the behaviors that measure personal attributes or predict an outcome; they obtain the sample of the test taker's behavior under standardized conditions; and they have rules for scoring:

1. *A psychological test representatively samples the behaviors that are thought to measure an attribute or are thought to predict an outcome.* For example, suppose we were interested in developing a test to measure your physical ability. One option would be to evaluate your performance in every sport you have ever played. Another option could be to have you run the 50-meter dash. Both of these options have drawbacks. The first option could be very precise, but not very practical. Imagine how much time and energy it would take to review how you have performed in every sport you have ever played. The second option is too narrow and unrepresentative. How fast you run the 50-meter dash does not tell us much about your physical ability in general. A better method would be to take a representative sample of your performance in sports. For example, we might require you to participate in some individual sports (e.g., running, tennis, and gymnastics) and some team sports (e.g., soccer and basketball) that involve different types of physical abilities (e.g., strength, endurance, precision). This option would include a more representative sample. Remember, whether a sample is representative depends on how the attribute is defined.

2. *A psychological test includes behavior samples that are obtained under standardized conditions.* That is, the test must be administered the same way to all test takers. When you take a test, various factors can affect your score besides the attribute that is being measured. Factors related to the environment (e.g., room temperature and lighting), the examiner (e.g., examiner attitude, how the instructions are read), the examinee (e.g., disease and fatigue), and the test (e.g., understandability of the questions) can all affect your score. If everyone is tested under the same conditions (e.g., same environment), we can be more confident that these factors will affect all test takers similarly. If all of these factors affect test takers similarly, we can be more certain that a person's test score accurately reflects the attribute being measured. Though it is possible for test developers to standardize factors related to the environment, the examiner, and the test, it is difficult to standardize examinee factors. For instance, test developers have little control over what test takers do the night before they take a test!

3. *A psychological test has rules for scoring.* These rules ensure that all examiners will score the same set of responses in the same way. For example, intelligence tests have detailed rules for calculating an intelligence quotient (IQ). Teachers also use rules for determining exam scores. They usually report exam scores as either the number correct or a percentage (the number of correct answers divided by the total number of questions on the test). Essay questions should also be scored based on a plan for awarding or deducting points depending on what is included in the answer.

Although all psychological tests have these characteristics, not all exhibit these characteristics to the same degree. For example, some tests might include a more representative sample of behavior than others. Some tests, like group-administered tests, may be more conducive to standardized conditions than individually administered tests. Some tests have well-defined rules for scoring; others do not. For example, tests that include objective questions can have more explicit scoring rules, such as "If Question 1 is marked True, then score 2 points." Tests that include subjective questions, like short answers, would have less explicit rules for scoring.

ASSUMPTIONS OF PSYCHOLOGICAL TESTS

There are many assumptions we must make when using psychological tests. The following are what we consider to be some of the most important assumptions.

1. *Psychological tests measure what they say they measure.* This is also called *test validity.* If a test says that it measures mechanical ability, and we use it, we must assume that it does indeed measure mechanical ability.

2. *An individual's behavior, and therefore test scores, will remain stable over time.* This is also called *test reliability.* If a test is administered at a specific point in time, and then we administer it again at a different point in time (for example, 2 weeks later), we must assume that the test taker will receive a similar score at both points in time.

3. *Individuals understand test items similarly* (Wiggins, 1973). For example, when asked to respond "true" or "false" to a test item such as "I am almost always healthy," we must assume that all test takers interpret "almost always" similarly.

4. *Individuals can report accurately about themselves* (for example, about their personalities, their likes, their dislikes) (Wiggins, 1973). When we ask people to remember something or to tell us how they feel about something, we must assume that they will remember accurately and that they have the ability to report accurately on their thoughts and feelings. For example, if we ask you to tell us whether you agree or disagree with the statement "I have always liked cats," you must remember not only how you now feel about cats, but how you felt previously.

5. *Individuals will report their thoughts and feelings honestly* (Wiggins, 1973). Even if people are able to correctly report about themselves, they might choose not to do so. Sometimes people respond in the way they think we want them to respond, or they lie so that the outcome benefits them. For example, if we ask an individual if they have ever taken a vacation, they might tell us that they have even if they really have not. Why? Because we expect most individuals to occasionally take vacations and therefore we would expect most individuals to answer yes to this question. It is also conceivable that criminals might respond to questions in a way that makes them appear unhealthy so that they can claim they were insane when they committed a crime. When people report about themselves, we must assume that they will report their thoughts and feelings honestly.

6. *The test score an individual receives is equal to his or her true ability plus some error, and this error might be attributable to the test itself, the examiner, the examinee, or the environment.* That is, a test taker's score might reflect not only the attribute being measured, but might reflect such things as awkward question wording, errors in administration of the test, examinee fatigue, or the temperature of the room in which the test was taken. When evaluating an individual's score, we must assume that it will include some error.

Although we must accept some of these assumptions at face value, we can increase our confidence in the accuracy of the test scores by following certain steps during test development. For example, in Section III of this book, which covers test construction, we will talk about how to design test questions that are universally understood and that reflect, as much as possible, the attribute being measured. We will also talk about the techniques that are available to promote honest answering. In Section II, which covers psychometric principles, we will discuss how to measure a test's reliability and validity.

Summary Box 1.3
Some Assumptions of Psychological Tests

- Psychological tests measure what they say they measure.
- An individual's behavior, and therefore test scores, will remain unchanged over time.
- Individuals understand test items similarly.

- Individuals can report accurately about themselves.
- Individuals will honestly report their thoughts and feelings.
- The test score an individual receives is equal to his or her true ability plus some error.

TEST CLASSIFICATION METHODS

There are thousands of psychological tests available, and professionals refer to these tests in various ways. Here we discuss the most common classifications of psychological tests.

Sometimes tests are categorized as being tests of maximal performance, behavior observation tests, or self-report tests. Tests are also often referred to as being standardized or nonstandardized, or as objective or projective. Tests are also described in terms of the dimension that they measure. Last, tests are sometimes categorized based on subject.

Maximal Performance, Behavior Observation, or Self-Report

Most psychological tests can be defined as being tests of maximal performance, behavioral observation tests, or self-report tests.

- **Tests of maximal performance** require test takers to perform a particular task, such as making a right-hand turn, arranging blocks from smallest to largest, tracing a pattern, or completing mathematical problems. Test takers try to do their best because their score is determined by their success in completing the task. Intelligence tests, tests of specific abilities (such as mechanical ability), driving tests (road and written), and classroom tests are all tests of maximal performance.

- **Behavior observation tests** involve observing a person's behavior and how they typically respond in a particular context. In such tests, unlike in tests of maximal performance, many times people do not know that they are being observed and there is no single, defined task for the individual to perform. Many restaurants use this technique to assess a food server's competence in dealing with customers. Sometimes managers hire trained observers to visit their restaurants disguised as typical customers. In exchange for a free meal, the observers agree to record specific behaviors performed by the food server, such as whether the food server greeted them in a friendly manner. Other examples of behavior observations include documenting job performance for performance appraisals or clinical interviews.

- **Self-report tests** require test takers to report or describe their feelings, beliefs, opinions, or mental states. Many personality inventories are self-report tests.

Most psychological tests fit one of the above categories, and some contain features of more than one category. For example, a structured job interview (which involves asking all job applicants a standard set of questions) could include both technical questions and questions about the applicant's beliefs or opinions. Technical questions that are very well defined for the interviewee qualify the interview as a test of maximal performance. Questions about beliefs and opinions qualify the interview as a self-report test. The interviewer might also observe the interviewee's behaviors, such as the interviewee's greeting; this would qualify the interview as a behavioral observation.

Standardized or Nonstandardized

Often tests are referred to as standardized or nonstandardized. **Standardized tests** are tests that have been administered to a large group of individuals who are similar to the group for whom the test has been designed. For example, if a test is designed to measure the writing ability of high school students, then the test would be administered to a large group of high school students. This group is called the **standardization sample**—people who are tested to obtain data to establish a frame of reference for interpreting individual test scores. These data, called **norms,** indicate the average performance of a group, and the distribution of scores above and below this average. For example, if you completed the SAT, the interpretation of your score included comparing your score to the SAT standardization sample to determine whether your score was high or low in comparison to others. You might have scored above average, average, or below average. In addition, standardized tests always have specific directions for administration and scoring.

Nonstandardized tests do not have standardization samples and are more common than standardized tests. Nonstandardized tests are usually constructed by a teacher or trainer in a less formal manner for a single administration. For example, many of the exams you take in your college courses are nonstandardized tests.

Objective or Projective

Sometimes people make a distinction between objective and projective tests. **Objective tests** are structured and require test takers to respond to structured true/false questions, multiple-choice questions, and rating scales. What the test taker must do is clear; for example, the test taker must answer true or false, circle the correct multiple-choice item, or circle the correct item on the rating scale. The MMPI, SAT, and most classroom tests are examples of objective tests. To see sample items from such an objective test—the NEO Personality Inventory—see For Your Information 1.1.

On the other hand, **projective tests** are unstructured. They require test takers to respond to unstructured or ambiguous stimuli such as incomplete sentences, inkblots, and abstract pictures. The role of the test taker is less clear than with a standardized test. People who use projective tests believe that test takers project themselves into the task they are asked to perform and their responses are based on what they believe the stimuli mean and the feelings they experience while responding. These tests tend to elicit highly personal concerns. They are often used to detect unconscious thoughts or personality characteristics, and they might be used to identify the need for psychological counseling. The Rorschach Inkblot Technique and the Thematic Apperception Test (TAT) are two common projective tests. The Rorschach Inkblot Technique requires test takers to view inkblots and describe to

---

For Your Information   1.1
Sample Items From the NEO Personality Inventory

The NEO Personality Inventory is an objective, self-report instrument that is designed to tell individuals what makes them unique in their thinking, feeling, and interaction with others. There are two forms of the inventory, but both measure five broad personality dimensions: neuroticism, extroversion, openness, agreeableness, and conscientiousness. Test takers must indicate whether they strongly disagree (SD), disagree (D), are neutral (N), agree (A), or strongly agree (SA) with each of 240 statements. These statements are about their thoughts, feelings, and goals. Below we have listed a sample item from each of the five scales.

Neuroticism
Frightening thoughts sometimes come into my head.   SD   D   N   A   SA

Extroversion
I don't get much pleasure from chatting with people.   SD   D   N   A   SA

Openness
I have a very active imagination.   SD   D   N   A   SA

Agreeableness
I believe that most people will take advantage of you if you let them.   SD   D   N   A   SA

Conscientiousness
I pay my debts promptly and in full.   SD   D   N   A   SA

the test examiner objects or people they think the inkblots resemble. Chapter 14 contains more information on the Rorschach Inkblot Technique and the TAT.

Dimension Measured

Psychological tests are often discussed in terms of the dimension they measure. For example, sometimes we distinguish among achievement tests, aptitude tests, intelligence tests, personality tests, and interest inventories. We refer to these as dimensions because they are broader than a single attribute or trait level. Often these types of tests measure various personal attributes or traits.

Achievement Tests. Achievement tests are designed to measure a person's previous learning in a specific academic area (e.g., computer programming, German, trigonometry, psychology). A test that asked you to list the three characteristics of psychological tests would be an achievement test. Achievement tests are also referred to as tests of knowledge.

Achievement tests are primarily used in educational settings to determine how much someone has learned or what they can do at that point in time. Many elementary schools and high schools rely on achievement tests to compare what students know at the beginning of the year and at the end of the year, to assign grades, to identify students with special educational disabilities, and to measure students' progress.

Aptitude Tests. Whereas achievement tests measure the test taker's knowledge in a specific area at a specific point in time, **aptitude tests** are designed to assess the test taker's potential for learning or their ability to perform in an area in which they have not been specifically trained. Aptitude tests measure the product of cumulative life experience—or what one has acquired over time. They help determine what "maximum" we can expect from a person.

Schools, businesses, and government agencies often use aptitude tests to predict how well someone will perform or to estimate the extent to which an individual will profit from a specified course of training. Vocational guidance counseling might involve aptitude testing to help clarify the test taker's career goals. If a person's score is similar to scores of others already working in a given occupation, the test will predict success in that field.

The distinction between achievement tests and aptitude tests is not always so clear. Some tests, like the SAT, measure not only unstandardized educational experiences, but fairly specific and uniform prior learning. The verbal section on the SAT more accurately reflects measurement of an aptitude, whereas the math section more accurately reflects the measurement of achievement (the verbal and math section collectively form what is referred to as the SAT I). The SAT II (the subject tests) measures achievement in a particular field of study.

Intelligence Tests. Intelligence tests, like aptitude tests, assess the test taker's ability to cope with the environment, but at a broader level. Intelligence tests are often used to screen individuals for specific programs (e.g., gifted or honors programs) or programs for persons with mental disabilities. Intelligence tests are typically used in educational and clinical settings.

Interest Inventories. Interest inventories are designed to assess a person's interests in educational programs and job settings and thereby provide information for making career decisions. Because these tests are often used to predict satisfaction in a particular academic area or employment setting, they are primarily used by counselors in high schools and colleges. They are not intended to predict success, but only to offer a framework for narrowing career possibilities.

Personality Tests. Personality tests are designed to measure human character or disposition. The first personality tests were designed to assess and predict clinical disorders. These tests remain useful today for determining who needs counseling and who will benefit from treatment programs. For example, the Minnesota Multiphasic Personality Inventory (MMPI), which was developed in the late 1930s, is used to diagnose various clinical disorders.

Newer personality tests are designed to measure "normal" personality traits. For example, the Myers-Briggs Type Indicator (MBTI) is used by career counselors to help students select majors and careers consistent with their personality. Some industrial/organizational psychologists use the MBTI to help construct more effective work teams.

Personality tests can be either objective or projective. The MMPI and the MBTI are both examples of objective personality tests. Projective personality tests such as the TAT serve the same purpose as some objective personality tests, but, as you will recall, they require test takers to respond to unstructured or ambiguous stimuli.

Subject Tests

Many popular psychological testing reference books classify tests by subject. For example, *The Twelfth Mental Measurements Yearbook (MMY)* (Conoley & Impara, 1995) classifies thousands of tests into 18 major subject categories, and alphabetically within each category:

- Achievement
- Behavior Assessment
- Developmental
- Education
- English
- Fine Arts
- Foreign Languages
- Intelligence
- Mathematics
- Miscellaneous (e.g., courtship and marriage, driving and safety education, etiquette)
- Multi-Aptitude Batteries
- Neuropsychological
- Personality
- Reading Science
- Sensory Motor
- Social Studies
- Speech and Hearing
- Vocations

Reference books such as the *MMY* often indicate whether a test is (1) a test of maximal performance, a behavior observation test, or a self-report test; (2) standardized or nonstandardized; and (3) objective or projective.

Summary Box 1.4
Test Classification Methods

Psychological tests are often classified

- as being tests of maximal performance, behavior observation tests, or self-report tests.

- as being standardized or nonstandardized.
- as being objective or projective.
- based on the dimension that they measure.
- based on subject.

PSYCHOLOGICAL ASSESSMENT, PSYCHOLOGICAL TESTS, MEASUREMENT, AND SURVEYS

Students often think of psychological assessment and psychological testing as one and the same. Similarly, students often do not understand the difference between psychological testing and measurement, or between psychological tests and surveys. This section is designed to help you distinguish among these terms that are commonly used in psychological testing.

Psychological Assessment and Psychological Tests

Psychological assessment and psychological testing are both methods for collecting important information about people, and both are also used to help understand and predict behavior (Maloney & Ward, 1976). Assessment, however, is a broader concept than psychological testing. **Psychological assessment** involves multiple methods—such as personal history interviews, behavioral observations, *and psychological tests*—for gathering information about an individual. Assessment involves an objective component and a subjective component (Matarazzo, 1990), and psychological tests are only one tool in the assessment process. For example, a clinical psychologist might conduct a psychological assessment of a patient and as a part of this assessment might administer a psychological test such as the MMPI.

Psychological Tests and Measurements

Although their meanings overlap, *psychological test* and *measurement* are not synonyms. **Measurement,** broadly defined, is the assignment of numbers according to specific rules. The concept of measurement is represented by the lefthand circle in Figure 1.2. Psychological tests require test takers to answer questions or perform tasks so that their personal attributes can be measured. The concept of a psychological test is represented by the righthand circle in Figure 1.2. With psychological tests, test takers' answers to questions or their performances on tasks are

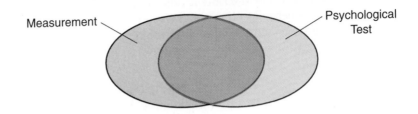

FIGURE 1.2. A comparison of measurement and psychological testing. The area of intersection represents samples of behavior expressed as numerical scores.

not initially expressed in physical units of any kind. Instead, scores are derived according to a predetermined method. In some cases, the end result of a psychological test is not a derived score at all, but a verbal description of an individual. For example, some personality tests have rules for scoring or summarizing information, but they do not produce overall scores. Instead, these tests yield profiles. The Myers-Briggs Type Indicator is an example of such a test.

Psychological tests can be considered psychological measurements when a sample of behavior can be expressed as a numerical score. This is represented by the overlapping section of the two circles in Figure 1.2.

You will find that many people use the terms *psychological test* and *psychological measurement* interchangeably. Although most psychological tests are measurements, not all psychological tests, strictly defined, meet the definition of measurement. Throughout the remainder of this text, we will follow the common practice of referring to all psychological tests as measurements, because most are; but keep in mind the distinctions we have drawn in this section.

Psychological Tests and Surveys

Surveys, like psychological tests (and psychological assessments), are used to collect important information from individuals. Surveys differ from psychological tests in two important ways. First, psychological tests focus on individual outcomes, whereas surveys focus on group outcomes. Psychological tests provide us with important information about individual differences and help individuals and institutions make important decisions about individuals. For example, a psychological test might suggest that a child is unusually intelligent and therefore should be placed in a gifted or honors program. Surveys, on the other hand, provide us with important information about groups and help us make important decisions about groups. For example, an organizational survey might suggest that employees are displeased with a company benefits program and that therefore a new benefits program is needed.

Second, the results of a psychological test are often reported in terms of an overall derived score, or scaled scores, whereas survey results are often reported at the question level by, for example, providing the percentage of respondents who selected each answer alternative. Of course, some surveys focus on individual outcomes and are constructed using scales. Such surveys approximate psychological tests. We have dedicated Chapter 12 to an in-depth discussion of surveys.

There are thousands of psychological tests. To choose an appropriate test for a particular circumstance, one must know the types of tests that are available and their merits and limitations.

Prior to the 1950s, test users had few resources for obtaining such information. Today, however, numerous resources are available. They all have the same general purpose—to help test users make informed decisions—but the information they contain varies. Some references give only general information about psychological tests, such as the test's name, author, and publisher. Others contain very detailed information including extensive test reviews and detailed bibliographies. Some resources include information about commercially published tests, and others include information about less-known, unpublished tests. Others include information about tests for particular groups (for example, children), or information on a broad range of tests for various populations. For Your Information 1.2 describes some commonly used reference books, including book title, a brief synopsis of the contents of the book, and a catalog number. Although different libraries might give the book different catalog numbers, the one we have supplied will direct you to the general area where you will find the book. If you cannot find a particular book, ask your librarian for assistance; if your library does not carry the book, the librarian can help you obtain it from another location.

Whether you are trying to locate tests that measure intelligence, self esteem, or some other attribute or trait, we suggest you begin your search with one of the reference books listed in For Your Information 1.2. The *Mental Measurements Yearbooks (MMY)* and *Tests in Print* are two of the most helpful references. Suppose you were interested in finding a test to measure intelligence in children. First you would look under *Intelligence* in the *Tests in Print* subject index. The subject index would list many different intelligence tests. To find the ones designed for children, you would turn to the more detailed test entries. The detailed entries tell you the appropriate test respondents (e.g., children or adults), the author and publisher, and other descriptive information. Once you have found one or more intelligence tests for children, you can consult the *MMY*. *Tests in Print* directs you to the volume of the *MMY* that contains additional information about the test including reliability and validity information and test reviews.

There are various other ways of locating information about psychological tests. For Your Information 1.3 discusses locating information about published tests using the World Wide Web. To read about how to locate unpublished psychological tests, see For Your Information 1.4.

SUMMARY

By now you should understand that psychological testing extends beyond the use of intelligence and personality tests. Anything that requires that you perform a behavior that is used to measure some personal attribute, trait, or characteristic or to predict an outcome can be considered a psychological test.

All psychological tests have three defining characteristics in common: They include a representative sample of behavior, they collect the sample under

Reference	Contents	Catalog #
Mental Measurements Yearbooks (multiple volumes)	Each volume contains a comprehensive set of consumer-oriented test reviews of new or revised tests. Most test entries include the name of the test, the intended population, publication dates, forms and prices, test author, and publisher. Most entries also include information about reliability and validity, one or two professional reviews, and a list of references to pertinent literature.	Ref LB 3051.M4
Tests in Print (multiple volumes)	These volumes contain a comprehensive bibliography of commercially available, English-language tests in psychology and achievement. Listings include the title of the test, intended population, publication data, author, publisher, foreign adaptations, pointers to reviews in the *Mental Measurements Yearbooks,* and a reference list of professional literature providing useful information about a specific test. Evaluative information is not included.	Ref LB3051.T47
Tests	This volume contains descriptions of a broad range of tests for use by psychologists, educators, and Human Resource professionals. Each entry includes the test title, author, publisher, intended population, test purpose, major features, administration time, cost, and availability. It does not contain information about test reliability or validity.	Ref BF176.T43
Test Critiques (multiple volumes)	These volumes contain reviews of some of the most frequently used psychological, business, and educational tests. Each review includes descriptive information about the test (e.g., author, attribute measured, and norms) and information on practical applications and uses, along with in-depth information on validity, reliability, and test construction.	Ref BF176 T418
Personality Test and Reviews (multiple volumes)	These volumes contain a bibliography of personality tests that are contained in the *Mental Measurements Yearbooks,* along with descriptive information about the tests and test reviews.	Ref BF698.5.B87
Tests in Education	This volume contains descriptive and detailed information about educational tests for use by teachers, administrators, and educational advisors.	Ref LB3056.G7.L49

Reference	Contents	Catalog #
Measures for Psychological Assessment	This volume contains annotated references to journal articles and other publications where measures of primarily mental health are described.	Ref BF698.5C45
Testing Children	This book describes tests available for use with children, including the knowledge, skills, and abilities measured by the test, the content, structure time required to administer, scores produced, cost, and publisher.	Ref BF722.T47
Test and Measurements in Child Development: A Handbook	This handbook lists unpublished measures for use with children. Detailed information about each measure is included.	Ref BF722.J64
Measures for Psychological Assessment: A Guide to 3,000 Original Sources and Their Applications	This guide contains annotated references to thousands of less-formal assessment devices developed and described in journal articles.	Ref 155.28016.C559

standardized conditions, and they have rules for scoring. When using psychological tests, we must assume that the test measures what its says it measures, that an individual's behavior and therefore test scores will remain stable over time, that individuals understand test items similarly, that individuals can and will report their thoughts and feelings accurately, and that the test score an individual receives is equal to her or his true ability plus some error.

Psychological tests can be classified in various ways: as being tests of maximal performance, behavior observations, or self-reports; as standardized or non-standardized; as objective or subjective. Tests are also classified according to the dimension they measure. There are other ways of classifying tests, but these are the most common.

A psychological test is only one of many tools available for psychological assessment. A psychological test can be considered a measurement when the sampled behavior can be expressed in a derived score. Psychological tests differ from surveys in various ways. For example, psychological tests focus on individual differences, whereas surveys focus on group similarities.

Various reference works and Web sites provide information about psychological tests. The *Mental Measurements Yearbooks* and *Tests in Print* are the most popular references. The APA, ERIC, and Buros Web sites are very popular sources of test information.

Computer technology now lets us connect to the World Wide Web to locate valuable information about psychological tests, such as:

- The names and addresses of test publishers
- The names of and descriptive information about thousands of psychological tests
- Reviews of psychological tests
- Information about how to select an appropriate test

Here we describe three of the most valuable Web sites.

AMERICAN PSYCHOLOGICAL ASSOCIATION

The American Psychological Association Science Directorate receives hundreds of letters and phone calls each year from people trying to locate tests. The APA does not sell or endorse specific testing instruments, but it does provide guidance on the testing resources that are available and how to find psychological tests. Some of the most frequently asked questions can be found at **http://www.APA.org/science/test.html.** One section of this Web site focuses on published psychological tests (those that can be purchased from a test publisher): how to locate such tests within a subject area, how to contact the test publisher, and where to find computerized testing materials and information. Another section of this Web site focuses on unpublished psychological tests and measures (those that are not available commercially). This section tells you how to find unpublished tests in your area of interest and informs you of your responsibilities as a user of unpublished tests.

ERIC

The Educational Resources Information Center (ERIC) Clearinghouse on Assessment and Evaluation Home Page, **http://www.cua.edu/www/eric_ae,** is the result of a joint project between the Educational Test-

ing Service (ETS) and ERIC. This Web site provides information on over 9,500 psychological tests and research instruments. Tests range from vocational and interest inventories, achievement and aptitude tests, to tests that measure managerial style or shyness or predict recidivism in released criminal offenders. For each testing instrument, you can access the title of the test, author, age/group for which the test is intended, what the test covers, how long it takes to administer the test, and the publisher's name and address.

From the ERIC home page you can also access *Tips for Test Selection* and *The Code of Fair Testing Practices.* The Code is discussed in more detail in Chapter 3. The Tips for Test Selection site provides detailed guidelines for deciding whether or not to use a specific test. This site includes the questions to ask about test coverage, reliability and validity, norming, test and item bias, before deciding to use a specific test. It also refers you to other sources.

From the ERIC home page you can access the *Pro-Ed Test Review Locator,* which contains information about which volume of the *Test Critiques* series (published by Pro-ED) contains information and reviews of the test you are considering. The *Test Critique* series contains information about how to administer, score, and interpret specific tests. It includes normative data, reliability and validity information, and criticisms of specific tests. This Web site also gives the addresses of hundreds of major test publishers.

BUROS

The Buros home page, **http://www.unl.edu/ buros,** contains user guides and articles about how to use the *Mental Measurements Yearbooks* and the *Tests in Print* series. From here, you can link to the Buros Test Review Locator, which tells you which publications, and which volumes, of the Buros Institute for Mental Measurements contain reviews and descriptions of the tests you are considering.

Tests in Microfiche contains information on a variety of educational and psychological tests that have been cited in the literature but are either out of date or have never been published commercially. There are over 800 tests on microfiche. Each year new tests are added. For more information you can write to Educational Testing Service Test Collection, Educational Testing Service, Princeton, NJ 08541, or call (609) 734-5686.

Health and Psychosocial Instruments (HAPI) is a computerized database of information on a variety of measures that have appeared in journals but have never been published for sale to the public. The database is updated each quarter and cov-

ers more than 15,000 instruments. Many college libraries gain access to HAPI through BRS Information Technologies. Some libraries maintain the database on CD-ROM. For more information, write to Behavior Measurement Database Services, P.O. Box 110287, Pittsburgh, PA 15232-0787.

PsycINFO Database, Psychological Abstracts, and PsycLIT are bibliographic databases that index published studies in psychology. By using key words you can find citations for articles in your area of interest (e.g., personality). The abstracts of the studies usually state whether the author developed a measure as a part of the study.

KEY CONCEPTS

achievement tests	measurement	psychometrics
aptitude tests	nonstandardized tests	self-report tests
behavior	norms	standardization sample
behavior observation tests	objective tests	standardized tests
emotional intelligence	personality tests	surveys
intelligence tests	projective tests	tests of maximal
interest inventories	psychological assessment	performance
	psychological tests	

LEARNING ACTIVITIES

1. Ask various professionals, in and outside of the psychology field to define what a psychological test is. Compare and contrast the different definitions. Compare these definitions to the definition provided in this textbook. Discuss why definitions might vary.

2. Construct a five-question quiz covering the material presented in Chapter 1. Give the quiz to your classmates (your instructor will determine the logistics of this). Have classmates discuss whether the quiz meets all of the characteristics of a psychological test. What were the strengths of your quiz? How could your quiz have been improved?

3. Select a psychological test that is mentioned in Chapter 1 or 2 or that is suggested by your instructor. Using the reference books that are available at your library and using the World Wide Web, collect as much of the following information as possible about your test. Keep track of where you found the following information.

- Name of test
- Attribute(s) measured or outcome predicted
- Author of test
- Publisher of test
- Target group
- Format of test
- Is it

    a. a test of maximal performance, a behavior observation, or self-report?
    b. standardized or nonstandardized?
    c. objective or subjective?

4. Select a couple of tests that measure the same attribute, characteristic, or trait. How are they similar? How are they different?

CHAPTER 2

Learning About Psychological Tests

"I have a 4.0 grade point average but I didn't do so well on the Law School Admissions Test (LSAT). To be safe, I think I will apply to some of the top-rated law schools as well as a few law schools that are less competitive in terms of test scores."

"They decided not to give me the scholarship I applied for. Because all of the applicants had similar grade point averages and great letters of recommendation, the scholarship review committee decided to give the scholarship to the applicant who had the highest SAT score."

"I told my academic counselor that I did not know what I wanted to do with my life. She referred me to the college career services office. A career counselor talked with me for a long time, asking me about my likes and dislikes and my hobbies. She had me take several interest and vocational tests. She used this information to help me focus on what direction I should take in terms of a major and career."

You have probably had to make some important decisions in your life, such as where to apply to college or what to major in. Likewise, others have probably made important decisions about you. For example, colleges may have decided to admit you, scholarship committees may have decided not to offer you a scholarship, organizations may have decided to hire you, or psychologists may have decided to place you in a gifted program. It is very likely that psychological tests were used to help make some of these important decisions.

In this chapter, we discuss the importance of psychological testing. We discuss who uses psychological tests and for what reasons. We also discuss the history of psychological testing, tracing the first psychological tests back to ancient China. Last, we discuss some of the concerns our society has about the use of psychological tests.

WHY IS PSYCHOLOGICAL TESTING IMPORTANT?

Psychological testing is important because people use tests to make important decisions—like those in the above anecdotes. The types of decisions that are made can be classified as *individual* versus *institutional* and *comparative* versus *absolute.*

Individual and Institutional Decisions

Psychological tests are used for individual decisions and institutional decisions. The person who takes the test uses the results to make an **individual decision.** For example, sometime in the future you might take the Law School Admissions Test (LSAT), which is required as a part of the application process for law school. Based on your score, you might decide to apply to certain law schools or none at all. Or perhaps sometime in the near future you might go to your college's career services center to discuss which career options you should explore (or perhaps you have done this already). As a part of the assessment process, a counselor might ask you to take an interest inventory. Based on the results of the interest inventory, you might decide to pursue a career in psychology.

Institutional decisions, on the other hand, are decisions that are made by the institution that administers the test or uses the results. The law schools that you apply to will look at your LSAT scores, among other things, to help them make a decision about whether they should admit you. Likewise, psychologists at a mental health clinic might use the results of a number of psychological tests to develop a treatment program for a patient.

Comparative and Absolute Decisions

Institutions make decisions using either a comparative or an absolute method. **Comparative decisions** are made by comparing test scores to see who has the best score. For example, imagine that, based on interviews and letters of recommendation, you are one of four finalists for a scholarship, and who gets the scholarship comes down to SAT scores. You scored 2 points lower than the top finalist. The other person gets the scholarship due to scoring the highest on the test. This would be a comparative decision because all of the SAT scores were compared and the highest scorer was selected. Or suppose you apply for a job that requires you to take a group of tests. Requiring you to score better than 75% of the applicants would be using the tests in a comparative manner. You must score in the top 25% in order to be considered for employment.

    Absolute decisions, on the other hand, are made by seeing who has the minimum score needed to qualify. For example, perhaps only those scholarship applicants who received a minimum combined score of 1,000 on their SAT were eligible for the scholarship. Or suppose that you apply for a job and are told that only the applicants who score 50 or better (out of a possible 70) will be asked to come in for interviews. This is an absolute decision, because you must score at least a 50 to be further considered for the job (see in Greater Depth 2.1).

IN GREATER DEPTH 2.1

Types of Decisions Made Using Psychological Tests

Individuals and institutions make decisions based on test scores. Institutions make decisions either by comparing you to other people or by determining whether you have the minimum to qualify.

An Individual Decision

- Based on your SAT scores, you decide to apply only to certain schools.
- Based on the results of an interest inventory, you decide to pursue a particular career.

An Institutional Decision

A Comparative Decision
- A college decides to admit you because your SAT score was better than the scores of most of the other applicants.
- An organization decides to hire you because you did better than everyone else in the assessment center.
- An elementary school suggests that a child be placed in a gifted program because an intelligence test placed her in the top 25% of her age group.

An Absolute Decision
- A college decides to admit you because you scored at least 1,000 on your SAT.
- An organization continues to evaluate your application because you scored the minimum score necessary to continue to be considered.

WHO USES PSYCHOLOGICAL TESTS
AND FOR WHAT REASONS?

Psychological tests are used by a variety of professionals in a variety of settings. Psychiatrists, psychologists, social workers, mental health counselors, industrial/organizational psychologists, career counselors, and many non-psychology-related professionals all use psychological tests, in a variety of educational, clinical, and organizational settings (see Table 2.1).

Educational Settings

Administrators, teachers, school psychologists, and career counselors use psychological tests in public and private schools, colleges, and universities. For example, college admissions administrators use psychological tests to help make admission decisions. Teachers use tests to determine whether children are ready for reading and writing programs and to assign grades. School psychologists use tests to determine eligibility for gifted programs, and to identify developmental, visual, and auditory problems for which a child might need special assistance. Career counselors use vocational and interest inventories to help students select a major area of concentration in college and a career that is consistent with their skills and interests. Chapter 13 is devoted to discussing how psychological tests are used in educational settings.

TABLE 2.1. Who Uses Psychological Tests and Why

Who	Where	Why
Administrators Teachers School psychologists Career counselors	Public schools Private schools Colleges Universities	To select students To place students in programs To assess student knowledge To counsel students To improve instruction To plan cirricula
Clinical psychologists Psychiatrists Social workers Counseling psychologists	Mental health clinics Residential programs Private practices	To diagnose To plan treatment programs To assess treatment outcomes
Industrial/organizational psychologists Human resource professionals	Organizations	To make hiring decisions To determine best fit within the organization To determine training opportunities To evaluate worker performance

Clinical Settings

Clinical psychologists, psychiatrists, social workers, and counseling psychologists and other health care professionals use psychological tests in clinical settings, such as mental health clinics, residential programs, and private practices. In clinical settings, tests are used for diagnostic purposes, to help plan treatment programs, and to assess the outcome of treatments. Chapter 14 is devoted to discussing the use of psychological tests in clinical settings.

Organizational Settings

Industrial/organizational psychologists and human resource professionals use psychological tests in organizations. Now more than ever, managers are concerned that the people they hire have the knowledge, skills, and abilities necessary to perform the job today and in the future. Poor hiring decisions are expensive to companies because they often result in lower productivity, increased training needs, and higher turnover. Therefore, many companies use psychological tests to help make decisions about whom to hire. Organizations also use psychological tests to place employees in the job they are suited for, to determine employees' training needs, and to evaluate worker performance. In Chapter 15 we will discuss how psychological tests are used in organizational settings.

Summary Box 2.1
Why Is Psychological Testing Important, and Who Uses Psychological Tests for What Reasons?

- Psychological testing is important because people use tests to make important decisions.
- Individual decisions are those that people make as a result of taking a test.
- Institutional decisions are those that institutions make as a result of an individual's performance on a test.
- Comparative decisions are made by institutions and involve comparing people's scores to see who has the best score.
- Absolute decisions are made by institutions and involve seeing who has the minimum score to qualify.
- Psychological tests are used by a variety of professionals in educational, clinical, and organizational settings for a variety of purposes.

- In educational settings, administrators, teachers, school psychologists, and career counselors use psychological tests to make variety of educational decisions, including admissions, grading, and career decisions.
- In clinical settings, clinical psychologists, psychiatrists, social workers, and other health care professionals use psychological tests to make diagnostic decisions, determine interventions, and assess the outcome of treatment programs.
- In organizational settings, industrial/organizational psychologists as well as other Human Resource professionals use psychological tests to make decisions in areas such as hiring, training, and performance evaluation.

THE HISTORY OF PSYCHOLOGICAL TESTING

Some scholars believe that the use of psychological tests can be traced back to 2200 B.C. in Ancient China. However, most scholars agree that serious research efforts on the use and usefulness of psychological tests did not begin until the 20th century. In Greater Depth 2.2 traces the history of the use of psychological tests up to the 20th century.

Intelligence Tests

Alfred Binet and the Binet-Simon Scale

Late in the 19th century, Alfred Binet founded the first experimental psychology research laboratory in France. In his lab, Binet attempted to develop experimental techniques to measure intelligence and reasoning ability. Binet believed that intelligence is a complex characteristic that can be determined by evaluating a person's reasoning, judgment, and problem-solving abilities. Binet tried out a variety of tasks to measure reasoning, judgment, and problem solving in his own children, as well as in other children in the French school systems.

Alfred Binet was successful, and in 1905, along with Théodore Simon, Binet published the first test of mental ability—the *Binet-Simon Scale*. This test was used to help Parisian school officials decide which children, no matter how hard they tried, were unable to profit from regular school programs (Binet & Simon, 1905).

Lewis Terman and the Stanford-Binet

Binet's work influenced psychologists across the globe and psychological testing took off. The Binet-Simon Scale was adapted for use in many countries. In 1916, Lewis Terman, an American psychologist, developed the *Stanford-Binet* test, an adaptation of Binet's original test. This test—developed for use with Americans age 3 to adulthood—was used for many years. A revised version of the Stanford-Binet remains one of the most widely used intelligence tests today.

The Weschler-Bellevue Intelligence Scale

By the 1930s there were thousands of psychological tests available, and psychologists as well as laypeople were debating the nature of intelligence (what intelligence is all about). The dispute over defining intelligence prompted the development of the *Wechsler-Bellevue Intelligence Scale* for adults, which provided an index of general mental ability (as did the Binet-Simon Scale) and revealed patterns of intellectual strengths and weaknesses. The Wechsler tests are now available in three forms—for adults, for children, and for preschoolers.

Personality Tests

In addition to intelligence testing, the 1930s brought an interest in measuring personality.

The Personal Data Sheet

In the 1930s the U.S. military wanted a test that could be used to help detect soldiers who would not be able to handle the stress associated with combat. As a

2200 B.C.E.: Xia Dynasty

Some scholars state that the use of psychological tests dates back approximately 4,000 years to 2200 B.C.E. when the Chinese emperor "Yushun" examined officials every third year to determine if they were suitable to continue in office (DuBois, 1970; Martin, 1870).

However, modern scholars of ancient China say that we have little archaeological evidence supporting these claims. Somewhere between 1766 and 1122 B.C.E. (Shang dynasty), the Chinese developed reliable writing systems (Bowman, 1989). Nowhere in the writings were there any hints that leaders were examined as described above. Even in 1115 B.C.E., when the writing systems became more elaborate, there were still no inscriptions or writings to suggest the existence of such an examination process (Martin, 1870).

200–100 B.C.E.: Late Qin, Early Han Dynasty

Most modern scholars of ancient China agree that royal examinations began around 200 to 100 B.C.E., in the late Qin (Ch'in) or early Han dynasties (Eberhard, 1977; Franke, 1960; Pirazzoli-t'Serstevens, 1982; Rodzinski, 1979). Hucker (1978) believes that the first written examinations in world history began in China in 165 B.C.E. when the emperor administered written examinations to all nominees. Pirazzoli-t'Serstevens (1982) also believes that this was the beginning of all examinations systems. Eberhard (1977), on the other hand, admits there may have been some assessment procedures before 165 B.C.E.

for selecting officials, who were probably tested more for literacy than for knowledge.

618–907 C.E.: T'ang Dynasty

Such examination systems seem to have been discontinued until the T'ang dynasty, when they become even stronger than ever (Bowman, 1989).

1368–1644: Ming Dynasty

During the Ming dynasty, the examinations became more formalized. There were different levels of examinations (municipal, county, provincial, and national) and the results of examinations were used to grant formal titles, similar to the university degrees that are granted today. Upon passing each level of examination, people were given more titles and were given increasingly more power in the civil service (Bowman, 1989). These examinations were distressful, and this distress became a part of Chinese culture and became a part of folk stories and the literature (poems, comedies, and tragedies). Nonetheless, this examination system seemed to work well. Today, many scholars believe that it kept talented individuals in the national government (Kracke, 1963) and it kept members of the national government from becoming nobility purely because of their descent.

Seeing the value of such examinations for making important decisions, Europeans and eventually the governments of the United Kingdom, the United States, Canada, and other countries adopted such examination systems.

Psychological Tests: From Ancient China to the 20th Century

1791: France and Britain

France initially adopted an examination system in 1791. Soon thereafter Napoleon temporarily abolished it. The system adopted by France served as a model for a system adopted by the British in 1833 to select trainees for the Indian civil service—the beginning of the British civil service.

1860s: United States

Due to the success of the British system, Senator Charles Sumner of Massachusetts and Representative Thomas Jenckes proposed to Congress in 1860 that the United States use a similar system. Thomas Jenckes's report, entitled "Civil Service in the United States," described the British and Chinese systems in detail. This report laid the foundation for the establishment of the Civil Service Act, which passed in January 1883.

20th Century: Western Europe and the United States

In 1879 Wilhelm Wundt created the first psychological laboratory, in Leipzig, Germany. At this time psychology was the study of the similarities among people. For example, physiological psychologists studied how the brain and the nervous system function, and experimental psychologists conducted research to discover how people learn and remember. Strongly influenced by James McKeen Cattell, an American researcher in Wundt's laboratory, psychologists turned their attention to exploring individual differences. Cattell and others realized that learning about the differences among people was just as important as learning about the similarities. They believed that by developing formal psychological tests to measure individual differences, we could help solve many of our social problems, such as who should be placed in remedial programs, who should be sent to battlefields, and who should be hired in particular jobs. At this time, scientists were particularly interested in finding a quantitative way of measuring general intelligence.

In the early 20th century, serious research efforts began on the use and the usefulness of various testing procedures. Research was conducted by scholars in the United States and in Germany, eventually leading to intelligence testing and the work of Alfred Binet.

result, American psychologist Robert Woodworth designed the *Personal Data Sheet* (PDS). The PDS was a paper-and-pencil psychiatric interview that required military recruits to respond yes or no to a series of questions that searched for mental disorders. One question asked, "Are you troubled with the idea that people are watching you on the street?" (as cited in Cohen, Swerdlik, & Phillips, 1996).

After World War II, Woodworth developed the *Woodworth Psychoneurotic Inventory*. Although the Personal Data Sheet is often referred to as the forerunner of the modern personality inventory, the Woodworth Psychoneurotic Inventory was the first widely used personality inventory.

The Rorschach and the TAT

Interest also grew in measuring personality by exploring the unconscious. With this interest came the development of two important projective techniques: the *Rorschach* and the *Thematic Apperception Test*. The Rorschach, which will be described in Chapter 14, was developed by Swiss psychiatrist Hermann Rorschach. The Thematic Apperception Test was developed by American psychologists Henry A. Murray and C. D. Morgan. Both tests were based on the personality theories of Carl Jung and are used today for personality assessment.

In the 1930s, there was also a need for **vocational tests.** The Public Employment Services needed tests because thousands of people had lost their jobs due to the Great Depression and thousands more were coming out of school seeking work. Because there were not enough jobs, people were being forced to look for new lines of work. As a result, there was a large-scale program to develop vocational aptitude tests to help predict how successful a person would be at an occupation before entering it. In 1947, the *General Aptitude Test Battery* (GATB) was developed by the Department of Labor to meet this need. The GATB was, and although it has been revised, it is still used today to make job referrals.

By the middle of the 20th century, there were many tests available, and they were being used by many to make important decisions about individuals. To help protect the rights of the test taker, in 1953 the American Psychological Association published the document *Ethical Standards of Psychologists* (American Psychological Association, 1953). Chapter 3 discusses these ethical standards.

For a time line of significant events in psychological testing in the 20th century, see Figure 2.1.

THE SOCIAL AND LEGAL IMPLICATIONS OF PSYCHOLOGICAL TESTING

Psychological testing is part of American culture, and it is big business. In the 1930s there were thousands of tests available (Buros, 1938). As we approach the 21st century, there are tens of thousands of commercially available psychological tests, as well as thousands of unpublished tests. Approximately 20 million Americans take standardized tests each year (Hunt, 1993). These tests are published by hundreds of test-publishing companies, who earn close to $200 million a year (Educational Testing Service, 1995).

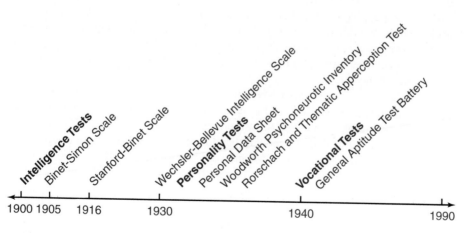

FIGURE 2.1. Significant events in the 20th century.

Psychological tests are used to make decisions, and they are meant to benefit people. Their widespread use suggests that, in general, they do serve their purpose. Nonetheless, psychological testing has always been controversial and probably always will be. Some of this controversy stems from people's misunderstandings about the nature and use of psychological tests. With education, some of this controversy is likely to disappear. Members of society are concerned that some types of psychological tests unfairly discriminate against certain racial and economic groups and that, as a result, members of these groups are not selected for educational programs or hired at the same rate as other groups.

This concern has influenced social movements and legislation as well as the standards of the psychology profession. Below we discuss some of society's concerns about psychological testing.

Intelligence Tests

The American public really began to express its concern when psychological testing became widespread in the 20th century. Much criticism was and continues to be targeted at intelligence tests.

Intelligence Testing in Education

It is well documented that middle- and upper-class White people, on average, score higher on intelligence tests than other economic and racial groups. Early in the 20th century, believing that this difference in intelligence was due to heredity, elementary schools began giving students intelligence tests and placing those with higher IQ scores in special academic programs and those with lower scores in more vocationally related programs (Hunt, 1993). Those who believed that intelligence was inherited had no problem using psychological tests in this manner. They believed that the people who do better on such tests are endowed by nature with superior intellects. If intelligence is indeed inherited, then using psychological tests in this manner is fair and in the best interest of individuals and society.

However, what if intelligence is not inherited, but the result of the environment in which one is raised? If this were the case, then all people would be born with the same potential, and, in general, only those who grew up in favorable backgrounds would score higher. Those who had disadvantaged backgrounds would score lower. In this case, the use of intelligence scores to determine an individual's educational opportunities is unfair. Hence, the public's concern over the use of intelligence tests.

Over the years, activists who believe that intelligence is determined primarily by environment have worked to eliminate what they consider to be the unfair use of intelligence tests. In the 1960s, in the heat of the Civil Rights Movement, activist groups demanded that schools abandon the use of intelligence tests. New York, Washington, D.C., and Los Angeles did just that (Hunt, 1993). For Your Information 2.1 discusses a court case in which, for exactly this reason, schools in California were ordered not to use intelligence tests for student placement. However, continued efforts to eliminate testing failed when it became apparent that the placement of slow learners and handicapped children in the same classrooms as normal and gifted children slowed learning.

Unless you live in California, you are probably not aware of the controversy about using IQ scores as a method for placing children in educable mentally retarded (EMR) classes. In 1979, in the case of *Larry P. V. Riles,* testimony suggested that IQ tests are biased against African American children. The plaintiff—the party bringing the suit—showed that six African American children who scored low on one intelligence test scored much higher on the same test when it was revised to reflect the African American children's cultural background. Although the African American children's first scores placed them in the range labeled "retarded," the scores from the revised test labeled them as "normal." In addition, evidence was given that there was a higher proportion of African American children in EMR classes than in the student body. This information caused the judge to rule that schools in California may not use IQ test scores to place African American children in EMR classes or their "substantial equivalent."

California abolished EMR classes, and in 1986, the same judge modified his ruling, banning the use of IQ tests to evaluate African American children referred for any special assessment. This ruling did not please all parents. For instance, Wendy Strong, mother of a 7-year-old, tried to get help for her daughter, Brianna, who had problems learning. Because her race was shown as African American on school records, school psychologists were not able to administer an IQ test to Brianna. Brianna's mother threatened to have her daughter's racial category changed so she could be tested. Such a change was possible, because Brianna had one African American parent and one White parent.

Eventually, another suit was brought by African American parents who wished to have their children tested. The Appeals Court ruled in 1994 that parents such as the Strongs were not adequately represented in the 1986 proceedings. Therefore, the court canceled the 1986 ruling, but upheld the original 1979 ruling.

Sources: Adapted from *Crawford v. Honig,* 1994; "Child Denied IQ Test Because of Her Race," 1994.

Students' performance on tests can be affected by their life experiences. To read about what one school in Florida is doing to expose students to different environments and raise their students' scores on standardized tests, see For Your Information 2.2.

Intelligence Testing in the Army

The U. S. Army was also using intelligence tests. Walter Lippmann (1922a–1992e), a popular newspaper columnist, criticized the Army's Alpha and Beta tests as having a great potential for abusing a process (psychological testing) that otherwise could be of great benefit to the army. Like others, he questioned whether intelligence tests actually measure "intelligence" and whether intelligence is determined by heredity—a question that came to be known as the **nature-vs.-nurture controversy.** Data collected using Army recruits suggested that mean intelligence scores of African American males were much lower than mean scores for White males. In addition, when scores of foreign-born recruits were sorted by their countries of origin, Eastern European recruits (e.g., Turks, Greeks, Poles, Russians) produced large numbers of scores that indicated a mental age of below 11 years—which for an adult is an indication of low intelligence (Yerkes, 1921). Political groups who resented the immigration of large numbers of families from Europe following World War I seized on these data to support their arguments that immigration was harmful to the United States.

Each year, thousands of elementary schools administer standardized tests to assess students' ability to read, write, and do math. Things are no different at Grand Avenue Elementary School in Orlando, Florida. However, their approach to preparing students for these tests is novel.

In 1995, mentors began working with fourth-graders who take the annual standardized tests. Mentors tutor fourth-graders in math and reading and expose the children to life experiences. Although all mentors meet weekly with fourth-graders, their activities vary. In one case, mentors took children on a trip to the beach. Children got to walk on the beach, feel the sand, and touch the water. Many of them did not know the water was salty, nor did they know the name of the ocean. One mentor had students use a compass to find the way to McDonald's. When they arrived at McDonalds, they ate lunch. Another mentor took students to the mall, but the children had to use maps to figure out how to get there. Another mentor took some students to a hotel. Students toured the hotel and got to see the presidential suite where pop star Whitney Houston once

stayed. Of course, the children had to use the hotel map to find the suite and other places included in the tour.

But why did this Florida school start using mentors? The school believed that many of their students were not doing well on some portions of standardized tests because the students could not relate to the material contained in the questions. For example, the reading and essay sections of standardized tests often require students to know about experiences that are more common to middle-class and upper-class families, such as going to the beach or taking out-of-state vacations. Ninety percent of the students at Grand Avenue come from low-income households. Most have never experienced an out-of-state vacation or a trip to the beach. The mentoring program is a way of leveling the playing field for students at this school. The mentoring program familiarizes students with what most middle- and upper-class students experience. According to the school, this approach seems to be working. Test scores were higher in the spring of 1996.

Source: Wertheimer, 1996.

Of course, for these immigrants the language and customs of the United States were unfamiliar, and their alleged stupidity was just lack of experience. In addition, the tests themselves and the instructions given during their administration were usually incomprehensible. The Army Beta tests, for example, required test takers to follow directions and perform a series of ballet movements that were highly confusing and distracting. Wood (1919) reports that fairly good results were obtained when orders were disobeyed!

The Army's Alpha and Beta tests were discontinued following World War I, but the nature-vs.-nurture debate continued. Its connection to psychological tests and intelligence raised public controversy again almost 50 years later, when the Civil Rights Movement was changing the American experience.

In 1969, Arthur Jensen published an article in the *Harvard Educational Review* that again pointed out a difference in average intelligence scores between African Americans and Whites—implying that Negroes were not as "intelligent" as Whites due to genetic factors. This time Jensen used later and more sophisticated tests than those the Army used in World War I, but the basic "pro-heredity" argument was still the same.

The debate that followed led professionals as well as the public to question how psychologists and test developers defined and measured intelligence. A number of psychologists (Eells et al., 1951; Harrington, 1975, 1976) also pointed out that the intelligence tests administered to African Americans had been developed for middle-class White children—whose experiences are different from those of children from other socioeconomic classes. Furthermore, Asa Hilliard (1984) questioned Jensen's underlying assumptions regarding an operational definition of race. He asked, "How do IQ researchers select 'African-American' or 'White' samples for comparison? Perhaps there is a secret method of selection, as no method has been publicly described" (p. 147).

This debate arose again in 1994 when Richard Herrnstein and Charles Murray published *The Bell Curve,* a book that reiterated many of the conclusions that Jensen drew in 1969. A review of their book in the *Scientific American,* Kamin, (1995) states:

> the caliber of the data in The Bell Curve is, at many critical points, pathetic. Further, the authors repeatedly fail to distinguish between correlation and causation and thus draw many inappropriate conclusions. (p. 99)

Aptitude and Integrity Tests

As with intelligence tests, the American public has expressed concern over the use of aptitude and integrity tests.

Aptitude Testing and the U.S. Employment Service

In the 1940s, the United States Employment Service (USES) developed the General Aptitude Test Battery (GATB), which measures a number of cognitive abilities and some aspects of manual dexterity. Like for intelligence tests, the average GATB scores of minority groups were well below those of the other groups. Because the USES and many of its state and local offices used GATB scores to make referrals to employers, this meant that more Whites than African Americans or Hispanics were being referred for jobs (Hunt, 1993). The amended Civil Rights Act made it illegal to use GATB scores in this way because national policy required giving the disadvantaged compensatory advantages (Wigdor, 1990). Rulings by the Equal Employment Opportunity Commission, and several court decisions, resulted in a solution that would be called "within-group norming" or "race norming." Based on within-group norming, test takers would be referred for jobs, based not on their raw test score but on where they ranked within their own racial or ethnic group. (We talk more about norms in Chapter 5). So, a minority who scored the same as a White would in fact be rated higher than the White. Employment services in 38 states used this "race norming."

Many psychologists were outraged about the use of race norming. They claimed it was a disgrace to the psychological testing industry, a distortion of a test's measure of job fitness (Gottfredson, 1991), and an illegal "quota system" that was unfair to Whites. In 1989, a study conducted by a committee of the National Research Council supported the use of race norming. However, the committee recommended that referrals by employment services be based not only on applicants' GATB score, but also on their experience, skills, and education. Several years later, race norming was outlawed, but not because it was unfair. In a struggle to pass the Civil Rights Act of 1991, congresspersons who favored race norming had to yield to those who did not. As passed, section 106 of the Civil Rights Act of 1991 prohibited employers from adjusting scores on the basis of race, color, religion, sex, or national origin (Hunt, 1993) when the sole purpose was to refer people for jobs or to select employees.

Aptitude Testing in Education

Another concern of Americans in the 1970s was a decline in Scholastic Assessment Test (SAT) scores (Haney, 1981). This time the concern was not with how "intelligent" Americans were, but how much American students were learning in public schools. A special panel was convened by the College Board and the Educational Testing Service (ETS), which concluded that a 14-year decline in average scores—almost 50 points in verbal scores and about 30 points in math scores—was due to two factors.

First, more students were taking the SAT, meaning that students came from more diverse backgrounds. Again, the implication was that the traditional test takers, middle- and upper-class White students, were more likely to make high grades. Second, the panel found that the type of educational experience students had in the late 1960s and early 1970s caused a decrease in performance on standardized tests. Among the reasons given were a "diminished seriousness of purpose and attention" and a "marked diminution in young people's learning motivation" (Haney, 1981, p. 1026).

Integrity Testing in Organizations

Integrity tests, or honesty tests, claim to measure an employee's honesty. Some such tests predict how honest an employee will be on the job. Employers have used these tests for many years both to screen applicants and to keep existing employees honest. Annually, integrity tests are given to approximately 15 million people (Gavzer, 1990), and their use is growing. Research by the Bureau of National Affairs suggests that their use is justified. The Bureau of National Affairs recently reported that employee theft costs American businesses upward of $25 billion a year (U.S. Congress, Office of Technology Assessment, 1990).

There are two types of **integrity tests.** One type tests honesty by directly asking employees about their attitudes toward honesty. Questions include these: "Do you think it is stealing to take small items home from work?" and "Do you always tell the truth?" Other integrity tests use a more personality-based measure that includes more indirect questions that are used to infer the applicant's attitude toward honesty. Questions include these: "How often do you blush?" "How often are you embarrassed?" and "Do you make your bed?" (U.S. Congress, Office of Technology Assessment, 1990).

Many labor groups oppose the use of such tests because they feel that such tests (1) are neither valid nor reliable and therefore falsely classify some honest people as dishonest; (2) are an invasion of privacy; and (3) adversely impact minority groups, eliminating higher percentages of them than of Whites from job opportunities (U.S. Congress, Office of Technology Assessment, 1990).

The American Psychological Association also expressed concern about the reliability and validity of such tests. After 2 years of research, an APA task force concluded that publishers of integrity tests have little information regarding whether integrity tests actually predict honesty (APA, Science Directorate, 1991). The APA urged employers to quit using the integrity tests for which little validity information was available. They suggested that employers instead rely on only those tests for which there is a preponderance of evidence in support of their predictive validity (APA, Science Directorate, 1991). Chapter 8 discusses predictive validity. For Your Information 2.3 discusses famous U.S. Supreme Court cases on testing.

For Your Information
Psychological Tests and the Law

2.3

When businesses began to use tests to decide which job applicants to hire, the public—particularly minorities and women—became concerned that tests were not being used fairly. Little was done to remedy this situation, however, until the Equal Opportunity Act was passed by Congress in 1964. Title VII of this act prohibited discrimination in hiring due to race, color, religion, sex, and national origin.

In 1971, Willie Griggs, an African American male who had been refused a job as coal handler at Duke Power Company, sued the company, charging that use of psychological tests had cost him a job for which he was qualified. The company hired only applicants who had a high school diploma or passing scores on the Wonderlic Personnel Test and the Bennett Mechanical Comprehension Test. Because these requirements excluded most African Americans, Griggs brought suit under Title VII of the Civil Rights Act.

The first court to hear the case ruled against Griggs, but the case was appealed all the way to the U.S. Supreme Court, where he won. The Supreme Court's landmark decision stated that any test that excludes minorities from employment must be shown to be related to job performance (*Griggs v. Duke Power,* 1971). As we will discuss in Chapter 4, the Civil Rights Act of 1964 and subsequent legislation and case law have significantly affected how psychological tests are used by businesses today.

Both the U.S. Congress and the New York state legislature became concerned about "truth in testing" in the late 1970s. The resulting legislation requires publishers of standardized educational tests to give test takers access to corrected test results after administration; to file information on test development, validity, reliability, and cost with the appropriate government agencies; and to give test takers information on the nature and intended use of tests before testing, along with a guarantee that their right to privacy will be respected (Haney, 1981). Many of these regulations reflect the ethical standards for testing adopted by the American Psychological Association and other groups. Since state and federal legislatures began passing laws concerning psychological tests, it has become not unusual for courts to try cases in which they pass judgment on how tests are used and interpreted.

In *Hobson v. Hansen* (1967), the Supreme Court ruled that ability tests developed using Whites as the test population could not be used to track African American students in a desegregated school. In Florida in 1981, 10 African American students who failed a statewide test of competency sued Ralph Turlington, the state commissioner of education at that time, causing Florida's testing program to be declared unconstitutional (*Debra P. v. Turlington,* 1981).

As you can see, psychological tests have sometimes been misused. When tests are not used properly by competent and sensitive professionals, the consequences can range from harming the individual who took the test to lawsuits against the person who misused the test outcomes. Like automobiles, psychological tests are marvelous developments made possible by our advances in scientific knowledge. They can be used to improve our lives, but when misused the consequences can be costly. Chapter 3 discusses ethical standards for responsible use of psychological tests.

Summary Box 2.2

History of Psychological Testing and Social/Legal Implications

---

- While the use of psychological tests can be traced to ancient China, the advent of formal psychological testing did not begin until 1905 when Binet published the first test of intelligence.
- The use and usefulness of psychological testing took off in the 20th century during which time various intelligence, personality, and aptitude tests were developed and used by a variety of individuals and institutions.
- Even with their widespread use by individuals and institutions, psychological tests are not without their critics.

- Many individuals are very concerned that psychological tests are biased and do not result in the correct institutional decisions.
- Psychological testing has influenced social movements and legislation in the 20th century.
- In the latter half of the 20th century, legislatures passed laws and courts have set case law that determine how psychological tests can and cannot be used.

SUMMARY

Psychological testing is important and is used by a variety of professionals and in a variety of settings. Testing is important because psychological tests are used to make important decisions about people. Based on test scores, individuals make decisions about themselves and institutions make decisions about individuals. Psychological tests are used in clinical settings, educational settings, and organizational settings.

Although the use of psychological tests might have originated in ancient China, the advent of formal psychological testing did not begin until Binet published the first test of intelligence. From then on, the value of psychological tests spread.

Even with the widespread use of psychological tests, they are not without their critics. Many people are very concerned that psychological tests are biased and do not result in the correct institutional decisions. Psychological testing has influenced social movements and legislation in the 20th century. The use of intelligence tests and their relation to the nature-vs.-nurture debate has been and continues to be controversial. In the latter half of the 20th century, legislatures have passed laws and courts have set case law that determine how psychological tests may and may not be used.

When tests are not used properly by competent and sensitive professionals, the consequences can range from harming the individual who took the test to lawsuits against the person who misused the test outcomes.

KEY CONCEPTS

absolute decisions
comparative decisions
individual decisions

institutional decisions
integrity tests

nature-vs.-nurture
controversy
vocational tests

1. Interview a professional who uses psychological tests (e.g., a career counselor, a clinician, an industrial/organizational psychologist, a professor) and individuals at organizations who use psychological tests (e.g., your college admissions office or Human Resource department). Find out what tests they use and what types of decisions they make based on the results of those tests.

2. As a class, classify the information collected in number one as (1) individual or institutional decisions, and (2) as comparative or absolute decisions.

3. Match the person(s) in Column A with their accomplishment in Column B.

Column A	Column B
Wilhelm Wundt	A. Designed a test to identify mentally retarded French schoolchildren
	B. Founded the first experimental psychology laboratory in France
Henry A. Murray and C. D. Morgan	C. Developed the Personal Data Sheet (PDS)
Alfred Binet	D. Founded the first psychological laboratory in Germany
Robert Woodworth	E. Developed a Psychoneurotic Inventory that was the first widely used personality inventory
	F. Developed the Thematic Apperception Test (TAT)
Lewis Terman	G. Developed the Stanford-Binet Scale

CHAPTER 3

Using Tests Ethically and Properly

"I'm an engineering major. Last week I took an interest inventory, and my skill and interest scores indicated that I should avoid engineering as a career. Instead, I scored higher in the careers that help people. I've wasted three years of college!"

"My roommate is taking a Personality class. Last week, after a long night of studying, she decided to give me a personality test. I came out neurotic. Since then, I've been too upset to go to class."

"My company hired a psychologist to give personality tests to all employees. Instead of using information about each individual's personality type to train employees how to work together, my boss went around asking people to transfer to other areas, telling them that he did not want certain personality types working in his office."

"I filled out an intelligence test in a popular woman's magazine. According to the test, I have an IQ of 85. I know I'm not a genius, but now I know I will never get into college."

"Can I please get a copy of the Weschler Intelligence Test? My son is going to be taking the test next week to determine if he should be put in a gifted program. I'd like to show him the test and give him a little experience."

You might have personally experienced or heard of situations like those described in the anecdotes that open this chapter. At first you might not see anything wrong; however, knowledgeable test users and consumers know that each one of the anecdotes illustrates a potential misuse of psychological tests.

Psychological tests are an essential tool of many professionals in a variety of settings, such as education, clinical psychology, and business. Unfortunately, misuse, by those administering and taking tests, is a chronic and disturbing problem that can harm individuals and society. For individuals, test misuse can result in inappropriate decisions and improper diagnoses. For society, test misuse reflects poorly on professional organizations and properly trained test users, and the resultant inappropriate decisions cost money and missed opportunities.

Test misuse often is unintentional, arising from inadequate technical knowledge and misinformation about proper testing procedures. To prevent test misuse, psychologists have developed technical and professional standards for the construction, evaluation, administration, and dissemination of psychological tests.

Test misuse can be overcome by understanding these technical and professional standards. This chapter introduces you to these issues. This chapter will enable you, at a very general level, to evaluate your own experience taking psychological tests, such as the Scholastic Assessment Test (SAT) or the American College Test (ACT) to gain entrance into college, various intelligence tests to determine your eligibility for gifted or honors programs, and classroom tests to determine your mastery of course material. Additionally, this chapter will help you evaluate other testing situations and perhaps to become an informed test examiner yourself.

To enhance your understanding of proper test use, we begin by introducing you to a very important component: ethical standards in psychological testing. We discuss what ethics are, the history of ethical standards, and specific ethical standards for psychological testing, including issues of privacy, anonymity, and informed consent. Along the way, we will introduce you to various publications that present ethical guidelines. Second, we introduce you to proper test use, focusing first on the responsibilities of test publishers, then on the responsibilities of test users. Finally, we define the different types of test users and provide you with a list of the knowledges, skills, abilities, and other characteristics necessary for proper test use.

ETHICAL STANDARDS
FOR PSYCHOLOGICAL TESTING

One day in 1954, Charlotte Elmore became concerned because her 6-year-old son, Michael, was not receiving the same instruction in reading as her neighbor's daughter. Both attended first grade at the same school, but Michael's class was only starting reading lessons, and the little girl was already reading to her parents.

Mrs. Elmore contacted the school principal, who made a shocking revelation. The school had administered an intelligence test to all students. Michael's score, the principal said, indicated that he was borderline retarded. Furthermore, the principal informed her, Michael would need to repeat first grade. When Mrs. Elmore asked why she and her husband had not been told of Michael's score, the principal explained that most parents have difficulty really understanding intelligence tests and that it was best for their children if parents leave such matters to school authorities. When the Elmores asked to have Michael retested, the principal refused, explaining that scores rarely change more than a few points.

Fortunately, the Elmores put more faith in their observations of Michael and his accomplishments than they did in the school's interpretation of one test score. They had Michael retested by an outside psychologist and his IQ score was 90. Although 100 is the mean of most intelligence tests, 90 is not considered low. (We will explain this concept in more detail in Section II, Chapter 5.) The outside psychologist did not agree that Michael needed to repeat first grade, and he contacted the principal on the Elmores' behalf. Eventually, with the help of remedial reading classes and a change of schools, Michael caught up with his classmates.

In high school, Michael enrolled in college preparatory classes, earned A's and B's, and became a member of the honor society. In 1965, he was accepted as a premedical student at Indiana University. While he was in medical school, he took another intelligence test and earned a score of 126—a "superior" score. He completed medical school and began practicing medicine as a gastroenterologist—a doctor who treats diseases of the digestive tract (Elmore, 1988).

Although Michael Elmore's story has a happy ending, a number of practices on the part of his elementary school could have prevented Michael from reaching his full potential and becoming a successful contributor to society. In this section, we will examine the ethical standards that today guide psychologists and others who use psychological tests and seek to protect children like Michael Elmore from test misuse.

What Are Ethics?

Whenever professionals offer advice or intervene in the affairs of individuals, questions arise concerning honesty, fairness, and conflicts of interest. **Ethics** refers to issues or practices that influence the decision-making process in terms of "doing the right thing." In other words, ethics reflect the morals—what is considered right or wrong—of a society or culture.

Most professional societies, including the American Psychological Association, have a set of professional practice guidelines, or codes, known as **ethical standards.** Members of professional societies vote on and adopt these codes after a good deal of discussion and debate. As you can imagine, it is often difficult for everyone to agree on the right thing to do.

For example, psychologists and other professionals often disagree about how to interpret a client's right to privacy. Should clients who have committed aggressive or sexually abusive acts be protected from legal inquiry about their psychological history? What about clients who are likely to harm themselves or others in the immediate future? Such situations pose **ethical dilemmas**—problems for which there are no clear or agreed-upon moral solutions.

For violations of ethical standards, there are various penalties—including expulsion from the society. Ethical standards are not laws established by governmental bodies. No one can be tried or sued in a court of law for violating an ethical standard. Rather, these standards are statements by professionals regarding what they believe are appropriate and inappropriate behaviors for anyone practicing their profession.

Psychological testing plays an important role in individuals' opportunities for education, employment, and mental health treatment. When tests are used improperly, there is great potential for harm to individuals, often without the victims being aware of it. Therefore, ethical use of psychological tests must be of paramount importance to psychologists and other professionals who use or rely on them.

A number of organizations, including the executive branch of the U.S. government, have issued codes of ethics or guidelines regarding test use. The largest and most influential professional society to do so is the American Psychological Association.

The History of Ethical Standards

Although the history of psychological testing reaches back into antiquity, the formulation of standards for proper use of tests was much longer in coming. In 1953, the American Psychological Association published the first ethical standards for psychologists. This document, called *Ethical Standards of Psychologists,* was the result of much discussion and study by the APA committee that wrote them as well as many other members of the APA.

Since then, the ethical principles of the American Psychological Association have been revised and updated. A portion of the most current set of ethical principles approved and adopted by the members of the American Psychological Association is presented in Appendix B of this text. The entire APA document consists of a preamble, six general principles that are goals to guide psychologists toward the highest ideals of psychology, and eight sets of ethical standards (APA, 1992). The eight sets of ethical standards are:

1. General Standards
2. Evaluation, Assessment, or Intervention
3. Advertising and Other Public Statement
4. Therapy

5. Privacy and Confidentiality
6. Teaching, Training Supervision, Research, and Publishing
7. Forensic Activities
8. Resolving Ethical Issues

Although the second set of standards—Evaluation, Assessment, or Intervention—is most directly related to the use of psychological tests, the principles in a number of areas are relevant for test users. For instance, compliance with the fifth set of standards—Privacy and Confidentiality—is critical to ethical testing.

Because testing is an important and often misunderstood area of psychology, the APA has also addressed and published ethical standards for a number of specific areas, including numerous documents on ethical issues that relate to psychological testing and assessment. For Your Information 3.1 lists those documents and their dates of publication.

Perhaps the most important of these documents is the *Standards for Educational and Psychological Testing* (APA, 1985), which was prepared by the APA in collaboration with the American Educational Research Association and the Na-

---

For Your Information   3.1
American Psychological Association Publications
on Ethics in Psychological Testing

Psychologists understand the importance of ethical and competent use of psychological tests. They are so concerned that tests be used correctly that the APA has expended a great deal of time and energy to provide specific details about proper test use. Each of the following publications was the result of the work of a committee that thoroughly investigated the area of concern before drafting standards and bringing them to the general membership for approval.

- *Technical Recommendations for Psychological Tests and Diagnostic Techniques* (APA, 1954)
- *Standards for Educational and Psychological Tests and Manuals* (APA, 1966b)
- "Automated Test Scoring and Interpretation Practices" (APA, 1966a)
- Standards for Educational and Psychological Tests (1974)
- *Principles for the Validation and Use of Personnel Selection Procedures* (APA, Division of I/O Psychology, 1980)
- "Specialty Guidelines for the Delivery of Services by Clinical Psychologists" (APA, Committee on Professional Standards, 1981a)
- "Specialty Guidelines for the Delivery of Services

by Counseling Psychologists" (APA, Committee on Professional Standards, 1981b)
- "Specialty Guidelines for the Delivery of Services by Industrial/Organizational Psychologists" (APA, Committee on Professional Standards, 1981c)
- "Specialty Guidelines for the Delivery of Services by School Psychologists" (APA, Committee on Professional Standards, 1981d)
- *Ethical Principles of Psychologists* (APA, 1981)
- Ethical Principles in the Conduct of Research with Human Participants (1982)
- *Standards for Educational and Psychological Testing* (APA, 1985)
- *Guidelines for Computer-Based Tests and Interpretations* (APA, 1986)
- Casebook on Ethical Principles of Psychologists (1987)
- "General Guidelines for Providers of Psychological Services" (APA, 1987)
- Principles for the Validation and Use of Personnel Selection Procedures (1987)
- "Ethical Principles of Psychologists and Code of Conduct" (APA, 1992)
- Standards for Educational and Psychological Testing (APA, 1985)

tional Council of Measurement in Education. The current edition of *Standards* has been under discussion and revision for more than 3 years. It summarizes the recommended practices for test construction, administration, and interpretation.

Another important document is the *Code of Fair Testing Practices in Education* (APA, 1988), which was developed in 1988 by a consortium of professional organizations and test publishers known as the Joint Committee on Testing Practices. This document, reproduced in Appendix C, describes the obligations of educational test developers and test users and will guide much of our discussion in the next section.

A number of professional associations related to the field of psychology have also expressed their concern about ethical standards. For instance, the National Association of School Psychologists established ethical standards in 1984 that address the selection, use, and interpretation of psychological tests in elementary and secondary schools (National Association of School Psychologists, 1984). In the field of counseling, some practitioners (Herlihy & Remley, 1995) have expressed dismay at the large number of sources of practice standards, ranging from the ethical codes of various associations to national certification boards and state licensure laws. To read about the rights that are accorded to test takers by the *Standards* and other ethical codes, see In Greater Depth 3.1.

Privacy, Anonymity, and Informed Consent

The many codes of conduct we have described cover a multitude of ethical issues and concerns. Their common purpose is to protect the rights of individuals who participate in psychological testing. The "Ethical Principles of Psychologists and Code

---

IN GREATER DEPTH 3.1

The Rights of Test Takers

Standards for Educational and Psychological Testing (APA, 1985) gives the following rights to people who take psychological tests.

A. *The right to informed consent.* Test takers have a right to know why they are being tested, how the test will be used, and how the test scores will be interpreted and used.

B. *The right to know and understand test results.* Test takers have a right to know their test results—not just their scores, but what the scores mean. Because some test results might affect the test taker's self-esteem or behavior, these results should be explained sensitively by a qualified professional.

C. *Protection from invasion of privacy.* Individuals may not be required to take psychological tests or be subjected to any other form of unwanted collection of personal information.

D. *Protection from stigma.* The least stigmatizing labels should be assigned when reporting test results. Although many tests suggest clinical diagnoses (e.g., *feebleminded, addictive personality*), these clinical terms can be harmful to individuals when used by family and friends. It is important that test results be provided to individuals and families in terms they understand and that facilitate positive growth and development.

E. *The right to confidentiality.* Individuals have a right to expect that none of their personal information or test scores will be disclosed to anyone without their consent. Test users must also take all necessary precautions to safeguard records by storing them in a secure location.

Source: Adapted from Cohen, Swerdlik, & Phillips, 1996.

of Conduct" (APA, 1992) affirm the importance of respect for individuals, establish the need to safeguard individual dignity and privacy, and condemn unfair discriminatory practices. How these goals are accomplished will be described in detail as we address the various topics in this chapter. However, the issues of privacy, anonymity, and informed consent are so important that they apply in all situations.

Privacy

The concepts of individual freedom and privacy are integral to the cultural heritage of Americans. The document Ethical Principles of Psychologists (APA, 1992) affirms the rights of individuals to privacy, confidentiality, and self-determination. **Confidentiality** means that individuals are assured that all personal information they disclose will be kept private and not disclosed without their explicit permission. In the case of minors or individuals who are unable to make personal decisions, the consent of a parent or guardian must be obtained before test results or interpretations can be disclosed to others.

Sometimes test users are tempted to violate ethical standards regarding confidentiality. For instance, managers might believe it is in the best interest of their company for them to have psychological information about employees. Teachers might seek students' test scores with the good intention of understanding a student's performance problems. Sometimes researchers simply are careless and leave files unattended that contain test scores and personal information about research participants. APA ethical standards emphasize, however, that regardless of good intentions or the apparently trivial nature of data collected, psychologists should not disclose information about a test taker without that individual's consent.

Anonymity

Anonymity is the practice of administering tests or obtaining information without obtaining the identity of the participant. Researchers believe that persons who complete surveys or tests anonymously often provide more honest information about themselves. On the other hand, it is often important for researchers to identify test takers in order to correlate test scores with other variables. Hence there is a strong temptation for investigators to code test materials or surveys in such a way that participants can be identified without the participants' knowledge. Such practices violate ethical standards that assure individual privacy.

The document "Ethical Principles of Psychologists and Code of Conduct" (APA, 1992) acknowledges that other obligations (e.g., knowledge that failure to disclose information would result in danger to others) can lead to a conflict among ethical standards. For most psychologists and test administrators, however, there are no ethical reasons for violating rights of confidentiality and anonymity.

Informed Consent

Individuals have the right of self-determination. This concept means that individuals are entitled to full explanations of why they are being tested, how the test data will be used, and what the test results mean. Such explanations, referred to as **informed consent,** should be communicated in language the test taker can understand. In the case of minors or persons of limited cognitive ability, both the test taker and his or her parent or guardian must give informed consent. In the case of Michael Elmore, the school administrators did not inform his parents that they would be administering the intelligence test, and they assumed that the Elmores were not capable of understanding the test and its implications.

It is important to note that "parental permission" is not the same as informed consent. It is the psychologist's responsibility to confirm that both the child and the parent understand to the best of their ability the implications of psychological testing before any test is administered. In addition, both child and parent are entitled to an explanation of the scores of all tests.

Summary Box 3.1
Ethical Standards for Psychological Testing

- Ethics reflect the morals—what is considered right or wrong—of a society or culture.
- Most professional societies have a set of professional practice guidelines known ethical standards.
- There are penalties for violating these ethical standards.
- In 1953 the American Psychological Association published the first ethical standards for psychologists—the document *Ethical Standards of Psychologists.*
- There are many publications on ethics in psychological testing.
- The purpose of these ethical standards is to protect the rights of individuals who are the recipients of psychological testing.
- Most notably, test takers have rights to privacy, anonymity, and informed consent.

APPROPRIATE USE OF PSYCHOLOGICAL TESTS

Psychological testing can be extremely useful for clinicians, counselors, teachers, managers, and others. Inappropriate or incompetent use of testing—as in the case of Michael Elmore—can have undesirable and harmful consequences for individuals. The proper use of tests is so important that we have dedicated the next section to discussing it in detail. In this section, we discuss the responsibilities of test publishers and test users to ensure proper test use.

Responsibilities of the Test Publisher

Test publishers have ethical and professional standards that they must follow. Publishers must sell psychological tests only to qualified users, must truthfully market psychological tests, and must provide comprehensive test manuals for each psychological test.

The Sale of Psychological Tests

Test publishers have requirements to ensure that only qualified persons purchase psychological tests (APA, 1985). Not all publishing firms place the same restrictions on the sale of psychological tests, but in general, publishers often require purchasers to have advanced coursework in psychology. Most publishers have detailed requirements depending on the type of psychological test being purchased. For example, some publishers use a three-level test classification system developed by the American Psychological Association (1954) to determine who is qualified to purchase specific tests. The differences between the levels reflect how much knowledge the test user must have of both **psychometrics**—the quantitative and technical aspect of mental measurement—and psychology.

1. *Level A tests* have minimal requirements. Tests in this level can be administered, scored, and interpreted by nonpsychologists, with the aid of the manual and general information about the purpose of the testing. They are usually achievement tests.
2. *Level B tests* have more stringent requirements. To purchase tests in this level, one must understand test construction and use, and have advanced coursework in areas such as statistics, individual differences, psychology of adjustment, personnel psychology, and guidance. Such tests are usually aptitude tests.
3. *Level C tests* have very strict requirements. To purchase tests in this level, one must have an advanced degree, substantial understanding of testing and supporting psychological fields, and supervised experience using the test. These tests usually are projective personality tests and individual intelligence tests.

Figures 3.1 and 3.2 show the test purchasing requirements of two publishers, Psychological Assessment Resources (PAR), Inc., and NCS Assessments. Note that both publishers use the three-level classification system we just mentioned, but their order is reversed. In addition, NCS Assessments includes a fourth, "M"

PAR, Inc. sells psychological tests and materials only to qualified professional users in accordance with the *Standards for Educational and Pyschological Testing* and PAR's qualification guidelines. Orders must include the name of a qualified individual who will be responsible for the use of the ordered materials. (Please complete the qualification form on the back of the order form if this is your first order with PAR.)

Qualification Level A—No special qualifications required although range of materials eligible for purchase is limited.

Qualification Level B—At least a B.A. in psychology, Counseling, or a closely related field, and relevant training or coursework in the interpretation of psychological tests and measurement at an accredited college or university; OR verification of membership in a professional association recognized to require training and experience in the ethical and competent use of psychological tests; OR licensed or certified by an agency which does the same.

Qualification Level C*—A graduate degree in Psychology, Education, or closely related field that includes advanced training in the administration and interpretation of psychological tests; OR membership in a professional association that requires training and experience in the ethical and competent use of psychological tests, OR licensed or certified by an agency which does the same.

*RIAP purchasers must additionally demonstrate knowledge of projective techniques.

FIGURE 3.1. Qualifications to purchase PAR materials

(Photocopy as needed)

First Order?

Please establish your qualification level for this and future purchases by providing the following information. For quickest service, qualify by phone at 1-800-627-7271, ext. 5151, or send this form along with your order.

Qualification Requirements

The psychological and educational assessment reports, forms, and hand-scoring materials offered in this catalog are intended for use by professionals who are specially trained and experienced in the appropriate professional use of these assessment instruments.

Given the potential for misuse of psychological testing materials, NCS Assessment has established qualification guidelines that restrict the sale and distribution of our testing products to those professionals who are appropriately trained to administer, score, and interpret psychological tests. These guidelines reflect the intent of the ethical guidelines established by the American Psychological Association and the American Counseling Association, as well as those published in the *Standards for Educational and Psychological Testing* by the American Educational Research Association, the American Psychological Association, and the national Council on Measurement in Education.

Qualification Criteria

All materials and reports offered by NCS have been assigned to one of four qualification levels (A, M, B, or C) according to the level of training necessary for their proper use.

Level A purchasers require: *(requires the highest level of training)*
Once qualified Level A can purchase tests from all four qualification levels, A, M, B, or C.

• Licensure to practice psychology independently.

• A graduate degree in psychology or a closely related field and either a graduate-level course in Tests and Measurements or participation in an NCS-approved workshop.

Level M purchasers require:
Once qualified Level M can purchase tests from three qualification levels, M, B, or C.

• A specialized degree in the healthcare field and an appropriate license or certification.

Level B purchasers require:
Once qualified Level B can purchase tests from two qualification levels, B, or C.

• A bachelor's degree in psychology, human relations, or a closely related field, and course work in the use of psychological assessment instruments (graduate or undergraduate level) or participation in an NCS-approved workshop.

Level C purchasers require:
Once qualified Level C can purchase tests from qualification level C.

• A bachelor's degree in psychology, education, human relations, or a closely related field. Specific course work or workshops are not required, although participation in an NCS-approved workshop is recommended.

Name _____

Telephone _____

Title _____

Organization Name _____

Address _____

City _____ State _____ ZIP _____

1. Your primary type of pratice:
   ☐ Private practice/personal   ☐ Organization/institute

2. Valid license or certificate issued by a state regulatory board:

   Certificate/Lincense _____ State _____

   Certifying or Licensing Agency _____

   Number _____ Expiration Date _____

3. Highest professional degree attained:

   Degree _____

   Major Field _____ Year _____

   Institution _____

4. Course work completed in Tests and Measurements

   Date _____ Course _____

   Institution _____

   ☐ graduate level   ☐ undergraduate level

   Date _____ Course _____

   Institution _____

   ☐ graduate level   ☐ undergraduate level

5. Participation in related NCS-approved workshop:

   ☐ MMPI–2™   ☐ MCMI–II™ or MCMI–III™   ☐ ISO–30™   ☐ T–JTA®

   ☐ MMPI–A™   ☐ MACI™   ☐ CISS™   ☐ CDS

   Date _____ Location _____

   Leader _____

I certify that all the information contained in this form is accurate. I certify that any test products that I purchase from NCS will be used by me and/or members of my institution or organization in accordance with the American Psychological Association's ethical principles and the Standards for Educational and Psychological Testing. I further agree to abide by the terms set forth in the NCS Assessments catalog.

Signature _____ Date _____

MMPI and MMPI–A are trademarks of the University of Minnesota. MCMI and MACI are trademarks of Diandrien, Inc. ISQ-30 is a trademark of NCS. CISS is a registered trademark of David Cambell, PhD. T-JTA is a registered trademark of Psychologial Publications, Inc.

VI

FIGURE 3.2. NCS test user's qualification form

level. Whether publishers use this system or not, the qualifications for specific tests can be found in test publishers' catalogues. Figures 3.3, 3.4, and 3.5 provide examples of representative tests and different qualification levels.

Unfortunately, there are no uniform guidelines for the purchase of psychological tests. To facilitate uniform guidelines, the Test User Qualifications Working Group (TUQWoG) of the American Psychological Association is currently working to define the essential qualifications needed by purchasers of various types of tests (personal communication, APA, March, 1999).

Sometimes students need to purchase psychological tests. For Your Information 3.2 discusses the sale of tests to students and shows a sample of a customer qualification form.

The Marketing of Psychological Tests

Test publishers should properly and truthfully market the psychological tests they publish. First, they should ensure **test security**—that the content of their psychological tests does not become public. Test security includes not printing parts of currently available tests or whole psychological tests in newspapers, magazines,

Obtain a rapid, reliable Five-Factor measure of adult personality . . .

This shortened version of the NEO-PI Form S provides a quick, reliable, and valid measure of the five domains of adult personality, and gives researchers and professionals a comprehensive Five-Factor measure of personality. The NEO-FFI provides:

Purpose: Quick five factor measure of personality
Suggested For: Adults
Administration: Individual or group
Time: 10–15 minutes
Qualification Level: B; see page 48 for details

- 60 items rated on a 5-point scale
- Administration in as little as 10–15 minutes
- Calculation of raw scores in 1–2 minutes
- Profile grid for plotting *T*-score profile
- Correlation of .77 to .92 with NEO PI-R domain scales
- Internal consistency values range from .68 to .86
- "Your NEO Summary" sheets for easy-to-understand client feedback

The NEO PI-R Professional Manual provides information on test development and use, as well as validation data and norms for male and female adults.

The 60-item NEO-FFI test booklet can be completed in 10–15 minutes by an adult with 6th-grade reading skills. It is designed without templates so that scale raw scores can be easily calculated in 1–2 minutes, and contains a profile grid for transforming raw scores and plotting a *T*-score profile.

FIGURE 3.3. NEO Five-Factor Inventory (NEO-FFI)

This comprehensive battery assesses short-term, verbal, and visual (nonverbal) memory functioning. This exceptionally well-normed instrument reliably and accurately differentiates normal from neurologically impaired individuals. Verbal and visual tasks use both recall and recognition formats and assess memory immediately after stimulus presentation as well as after a delay period.

Purpose: Comprehensive assessment of memory functioning
Suggested For: Ages 18–90
Administration: Individual
Time: 40–45 minutes
Qualification Level: C; see page 48 for details

The MAS has been designed for use by clinical and consulting psychologists, as well as researchers. Its self-contained easel format increases ease of use and greatly simplifies administration.

The MAS consists of 12 subtests based on the following 7 memory tasks: Verbal Span, List Learning, Prose Memory, Visual Span, Visual Recognition, Visual Reproduction, Names-Faces. The 16-page record form contains instructions for the clinician to use during administration of the 7 memory tasks. Three of the tasks are administered entirely from the record form. The Visual Span, Visual Recognition, Visual Reproduction, and Names-Faces tasks require the accompanying stimulus card set for administration.

FIGURE 3.4. Memory Assessment Scales (MAS)

or popular books. Not only does a lack of test security invalidate future use of the test, but also it can result in psychological injury to the individuals who take and attempt to interpret the test. Such test misuse creates further resistance on the part of the public toward all psychological testing.

It is not uncommon, however, for test publishers to print examples of outdated test items. For example, the Educational Testing Service (ETS) releases previously administered tests in the form of practice tests (ETS, 1996). All portions of tests shown in this text have been published with the permission of their publishers.

The Availability of Comprehensive Test Manuals

Publishers should ensure that every psychological test has an accompanying test manual. The test manual should include (1) information that enables the test purchaser to evaluate the psychometric characteristics of the test (e.g., how the test was constructed, its reliability and validity, composition of norm groups); (2) detailed information about proper administration and scoring procedures; and (3) an explanation of how to compare test scores to those of norm groups. You will find more information on test manuals in Chapter 11.

Test publishers try to comply with these objectives, but sometimes the system fails and unqualified people purchase and use psychological tests, or a test is released before it is complete or with misleading or incomplete information in the

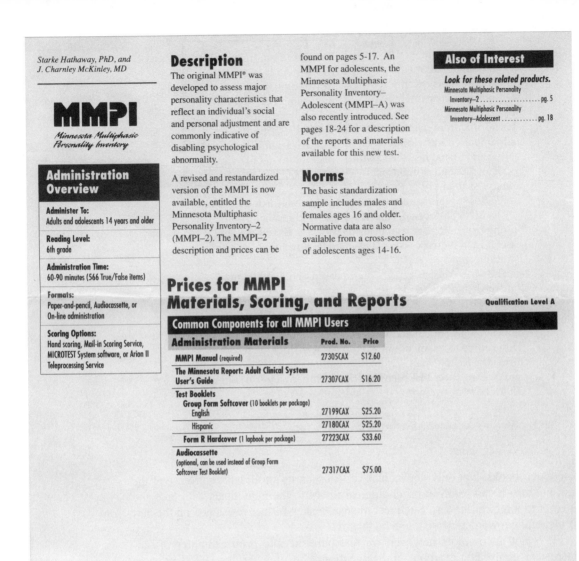

FIGURE 3.5. Minnesota Multiphasic Personality Inventory (MMPI)

Sometimes undergraduate and graduate students need to purchase a psychological test for a class assignment or a research project. For example, in your Tests and Measurements class you might be required to evaluate a psychological test. A thorough evaluation requires not only library research, but also access to the psychological test of interest and the test manual. Likewise, students might be interested in conducting an independent research study. They might wish to explore the relationship between some psychological attribute (e.g., self-esteem) and an outcome (e.g., grade point average). To conduct this research, the student will need a psychological test to measure the psychological attribute.

In most cases, students do not meet the qualifications required by test publishers to purchase psychological tests. Because publishers recognize how valuable reviewing and/or using psychological tests can be to the learning experience, they often allow students to purchase tests if they obtain a letter or complete a qualification form signed by a qualified psychology instructor. By signing the letter or the qualification form, the instructor assumes responsibility for the proper use of the test purchased by the student.

PAR Qualification Form

PAR Customer Qualification Form

In accordance with the *Standards for Educational and Psychological Testing* and PAR's qualification guidelines, many tests and materials sold by PAR are available only to those professionals who are appropriately trained to administer, score, and interpret psychological tests. Eligibility to purchase restricted materials is determined on the basis of training, education, and experience. If you have not already established a qualification level with PAR, please complete this form and send it with your first order.

Name _____ Telephone _____ Customer # _____
Job Title _____ Organization Name _____
Address _____
City _____ State ____ Zip _____ Country _____

Please provide the information requested in each category

Educational background
Highest Degree Attained _____ Major Field _____
Year _____ Institution _____

Licenses/Certificates
Certificate/License _____ State _____
Certifying or Licensing Agency _____ Number _____ Expiration Date _____

Training/Courses completed in use of tests

Course	Date	Institution	Level

Other applicable courses/Workshops completed

Title	Date	Leader

Professional experience using tests

Date	Organization	Tests Used

Membership in professional organizations (check all that apply)

_____ APA   _____ APS   _____ ACA   _____ NCME   _____ AERA   _____ NASP
_____ ASHA   _____ NBCC   _____ CPA   _____ Other

I certify that all information contained in this form is accurate. I certify that I and/or other persons who may use any test materials I order have a general knowledge of measurement principles and of appropriate and ethical test use and interpretation as called for in the *Standards for Educational and Psychological Testing*. I also certify that I/we are qualified to use and interpret the results of these tests as recommended in the *Standards*, and I assume full responsibility for the proper use of all materials I order from PAR.

Signature _____ Date _____

☐ I am a graduate student. My professor has endorsed my order below.
☐ I agree to supervise this student's use of items ordered and endorse the statement above.

Professor's Name _____ Department _____ Institution _____
Signature _____ Date _____

Complete and mail to: **PAR Qualifications Department, P.O. Box 998, Odessa, FL 33556**

Psychological Assessment Resources, Inc. / Fall 1996

manual. For this reason, proper test use ultimately resides with the individual using the psychological test.

Responsibilities of the Test User

Test users have the responsibility to ensure that they have the necessary training and experience to purchase and use psychological tests (APA, 1985). Various publications make this point. For example, "Principles for Professional Ethics" by the National Association for School Psychologists (NASP, 1992) states that school psychologists should only practice what the strengths and limitations of their training and experience qualify them for. Similarly, the American Psychological Association's "Ethical Principles of Psychologists and Code of Conduct" (1992) says that psychologists should avoid misuse of assessment techniques, interventions, results, and interpretations and use only those techniques that their education, training, or experience qualifies them to use. Psychologists should also do what they can to keep others from misusing the information provided by assessments, interventions, results, and interpretations.

Who Is a Test User?

A **test user** is anyone who participates in purchasing, administering, interpreting, or using the results of a psychological test. A **test taker** is the person who responds to test questions or whose behavior is being measured. It is easy to understand what is meant by *test user* if you think of the various stages that are involved in the psychological testing process:

1. We determine a need for psychological testing.
2. We select the psychological test(s) to use.
3. We administer the psychological test(s) to the test takers.
4. We score the test(s).
5. We interpret the scores.
6. We communicate the test results to the test taker or to some separate decision maker.

Sometimes all stages are carried out by the same person. For example, in the case of Michael Elmore, the outside psychologist might have (1) determined that Michael's intelligence needed to be retested, (2) selected which intelligence test to administer, (3) administered the intelligence test, (4) scored the test, (5) interpreted the results, and (6) communicated the results to Michael's parents and Michael's principal.

However, sometimes there are various people involved in the different stages. For example, suppose the outside psychologist determined that Michael should be retested and selected the appropriate intelligence test and that one of her or his assistants administered the intelligence test. The test might have been mailed away to a test publishing company to be scored. The outside psychologist might have taken Michael's scores and, along with other information, interpreted these scores, and then communicated these results first to Michael's parents and then to the school principal.

Thus, a number of people can be involved in the test administration process. Each of these parties is a test user and must act responsibly to contribute to the effective delivery of testing services. Acting responsibly means ensuring that one is qualified for each of the roles one plays.

Test Users' Knowledge, Skills, Abilities, and Other Characteristics

Knowledgeable test users have developed specific knowledge, skills, abilities, and other characteristics—what we call KSAOs—related to proper test use. The documents "Ethical Principles of Psychologists and Code of Conduct" (APA, 1992) and *Standards for Educational and Psychological Testing* (APA, 1985) guide the KSAOs of proper test use. In addition to these two guiding documents, students can read other documents such as those presented in For Your Information 3.1.

To provide you with a general understanding of the KSAOs that are necessary to properly use tests, we have constructed a list reflecting what knowledgeable test users do. This list, presented in Table 3.1, is based on ethical and technical standards of various professional organizations concerned with psychological testing, such as the Joint Committee on Testing Practices' Test Users Quality Working Group (TUQWoG) (APA, 1993). The list is divided into seven categories, reflecting various stages in the testing process. The first category reflects professionals' belief in comprehensive assessment and the notion that people should not make decisions about themselves, nor have decisions made about them, based solely on the outcome of one test—other factors should be taken into account.

The second category pertains to appropriate test use, which is competently using tests and exercising appropriate quality-control procedures over all aspects of test use. The third and fourth categories are concerned with test users' having

TABLE 3.1. KSAOs for Proper Test Use

Comprehensive Assessment

- Select tests that sufficiently sample the behaviors for a specific purpose.
- Include a personal history to integrate with test results.
- Base any decisions that must be made on wider information than a single test score.
- Base any decisions that must be made on multiple sources of convergent data.

Proper Test Use

- Accept full responsibility for using psychological tests ethically and competently.
- Gain the appropriate consent.
- Inform test takers why they are being tested and how the test scores will be interpreted and used.
- Select tests that are appropriate to both the purpose of measurement and the test taker.
- Select quality tests.
- Refrain from using research versions of a test when important decisions are involved.
- Select tests that are as free from discrimination as possible.
- Use tests only for the purpose for which they were designed.
- Know the tests you use and their limitations.
- Only allow qualified personnel to administer, score, or interpret tests.
- Use settings for testing that allow for optimum performance by test takers.
- Prevent participants from reviewing actual tests prior to administration.
- Establish rapport with test takers to obtain accurate scores.
- Do not make photocopies of copyrighted test materials.
- Ensure that test takers follow directions.

(continued)

TABLE 3.1. KSAOs for Proper Test Use (*continued*)

- Do not modify prescribed test administration procedures.
- Read standard directions as written.
- Follow timing instructions accurately.
- Do not answer questions from test takers in greater detail than the test manual permits.
- Do not help a favored person earn a good score.
- Maintain proper actions regardless of management pressure.
- Resist pressures to unduly shorten the planning, diagnostic, and interpretive process.
- Do not disclose personal information and test scores to anyone without the test taker's consent.
- Safeguard records by storing them in a secure location.
- Keep up with your field.

Psychometric Knowledge
- Know the factors that can affect the accuracy of a test score.
- Consider the standard error of measurement when interpreting scores.
- Appreciate the implications of test reliability.
- Appreciate the implications of test validity.
- Understand why raw scores are transformed into standard scores and percentile ranks.
- Understand the various transformed scores.

Use of Norms
- Know what norms are.
- Know the different types of norms.
- Know how to use norms and know their limitations.
- Select the appropriate norm group for interpreting test scores.

Maintaining Integrity of Test Results
- Investigate low or deviant scores to determine their causes (e.g., low motivation).
- Avoid interpreting scores beyond the limits of the test.
- Appreciate the individual differences of test takers instead of presenting test scores directly from descriptions in the manual or computer printout.
- Understand that absolute cutoff scores are questionable because they ignore measurement error.
- Understand that test scores represent only one point in time and they are subject to change over time from experience.

Accuracy of Scoring
- Follow the scoring directions.
- Carefully score the test to avoid scoring and recording errors.
- Use checks to ensure scoring accuracy.

Feedback to Test Takers
- Have qualified staff who are willing and available to provide counseling to test takers and significant others (e.g., parents).
- Provide feedback to test takers in a language they can understand, using the least stigmatizing language possible.
- Allow only qualified staff to provide feedback.

Source: Adapted from *Responsible Test Use: Case Studies for Assessing Human Behavior* (APA, 1993).

appropriate psychometric knowledge and appropriately using norms. That is, they should know and correctly use basic statistical principles of measurement (e.g., reliability, validity, standard error of measurement) and the various types of norms. The fifth category is concerned with test users' maintaining the integrity of test results. This refers to correctly applying psychometric principles to the interpretation of test scores and understanding the limitations of test scores. The sixth category pertains to accurate scoring of tests by test users. The seventh category is concerned with communicating correct interpretations of test scores to test takers.

This list is not necessarily inclusive. Your instructor may have items to add. Also, not all categories are relevant to all test users and not all items are appropriate for all testing situations.

Summary Box 3.2
Responsibilities of Test Publishers and Test Users

Test publishers and test users are responsible for the proper use of psychological tests.

Test publishers should

- ensure that only qualified persons purchase psychological tests.
- properly and truthfully market the psychological tests that they publish.
- ensure that every psychological test has an accom-

panying test manual that contains factual information that enables test users to use the test properly.

Test users should

- ensure that they have the necessary training and experience to purchase and use psychological tests.
- ensure they have the knowledge, skills, abilities, and other characteristics required for proper test use.

SUMMARY

Most professional societies, including the American Psychological Association, have a set of professional practice guidelines known as ethical standards. Because testing is an important and often misunderstood area of psychology, the APA and other professional societies have published numerous documents on ethical issues that relate to psychological testing and assessment. The most important of these documents is the latest revision of *Standards for Educational and Psychological Testing* (APA, 1985). Another important document is the *Code of Fair Testing Practices in Education* (APA, 1988), which describes the obligations of test developers and test users.

These ethical codes affirm the importance of respect for individuals, establish the need to safeguard individual dignity and privacy, and condemn unfair discriminatory practices. Particular issues of importance include maintaining confidentiality and anonymity, obtaining informed consent, and using tests appropriately.

Test publishers also have ethical and professional standards that they must follow. Publishers should sell psychological tests only to qualified users, market psychological tests truthfully, and provide comprehensive test manuals for each psychological test. Test users have the responsibility to ensure that they have the necessary training and experience to purchase and use psychological tests.

anonymity
confidentiality
ethical dilemmas

ethical standards
ethics
informed consent
psychometrics

test security
test taker
test user

LEARNING ACTIVITIES

College students, particularly those majoring in psychology, take psychological tests often. Not only are you tested on your academic knowledge, but you also might be asked to participate in class exercises or research studies that call for testing participants on psychological constructs. The following situations are adapted from a casebook on ethical teaching (Keith-Spiegel et al., 1994). Read each situation and determine the following:

- Is there an ethical issue? If so, what is it?
- Is there an ethical dilemma or has an ethical standard clearly been violated? Explain.
- Propose how such a situation can be avoided.

1. *Marketing Research Participation.* A professor teaching an introductory psychology course informs his students at the beginning of the semester that they will be required either to participate in a research study or to complete another assignment that takes about the same amount of time and effort. The study is one that he is conducting on intelligence in which they will take a number of psychological tests, including IQ tests. He describes to them the department's rules on test administration, which follow APA guidelines regarding confidentiality, informed consent, and debriefing (explanation of test results). He then tells the students that he definitely prefers that they serve as research participants.

2. *Class Demonstrations of Secure Tests.* In an upper-division undergraduate course on psychological testing, the professor demonstrates two psychodiagnostic tests designated as "secure." Although she does not teach students how to score or interpret them, she does show actual Rorschach cards to the students and reads actual items from the MMPI (Minnesota Multiphasic Personality Inventory).

3. *Student Disclosures in Class.* A professor in a social psychology class likes to give attitude scales as class demonstrations and exercises. His scales cover topics such as attitudes toward women and the "Just World" theory and personality traits such as locus of control and self-efficacy. He asks the students to complete the scale and then gives them the key for scoring it. (He uses only scales that are published in professional journals for public access.) After the students have determined their scores, he asks them to form groups and discuss their results. Often he also requires students to include their test results in their journals.

CHAPTER 4

Testing With Computers and Testing Special Populations

"I want to apply to graduate school this spring but I missed the GRE paper-and-pencil administration. I've heard there is a computerized version that I can take whenever I want. Is this true? Is there any reason I shouldn't take the computerized version?"

"I took a vocational interest inventory at our Career Services Center a couple of weeks ago. The counselor said she would give me a call when my results came in. She said that they sent my answers off to be computer scored. Is this common?"

"I have a friend who wants to go to graduate school. Graduate schools require that you take the GRE. How can she take the GRE when she is blind?"

"I'm having a really hard time in college. I don't seem to understand the material and I am not doing well at all on my tests. I was diagnosed with a learning disability in high school—maybe this has something to do with it. Is there something I can do to improve my study and testing-taking skills?"

Some of you have probably taken a computer-administered test, or you have had your tests scored by computers. Computer technology is becoming more popular in every phase of testing, and computers are making it possible to construct better tests by streamlining the testing process and ensuring standardized administration procedures. Computers are also decreasing the errors in test scoring. Although there are many advantages to computer-based testing, some people also believe that there are many disadvantages.

Some of you probably know someone who is physically or mentally challenged. Such people might need changes in the testing process so their knowledge, skills, abilities, and traits can be properly measured. When appropriate, test administrators may modify the testing process to accommodate the needs of people who are physically or mentally challenged.

Some of you probably also know someone who has a learning disability. Students with learning disabilities, like persons who are physically or mentally challenged, can benefit from modifications to test-taking procedures (and learning strategies) to help them succeed in school.

In this chapter, we discuss these three important issues, each of which is very important in the field of psychological testing. First, we discuss computer-based testing. We discuss how computers are used in the psychological testing process and their advantages and disadvantages, including the ethical use of computer-based tests. Second, we discuss special tests or modifications to the testing practice that may be necessary to accommodate the person who is physically or mentally challenged. Third, we discuss learning and testing modifications that allow students with learning disabilities to learn and test more effectively.

COMPUTERIZED TESTING

Computers are increasingly becoming a way of life for the psychological testing industry. Though the use of computers for scoring and interpreting tests is not entirely new (e.g., Campbell, 1971; Dahlstrom, Welsh, & Dahlstrom, 1972), computers are now useful in all phases of the testing process. Some of the first computerized tests were used to make hiring decisions in organizational settings and included tests to see how well an individual typed, used a word processor, and entered data into a spreadsheet. These tests replicated the types of tasks that are most often encountered in the automated office. Job applicants demonstrated their proficiency on each task and were evaluated on a standardized basis.

Today, a wide variety of computerized tests are available from test publishers and they are used for a variety of purposes. Social workers, psychiatrists, psychologists, counselors, educational psychologists, industrial/organizational psychologists, and other professionals rely on computers to help them develop, administer, score, and interpret tests (Groth-Marnat & Schumaker, 1989; Sillup, 1992). In this section, we discuss the use of computers in test development, test administration, and test scoring and interpretation. We also discuss the advantages and disadvantages of computerized testing.

Test Development

Computers have made it possible to construct better and more valid tests. In education, for example, textbook publishers now offer professors computerized test-construction software programs to help them prepare course exams. These programs contain a **test bank**—a large number of multiple-choice, true/false, matching, short-answer, and essay questions. The questions are classified by chapter and sometimes by difficulty. These classification items help professors increase their exams' content validity (which we will discuss in more detail in Chapter 7) by making it easier to choose a representative sample of questions from each chapter. Figures 4.1 and 4.2 give an overview of one such program, the Test Construction Set published by the Computer Training and Support Corporation.

Test Administration

Psychological tests can also be administered on computers. Some computer-based tests are exact copies of their paper-and-pencil counterparts. Others are **adaptive tests**—tests made up of questions chosen from a large test bank to match the skill and ability level of the test taker. In adaptive tests, all test takers start with the same set of questions—usually those of moderate difficulty. As the test progresses, the computer software chooses and presents the test taker with harder or easier questions, depending on how well he or she answered previous questions (Jacobson, 1994). According to test developers, these types of tests provide a fuller profile of a person in a shorter period of time (ETS, 1993; Jacobson, 1994). Time is not wasted on questions that are too easy or too hard, and a test that once took 4 or 5 hours might now take only 2 or 3 hours (Weiss, 1985).

Many testing organizations offer computer-administered tests. For example, the Educational Testing Service offers the NCLEX test for the National Council of State Boards of Nursing and the Graduate Record (GRE) General Test on computer. Business organizations purchase psychological tests on floppy disks or CD-ROM and use these tests to screen, hire, and train employees. For example, Connecticut General Life Insurance Company, a CIGNA company, uses Claim Processing Proficiency Assessment (CPPA) software to screen applicants for claim processor positions. Claims processing requires typing and intellectual skills

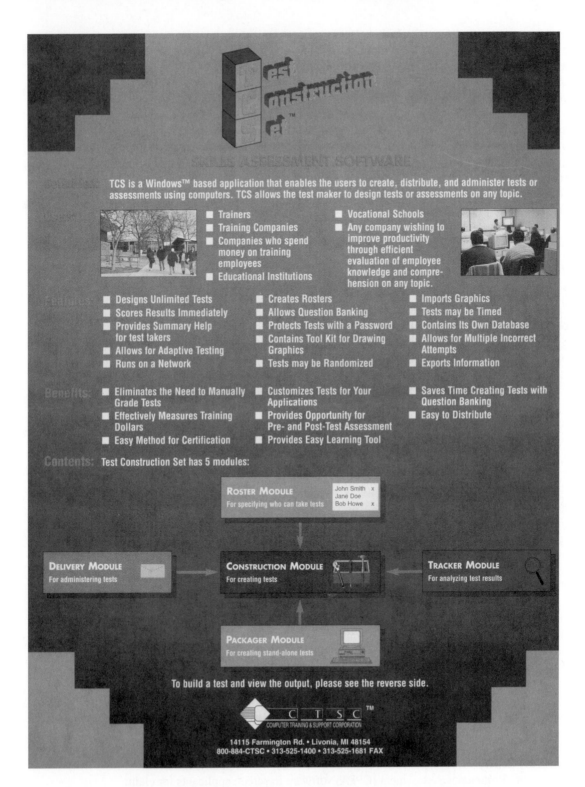

62 FIGURE 4.1. Overview of skills assessment using Test Construction Set software

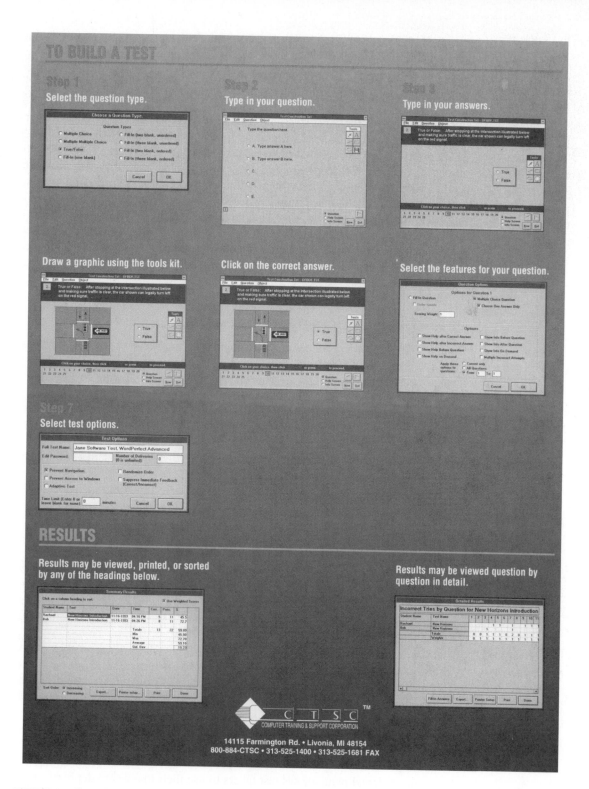

FIGURE 4.2. Steps for building a test using Test Construction Set software

(comprehension, coding, and calculation). The CPPA tests an applicant's typing speed and accuracy and ability to process a claim document (Sillup, 1992).

Test Scoring and Interpretation

For decades, test users have been able to mail test answer sheets to a scoring service that scores, interprets, and generates reports—all done by computer. Today, it is not always necessary to mail answer sheets to scoring services. Test users can purchase computerized scoring programs, and within minutes they can have test scores and interpretations, saving them both time and money. Your college's career services center probably has computerized vocational tests and the ability to immediately score your answers. Likewise, organizations are relying more and more on the use of computerized assessment centers (assessment centers are discussed in Chapter 15) to decrease the time it takes to assess an individual's performance and produce a report outlining their strengths and development opportunities (areas needing improvement).

Advantages of Computerized Testing

Computer-based tests are becoming more popular because of their many advantages. In fact, we believe that national standardized paper-and-pencil tests will be rare by the next decade. Computer tests are popular for many of the following reasons:

- *They are efficient.* Whether the computer is used to administer or score tests, computers save test users both money and time (e.g., they save the test user the cost of sending off scoring sheets for analysis, and they allow test users to have test results almost immediately).
- *They can be scheduled at a test taker's convenience.* Rather than having to wait for a national group test administration (as used to be the case with most college entrance exams), test takers can schedule testing at a time that is convenient for them.
- *They can be administered individually in comfortable settings.* Paper-and-pencil tests are often administered to groups in large rooms where it is difficult to control room temperature or provide enough comfortable seats.
- *They facilitate standardized administration procedures by eliminating human error.* Test administrators are not as involved in the computerized testing process (e.g., most of the time they are not required to read instructions to test takers), and therefore standardized administration procedures are less likely to be compromised.
- *They allow for more technologically advanced testing procedures.* For example, computers can simulate real-life situations, present three-dimensional graphics, respond to voice-activated responses, and provide on-screen calculators. They also allow for split screens that show reading passages and questions at the same time.
- *They allow more opportunities for testing persons who are physically or mentally challenged.* For example, Wilson et al. (1982, as cited in Jackson, 1986) developed a test response device for people with hearing or physical impairments: A dental plate allows test takers to use their tongues to depress certain areas on the plate to indicate their response to test questions.

- *They can be administered in an adaptive format.* With an adaptive format, a test taker's time is not wasted on questions that are too easy or too hard.
- *They decrease the errors associated with scoring.* Once again, humans are not as involved in the process, and therefore it is less likely that a person's score will be affected by errors associated with factors such as data entry.

Disadvantages of Computerized Testing

The use of computer-based tests is controversial (Groth-Marnat & Schumaker, 1989; Jacobson, 1994), due to some popularly perceived disadvantages. Below are some of the often discussed disadvantages along with a few of our thoughts.

- *Computer-based tests are unfair to computer-illiterate and computer-phobic test takers. Some people claim that taking a psychological test is intimidating enough—if a person is computer illiterate or computer phobic, the experience could be even more anxiety provoking, and thus these people will probably score lower on the computer-based version of the test.* Common sense tells us that experience with computers will better prepare us for computer-based testing. However, research suggests that if a properly developed introductory tutorial is included in the testing process, test takers can learn all they need to know in several minutes. They can learn how to move the cursor, how to scroll between screens, and how to hit the enter key. Those who do not learn quickly can be allowed to complete the tutorial as many times as necessary. In fact, research suggests that people familiar with computers do not score significantly higher than those unfamiliar with computers. Research (ETS, 1993) also suggests that people's scores on paper-and-pencil tests and computer-based tests do not differ significantly. However, if the computer test requires more technique than can be taught in the tutorial, one might have a valid concern about the equity of the tests. For another individual's viewpoint on this issue, see For Your Information 4.1.
- *Computer-based tests are unfair to some groups, such as women and minorities. Men are seen as having an advantage because they are thought to be better at "computer-related stuff" than women are.* Research does not support this notion. Research (ETS, 1993) suggests that there are no significant differences between how men and women of similar ability perform on computer and paper-and-pencil tests. Women who are not computer literate might become anxious when first introduced to computers, but their final performance seems relatively unaffected (ETS, 1993). Other research confirms this finding, suggesting that when there is no change in format, tests of intellectual abilities are not likely to result in differences between men and women (Sacher & Fletcher, 1978). Research using minorities suggests that African Americans perform better on computer-administered IQ tests than on individually administered versions, and scores of Whites do not change (Johnson & Mihal, 1973). The ETS suggests that after test takers have hands-on experience, African American and White students have a similar preference for computer-based tests (ETS, 1993).
- *Computer-based test administration practices can compromise the psychometric quality of tests.* Computer-based tests are offered more frequently than their paper-and-pencil counterparts. For each test taker, questions are randomly selected from a pool of test questions. If a test is offered over and over,

By Bonnie J. Walker, Assistant Professor of Psychology, Rollins College

For many of us, when we examine our current everyday activities, we see that our dependence on computers and technologically sophisticated systems is extensive. With improvements in their accessibility and dependability, computer systems are becoming more commonplace tools of psychological assessment (Lankford, Bell, & Elias, 1994; Eckert et al., 1997). Computer-assisted assessment has many advantages, including consistent and efficient administration and scoring, adaptability, cost effectiveness, and database development. However, increased dependence on computer-assisted assessment can also produce problems for both test administrators and test takers, such as increased levels of frustration **(technostress),** anxiety, and fear **(computer phobia).** These potential problems are related to system and software design, as well as system reliability, training effectiveness, and user variability. According to Turnage and Greenis (1994), user variability is a significant factor affecting performance on computer-based tasks and a factor most often overlooked by system and software designers. User variability includes such individual differences as age, gender, education, and computer experience, as well as a number of personality traits.

Many research efforts have been directed at exploring what user variability factors affect a person's potential and continued success at technological interaction (Turnage & Greenis, 1994). A number of studies (e.g., Pope-Davis & Twing, 1991; Rosen, Sears, & Weil, 1987) have found that older people experience more anxiety using computerized equipment than younger people do. Lankford, Bell,

and Elias (1994) also pointed out that computer anxiety can alter the validity of computer-administered tests. The relationship between gender and computer anxiety is not as clear (Ray & Minch, 1990), and the effects might be confounded by gender-role identity (Rosen, Sears, & Weil, 1987). Although computer experience is related to decreased levels of anxiety (e.g., Igbaria & Parasuraman, 1989), such experience has not been found to affect the perceived stress related to computer interactions (Ballance & Ballance, 1996). A number of studies have demonstrated that anxiety and somatic complaints are related to computer stress (Hudiburg, 1990; Hudiburg, 1991; Hudiburg & Jones, 1991) and moderated by individual self-concept (Hudiburg & Necessary, 1996). Unfortunately, the interactions among all these factors in relation to computer-assisted testing have not been evaluated.

On an individual basis, when considering the administration of a computer-assisted versus standard form assessment, factors such as age, education, and computer experience should initially be taken into consideration. If equivalent forms in both modalities are not available, outcomes for particularly anxious or technically unskilled persons completing a computer-assisted assessment might have to be adjusted accordingly. At the least, individual adverse reactions to such situations and personal attributes should be noted for use in later evaluations. Eventually, as more and more individuals are exposed to computers, as computer-assisted assessment becomes more prevalent, and as the design of such materials becomes more sophisticated, there will be less need for such close monitoring. Until then, it is best to remember that the computer is a tool that not everyone has learned to use.

the chances of questions being selected increases and therefore they do tend to become well known (Jacobson, 1994).

- *Computer-based tests are not fair to older test takers.* In fact, although older test takers might be inclined to be nervous, researchers have found that such apprehension does not significantly affect test-taking performance (ETS, 1993).
- *Computer-based tests might require motor skills or sensory abilities not possessed by persons who are physically or mentally challenged.* This could be true, but computer-based tests can be more flexible than paper-and-pencil

tests. For example, in the future it might be possible for persons with hearing impairments to have testing materials presented on the screen in sign language; for persons with visual impairments, testing materials might be presented on the screen in much larger type than usual.

- *Computer-based test interpretations can result in inaccurate interpretations of test scores, making them invalid.* With computer-based test interpretation, only one narrative interpretation is usually produced with a given set of scores (Matarazzo, 1986; Walker & Myrick, 1985). This indeed contradicts test users' training, which says that test score interpretation depends on the specific context and history of the test taker (Groth-Marnat & Schumaker, 1989).

- *Computer-based tests do not allow test takers to use the same strategies they use when answering paper-and-pencil test questions. For example, with some computer-based tests, test takers are not allowed to scan through the test to preview the items or, when done with the test, go back and change answers to previous questions* (Jacobson, 1994). True, computerized testing does not allow the test taker to scan through the test or go back to change answers to previous questions. However, test developers point out that an inability to scan through the test is an advantage for some people. Some test takers get anxious when they can see how many questions are on a test. They often hurry through the test in order to finish. When items are presented one at a time on a computer monitor, test takers can pay more attention to each question and will be less likely to hurry through the test (Cohen, Swerdlik, & Phillips, 1996).

- *Computerized tests are not psychometrically equivalent to their paper-and-pencil counterparts. For example, with standardized achievement tests (e.g., the SAT), of two students who are similar in terms of their achievement, one might score higher because of the way the test is being administered—on the computer or in paper-and-pencil format.* Research indicates that sometimes there are major psychometric differences between traditional formats and computer-based test formats (French & Beaumont, 1991) and sometimes there are relatively few psychometric differences (Kobak, Reynolds, & Greist, 1993; Watson, Thomas, & Anderson, 1992). Whether there are differences seems to depend on the format of the test and item content. Multiple-choice and true/false computer-based and paper-and-pencil tests seem to produce equivalent scores (Hoffman & Lundberg, 1976). On the other hand, math tests with a time limit and matching-type tests tend to produce nonequivalent scores (Greaud & Green, 1986). Regarding content, some researchers report that there are no differences between computer-administered tests and paper-and-pencil tests (e.g., Skinner & Allen, 1983), whereas others do report differences (Evan & Miller, 1969; Hart & Goldstein, 1985). Research indicates that females are more honest on computerized tests than males are (Kosen et al., 1970) and that computerized tests tend to result in more extreme scores (Rezmovic, 1977). Further research is needed.

Ethical and Proper Use of Computer-Based Tests

As with traditional tests, it is crucial that the developers, distributors, and users of computer-based tests, computer-based scoring services, and computer-based interpretation services abide by the ethical, professional, and technical standards that we have already mentioned. Several publications reinforce this notion. The *Standards for Educational and Psychological Testing* (APA, 1985) contains many references to computer-based testing. The *Guidelines for Computer-Based Tests and Interpretations* (APA, 1986) takes these standards one step further and explains them as they relate to the use of computer administration, scoring, and interpretation of psychological tests.

Summary Box 4.1
Computerized Testing

- Computers are used in all phases of the testing process.
- Computers are used to facilitate the development of psychological tests.
- Computers are used to administer psychological tests.
- Computers are used to score and interpret scores of psychological tests.

- Computerized testing is popular because of its many advantages.
- Computerized testing is also controversial.
- Users of computerized tests, like users of other tests, must abide by ethical, professional, and technical standards.

TESTING PERSONS WHO ARE PHYSICALLY AND MENTALLY CHALLENGED

Some people who are physically and mentally challenged might have special needs in psychological testing. By **physical and mental challenges,** we mean sensory, motor, or cognitive impairments. **Sensory impairments** include deafness and blindness. **Motor impairments** include disabilities such as paralysis or missing limbs. **Cognitive impairments** include mental retardation, learning disabilities, and traumatic brain injuries.

Various laws protect persons who are physically or mentally challenged. These include the Rehabilitation Act of 1973 (which was amended in 1978, 1986, and 1987), the Americans with Disabilities Act (ADA) of 1990, and the Education for All Handicapped Children Act of 1990. These laws, and others, guide our understanding of what we must consider when testing someone who is physically or mentally challenged. Often such test takers have special needs that require modifications to the testing process. For instance, these laws state that test users must modify the testing format and the test interpretation process to reflect accurately whatever factor the psychological test measures. In other words, an individual's impairment must not influence the test outcome if the test is measuring a concept unrelated to the disability.

The modifications that are made depend on the specific disability. In Greater Depth 4.1 highlights some of the major administration and interpretation modifications for four categories of disabilities: visual impairment, hearing impairment, motor impairment, and cognitive impairment. Of course, not all psychological tests can be appropriately modified using these methods. Therefore, tests have been developed specifically for individuals who are physically or mentally chal-

Administration and Interpretation Modifications for Persons Who Are Physically and Mentally Challenged

Visual Impairment (Totally Blind and Partially Blind)

- The room should be free of distractions because the visually impaired are easily distracted by extraneous events.
- The test taker should be given ample time for testing to allow for dictation of instructions, slower reading of instructions, or time for the examinee to touch the testing materials.
- All materials should be put within reach of the examinee.
- The room lighting should be modified for optimal vision for the partially blind.
- The size of the test print should be increased for the partially blind.
- The appropriate writing instruments and materials (e.g., thicker writing pens) should be available for the partially blind.
- The test should be administered in Braille if the examinee uses Braille to read.
- Test scores of modified standardized tests should be cautiously interpreted unless there are norms for visually impaired test takers.

Hearing Impairment (Deaf and Partially Deaf)

- The test taker who has a mild hearing impairment should be provided the option of amplifying the examiner's voice using an electronic amplification apparatus.
- The test taker who has a severe hearing impairment should be provided the option of having written instructions and questions pantomimed or having an interpreter sign instructions, questions, and examinee's responses. However, the test administrator should be aware that substituting written instructions for verbal instructions introduces another variable (reading proficiency) into the testing situation and that pantomiming can compromise the standardization of instructions.
- When interpreting scores, test users should understand that the communication of the deaf is often fragmented (similar to that of individuals who are not very intelligent or who have a psychopathology, but this does not indicate low intelligence or psychopathology).

Motor Impairment

- Test administrators should select tests that do not need to be modified due to the test taker's motor impairment, or they should select tests that require very little modification. (Often intelligence tests include verbal and motor performance measures. Not using motor performance measures could put too much weight on verbal intelligence.)
- The test administrator should have a writer available to enter responses on paper-and-pencil tasks that require fine motor coordination.

Cognitive Impairment

- Test takers with cognitive impairments should, in many cases, be tested using a structured interview, usually with family members or friends of the examinee.

Source: Adapted from, Cohen Swerdlik, Phillips, 1996.

TABLE 4.1. Tests Developed Specifically for Persons Who Are physically or Mentally Challenged

Disability	Attribute Measured	Name of Test
Visual Impairment	Intelligence	Haptic Intelligence Scale
	Intelligence	Intelligence Test for Visually Impaired Children
	Intelligence	Perkins Binet Tests of Intelligence for the Blind
	Cognitive ability	Cognitive Test for the Blind and Visually Impaired
	Development	Skills Inventory
	Learning/job success	Non-Language Learning Test
	Learning potential	The Blind Learning Aptitude Test
	Personality	Adolescent Emotional Factors Inventory
	Personality	Sound Test
	Vocational functioning	Comprehensive Vocational Evaluation System
	Vocational and interest	PRG Interest Inventory
Hearing Impairment	Cognitive ability	Test of Nonverbal Intelligence
	Intelligence	Child Behavior Checklist
	Behavior	Devereaux Adolescent Behavior Rating Scale
	Behavior disorders	Walker Problem Behavior Identification Checklist
Motor Disabilities	Perceptual-motor skills	Purdue Perceptual-Motor Survey
	Sensory-motor skills	Frostig Movement Skills Test Battery
Cognitive Disabilities	Adaptive behavior	Vineland Adaptive Behavior Scales
	Career assessment	Career Assessment Inventories for the Learning Disabled
	Sexual knowledge and attitudes	Socio-Sexual Knowledge and Attitudes Test
	Vocational preference	Reading Free Vocational Inventory

lenged. Some of these tests are listed in Table 4.1, where they are classified by disability and attribute measured.

TESTING STUDENTS WHO HAVE LEARNING DISABILITIES

Some students have learning disabilities. However, unlike the physical and mental disabilities already discussed, such as paralysis or blindness, a **learning disability** does not have visible signs. Learning disabilities can be divided into three broad categories (National Institute of Mental Health, 1993):

1. *Developmental speech and language disorders.* These include:
   - *Developmental articulation disorder,* characterized by having trouble controlling speech rate or learning to make speech sounds.

- *Developmental expressive language disorder,* characterized by problems expressing oneself in speech.
- *Developmental receptive language disorder,* characterized by difficulty understanding certain aspects of speech.

2. *Academic skills disorders.* These include:
   - *Developmental reading disorder (dyslexia),* characterized by problems with reading tasks.
   - *Developmental writing disorder,* characterized by problems with writing.
   - *Developmental arithmetic disorder,* characterized by problems recognizing numbers and symbols, memorizing facts involving numbers, aligning numbers, and understanding abstract concepts like fractions.

3. *"Other,"* a catch-all that includes *motor skills disorders* and *specific developmental disorders not otherwise specified.* These include various coordination, spelling, and memory disorders.

Attention deficit hyperactivity disorder (ADHD), which is often characterized by excessive daydreaming and distraction, is not considered a learning disability. But, because it typically interferes with academic performance, ADHD often accompanies academic skills disorders (National Institute of Mental Health, 1993).

In most cases, students develop learning and test-taking strategies to compensate for their learning disabilities. These strategies depend on the type and severity of the disability and vary from one person to the next, with some students requiring more help than others. Given the right resources and support, most students with learning disabilities are very capable of performing well in school.

Faculty are an important resource for students with learning disabilities. Faculty can make course adjustments that allow these students to learn and test more effectively. For example, faculty can do the following (Association on Handicapped Student Service Programs in Postsecondary Education, 1991):

- Encourage students with learning disabilities to self-disclose—that is, encourage students to tell their teachers and academic resource center professionals about their disability.
- Ask students with learning disabilities what they can do to facilitate their mastery of course material.
- Provide these students with a detailed course syllabus, with clearly defined course expectations, prior to registration or the start of class.
- Select texts with study guides.
- Begin each class session with an overview of the material to be covered.
- Speak directly to students, using gestures and expressions to make points and use blackboards, transparencies, and handouts for new or difficult information.
- Announce assignments in advance and in both oral and written form.
- Allow ample time for questions and answers.
- Allow students to tape record lectures to facilitate their note taking.
- Provide study questions for exams in advance.
- Inform students of the format of exams (for example, multiple choice) and what constitutes a good answer for open-ended or essay questions.

- Modify the testing process to allow students with learning disabilities to show their mastery of material by alternative methods (for example, allow them more testing time, allow oral exams).
- Encourage students to use campus support services, such as academic resource centers and writing centers.

Some of these suggestions facilitate learning for all students, others require students with learning disabilities to first self-disclose. If you know you have a learning disability, it might be a good idea to tell your instructors. If you wonder whether you have a learning disability, go to your school's center for services for students with disabilities or academic resource center. They can help determine whether you do or do not have a learning disability.

There are other things that students with learning disabilities can do to facilitate their academic performance, including the following (see Association on Handicapped Student Service Programs, 1991):

- Request "reasonable accommodations" to facilitate their learning. Section 504 of the Rehabilitation Act of 1973 prohibits discrimination because of a handicap.
- Learn how to describe their learning disability so that they can clearly convey their needs.
- Set realistic goals for their coursework and themselves.
- Use external aids, such as a calendar to keep track of assignments.
- Sit in the front of the classroom to reduce distractions and maximize contact with the professor.
- Tape-record lectures to facilitate note taking.
- Determine how they learn best. Students who learn by discussing things with others can start a study group. Students who learn best studying alone can set time aside to study.
- When studying, write down questions and bring them to class.
- If overwhelmed, seek help. Speak to the professor immediately or go to the college's academic resource center.

Summary Box 4.2
Testing Physically and Mentally Challenged Individuals and Individuals With Learning Disabilities

- Sometimes we must modify the psychological testing process to meet the needs of persons who are physically and mentally challenged.
- Various laws protect physically and mentally challenged individuals and these laws make it clear that an individual's impairment must not influence the test outcome if the test is measuring a concept unrelated to the disability.
- The modifications that are made to the testing process depend on the specific disability.

- Sometimes we must also modify the testing (and learning) process for students with learning disabilities.
- These modifications range from providing the student who has a disability with detailed course syllabi with clearly defined expectations, to modifying the testing process to allow them to show their mastery of material by alternative methods (e.g., allow more testing time, allow oral exams).

SUMMARY

73

CHAPTER 4
Testing With
Computers and
Testing Special
Populations

Computer technology is becoming useful in every phase of the testing process. Computers have made it possible to construct better and more valid tests. For instance, psychological tests can now be scored and interpreted by computer. Research suggests that, used appropriately, computer-administered tests do not disadvantage any group. As with traditional tests, developers, distributors, and users of computer-based tests should abide by the ethical, professional, and technical standards that have been set by the psychological testing industry.

Persons who are physically or mentally challenged might have special needs in psychological testing that require modifying the testing process. The modifications that are made depend on the specific disability of the test taker. When testing someone who is physically or mentally challenged, standards, along with certain laws, require that test administrators modify traditional testing formats and test interpretation processes to ensure that an individual's impairment does not influence the test outcome.

Another group of people who might need test modifications are those with learning disabilities. Students and faculty can work together to develop learning and test-taking strategies to help these students succeed in college.

KEY CONCEPTS

adaptive tests
attention deficit
  hyperactivity disorder
  (ADHD)
cognitive impairments

computer phobia
learning disability
motor impairments
physical and mental
  challenges

sensory impairments
technostress
test bank

LEARNING ACTIVITIES

1. Read the following incident and answer the questions that follow (adapted from Responsible Test Use: Case Studies for Assessing Human Behavior [APA, 1993]):

Incident: A physically challenged person applied to take a professional certification examination. Because the applicant was blind, she requested and was allowed to bring with her readers to facilitate the testing process. Readers are people who read test instructions and questions for the blind applicant. The only constraint was that she not bring readers who were experts in the subject matter.

The exam was to be administered nationwide on one test date. Normally the test is divided into two 3-hour sessions. One session is in the morning and one is in the afternoon. The blind test taker was told that she had to complete the exam on the nationwide test date. However, she was allowed to start the exam at 6 A.M. and work continuously until 6 P.M. During 12 hours of testing, she took one 10-minute break. At the end of the day, the blind applicant was very fatigued and complained that she could not think at all.

- What is right and what is wrong with this incident?
- What modifications could have been made to the testing process to best serve the applicant and to ensure that the test scores would have remained valid?

2. Read the following incident and answer the questions that follow (adapted from Responsible Test Use: Case Studies for Assessing Human Behavior [APA, 1993]).

Incident: The president of a computer manufacturing company wanted to start a career development program for his employees. He wanted his employees to have access to specific assessment instruments to help them understand themselves and to develop career plans. He was most interested in the Strong Interest Inventory and the Myers-Briggs Type Indicator (MBTI). The president wanted to offer such assessments on computer because most of his employees had individual computers that were connected to a network with confidential, password protected, electronic mail.

The president contacted the publisher of the Strong Interest Inventory and the Myers-Briggs Type Indicator to have them set up the program. The publisher and the president came up with the following plan: The Strong and the Myers-Briggs would be loaded onto a central computer in the career development office. All employees would be informed of the program, and any employee who wanted to take either instrument would make the request on the computer, which would explain the purpose of the instruments and administer the items. When the individual had completed either or both instruments, the test would be computer-scored and the results sent to the individual via e-mail. The results were written clearly, in language that could be understood by nonprofessionals. A copy would also be sent to a certified counselor in the career development office who was qualified to interpret either instrument. Included with the results would be an offer to the individual to speak with the counselor about their test results, either via e-mail or in a face-to-face feedback session.

- What are the advantages and disadvantages of computer testing and interpretation in this situation?
- What information other than test scores might be useful for helping the employees of this computer manufacturing company with their career concerns?

Psychometric Principles

Section II consists of five chapters. These chapters introduce the psychometric principles of psychological testing.

- **CHAPTER 5—Interpreting Test Scores**   In Chapter 5, we discuss the procedures used to calculate and interpret test scores. We begin with a discussion of the levels of measurement of test data. We discuss frequency distributions, measures of central tendency (mean, mode, median), measures of variability (range, variance, and standard deviation), and one measure of relation (correlation). Chapter 5 ends with a discussion of how to convert test scores into more meaningful units of measure and the role of norms in interpreting test scores.

- **CHAPTER 6—Estimating Consistency and Accuracy**   In Chapter 6, we explain what reliability is and why it is important that a psychological test be reliable. We discuss four different ways of estimating reliability—test-retest, parallel forms, internal consistency, and scorer reliability. We discuss how to estimate the reliability of speeded tests. After discussing the concepts of true score and error, we introduce the reliability coefficient, how to calculate it, and how to interpret it. Chapter 6 ends with a discussion of the various factors that can influence the reliability of a test.

- **CHAPTER 7—Evaluating What a Test Really Measures**   In Chapter 7, we explain what validity is and why it is important that a test be valid. Although we introduce three methods of estimating validity (content validity, criterion-related validity, and construct validity), we focus on defining and discussing two methods for evaluating the content validity of a test. Last, we discuss the notion of face validity.

- **CHAPTER 8—Using Tests to Make Decisions**   In Chapter 8, we focus on criterion-related validity. We discuss what criterion-related validity is and the different methods for demonstrating criterion-related validity. We discuss how to make predictions with linear regression and how to estimate criterion-related validity. After discussing how to select a criterion, we turn our attention to calculating and evaluating validity coefficients. Last, we discuss the ethical issues associated with test validation.

- **CHAPTER 9—Consolidating Evidence of Validity**   In Chapter 9, we continue our discussion of validity, focusing on construct validity. We discuss what a construct is and the method for gathering theoretical and psychometric evidence of construct validity. Chapter 9 ends with a discussion of confirmatory factor analysis.

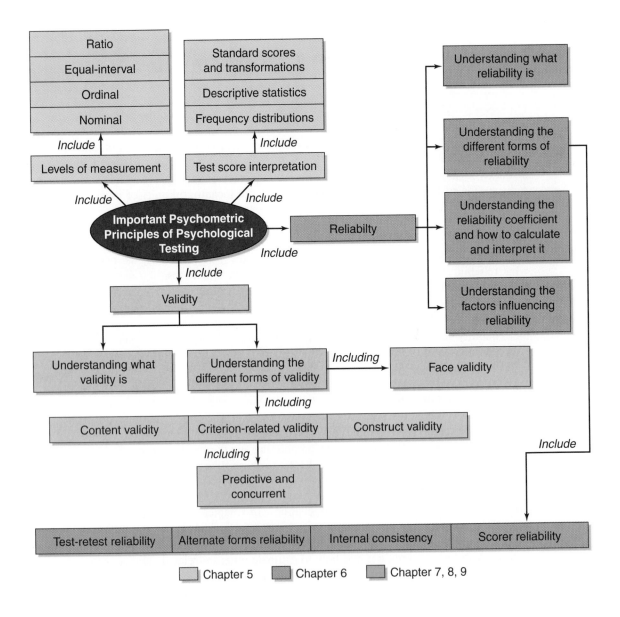

Interpreting Test Scores

"My professor wrote all our midterm exam scores on the blackboard. She asked us to look over the scores and then describe to her how the class performed and how each of us performed in comparison to the rest of the class. Besides saying that everyone did 'okay' and calculating the average exam score, none of us had much to say. Our professor then spent the entire class period explaining the different ways to describe a group of scores and compare one score to a group of scores. I didn't know there were so many ways to describe the results of a test."

"For a class assignment, I had to select a psychological test and critique it. As I was searching through some testing manuals to find a test that interested me, I noticed that in addition to what they call raw scores, some tests report their scores in T scores and Z scores. What are raw scores, T scores, and Z scores?"

"My son recently took an intelligence test to see if he qualified for his school's gifted program. The school psychologist told me he scored in the 98th percentile. What does this mean?"

If a friend of yours told you she had answered 20 problems correctly on her math midterm, had correctly identified 18 of the organisms on her biology exam, or had correctly answered 67 questions on her psychology exam, what would you think about her performance? Although your friend's attitude would probably give you a clue to how well (or poorly) she did, her raw scores (the 20 problems, 18 organisms, and 67 questions) would tell you little about her test performance. To properly understand and interpret test performance, you need additional information.

In this chapter we seek to increase your understanding of the procedures used to calculate test scores so they can be properly interpreted. Because the procedures used to calculate and interpret test scores depend on the type of data that a test produces, we begin with a discussion of the four levels of measurement of psychological test data. We then discuss how to create frequency distributions, how to calculate measures of central tendency (for example, the mean), measures of variability (for example, the standard deviation), and measures of relationship (for example, correlation). After discussing how to convert raw scores into more meaningful units (for example, Z scores, T scores), we discuss the role of norms in interpreting test scores.

LEVELS OF MEASUREMENT

In Chapter 1, we explained that not all psychological tests are measurement instruments. We said that a psychological test is a true measurement instrument when numbers are assigned to the results of a psychological test according to rules. The numbers we assign are used to measure attributes of individuals (such as their intelligence). The claims we can make about the results of psychological tests depend on the properties of these numbers, or what we call a test's **level of measurement.** For example, if the level of measurement is appropriate, the results of a psychological test allow us to say that Johnny is twice as intelligent as Susan is. However, if the level of measurement does not allow for this type of explanation, the test user might only be able to say that Johnny is more intelligent than Susan is.

Most measurement experts think in terms of four levels of measurement based on the mathematical operations that can be performed with the data at each level (Stevens, 1946, 1951, 1961). These four levels are nominal, ordinal, equal-interval, and ratio levels of measurement. As you read on, notice that we can perform more mathematical operations (addition, subtraction, multiplication and division) as we move from one level of measurement to the next.

Nominal Scales

The most basic measurement level is the **nominal scale.** In nominal scales, numbers are assigned to groups or categories of information. We can think of the numbers in this scale as labels that identify data, because they are not intended for use in calculations. Nominal scales are generally used for demographic data, such as grouping people based on their gender, race, or place of residence. For example, we can assign 0 to women and 1 to men. Or we can assign 0 to Caucasians, 1 to Hispanics, 2 to African Americans, and so on. Although a researcher might assign 0 to women and 1 to men, these numbers do not represent quantitative values. (In other words, men are not *worth more* than women are because the number assigned to them is higher.) Instead, the numbers simply give the categories a numeric label. Another example of nominal scaling is the numbers marked on football or baseball players' uniforms. Again, such numbers are labels used for identification—they do not imply that one player is superior to another.

In psychological research, nominal scales are very important. For example, a psychologist might use the results of an intelligence test (or battery of tests) to classify an individual as normal or gifted. Normal individuals might be assigned the label 1 and gifted individuals the label 2. Similarly, a personality test might be used to determine whether an individual has a psychological disorder, and the psychological disorders could be assigned numbers (for example, manic depressive = 1, bipolar disorder = 2, and so on.).

Because nominal scales yield only categorical data, there are few ways that we can describe or manipulate the data they yield. Usually researchers report nominal data in terms of how many occur in each category. For example, a psychologist can report how many men and women scored as a 1 (normal) or as a 2 (gifted) or how many individuals were diagnosed as manic depressive or bipolar.

Ordinal Scales

Ordinal scales are the second level of measurement. In ordinal scales, numbers are assigned to order or rank individuals or objects from greatest to least (or vice versa) on the attribute being measured. If a teacher asks children to line up in order of their height, placing the shortest child first and the tallest last, the teacher can then assign numbers to the children based on their height. The smallest child is then ranked 1, the next-smallest child 2, and so on. If there are 20 children, the tallest child will receive the number 20. The teacher has then created an ordinal scale based on the children's height. An ordinal scale indicates an individual's or object's value *based on its relationship to others in the group*. If a child who is shorter than the others joins the group, then that child will be labeled 1 and the numbers assigned to each of the other children will change in relationship to the new child.

There are a number of practical uses for ordinal scales. Car dealerships often rank their salespeople based on the number of cars they sell each month. High schools and colleges rank students by GPA, yielding a measure of class standing. Some magazines rank colleges. For example, in 1998, *U.S. News and World Report* ranked Rollins College, the college where your authors teach, the #2 Comprehensive University in the South and the #1 Comprehensive University in Florida!

There are two important points to remember about ordinal scales. First, the number or rank has meaning *only within the group being compared* and provides no information about the group as a whole. For instance, the top student in your class might have a grade point average (GPA) of 3.98, but next year another student could receive the top ranking with a GPA of only 3.75. The ranks are assigned based the comparison group and have little meaning outside the group, and they do not indicate which group performed better as a whole.

Second, an ordinal scale gives *no information about how closely two individuals or objects are related*. The student with the highest GPA (ranked first) might be only a little better, or a lot better, than the student with the next-highest GPA (ranked second). If the top student has a GPA of 3.98, the student ranked next will be second whether her GPA is 3.97 or 3.50, as long as her score is higher than that of the rest of the students.

Age equivalents, grade equivalents, and percentile scores (which are discussed later in this chapter) all represent ordinal scales. Most psychological scales produce ordinal data. However, we cannot add, subtract, multiply, or divide ordinal scores (nor can we compute means or standard deviations), so ordinal scales are limited in their usefulness to psychologists. Therefore, test developers often make the assumption that their scale produces equal-interval data.

Equal-Interval Scales

Equal-interval scales are the next level of measurement. In equal-interval scales, numbers are assigned with the assumption that each number represents a point that is an equal distance from the points adjacent to it. For instance, an increase of 1 degree on a temperature scale represents the same amount of increase in heat at any point on the scale. In terms of a psychological measure, on a 5-point rating scale labeled "1 = worst, 2 = poor, 3 = average, 4 = good, 5 = best," we often assume that each point on the rating scale represents an equal distance or amount of the attribute being measured.

The advantage of an equal-interval scale is that means and standard deviations (we will discuss these later in this chapter) can be calculated for these scores. These statistics allow us to compare the performance of one group to that of another, or of one individual to that of another. We also use these statistics to calculate test norms and standard scores.

A drawback of the equal-interval scale (and the previous two scales) is that it does not have a point that indicates an absolute absence of the property being measured. Temperature scales (both Fahrenheit and Celsius) have a point that is labeled "zero," but that point does not represent a total absence of heat. In other words, the zero point on an equal-interval scale is arbitrary and does not represent the point at which the attribute being measured does not exist.

When we think about psychological attributes or attitudes, this property makes sense. Although we can compare individuals' levels of anxiety, intelligence, or mechanical aptitude, it is difficult to establish the point at which an individual totally lacks anxiety, intelligence, or mechanical aptitude. The equal-interval scale allows us to compare groups and individuals, even though we cannot specify at what point the attribute is totally absent. In a joking manner, we sometimes tell our students that a "0%" on an exam does not really mean that they have no knowledge of the subject matter, rather the exam did not sample the knowledge that they do have. This makes our students feel better for about a minute!

Ratio Scales

Ratio scales are a fourth level of measurement. In ratio scales, numbers are assigned to points with the assumption that each point is an equal distance from the numbers adjacent to it. In addition on ratio scales, there is a point that represents an absolute absence of the property being measured, and that point is called "zero." Most measurement scales we use in everyday life for physical measurements are ratio scales. For instance, stepping on your bathroom scale gives a measure of your weight in pounds. Suppose you weigh 150 pounds and your roommate weighs 165 pounds. If each of you gains one pound, you have gained the same amount. When nothing is on the scale, it registers "zero"—an absence of any weight. Ratio scales also allow ratio comparisons. For example, a person who weighs 160 pounds is *twice* as heavy as a person who weighs 80 pounds. In other words, scores can be compared by calculating their proportion to each other.

Although most measures of psychological attributes do not meet the requirements of a ratio scale, those that use common measures of time or distance do qualify as ratio measures. For instance, the time required to complete a task or the distance between two individuals might be used to infer attributes such as performance or preference.

Table 5.1 provides an overview of the four levels of measurement. We will introduce and explain the statistical procedures associated with them in the remainder of this chapter.

Summary Box 5.1
Levels of Measurement

- Test scores can be classified into one of four levels of measurement: nominal, ordinal, equal-interval, or ratio scales.
- With nominal scales, we assign numbers to represent categories.
- With ordinal scales, we assign numbers to order things.
- With equal-interval scales, we assign numbers to order things and we are able to determine the distance between two numbers.
- With ratio scales, we assign numbers to order things, we are able to determine the distance between two numbers, and there is a true zero point.
- The level of measurement of the data determines the statistical operations that we can perform and thus the claims we can make based on the data.

TABLE 5.1. Levels of Measurement

Level	Definition	Example	Appropriate Statistics
Nominal	The numbers represent labels or categories of data. The numbers have no quantitative value.	The numbers on a basketball player's uniform.	Frequencies
Ordinal	The numbers rank or order people or objects based on the attribute being measured. Distance between the numbers varies. The numbers have meaning only within the group.	Rankings given to basketball players before the draft.	Medians, percentiles, correlation
Equal-Interval	Points on the scale are an equal distance apart. The scale does not contain an absolute zero point.	Measures of each basketball player's "desire to win."	Mean, median, mode, standard deviation, correlation
Ratio	Points on the scale are an equal distance apart and there is an absolute zero point.	Players' height and game scores.	Mean, median, mode, standard deviation, correlation, proportions

PROCEDURES FOR INTERPRETING TEST SCORES

Raw scores are the basic scores calculated from a psychological test. Raw scores tell us very little about how your friend did on each of her tests individually, how your friend did in comparison to others who took the tests, or how your friend did on her math test compared to her biology test. Raw scores are not very useful at all without additional interpretive information. To make sense of raw scores, test users rely on a number of techniques. Often they create frequency distributions from raw test scores and draw a picture of them on a graph. Test users also use raw scores to calculate descriptive statistics, including measures of central tendency, measures of variability, and measures of relationship. These descriptive statistics tell test users about the average test score, the spread of the scores, and whether individuals' scores on one test are related to their scores on another test. Test users also convert raw scores to a standard unit of measurement, and then compare them to what we call a **norm group**—a previously tested group of individuals. This allows test users to determine if a person scored about average, better than average, or below average compared to other similar individuals.

Over the years, test developers have worked hard to improve the reliability and validity of tests, but unfortunately many test users still do not understand how to properly interpret test scores (Lyman, 1998). When tests are improperly used or interpreted, people are likely to make the wrong decisions about themselves and others. Howard B. Lyman (1998) provides the following examples of what can happen:

- A college freshman, told that she had "average ability," withdrew from college. Her counselor had not added, "when compared with other students at her top flight college." The freshman reasoned that if she had only average ability compared with people in general, she must be very unintelligent when compared with college students. Rather than face the situation, she dropped out of college. (There may have been other reasons, too, but this seemed to be the principle one.) (p. 2)
- "When am I going to start failing?" a student once asked me. Upon being questioned, he told me this story: "My high school teacher told me that I had an IQ of only 88. She said that I might be able to get into college because I was an All State football player, but that I'd be certain to flunk out—with an IQ like that!" I pointed out to Don that he had been doing well in my course. I discovered that he had earned a B+ average during his first two years at our university. I reminded Don that the proof of a pudding lies in its eating— and that the proof of scholastic achievement lies in earned grades, not in a single test designed to predict grades. Two years later, Don graduated with honors. (p. 2)

Although there are a variety of questions we want to ask about the use of these tests (for example, Were they reliable and valid tests? Were the tests administered properly? Were the tests scored properly?), there is one question that is most important to this chapter: Were the test scores properly interpreted? In the situations Lyman described, it seems likely that the test user made unacceptable errors in interpreting these students' test scores. Is it possible that, if the college counselor had compared the college freshman's ability to that of college students, she would have scored "above average"? Given that he was doing so well in school, is it possible that Don's IQ score of 88 might have been a percentile rank (which we will discuss later in this chapter)?

Frequency Distributions

When a group of people take a test, we can summarize their scores using a frequency distribution. A **frequency distribution** is an orderly arrangement of a group of numbers (or test scores). We often group the scores in frequency distributions in **class intervals.** Class intervals are a way to group scores for the purpose of displaying them. Lyman (1998) suggests that we aim for approximately 15 groups of scores. To determine the size of the interval, take the highest score and subtract the lowest score. Then divide this number by 15 or the number of intervals you want. This will give the width of each interval. If the width is an even number, add one to the width so that each interval will have a midpoint. Table 5.2 shows raw test scores for 27 children. Table 5.3 shows their frequency distribution, and Table 5.4 shows their class intervals.

In psychological testing, it is common to display frequency distributions graphically on a horizontal (x) axis and a vertical (y) axis. The horizontal axis represents all of the possible values of some variable (represented in intervals), and the vertical axis represents the number of people (frequency) who scored each value on the x axis. Test scores are organized and ordered, and a point is found on the x and y axes to represent the number of people who scored a particular value. Each point is connected by a line to complete the graphical presentation of the frequency distribution. If the distribution of scores is symmetrical (balanced on both sides) then the frequency distribution will form a bell-shaped curve, or what we call a **normal curve.** Distributions become more symmetrical when the sample of scores is large, because they more closely represent the entire population of scores.

The Normal Curve

When we give a psychological test to a group of individuals, we obtain a distribution of real scores from real people. Unlike this distribution of scores (or what we call the obtained distribution of scores), the **normal probability distribution** (also referred to as the normal curve) is a theoretical distribution. It exists in our imagination as a perfect and symmetrical distribution. The normal probability distribution has a number of characteristics that are important for the interpretation of test scores. In Greater Depth 5.1 lists these characteristics and shows a graph of the normal probability distribution.

TABLE 5.2. Raw Test Scores for 27 Children

Child	Test Score	Child	Test Score
1	21	15	29
2	22	16	16
3	25	17	23
4	14	18	27
5	25	19	27
6	26	20	28
7	28	21	30
8	17	22	24
9	22	23	19
10	10	24	31
11	34	25	31
12	36	26	32
13	37	27	40
14	20		

TABLE 5.3. The Frequency Distribution of the 27 Test Scores

Score	Frequency	Score	Frequency
10	1	26	1
11	0	27	2
12	0	28	2
13	0	29	1
14	1	30	1
15	0	31	2
16	1	32	1
17	1	33	0
18	0	34	1
19	1	35	0
20	1	36	1
21	1	37	1
22	2	38	0
23	1	39	0
24	1	40	1
25	2		

Most distributions of human traits—from height and weight to aptitudes and personality characteristics—form a normal curve when we plot the frequency distribution. For example, most people might fall between 5 feet 2 inches tall and 5 feet 9 inches tall, but a few are 4 feet tall and a few others are 6 feet 5 inches tall. Of course, many individuals will fall between these values. Most psychological tests, when given to large groups of individuals, approximate the normal curve. Not all psychological measurements, however, yield normal or bell-shaped curves.

TABLE 5.4. The Class Intervals for the 27 Scores

High score = 40 Low score = 10	*Class interval width = 40 (high score) − 10 (low score) = 30* *30 (difference) / 15 (ideal number of intervals) = 2* ***Because 2 is an even number, we will add 1 to create*** ***an interval width of 3.***

Class Interval	Frequency
10–12	1
13–15	1
16–18	2
19–21	3
22–24	4
25–27	5
28–30	4
31–33	3
34–36	2
37–39	1
40–42	1

The Characteristics of the Normal Probability Distribution

The normal probability distribution has a number of important characteristics.

- In a *normal curve,* most test scores cluster or fall near the middle of the distribution, forming what we refer to as the average or central tendency. The farther to the right or to the left you get from the central tendency, the fewer the number of scores.
- Most people will score near the middle of the distribution, making the center of the distribution the highest point.
- The curve can continue to infinity, and thus the right and left tails of the curve will never touch the baseline.
- Overall approximately 50% of the population will score above the mean, and 50% will score below the mean.
- Approximately 34.1% of the population will score

one standard deviation (we will explain this term later in this chapter) above the mean, and 34.1% will score one standard deviation below the mean. Approximately 13.6% of the population will score between one and two standard deviations above the mean, 13.6% will score between one and two standard deviations below the mean. Approximately 2.1% of the population will score between two and three standard deviations above the mean, and 2.1% will score between two and three standard deviations below the mean. This captures about 99.7% of the scores in a population.

- The curve is convex at its highest point and changes to concave at one standard deviation above and one standard deviation below the mean.

Source: Lyman, 1998.

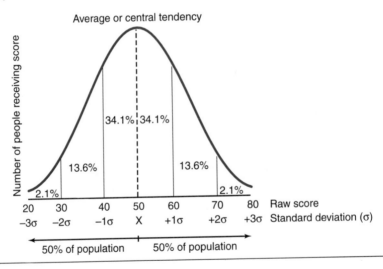

Some are negatively skewed (in which case there are many high scores). Some are positively skewed (in which case there are many low scores). Some are peaked (in which case most individuals have the same score and few have higher or lower scores). Finally, some are bimodal (in which case there are many low scores and many high scores). In Greater Depth 5.2 provides examples of evenly distributed, negatively skewed, positively skewed, peaked, and bimodal distributions.

Evenly Distributed, Skewed, Peaked, and Bimodal Distributions

Evenly Distributed Distributions

In evenly distributed distributions, most test scores cluster near the middle of the distribution, forming what we refer to as the average or central tendency. The farther a point is to the right or to the left from the central tendency, the fewer the number of individuals represented at that point.

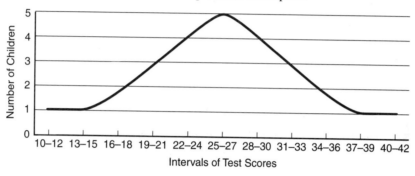

Negatively Skewed Distributions

Negative skewed distributions have one high point and are skewed to the left. In negatively skewed distributions, there are more high scores than low scores.

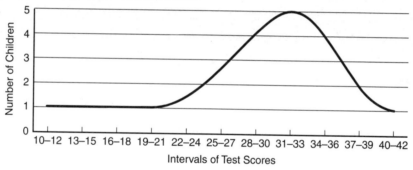

Positively Skewed Distributions

Positively skewed distributions have one high point and are skewed to the right. In positively skewed distributions, there are more low scores than high scores.

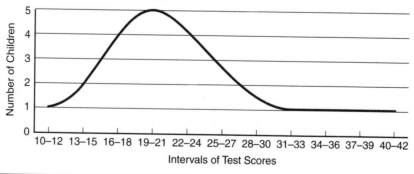

(continued)

Evenly Distributed, Skewed, Peaked, and Bimodal Distributions

Peaked Distributions

Peaked distributions have one high point and result when many individuals score near the center of the distribution.

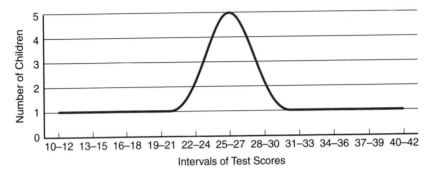

Bimodal Distributions

Bimodal distributions have two high points. Bimodal distributions result when many people score low, many people score high, and few score in the middle.

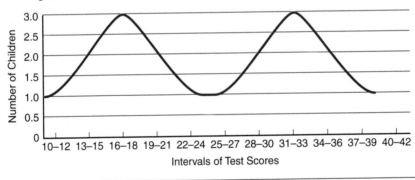

Descriptive Statistics

Have you ever told a friend about a movie you saw? Instead of relating every little detail, you probably summarized the movie by giving your friend just the main points. That is what **descriptive statistics** are all about. Whereas frequency distributions provide you with a visual image of a distribution of scores, descriptive statistics describe or summarize a distribution of test scores (instead of a movie) numerically. They allow us to determine the main points of a group of scores. These descriptive statistics include measures of central tendency, measures of variability, and measures of relationship.

Three common **measures of central tendency** are the mean (the arithmetic average), the median, and the mode. Each tells us about the middle of a set of numbers. The **mean** (which is symbolized as $\bar{X}$) is the average score in a distribution. The formula for the mean is: $\bar{X} = \Sigma X/N$. The mean is calculated by adding all of the scores in a distribution (ΣX) and dividing by the total number of scores (N). You probably learned to calculate averages in elementary school—this is the same thing.

The **median** is the middle score in a distribution. The median is determined by ordering all scores from lowest to highest, or highest to lowest, and selecting the middle score. If there is an even number of scores, you can find the middle score by adding the two middle scores and dividing by two. Be careful with this one! Students sometimes forget to order the scores before selecting the median.

The **mode** is the most common score in a distribution. The mode is calculated by ordering the scores in a distribution and seeing which score occurs most often. There could be more than one mode, or no mode at all.

In Greater Depth 5.3 provides an example of how to calculate these three measures of central tendency. As you may recall, Table 5.1 shows which measures of central tendency can be calculated at each level of measurement.

Which is a better measure of central tendency? It depends. Let's answer this question by looking at some examples. When my daughter Kia lost her first tooth, one of the first things I thought about was how much money I (a.k.a., the Tooth Fairy) would leave under her pillow. I could have collected data to help me make my decision. I could have asked other parents how much money they left under their children's pillow when their children lost a tooth. Using these amounts I could have calculated the average amount and paid Kia the mean. However, what if 2 of 20 parents I asked had really wealthy tooth fairies who paid $20 per tooth,

---

IN GREATER DEPTH 5.3

Calculating Measures of Central Tendency

The following scores might represent the going rate for a lost tooth according to 10 "tooth fairies."

Tooth Fairy	Going Rate
1	$1.00
2	$1.25
3	$1.00
4	$1.25
5	$1.00
6	$1.50
7	$5.00
8	$2.00
9	$1.25
10	$1.25

Here are calculations of the measures of central tendency:

Mean $= \Sigma \bar{X}/N = \$16.50/10 = $**$1.65**
Mode $=$ **1.25** (1.00, 1.00, 1.00, 1.25, 1.25, 1.25, 1.25, 1.50, 2.00, 5.00)
Median $=$ **1.25**
Because there is an even number of scores (10), we arrange the scores in order and we add the middle two scores (1.25 and 1.25) and divide by two (1.25 + 1.25/2 = 1.25)

while everyone else's tooth fairy paid between $2 and $4 per tooth? These two $20 tooth fairies would have raised the mean to a level that would have made me think most people paid more for teeth than they really did. The point is this: When there are a few extreme scores, or what we call **outliers,** in a distribution—that is, a few values that are significantly higher or lower than most of the values—it is a good idea to report the median or the mode instead of the mean.

If a distribution of scores represents a normal distribution, then the mean, mode, and median are equal. In skewed distributions, the mode is always (when enough data points are available) at the highest point of the distribution, and the mean is lower than the mode or median on the slowly descending side of the distribution. The median, the exact middle point, will fall between the mode and the mean.

Measures of Variability

Measures of variability also describe a set of scores in numerical form. However, whereas measures of central tendency tell us about the center of a distribution of scores, **measures of variability** represent the spread of the scores in the distribution and provide us with more information about individual differences. There are three commonly used measures of variability—the range, the variance, and the standard deviation.

We already introduced you to the range. Remember when we were determining the intervals for our graphical presentation of the frequency distribution? The first thing we did was to subtract the lowest score in the distribution from the highest score. What we did was calculate the range. The **range** is the high score in a distribution minus the low score in a distribution. The range of the distribution of scores presented in In Greater Depth 5.3 would be: *$5.00 – $1.00 = $4.00.*

How can calculating the range of a distribution of scores help us? Let's say that an elementary school decides to give a math test to each of its incoming second-grade students to determine their math skills. There are 150 questions on the test. Suppose each second-grade class has a mean of 100 correct answers. Does this mean that all of the second-grade classes have about the same math skills? Yes and no. Yes, all of the classes have the same mean math knowledge. But no, the individuals in each class do not necessarily all have similar math skills. Although the mean tells us the average math knowledge of each class, it does not tell us how *varied* the math knowledge is within each of the classes. It is possible that one of the second-grade classes had math scores as low as 50 and as high as 150 (a range of 100), while another had scores as low as 90 and as high as 110 (a range of 20). Although their mean scores are the same, the first class has a larger range and is going to require more varied math instruction than the other second-grade class.

Although the range is easy to calculate, be careful using it when a distribution of scores has outlying low and/or high scores. The low and/or the high scores do not accurately represent the entire distribution of scores and can misrepresent the true range of the distribution. For example, most of the tooth fairies in In Greater Depth 5.3 reported that the going rate for a lost tooth was between $1.00 and $1.25, but one tooth fairy reported that the going rate was $5.00. A range of $4.00 would be misleading in this case.

Like the range, the variance and the standard deviation tell us about the spread in a distribution of scores. The variance and the standard deviation are more satisfactory indexes of variability than the range is. The **variance** tells us whether individual scores tend to be similar to or substantially different from the mean. In most cases, a large variance tells us that individual scores differ substantially from the mean. A small variance tells us that individual scores are very similar to the mean. What is a "large" variance and what is a "small" variance? "Large" and "small" depend on the range of the test scores. If the range of test scores is 10, then 7 would be considered a large variance, 1 a small variance.

We said above that in most cases a large variance tells us that individual scores differ substantially from the mean. In some cases, however, a large variance can be due to outliers. For example, if there are 100 scores and 99 of them are close to the mean and one is very far from the mean, there might be a large variance due to this one outlier score.

The formula for the variance requires squaring the deviations (differences) of each score from the mean. This calculation changes the unit of measurement, making it difficult to interpret the variance. Therefore, we often take the square root of the variance, which gives us what we call the **standard deviation** (S). The standard deviation is the measure of variability most often reported. Mathematically, the standard deviation is this:

$$S_X = \sqrt{\frac{\Sigma (X - \bar{X})^2}{N}}$$

Where

S_X	=	standard deviation of a distribution of scores
$\sqrt{}$	=	square root
Σ	=	sum of the values
X	=	the raw scores
$\bar{X}$	=	the mean of the distribution of scores
2	=	squared
N	=	the number of scores

In Greater Depth 5.4 explains how, step by step, to calculate the variance and the standard deviation of a distribution of scores.

The standard deviation is a useful descriptive statistic. When we know the mean and the standard deviation of a distribution of scores, we can draw a picture of what the distribution of scores probably looks like. In Greater Depth 5.5 shows how to do this.

Measures of Relationship

Measures of relationship also help us describe distributions of scores. However, unlike measures of central tendency and measures of variability, you must have *two sets of scores* to calculate measures of relationship. The **correlation coefficient** is a statistic that describes the relationship between two distributions of scores. Using a correlation coefficient, we can relate one set of scores to another to see whether people who score high on one distribution (for example, on a math test) also tend to score high on another distribution (for example, on an English test). Such a relationship is described as a positive correlation. Likewise, if people who score high on one distribution are likely to score low on the other and vice versa, then the relationship is described as a negative correlation.

There are many ways of computing correlations. The most common technique

IN GREATER DEPTH 5.4

Calculating the Variance and Standard Deviation of a Distribution of Scores

Child	Raw Score	Deviation from Mean $x - \bar{x}$	Squared Deviation $(x - \bar{x})^2$
1	20	$20 - 14 = 6$	$6 \times 6 = 36$
2	18	$18 - 14 = 4$	$4 \times 4 = 16$
3	15	$15 - 14 = 1$	$1 \times 1 = 1$
4	15	$15 - 14 = 1$	$1 \times 1 = 1$
5	14	$14 - 14 = 0$	$0 \times 0 = 0$
6	14	$14 - 14 = 0$	$0 \times 0 = 0$
7	14	$14 - 14 = 0$	$0 \times 0 = 0$
8	13	$13 - 14 = -1$	$1 \times 1 = 1$
9	13	$13 - 14 = -1$	$1 \times 1 = 1$
10	10	$10 - 14 = -4$	$4 \times 4 = 16$
11	8	$8 - 14 = -6$	$6 \times 6 = 36$
	Total = 154		Total = 108

FORMULA FOR STANDARD DEVIATION

$$S_X = \sqrt{\frac{\Sigma\,(X - \bar{X})^2}{N}}$$

1. List each individual score.
2. Calculate the mean test score.
3. Subtract the mean from each individual score to determine the deviation from the mean.
4. Square each deviation.
5. Divide the total of the squared deviations by the number of cases. This equals the variance of the distribution.
6. Take the square root of the variance to get the standard deviation.

Mean = 154/11 = 14

Variance = 108/11 = 9.82

Standard Deviation = $\sqrt{9.82}$ = 3.1

---

yields an index called the **Pearson product moment coefficient.** The formula for the Pearson product moment coefficient is this:

$$r = \frac{\Sigma\,(d_x)\,(d_y)}{N\,(S_x)\,(S_y)}$$

Where

r = the correlation coefficient
Σ = the sum of the values
d_x = deviation from the mean for the first set of scores
d_y = deviation from the mean for the second set of scores
N = number of scores
S_x = standard deviation of first set of scores
S_y = standard deviation of second set of scores

Using the mean and standard deviation of a distribution, we can draw what the distribution most likely looks like, assuming that these statistics are calculated from a large sample and that the distribution is nearly bell-shaped or normal.

For example, if the mean is 14 and the standard deviation is 3.1, we can plot the distribution by doing the following:

1. Draw an *x*-axis that shows the test scores.
2. Place the mean in the center of the range of scores on the *x*-axis.
3. Add the standard deviation to the mean, and place this number one standard deviation above the mean ($14 + 3.1 = 17.1$). Add the standard deviation to this number, and place the sum two standard deviations from the mean ($17.1 + 3.1 = 20.2$). Add the standard deviation to this number, and place the sum three standard deviations above the mean ($20.2 + 3.1 = 23.3$). Do the same to label the opposite side of the distribution, but subtract the standard deviation from the mean ($14 - 3.1 = 10.9$; $10.9 - 3.1 = 7.8$; $7.8 - 3.1 = 4.7$).

4. According to the characteristics of the normal distribution, approximately 34% of the population will score between 14 and 17.1 and 34% will score between 14 and 10.9, and so on.

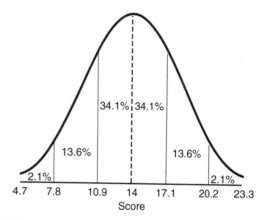

The correlation (*r*) between two distributions of scores can range from −1.0 to 1.0. If there is a perfect negative correlation (those who score high on one distribution score low on the other and vice versa), *r* will be −1.0. If the relation between the two variables is perfect (those who score high on one distribution also score high on the other), *r* will be 1.0. If there is no correlation, the *r* will be 0. In Greater Depth 5.6 shows you how to calculate the Pearson product moment correlation between two distributions of test scores.

Summary Box 5.2
Procedures for Interpreting Test Scores

- Because raw test scores tell us very little, we use descriptive statistics to describe or summarize a group of test scores.
- Frequency distributions are graphical pictures that help us understand the shape of the distribution.
- The normal probability distribution is a theoretical distribution that helps us understand collected distributions of scores.
- Measures of central tendency are numerical tools that help us understand the middle of a distribution of scores. They include the mean, mode, and median.
- Measures of variability are numerical tools that help us understand the spread of a distribution of scores. These include the range, variance, and standard deviation.
- Measures of relationship are numerical tools that help us understand how two sets of data are related. The Pearson product moment correlation is a common measure of relationship.

The Pearson Product Moment Correlation

Individual	Midterm Exam Score X	Final Exam Score Y	Midterm Deviation d_x	Midterm Deviation Squared d_x^2	Final Deviation d_y	Final Deviation Squared d_y^2	Product of Midterm and Final Deviations $(d_x)(d_y)$
1	95	90	15.3	234.09	11.4	129.96	174.42
2	86	80	6.3	39.69	1.4	1.96	8.82
3	76	66	− 3.7	13.69	− 12.6	158.76	46.62
4	55	70	− 24.7	610.09	− 8.6	73.96	212.42
5	67	67	− 12.7	161.29	− 11.6	134.56	147.32
6	90	89	10.3	106.09	10.4	108.16	107.12
7	100	92	20.3	412.09	13.4	179.56	272.02
8	56	67	− 23.7	561.69	− 11.6	134.56	274.92
9	78	80	− 1.7	2.89	1.4	1.96	− 2.38
10	94	85	14.3	204.49	6.4	40.96	91.52
Total				**2346.10**		**964.40**	**1332.80**

1. List both sets of scores for each individual.
2. Calculate the mean for both tests.

$$\overline{X}_x = 797/10 = 79.7 \quad \overline{X}_y = 786/10 = 78.6$$

3. Calculate the deviations (d_x and d_y) and the deviation squared (d_x^2 and d_y^2) for both tests.
4. Calculate the standard deviation for both tests.

$$S_X = \sqrt{\frac{\Sigma (X - \overline{X})^2}{N}} \qquad S_y = \sqrt{\frac{\Sigma (X - \overline{X})^2}{N}}$$

$$S_X = \sqrt{\frac{2346.10}{10}} = \sqrt{234.61} = 15.31 \qquad S_y = \sqrt{\frac{964.40}{10}} = \sqrt{96.44} = 9.82$$

5. Multiply the deviations for each individual ((d_x)(d_y)).
6. Calculate the product moment correlation.

$$r = \frac{\Sigma (d_y)(d_y)}{N(S_x)(S_y)} = \frac{1332.80}{10(15.31)(9.82)} = .8865$$

Although we can use most raw scores to calculate measures of central tendency, measures of variability, and measures of relationship, we need to convert raw scores to more meaningful units in order to make more sense out of individual scores. Why? Raw scores often have different denominators (for example, the raw score may represent the *number correct* out of 50 or the *number correct* out of 75). Although we can use raw scores to find a mean score, the range, the standard deviation, and the correlation of a group of scores, it is very difficult to compare one person's score with another person's score on a particular test unless we transform their scores into more meaningful units. These more meaningful units, called **standard scores,** are universally understood units in testing that allow the test user to evaluate a person's performance in reference to other persons who took the same or a similar test.

For example, if my son Zachary brought home a report that showed that he had scored a 47 on his arithmetic test and a 63 on his English test, the first questions I would ask him would be "What is the maximum you could have gotten correct?" and "What kind of scores did the other children get?" Does a 47 on his arithmetic test mean he did well? The number 47 is concrete, it is not necessarily informative. If I knew that the mean on the arithmetic test was 40 and the mean on the English test was 60, all I would know is that Zachary did better than average. I would not know if he had a C+ or an A.

Transformed scores are used with standardized tests of aptitudes, achievements, and personality and are designed to help us compare individual scores with group norms and to compare one individual's score on one test with the same individual's score on another test. Using transformed scores (which we will discuss in more detail later in this chapter), I can determine whether my son scored about average, better than average, or below average in comparison to the other children. I could also tell if he did better on his arithmetic test than on his English test.

When we transform raw test scores, we create a more informative scale. A **scale** is a set of transformed scores that are often reported for a test. There are linear transformations and area transformations. **Linear transformations** change the unit of measurement but do not change the characteristics of the raw data in any way. **Area transformations,** on the other hand, change not only the unit of measurement but also the unit of reference. Area transformations rely on the normal curve. They magnify the differences between individuals at the middle of the distribution and compress the differences between individuals at the extremes of the distribution. The most popular linear transformations include percentages, Z scores and T scores, both based on the standard deviation. The most common area transformations are percentiles.

Linear Transformations

Percentages. You are most likely most familiar with percentages. Most of the time, your professors probably convert and report the results of your classroom exams in percentages. To calculate a **percentage,** divide the raw score by the total number of questions. So, if you correctly answered 90 out of 100 questions, your transformed percentage score would be 90%.

Standard Deviation Units. Recall our discussion of the normal distribution. We said that in a normal distribution, the mean is the same as the median—the middle of the distribution. Fifty percent fall above or at the mean, and 50% fall below or at the mean. We said that if we take the mean of a distribution and add the standard deviation, approximately 34% of the population score in this range. If we add two standard deviations to the mean, approximately 48% of the population score in this range. If we add three standard deviations to the mean, approximately 50% of the population score in this range. The same is true when we subtract the standard deviation from the mean. If we subtract the standard deviation from the mean, approximately 34% of the population score in this range. If we subtract two standard deviations from the mean, approximately 48% score in this range. Last, if we subtract three standard deviations from the mean, approximately 50% of the population score in this range.

Standard deviation units refer to how many standard deviations an individual score falls away from the mean. The mean always has a standard deviation unit of zero. One standard deviation above the mean has a standard deviation unit of 1, two standard deviations above the mean has a standard deviation unit of 2, and three standard deviations above the mean has a standard deviation of 3. Standard deviation units below the mean are represented with a negative (–) sign.

For example, if the mean of a distribution is 6 and the standard deviation is 2, one standard deviation unit would represent a score of 8. This means that approximately 34% of the population will score between a 6 and an 8. An individual who scores a 7 falls within one standard deviation of the mean. A person who scores a 9 falls between one and two standard deviations above the mean. If they score a 5, they fall within one standard deviation below the mean.

Z Scores. *Z* scores are very similar to standard deviation units except they can be represented in whole numbers and decimal points. As with standard deviation units, the mean of a distribution always has a *Z* score of zero. A *Z* score of 1 is always one standard deviation above the mean. A *Z* score of –1 is always one standard deviation below the mean. The formula for the *Z* score is this:

$$Z \text{ score} = \frac{X - \bar{X}}{S}$$

Where

X = raw score
$\bar{X}$ = mean
S = standard deviation

T Scores. Unlike standard deviation units and *Z* scores, **T scores** always have a mean of 50 and a standard deviation of 10. The formula for the *T* score is this:

$$T \text{ score} = (Z \times 10) + 50$$

Many test users prefer to use *T* scores rather than *Z* scores because one half of the *Z* scores in a distribution will be negative. *T* scores are always positive. These scores also are easier for many people to understand, because they place the raw scores on a 100-point scale.

Percentile Rank. The mean of a distribution always has a percentile rank of 50. That means that 50% of the people scored at or above the mean and 50% of the people scored at or below the mean. To find an individual's percentile rank, find the number of individuals who scored below the individual and find the number of individuals who scored exactly the same score. Take the number of individuals who scored below a specific raw score, add half (.5) of those who scored exactly the same raw score, then divide it by the total number of people who took the test. Multiply by 100 to make the decimal answer a whole number. For example, let's say I got a 5 on a test. If 100 people took the test, 50 scored below me, and 2 scored the same as me, my percentile rank would be

$$\frac{50 + (.5)(2)}{100} = .51 \times 100 = 51\%$$

In Greater Depth 5.7 shows you all of the transformations described above using a normal distribution.

IN GREATER DEPTH 5.7

Linear and Area Transformations

Let's imagine that your class took a test that had 50 questions on it. Given the information below (which you should now know how to calculate), we can draw a picture of what the distribution of the test scores would look like.

Assumptions

- Number of correct questions out of 50
- Number of people who took the test = 100
- Mean = 31
- Range = 36
- Variance = 36
- Standard deviation = 6

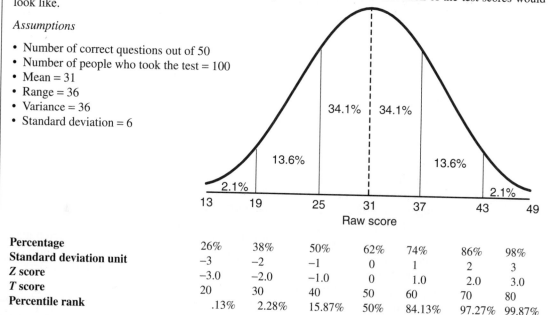

Percentage	26%	38%	50%	62%	74%	86%	98%
Standard deviation unit	−3	−2	−1	0	1	2	3
Z score	−3.0	−2.0	−1.0	0	1.0	2.0	3.0
T score	20	30	40	50	60	70	80
Percentile rank	.13%	2.28%	15.87%	50%	84.13%	97.27%	99.87%

Because few psychological measures produce ratio scale measures, we cannot say how much of an attribute one person has. For example, without a ratio scale measure, we cannot say how much intelligence Robert has. Most test scores provide us with relative measures that allow us to conclude only such things as that Robert is more intelligent than John, Robert scored three standard deviations above the mean, or Robert scored better than 75% of the people who took the test.

As we said earlier, we often transform an individual's test score to a more informative unit of measurement (for example, a Z score of a T score) to understand it better. Then, to help describe the individual's performance, we typically compare her or his transformed test score to the test scores of some other person or group of people who already took the test. When we compare an individual's score to the scores of another group of people who took the same test, the process is called **norm-based interpretation.** As you will recall, norms are distributions of scores obtained when the test has been given to a large number of people. We compare the individual's score to this distribution, which provides a standard for interpreting individual scores. Norms help us answer the question "Where does Robert stand in comparison to a group that defines our standards?" Chapter 11 describes how norms are developed.

Types of Norms

Percentile Ranks

The percentile rank is the simplest and most common form of norm. We showed you how to calculate a percentile in the previous section. An individual's **percentile rank** represents the percentage of the norm group that scored less than or equal to that individual. For example, if your raw score on a test is calculated to be equivalent to a percentile rank of 67, this means that 67% of the norm group scored less than or equal to you, or you scored as well as or better than 67% of the norm group.

The Scholastic Assessment Test provides a raw score and a percentile rank. Figure 5.1 shows how the College Board displays norm data in a percentile rank format.

Age and Grade Norms

Age and grade norms allow test users to compare an individual's test score to the scores of people of different ages and in different grades. Test users can determine whether an individual's scores are similar to, below, or above the scores for others their age or at their grade level. Age and grade norms are frequently used in educational settings. Age and grade norms provide us with information on the average performance of test takers at various ages and in various grades. Age and grade norms are typically developed by administering the test to (1) the targeted age or grade (e.g., 10-year-olds or fourth-graders) and (2) students of the ages and grades immediately below and immediately above (e.g., 9-year-olds or third-graders, and 11-year-olds and fifth-graders) the targeted age or grade (Kubiszyn & Borich, 1996). Age and grade norms typically present scores for a broader age and grade than that mentioned above, but sometimes the scores that are presented in the

 **SAT® Program**
The College Board

Your Scores

Test Date: **MARCH 1998**
R = Recentered score (test dates on or after April 1, 1995)

SAT I: Reasoning Test	Score	Score Range	Percentiles College-bound Seniors	
			National	State
Verbal	R 550	520-580	64	67
Math	R 540	510-570	59	63

WHAT DOES YOUR SCORE RANGE MEAN?
No single numerical score can exactly represent your reasoning skills. If you had taken different editions of the test within a short period of time, your performance would probably vary somewhat on the 200 to 800 scale.

HOW DO YOU COMPARE WITH COLLEGE-BOUND SENIORS?
Percentiles indicate what percentage of test takers earned a score lower than yours. The national percentile for your verbal score of 550 is 64, indicating you did better than 64% of the national group of college-bound seniors. The national percentile for your math score of 540 is 59, indicating you did better than 59% of the national group of college-bound seniors.

DID YOU DO BETTER IN VERBAL OR MATH?
Your scores indicate that you performed similar on the math test and the verbal test.

WHAT'S THE AVERAGE VERBAL OR MATH SCORE?
For college-bound seniors in the class of 1997, the average verbal score was 505 and the average math score was 511.

WILL YOUR SCORES CHANGE IF YOU TAKE THE TEST AGAIN?
If you take the test again, especially if you study between now and then, your scores may go up.

Among students with verbal scores of 550, 53% score higher on a second testing, 37% score lower, and 9% receive the same score. On average, a person with a verbal score of 550 gains 9 point(s) on a second testing.

Among students with math scores of 540, 59% score higher on a second testing, 32% score lower, and 9% receive the same score. On average, a person with a math score of 540 gains 14 point(s) on a second testing.

HOW DID YOU DO ON EACH TYPE OF QUESTION?

	Type of Question	Number Right	Number Wrong	Number Omitted	Number of Questions	Raw Score	Estimated Percentile College-bound Seniors
VERBAL	Critical Reading	28	11	1	40	25	75
	Analogies	9	3	7	19	8	45
	Sentence Completion	12	6	1	19	11	55
MATH	Arithmetic and Algebraic Reasoning		10	7	42	22	45
	Geometric Reasoning	13	5	0	18	12	75

Your responses to specific types of questions are presented as number right, number wrong, and number omitted. Raw scores are based on the specific edition of the test that you took (form code HY). You cannot compare raw scores on different editions of the test or across different types of questions. For each type of question, you can compare your performance to college-bound seniors who took this test. This percentile is an estimate of the percentage of college-bound seniors who earned a raw score lower than yours on each type of question.

SUMMARY OF SCORES

SAT I: Reasoning Test											Writing Subscores[1]	Listening Subscores[1]					
Test Date	Grade Level	Verbal	Math	Reading	Vocab.	TSWE	Test Date	Grade Level	Test 1	Score	Multiple Choice	Writing Sample	Reading	Listening	Usage/Prof Scores	Test 2	Score	Test 3	Score
Mar 98	11	R 550	R 540															

[1]Not all tests have subscores

FIGURE 5.1. SAT norm data in percentile rank format.

norms are only estimates of what a younger child (e.g., an 8-year-old or a second-grader) or older student (e.g., a 12-year-old or a sixth-grader) would likely obtain.

For Your Information 5.1 provides an example of grade norms from the California Achievement Tests.

The Careful Use of Norms

It is important that test users use the appropriate norms when interpreting test scores and that they use those norms correctly. First, there is not one right population that is regarded as the normative group. The test user must choose the appropriate group for comparison. For example, let's say that a teacher administered an achievement test to his third-grade students. He could compare his students' scores to different types of groups. He could compare his third-graders' achievement test scores to

1. the scores of all first- to third-grade children (in which case, many of his third-graders might score high),
2. all school-age children (in which case, many of his third-graders might score low), or
3. other third-graders (in which case, many of his third-graders might score near the mean).

Furthermore, he must decide if he wants to compare his third-graders to a national norm group of third-graders, to a regional norm group of third-graders, or to only third-graders in their school district.

As you can see, it can be difficult to select the appropriate norm group. Test users do not want to end up with a norm group that is too broad or too specific for their purpose. For this reason, test developers often develop and publish the results of various norm groups. Test users then select the norm group that is most appropriate for their needs.

Test users should also be careful to use up-to-date norms. Over time, the characteristics of populations change, and thus their test scores change. For example, SAT norms were recently updated to reflect more current data. Likewise, over time, tests get modified and updated. It is not fair to test takers for their test scores to be compared to the scores of outdated populations or to norms that were used for older versions of a test.

Test users should also be careful to look at the size of the norm group. The smaller the norm group, the greater the chance that the norm group is not representative of the entire population. What is an adequate size for a norm group? This is a difficult question to answer. Many norm groups for educational tests contain thousands of individuals. Norm groups for research instruments are often smaller—in the hundreds.

Test users should also be careful when using age and grade norms. If an individual child scores at a higher age level or at a higher grade level on a particular test, that test result *alone* is not a good reason for placing the individual with older children or in a higher grade.

The table here shows an example of grade norms from the 1970 edition of the California Achievement Tests. These norms are from the Vocabulary subtest, which has two parts. The overall score is determined by summing the subtest together. The total score can range from 0 to 40.

Grade Equivalents for Vocabulary Scale Scores on the California Achievement Tests

Grade Equivalent	Vocabulary Score	Grade Equivalent	Vocabulary Score	Grade Equivalent	Vocabulary Score
0.6	0–12	2.6	29	5.1	
0.7	13	2.7	30–31	5.2	
0.8		2.8		5.3	39
0.9	14	2.9	32	5.4	
1.0		3.0	33	5.5	
1.1	15	3.1	34	5.6	
1.2		3.2		5.7	
1.3	16	3.3	35	5.8	
1.4	17	3.4		5.9	
1.5		3.5		6.0	
1.6	18	3.6	36	6.1	
1.7	19	3.7		6.2	
1.8	20	3.8		6.3	
1.9	21	3.9		6.4	40
2.0	22	4.0	37	6.5	
2.1	23–24	4.1		6.6	
2.2	25	4.2		6.7	
2.3	26	4.3		6.8	
2.4	27	4.4		6.9	
2.5	28	4.5		7.0	
		4.6	38	7.1	
		4.7			
		4.8			
		4.9			
		5.0			

Source: Adapted from *Examiner's Manual for the California Achievement Tests, Complete Battery, Level 2 Form A,* 1970 McGraw-Hill, Inc.

Based on these norms, the median score for children just beginning the third grade is approximately 33. What if a third-grade student obtains a score of 40? Does this mean that the child is achieving at the level of a sixth-grader? Does this mean that the child should be put in the sixth grade? What this means is that this third-grade student has achieved a score that we would expect a typical sixth-grader to obtain if the sixth-grader took this test. It does not mean that this third-grade student is achieving at the level of a sixth-grader or that the third-grader should be advanced to the sixth grade. To determine whether this third-grader should be advanced into a higher grade, a broader assessment would be necessary to determine whether the third-grader would be able to achieve at the sixth-grade level in other achievement areas (e.g., math) and to determine whether the student would be able to cope with the social and emotional issues faced by students in higher grades.

- Standard scores are universally understood units of measurement in testing that allow us to evaluate how well an individual did on a test in comparison to others.
- We transform raw scores into standard scores to make comparisons.
- The most popular transformations are percentages, Z scores, standard deviation units, T scores, and percentiles.
- Because most test scores provide us with relative measures, we often rely on norms to describe the person's performance.
- Norms provide us with standards for interpreting scores.

- There are many types of norms, including percentile ranks, age norms, and grade norms.
- Percentile rank tells us the percentage of the norm group that scored less than or equal to that individual.
- Age and grade norms tell us whether an individual scored below, similar to, or above their age or grade level.
- Norms must be used carefully. Test users should be careful to select the appropriate norm group, evaluate the size of the norm group, and use the appropriate norm group when making decisions.

SUMMARY

Most psychological tests produce raw scores. For example, you might score "5 correct." Alone, raw scores tell very little. Is this 5 out of 10? 5 out of 20? 5 out of 5? To make sense of raw scores, we rely on a number of techniques. We plot frequency distributions. We calculate measures of central tendency, measures of variability, and measures of relationship. We also convert raw scores to standard scores and compare them to norms. The techniques we use and the claims we can make about test scores depend on their level of measurement (nominal, ordinal, equal-interval, ratio).

Each technique we use has a different purpose. We plot frequency distributions to see what a group of raw scores look like. We calculate measures of central tendency (mean, mode, and median) to determine where the center of the distribution is. We calculate measures of variation (range, variance, and standard deviation) to calculate the spread of scores in a distribution. We calculate measures of relationship (correlation) to determine the relationship between to sets of scores. We convert raw scores to a standard unit of measurement (percentage, Z score, standard deviation unit, T score, or percentile) so we can compare individual scores with a previously tested group or norm group. Comparing scores to norms allows us to determine whether a person scored about average, better than average, or below average when compared to similar individuals.

By using these techniques we can properly understand and interpret an individual's test performance. We can clearly understand the 20 problems your friend got correct on her math midterm, the 18 organisms she correctly identified on her biology exam, and the 67 questions she answered correctly on her psychology exam.

age norms
area transformations
class interval
correlation coefficient
descriptive statistics
equal-interval scales
frequency distribution
grade norms
level of measurement
linear transformations
mean
measures of central
   tendency
measures of relationship

measures of variability
median
mode
nominal scales
norm-based
   interpretation
norm group
normal curve
normal probability
   distribution
ordinal scales
outliers
percentages
percentile rank

product moment
   coefficient
range
ratio scales
raw scores
scale
standard deviation
standard deviation units
standard scores
T scores
variance
Z scores

LEARNING ACTIVITIES

1. Communicating the Results of Two Exams

Suppose you have magically changed places with the professor teaching this course. During the middle of the semester you administered a midterm exam to your students. Now it is the end of the semester, and you have just administered the final examination. Both exams consisted of 100 multiple-choice items, with 1 point awarded for each correct answer. The scores for the 25 students enrolled in your class could theoretically range from 0 (zero correct) to 100 (all correct).

Assume it is the day after your final examination, and you are sitting in your office with the test scores listed below. One task at hand is to communicate the test results to your class in a way that will best help each student understand how she or he performed on the test in comparison to the other test takers in the class. How do you accomplish this objective? For example, if Sally scored a 79 on the midterm and an 89 on the final, how did she do compared to her classmates?

Name	Midterm	Final
John	78	75
David	67	63
Kate	69	55
Zachary	63	60
Taylor	85	100
Peter	72	0
Kia	92	91
Jackie	67	75
Roger	94	90
Bill	62	65
Monique	61	60
Iara	44	55
Tonya	66	66
Amanda	87	88

Cindy	76	79
Terry	83	88
Robert	42	50
Linda	82	80
Ruth	84	82
Tara	51	50
Kristen	69	60
Nancy	61	60
Bo	96	100
William	73	77
Sally	79	89

2. Interpreting Test Scores in an Organization

Let's say that you work for a company that sells computer software at two locations. You are interested in assessing how much computer knowledge each of your employees has. You are interested in developing a software training program, but you are not sure how much your employees already know. You administer a test at both locations that assesses employees' computer knowledge. You get back the scores from each office. How would you interpret the scores? In addition, you wanted to see whether your employees' scores on the software test are related to their scores on their annual performance appraisal. Interpret the following data.

Office Location 1

Individual	Software Test Score	Performance Appraisal
1	33	100
2	45	105
3	77	110
4	28	105
5	45	95
6	67	110
7	28	100

Office Location 2

Individual	Software Test Score	Performance Appraisal
1	76	100
2	78	100
3	63	130
4	80	120
5	69	100
6	59	110
7	70	110

3. Interpreting the Wallibee Test

You are a clinical psychologist. While conducting a comprehensive assessment of your client Hulbert, you decided to administer various psychological tests to him.

One of these tests is the Wallibee Test of anxiety (this is not a real test). The Wallibee Test has 50 questions. Hulbert correctly answers 32. You are given the following information:

- The appropriate norm group has a mean of 28.
- The standard deviation of the norm group is 6.

Do the following:

1. Assuming the scores from the norm group are normally distributed, plot the scores (using the standard deviation) of the norm group.
2. Describe Hulbert's score in terms of standard deviation units and percentages. Calculate Hulbert's percentile, Z score, and T score.

4. Identifying Levels of Measurement

The table below describes various measurement tasks. Read each description, then write in under "Level" the level of measurement: nominal (N), ordinal (O), equal-interval (EI), or ratio (R).

Measurement Task	Level
1. A professor develops a multiple-choice test and scores it by counting the number of correct answers.	
2. Eggs in the supermarket are graded as "small," "medium," "large," and "jumbo."	
3. A teacher measures the height of her first-grade students.	
4. A trucking company has 10 vehicles, which it numbers 1 to 10.	
5. The months of the year are numbered "1 for January," "2 for February," and so on.	
6. An intelligence test is normed so that the average score is 100.	
7. Employees are assigned ID numbers.	
8. My daughter's hockey team is ranked best in her conference because they won the most games.	

CHAPTER 6

Estimating Consistency and Accuracy

"My statistics instructor let me take the midterm exam a second time because I was distracted by noise in the hallway. I scored 2 points higher the second time, but she says my true score probably didn't change. What does that mean?"

"I don't understand that test. It asked the same questions—only in different words—over and over."

"The County hired a woman firefighter even though she scored lower than someone else on the qualifying test. A man scored highest with a 99, and this woman only scored 97! Doesn't that mean they hired a less qualified candidate?"

"I took the same personality test in high school and again in college. My scores changed a lot. Has my personality really changed that much?"

Have you ever wondered just how accurate psychological tests are? How precise is the score on an IQ test or an employment test? If a student retakes a test, such as the Graduate Record Exam (GRE), can she or he expect to do better the second time without extra preparation? Are some tests more accurate than others? How do we know?

If you have found yourself making statements or asking questions like those at the beginning of this chapter, or if you have ever wondered about the accuracy of a psychological test, the questions you raised concern test reliability. As you will learn in this chapter, we use the term *reliability* to refer to the consistency and accuracy of test scores. All test scores—just like any other measurement—contain some error.

This chapter describes four methods of estimating a test's reliability: test-retest, alternate forms, internal consistency, and scorer reliability. You will learn how to calculate an index of reliability called the reliability coefficient as well as an index of error called the standard error of measurement. Finally, this chapter discusses factors that increase and decrease a test's reliability.

WHAT IS RELIABILITY?

As you are aware by now, psychological tests are measurement instruments. In this sense, they are no different from yardsticks, speedometers, or thermometers. A psychological test measures how much the test taker has of whatever quality the test measures. A driving test, for instance, measures how well the test taker drives. A self-esteem test measures whether the test taker's self-esteem is high, low, or average when compared to others.

The most important attribute of a measurement instrument is consistency. In psychology, we refer to consistency as **reliability.** A yardstick, for example, is a reliable or consistent measuring instrument, because each time it measures an article, such as a room, it gives approximately the same answer. Variations in the measurements of the room—perhaps a fraction of an inch from time to time—can be referred to as **measurement error.** Such errors are probably due to mistakes or inconsistencies of the person using the yardstick or due to the fact that the smallest increment on a yardstick is often a quarter of an inch, making finer distinctions difficult.

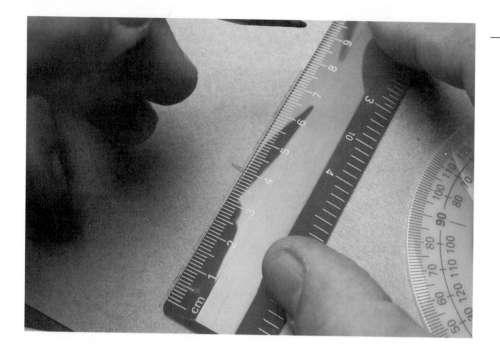

A yardstick also has **internal reliability** or consistency. The first foot on the yardstick is the same length as the second and third feet, and the length of every inch is uniform.

Reliability is one of the most important standards for determining how accurate and trustworthy a psychological test is. A reliable test is one we can trust to measure each person in approximately the same way every time it is used. A test must also be reliable if it is to be used to measure and compare people, much as a yardstick can be used to measure and compare rooms. Although a yardstick can help you understand the concept of reliability, you should keep in mind that psychological tests do not measure physical objects like yardsticks do and therefore psychological tests cannot be expected to be as reliable as a yardstick in making a measurement.

Also remember that just because a test has been shown to be reliable does not mean that the test is also *valid.* In other words, *evidence of reliability does not mean that the test measures what it is intended to measure or that it is being used properly.* We will address questions of test validity in Chapters 7, 8, and 9.

FOUR TYPES OF RELIABILITY

If you measure a room, but you are not sure whether your measurement is correct, what would you do? Most people would measure the room a second time, using either the same or a different tape measure.

Psychologists use the same strategies of remeasurement to check psychological measurements. These strategies establish evidence of the test's reliability. Basically, there are four methods for checking reliability: the test-retest method, alternate or parallel forms, internal consistency (using split halves or coefficient alpha), and scorer reliability. Each of these methods takes into account various conditions that could produce differences in test scores. Not all strategies are used for all tests. The strategy chosen to determine reliability depends on the test itself and the conditions under which it can be administered. The four strategies are discussed in detail below.

Test-Retest Reliability

To estimate how reliable a test is using the **test-retest method,** a test developer gives the same test to the same group of test takers on two different occasions. The scores from the first and second administrations are then compared using correlation—a statistical technique discussed in Chapter 5. This method examines the performance of a test over *time* and provides an estimate of the test's *stability.* The interval between the two administrations of the test might vary from a few hours up to several years. As the interval lengthens, test-retest reliability can be expected to decline, because the number of opportunities for test takers or the testing situation to change increases over time. For example, if we give a math achievement test to an individual today and then again tomorrow, there probably is little chance that the individual's knowledge of math changed overnight. But if we give an individual a math achievement test today and then again in two months, it is very likely that something will happen during the next two months that will increase (or decrease) the individual's knowledge of math. When test developers or researchers report test-retest reliability, they need to state the length of time that elapsed between the two test administrations.

Using test-retest reliability, the assumption is that the test takers have not changed in terms of the quality the test measures between the first administration and the second administration of the test. Changes in mood, fatigue or personal problems from one administration to another can affect an individual's test score. In addition, the circumstances under which the test is administered, such as the test instructions, lighting, or distractions, must be alike. Any differences in administration or the individuals themselves will introduce error and reduce reliability.

The greatest danger in using the test-retest method of estimating reliability is that the test takers will score differently (usually higher) on the test because of **practice effects.** For example, when test takers benefit from taking the test the first time (practice), they are able to solve problems more quickly and correctly the second time. (If all test takers benefited the same amount from practice, it would not affect reliability. However, it is likely that some will benefit from practice more than others.) Therefore, the test-retest method is appropriate only when test takers are not permanently changed by taking the test or the interval between the two administrations is long enough to offset the effect of practice.

The test developer makes the first estimates of a test's reliability. For instance, the developer of the Personality Assessment Inventory (PAI)—a test designed for clinical assessment of adults—collected data on test reliability from a variety of test takers before the test was published for general use, to assure that the PAI is a reliable measure (Morey, 1991). The PAI is featured in In Greater Depth 6.1, which describes the test's purpose, format, and development.

To determine the PAI's test-retest reliability, researchers administered it to two

Personality Assessment Inventory (PAI)

The Personality Assessment Inventory (PAI) is an objective personality test designed to gather information on a number of clinical syndromes in adults. The PAI contains 11 clinical scales (Somatic Complaints, Anxiety, Anxiety-Related Disorders, Depression, Mania, Paranoia, Schizophrenia, Borderline Features, Antisocial Features, Alcohol Problems, and Drug Problems) that measure clinical constructs. It also contains five treatment scales (Aggression, Suicidal Ideation, Stress, Nonsupport, and Treatment Rejection) that measure characteristics that affect treatment. The PAI has two interpersonal scales (Dominance and Warmth) that provide information about the client's relationships with others, and four validity scales (Inconsistency, Infrequency, Negative Impression, and Positive Impression) that are used to determine whether the respondent answered the questions consistently and in good faith.

The PAI contains 344 statements for which the test taker must choose one of four responses: "False, not at all true," "Slightly True," "Mainly True," and "Very True." This format provides more information than a true/false format, yet it prevents the respon-

dent from taking a neutral stance. Sample statements on the PAI resemble the following:

My friends are available if I need them.
Much of the time I'm sad for no real reason.
My relationships have been stormy.
I have many brilliant ideas.

Test takers answer the PAI on a "bubble sheet" that can be hand-scored or electronically scanned. Scoring generates a profile that shows the respondent's score on each of the scales. A clinical professional who is familiar with the properties of the PAI as well as common diagnostic schemas, theories of personality, and psychopathology then examines the profile and interprets the test outcomes.

To determine the PAI's test-retest reliability, researchers conducted two studies that calculated reliability estimates for each scale. The two studies yielded similar results, showing acceptable estimates of test-retest reliability for the PAI.

Source: Morey (1991). Test items reprinted with permission from PAR, Inc.

samples of individuals not in clinical treatment. Although the test was designed for use in a clinical setting, using a clinical sample for estimating reliability would have been difficult because changes due to a disorder or due to treatment would have confused interpretation of the results of the reliability studies. Therefore, they administered the PAI twice to 75 normal adults. The second administration followed the first by an average of 24 days. They also administered the PAI to 80 normal college students who took the test twice with an interval of 28 days. In each case, the set of scores from the first administration was correlated with the set of scores from the second administration. Both studies yielded similar results, showing acceptable estimates of test-retest reliability for the PAI. (Later in this chapter we will discuss what "acceptable level of reliability" means.)

Alternate Forms

To overcome problems such as practice effects, psychologists often give two forms of the test to the same people at the same time. This strategy requires the test developer to create two tests that follow the same test plan but have different content. These tests are referred to as **alternate forms** or **parallel forms**. Again, the sets of scores from the two tests are compared using correlation. This method provides a test of equivalence. The two forms (Form A and Form B) are administered as close in time as possible—usually on the same day. To guard against any **order effects,** changes in test scores resulting from the order in which the tests were taken, half the test takers receive Form A first and the other half receive Form B first.

The greatest danger when using this method is that the two forms will not be equivalent. Alternate forms are much easier to develop for well-defined characteristics, such as mathematical ability, than for personality traits, such as self-esteem or need for affiliation. For example, achievement tests that are given to students at the beginning and end of the school year are alternate forms. Although we check the reliability of alternate forms by administering them at the same time, their practical advantage is that they can be used as pre- and post-tests because they are equivalent measures. The developers of the PAI did not have an alternate form of the test, so they were not able to estimate reliability using this method.

Internal Consistency

What if you can give the test only once, and you do not have alternate forms? How can you estimate the test's reliability? We can measure the **internal consistency** or reliability of a test by giving the test once to one group of people. To make a comparison of scores, we divide the test into halves—called the **split-half method**— then compare the set of scores on the first half with the set of scores on the second half. The two halves must be equivalent in length and content for this method to yield an accurate estimate of reliability.

The best way to divide the test is to use random assignment to place each question in one half or the other. Random assignment is likely to balance errors in the score that can result from order effects (the order in which the questions are answered), difficulty, and content. For Your Information 6.1 shows how a 10-

---

For Your Information   6.1
Dividing the Test Into Halves, Using Random Assignment

Test questions in the original test were assigned to either Split Half 1 or Split Half 2 using the method of random assignment. This procedure resulted in two tests, each one half as long as the original test.

Original Test	**Split Half 1**	**Split Half 2**
Question 1	Question 2	Question 3
Question 2	Question 1	Question 10
Question 3	Question 6	Question 4
Question 4	Question 7	Question 5
Question 5	Question 9	Question 8
Question 6		
Question 7		
Question 8		
Question 9		
Question 10		

question test has been divided into two 5-question tests using random assignment. As in the last two methods, the scores of the first and second halves are compared using correlation.

If we split a test with 100 questions into two halves, we have two short tests instead of one long test. As we will explain later in this chapter, shortening a test decreases its reliability. Therefore, when using the split-half method, an adjustment must be made to compensate for splitting the test into halves. This adjustment uses the Spearman-Brown formula and is discussed in the next section.

An even better way to measure internal consistency is to compare individuals' scores on all possible ways of splitting the test in halves. This method compensates for any error introduced by any lack of equivalence in the two halves. Kuder and Richardson (1937, 1939) first proposed the "KR-20" formula for calculating internal consistency for tests whose questions can be scored as either right or wrong. In 1951, Cronbach proposed a formula called "coefficient alpha" that calculates internal consistency for questions that have more than two possible responses.

This method of estimating reliability is appropriate only for tests that are **homogeneous**—tests that measure only one trait or characteristic. For **heterogeneous** tests, which measure more than one trait or characteristic, estimates of internal consistency are likely to be low. For example, a test for people who are applying for the job of accountant might measure knowledge of accounting principles, calculation skills, and ability to use a computer spreadsheet. Such a test is heterogeneous because it measures three distinct factors of performance for an accountant.

An overall estimate of reliability is not appropriate to test the internal consistency of a heterogeneous test. Instead, the test developer should calculate and report an estimate of internal reliability for each homogeneous subtest or factor. In addition, Schmitt (1996) notes that the test developer should report the relationships or correlations among the subtests or factors of a test. In our example of a test for accountants, there would be three estimates of internal reliability—one for the part that measures knowledge of accounting principles, one for the part that measures calculation skills, and one for the part that measures ability to use a computer spreadsheet. The estimates for each part as well as their intercorrelations should be reported to test users. For Your Information 6.2 presents simulated data in a correlation matrix for our example of a test for accountants.

Furthermore, Schmitt (1996) emphasizes that the concepts of internal consistency and homogeneity are not the same. Coefficient alpha describes the amount of interrelation between questions on a test or subscale. Homogeneity refers to whether the questions measure the same trait or dimension. It is possible for a test

---

For Your Information   6.2
Simulated Data for a Test for Accountants

Test	1	2	3	
1. Accounting skills	(.90)	.70	.51	Coefficient alphas are listed in parentheses forming
2. Calculation skills		(.85)	.47	a diagonal. Correlations between the subtests are
3. Use of spreadsheet			(.95)	listed above the diagonal.

to contain questions that are highly interrelated even though the questions measure two factors. Therefore, a high coefficient alpha should not be used as "proof" that a test measures only one skill, trait, or dimension.

The developers of the PAI also conducted studies to determine its internal consistency. Because the PAI requires test takers to provide ratings on a response scale that has four options—"False, not at all true," "Slightly True," "Mainly True," and "Very True"—they used the coefficient alpha formula.

In these studies, the PAI was administered to three samples: a sample of 1,000 persons drawn to match the U.S. Census, another sample of 1,051 college students, and a clinical sample of 1,246 persons. Large numbers of respondents are needed to estimate internal consistency using coefficient alpha, because violation of assumptions underlying the formula cause coefficient alpha to overestimate or underestimate the population reliability when the number of respondents is small (Zimmerman, Zumbo, & Lalonde, 1993).

Table 6.1 shows the estimates of internal consistency for the scales and subscales of the PAI. Again, the studies yielded levels of reliability considered acceptable by the test developer for most of the scales and subscales of the PAI. Two scales on the test—Inconsistency and Infrequency—yielded low estimates of inter-

TABLE 6.1. Internal Consistency of the Personal Assessment Inventory

Scale	Alpha		
	Census	College	Clinical
Inconsistency *(ICN)*	.45	.26	.23
Infrequency *(INF)*	.52	.22	.40
Negative Impression *(NIM)*	.72	.63	.74
Positive Impression *(PIM)*	.71	.73	.77
Somatic Complaints *(SOM)*	.89	.83	.92
Anxiety *(ANX)*	.90	.89	.94
Anxiety-Related Disorders *(ARD)*	.76	.80	.86
Depression *(DEP)*	.87	.87	.93
Mania *(MAN)*	.82	.82	.82
Paranoia *(PAR)*	.85	.88	.89
Schizophrenia *(SCZ)*	.81	.82	.89
Borderline Features *(BOR)*	.87	.86	.91
Antisocial Features *(ANT)*	.84	.85	.86
Alcohol Problems *(ALC)*	.84	.83	.93
Drug Problems *(DRG)*	.74	.66	.89
Aggression *(AGG)*	.85	.89	.90
Suicidal Ideation *(SUI)*	.85	.87	.93
Stress *(STR)*	.76	.69	.79
Nonsupport *(NON)*	.72	.75	.80
Treatment Rejection *(RXR)*	.76	.72	.80
Dominance *(DOM)*	.78	.81	.82
Warmth *(WRM)*	.79	.80	.83
Median across 22 scales	.81	.82	.86

Source: Morey, L. C. (1991). Personality Assessment Inventory. Odessa, FL: Psychological Assessment Resources. p. 86. Reprinted with permission.

nal consistency. The test developer, however, anticipated lower alphas because these scales measure the care used by the test taker in completing the test, and careless responding could vary during the testing period. For instance, a test taker might complete the first half of the test accurately, but then become tired and complete the second half haphazardly.

Scorer Reliability

The three methods we have already discussed are concerned with whether or not the test yields consistent scores. But what about the person who scores the test? Individuals can make mistakes in scoring that add error to test scores. Therefore, the judgments or ratings that each scorer made about each answer are compared using correlation to see how much they agree. When there is strong agreement between scorers or raters, then the **scorer reliability,** also known as **inter-rater reliability,** will be high.

Some tests, such as those that require the administrator to rate behaviors, have complicated scoring schemes and the test score depends on the judgment of the test administrator. Such tests have manuals that provide explicit instructions for making these scoring judgments. Deviation from the scoring instructions or a variation in the interpretation of the instructions introduces error into the final score. Therefore, inter-rater reliability becomes an important consideration for tests that require judgment decisions by the administrator or scorer.

The Wisconsin Card Sorting Test (WCST) is used to assess brain damage. The test requires respondents to sort cards according to directions given by the administrator. Researchers (Axelrod, Goldman, & Woodard, 1992) conducted two studies on the reliability of scoring the WCST administered to adult psychiatric inpatients. In these studies, the test was administered by one person and then scored by another. In the first study, three clinicians experienced in neuropsychological assessment independently scored the WCST data according to instructions given in an early edition of the test manual (Heaton, 1981). Their agreement was measured using a statistical procedure called intraclass correlation, a special type of correlation appropriate for comparing responses of more than two raters or more than two sets of scores. The study focused on their scoring of three subscales for 30 psychiatric adult inpatients. Their scores for the three subscales correlated at .93, .92, and .88—indicating very high agreement. The studies also looked at **intrascorer consistency**—whether the each clinician was consistent in the way he or she assigned scores from test to test. Again the correlations, all above .90, were excellent.

In the second study, six novice scorers, who did not have previous experience scoring the WCST, scored 30 tests. The researchers divided the scorers into two groups. One group received only the scoring procedures in the test manual (Heaton, 1981) and the other group received supplemental scoring instructions in addition to those in the manual. All scorers independently scored the WCST. The consistency level was very high and consistent with the results of the first study. Although there were not significant differences between groups, those receiving the supplemental scoring material were able to score the WCST in less time. Conducting studies of interscorer reliability for a test, such as those of Axelrod et al. (1992), assures that the instructions for scoring are clear and unambiguous so that multiple scorers arrive at the same results.

The Bayley Scales for Infant Development, second edition (Bayley, 1993), is a test designed to assess the developmental level of children between the ages of one month and 3.5 years. Qualified developmental and child psychologists use the Bayley Scales to identify children who are developing slowly and who might benefit from cognitive intervention. The test has three scales:

- *The Motor Scale* measures the control and skill the child uses in moving its body.
- *The Mental Scale* measures cognitive abilities.
- *The Behavior Rating Scale* assesses behavior problems such as lack of attention.

The test is administered one-on-one—that is, the psychologist administers the test to one child at a time. The child is given a variety of age-specific objects or toys, and the psychologist observes how the child uses the object and then assigns a score based on a detailed scoring scheme provided by the test developer. The psychologist who purchases this test receives a large case containing all the objects used in administering the test. Figure 6.1 shows some of the Bayley Scales' test materials.

The test manual for the Bayley Scales reports three estimates of reliability:

- *Internal consistency.* Because the Motor Scale, Mental Scale, and Behavior Rating Scale measure different aspects of child development, internal consistency was assessed separately for each scale for each of 17 age groups. This strategy is appropriate because each scale is homogeneous and abilities are not expected to change during the 30- to 60-minute testing session. The reliability studies showed coefficient alphas ranging from .75 to .91 for the Motor Scale, .78 to .93 for the Mental Scale, and .64 to .92 for the Behavior Rating Scale. From these studies, Bayley concluded that the test is internally consistent.

- *Test-retest reliability.* Estimating the test-retest reliability of the Bayley Scales presented a problem unique to testing instruments that measure the abilities and behavior of infants. Cognitive development during the first months and years of life is uneven and sometimes fast. Young children often grow in spurts, changing dramatically over a few days. Testing a child before and after a developmental advance is likely to yield very different results on the two test administrations. Such changes in a test score would reflect actual changes in the child's skills, not error in the test itself or in test administration. Bayley's solution to this dilemma was to examine test-retest reliability over very short periods of time—from 1 to 16 days. Correlations between the two testing sessions across a number of studies were strong for the Motor Scale (.77) and the Mental Scale (.83). The Behavior Rating Scale had a wide range of test-retest reliability coefficients (.55 for 1-month-olds and .90 for 12-month-olds).

- *Scorer reliability.* Interscorer reliability is an important concern for the Bayley Scales because a lot of the scoring depends on the judgment of the examiner. The test manual provides clear scoring instructions, but the examiner's judgment is still necessary to assign scores accurately. For example, one item of the Motor Scale is "keep hands open." The scoring scheme instructs the examiner to give credit for this item if the child holds her or his hands open most of the time when she or he is following her or

Shield   Clear box   Picture book   Easel   Button sleeve

FIGURE 6.1. Sample test materials from the Bayley Scales

Source: Bayley, N. (1993). *Bayley Scales for Infant Development* (2nd ed.). San Antonio, TX. p. 38. Reprinted with permission.

his own interests. Sources of error in scoring this item include: examiners noting the position of the hands at varying times; examiners defining differently when the child is free to follow his or her own interests; and examiners disagreeing about what is meant by "most" of the time. Correlations between the scores assigned by the examiner and an observer sitting nearby during the same testing session were

.75 for the Motor Scale, .96 for the Mental Scale, and .80 for the Behavior Rating Scale.

- *Alternate forms.* As you can imagine, developing two equivalent tests like the Bayley Scales would be extremely difficult and time consuming. Therefore, an alternate or parallel form of the Bayley Scales does not exist, and alternate forms reliability could not be assessed.

As you can see, the answer to whether a test is reliable can depend upon how you decide to measure reliability. The first three types of reliability we discussed—test-retest, alternate forms, and internal consistency—look at the test itself. Scorer reliability involves an examination of how consistently the person scoring the test followed the scoring directions. For Your Information 6.3 describes how three of these four methods were used to estimate the reliability of the Bayley Scales for Infant Development.

The test developer needs to report to the test user which method was used to determine reliability. For some tests, such as the PAI and the Bayley Scales, more than one method is appropriate. Each method provides evidence that the test is consistent under certain circumstances. Using more than one method provides strong, corroborative evidence that the test is reliable.

Summary Box 6.1
Four Types of Reliability

- The test-retest method compares the scores of the same test takers taking the same test at two different times. This method is appropriate when the test takers have not changed on the ability, trait, or attitude the test measures.
- The alternate forms method compares the scores of the same test takers on two equivalent forms of the test taken at the same time.
- The internal consistency method compares the scores of test takers on two halves of the test taken at the same time *(split-halves method)*. Scores of test takers on all possible halves can be calculated using the *coefficient alpha* or *KR-20* formulas. This is appropriate only with tests whose questions are homogeneous.
- Scorer reliability is a measure of the accuracy of those scoring the test or making judgments. The judgments or ratings each scorer made are compared to see how much they agree.

ESTIMATING RELIABILITY FOR SPEED TESTS

Our discussion so far in this chapter assumes that the test for which we are estimating reliability is a **power test**—one in which respondents have ample time to respond to all questions. Although the test might have a time limit, the length of the test period has been set with the expectation that everyone will complete the test.

Another type of test—the **speed test**—relies for scoring on the number of correct answers supplied by the test taker in a short amount of time. In other words, the test is designed to be too long for anyone to finish in the time allotted. Furthermore, the speed test is one in which the differences in individual scores depends not on errors made by the test taker, but on the speed with which the test taker can generate correct answers (Anastasi, 1988). Speed tests are often skills tests that require the test taker to demonstrate proficiency in a skill such as sorting, attending to detail, or recognizing discrepancies.

Because each test taker completes a different number of questions on a speed test, estimates of internal consistency are difficult to obtain. If the test developer estimates internal consistency using the strategies described for a power test, the resulting reliability could be overestimated (too high). Therefore, special methods must be used to estimate internal consistency for speed tests. Instead of splitting the test according to the number of questions, the split should be made in terms of the time taken to complete each half. In other words, two separately timed parts of the test must be administered.

For example, using the split-halves procedure one could print the odd-numbered questions on one page and the even-numbered questions on another and administer each in a separately timed session. Then the scores for each half could be correlated and adjusted using the Spearman-Brown formula. An alternative procedure would be to divide the testing period into quarters and ask the test takers to mark the question on which they were working when the examiner gives a pre-arranged signal at the end of each quarter. In this case, the number of questions correctly completed in two quarters can be compared to the number correctly completed in the other two quarters. To use either of these methods, the questions must be similar in difficulty throughout the test.

TRUE SCORES AND ERROR

No measurement instrument is perfectly reliable or consistent. Many clocks are slow or fast, even if their errors must be measured in nanoseconds. Unfortunately, psychologists are not able to measure psychological qualities as precisely as engineers can measure speed or physicists can measure distance.

Psychologists know that a portion of every test score contains error. Classical test theory expresses this idea by saying that each observed test score *(X)* contains two parts—a true score *(T)* and error *(E)*. Therefore,

$$X = T + E$$

There are two types of error that appear in test scores—random error and systematic error.

Random Error

Random error is the *unexplained* difference between the true score *(T)* and the obtained score *(X)*. Theoretically, if the test could be given an infinite number of times and an average score calculated from those administrations, the average test score would equal the true test score. Furthermore, if the average error from all those administrations were calculated, it would equal zero.

Systematic Error

One way to reduce random error is to find out what is causing the error and then eliminate or control it. When a single source of error can be identified, we can often calculate the amount and direction (positive or negative) of the error and take its source into account when we interpret test scores. Such known error is identified as **systematic error.** For instance, if you know that the scale in your bathroom regularly adds 3 pounds to anyone's weight, then you can simply subtract 3 pounds from whatever the scale says to get your true weight. The error your scale makes is predictable and systematic.

Let's look at an example of the difference between random and systematic error proposed by Nunnally (1978). If a chemist uses a thermometer that always reads 2 degrees higher than the actual temperature, then the error that results is *systematic*—it can be predicted and taken into account. If, however, the chemist is nearsighted and he reads the thermometer with a different amount and direction of inaccuracy each time, his readings will be wrong, but the error will be *random.*

Systematic error is often difficult to identify. However, two problems we discussed above—practice effects and order effects—can add systematic as well as random error to test scores. For instance, if test takers learn the answer to a question in the first test administration (practice effect) or they can derive the answer from a previous question (order effect), then everyone will get the question right. Such occurrences systematically raise test scores. In such cases, the error can be eliminated by removing the question or replacing it with another that will be unaffected by practice or order.

Another important distinction between random and systematic error is that random error lowers the reliability of a test. Systematic error does not—the test is reliably inaccurate the same amount each time! This concept will become apparent when we begin calculating reliability using correlation.

THE RELIABILITY COEFFICIENT

We need to be as accurate as possible in describing our estimates of test reliability. Therefore, we use **correlation** (discussed in Chapter 5) to provide an index of the strength and direction of the linear relationship between two variables. For test-retest reliability, the two variables are the scores when the test was administered the first time and the second time—or, in the case of alternate forms and internal consistency, the scores of the first test and the second test.

The symbol that is used to denote a correlation coefficient is r. To show that the correlation coefficient represents a reliability coefficient, we add two subscripts of the same letter—such as r_{xx} or r_{aa}. Chapter 5 explains how to calculate a reliability coefficient.

Adjusting Split-Half Reliability Estimates

As we mentioned before, the number of questions on a test is directly related to the test's reliability—the more questions on the test, the higher the reliability, provided that the test questions are equivalent in content and difficulty. When a test is divided into halves to calculate internal reliability, the test length is also reduced by half. Therefore, psychologists adjust the reliability coefficient (obtained when scores on each half are correlated) using the formula developed by Spearman and Brown. *This formula is used only when adjusting reliability coefficients derived using two halves of one test. Other reliability coefficients, such as test-retest or coefficient alpha, should not be adjusted.* In Greater Depth 6.2 gives the Spearman-Brown formula and shows how to calculate an adjusted reliability coefficient.

The Spearman-Brown formula is also helpful to test developers who wish to increase the reliability of a test. The length of the test influences the reliability of the test: The more *homogeneous* questions (questions about the same issue or trait) the respondent answers, the more information the test yields about the respondent's knowledge, skill, or attitude. This increase in information yields more distinctive information about each respondent and produces more variation in test scores. Test developers who wish to increase the reliability of a test use the Spearman-Brown formula to estimate how many homogeneous test questions should be added to a test to raise its reliability to the desired level.

Other Methods of Calculating Internal Consistency

As you recall, a better way to measure internal consistency is to compare individuals' scores on all possible ways of splitting the test into halves. This method compensates for any error introduced by any lack of equivalence in the two halves. The two formulas used for estimating internal consistency are the KR-20 (Kuder & Richardson, 1937, 1939), which is used for tests whose questions, such as

---

IN GREATER DEPTH 6.2

Using the Spearman-Brown Formula

The Spearman-Brown formula below represents the relationship between reliability and test length; it is used to adjust the correlation coefficient obtained when using the split-halves method for estimating reliability:

$$r_{xx} = \frac{nr}{1 + (n - 1)r}$$

where

r_{xx} = the estimated reliability of the test
n = the number of questions in the revised version divided by the number of questions in the original version of the test
r = the calculated correlation coefficient

Suppose you calculated a correlation coefficient of .80 for the split halves shown in For Your Infor-

mation 6.1. Because the whole test is twice as long as each half, n is 2. You can then follow these steps to adjust the coefficient obtained and estimate the reliability of the test:

Step 1: Substitute values of r and n into the equation.

$$r_{xx} = \frac{2(.80)}{1 + (2 - 1)(.80)}$$

Step 2: Complete the algebraic calculations.

$$r_{xx} = .89$$

Step 3: Our best estimate of the reliability of the test is .89.

true/false or multiple-choice, can be scored as either right or wrong. (Note that although multiple-choice questions have a number of possible answers, only one is correct.) Coefficient alpha (Cronbach, 1951) is used for questions, such as rating scales, that have more than two possible answers. Coefficient alpha may also be used for scales made up of questions with only one right answer.

In Greater Depth 6.3 provides the equations used to calculate these estimates of internal consistency.

For an overview of the types of reliability we have discussed and the appropriate formula to use for each, see Table 6.2.

Using Computer Software to Calculate Reliability

When you begin developing or using tests, you will not want to calculate reliability by hand. All statistical software programs and many spreadsheet programs will calculate Pearson's product-moment correlation. The user simply enters the test scores for the first and second administration (or halves) and chooses the menu command called "correlation." If you calculate the correlation coefficient to estimate split-halves reliability, you will need to adjust the correlation coefficient by hand using the Spearman-Brown formula, because it is rarely found on software.

Computing coefficient alpha and KR-20 is more complicated. Coefficient alpha and KR-20 are not found on spreadsheet software, but they are available on

---

IN GREATER DEPTH 6.3

Formulas for KR-20 and Coefficient Alpha

Two formulas for estimating internal reliability are the KR-20 formula and the coefficient alpha formula. KR-20 is used for scales that have questions that are scored either right or wrong, such as true/false or multiple-choice questions. The formula for coefficient alpha is an expansion of the KR-20 formula and is used when test questions have a range of possible answers, such as a rating scale. Coefficient alpha may also be used for scales made up of questions with only one right answer.

$$r_{KR20} = \left(\frac{k}{k-1} \right) \left(1 - \frac{\Sigma\, pq}{\sigma^2} \right)$$

where

r_{KR20} = the Kuder-Richardson formula 20 reliability coefficient
k = the number of questions on the test
σ^2 = the variance of all the test scores

p = the proportion of test takers who gave the correct answer to the question
q = the proportion of test takers who gave an incorrect answer to the question

The formula for coefficient alpha is similar to the KR-20 formula and is used when test takers have a number of answers from which to choose their response.

$$r_\alpha = \left(\frac{k}{k-1} \right) \left(1 - \frac{\Sigma\, \sigma^2 i}{\sigma^2} \right)$$

where

r_α = the coefficient alpha estimate of reliability
k = the number of questions on the test
σ^2_i = the variance of the scores on one question
σ^2 = the variance of all the test scores

TABLE 6.2. Methods of Estimating Reliability

Method	Test Administration	Formula for Calculating Reliability Coefficient
Test-retest reliability	Same test administered to the same people at two points in time	Pearson product-moment correlation
Alternate forms or parallel forms	Two forms of the test administered to the same people	Pearson product-moment correlation
Internal consistency	Give the test in one administration, then split the test into two halves for scoring	Pearson product-moment correlation corrected for length by the Spearman-Brown formula
Internal consistency	Give the test in one administration, then compare all possible split halves	Coefficient alpha or KR-20
Inter-rater reliability	Give the test once, but have it scored by two raters	Pearson product-moment correlation

the larger, better-known statistical packages, such as SAS and SPSS. Consult your software manual for instructions on how to use these equations.

INTERPRETING THE RELIABILITY COEFFICIENT

We look at a correlation coefficient—and a reliability coefficient—in two ways to interpret its meaning. First, we are interested in its sign—whether it is positive or negative. The sign tells us whether the two variables increase or decrease together (positive sign) or one variable increases as the other decreases (negative sign). We expect that reliable tests will always have positive signs.

Second, we look at the number itself. As you recall from Chapter 5, correlation coefficients range from −1 (a perfect negative correlation) to +1 (a perfect positive correlation). Most often the coefficient's number will fall in between. Therefore, if a test's reliability estimate is +.91, we know that its sign is positive—people who made high scores on the first administration made similarly high scores on the second, and people who made low scores on the first administration made similarly low scores on the second. Furthermore, the coefficient .91 is very close to +1.00, or perfect agreement, so the test appears to be very reliable.

Psychologists have not set a fixed value at which reliability can be interpreted as satisfactory or unsatisfactory. The amount of reliability necessary, and the amount of error that can be tolerated, depends on the purpose of the test. Cascio (1991), when referring to employment tests, suggests that reliability should be above .90 if the test compares individuals. He notes, however, that tests with reliabilities as low as .70 have proven useful in certain situations. Schmitt (1996) notes (but does not necessarily agree with) a common presumption among many researchers that a coefficient alpha of .70 is adequate.

To better understand the amount of error in a test score, we use another statistic called the standard error of measurement.

Calculating the Standard Error of Measurement

Psychologists use the **standard error of measurement (SEM)** as an index of the amount of inconsistency or error expected in an individual's test score. In other words, the SEM is a measure of how much the individual's test score *(X)* is likely to differ from the individual's true test score *(T)*. As you recall, the true test score is the theoretical score that would occur if there were no measurement errors. To see how to calculate the SEM, see In Greater Depth 6.4.

Interpreting the Standard Error of Measurement

To understand what the SEM means, we must apply it to an individual's test score. Because the SEM acts as a measure of variation, we can assume that if the individual took the test an infinite number of times:

- 68% of the observed test scores *(X)* would occur within ± 1 SEM of the true score *(T);*
- 95% of the observed test scores *(X)* would occur within ± 2 SEM of the true score *(T);* and
- 99.7% of the observed test scores *(X)* would occur within ± 3 SEM of the true score *(T).*

To understand this assumption, refer to our discussion of the properties of the normal curve in Chapter 5.

We can then use the information above to construct a **confidence interval**—a range of scores that we feel comfortable includes the true score. In Greater Depth 6.5 shows how to calculate a confidence interval for an observed score.

Confidence intervals are important because they give us a realistic estimate of

IN GREATER DEPTH 6.4

Calculating the Standard Error of Measurement (SEM)

The formula for calculating the standard error of measurement is:

$$SEM = \sigma \sqrt{1 - r_{xx}}$$

where

SEM = the standard error of measurement
σ = the standard deviation of one administration of the test scores
r_{xx} = the reliability coefficient

If $\sigma = 14.327$ and $r_{xx} = .91$, then you can calculate the standard error of measurement by substituting these values into the equation and completing the algebraic calculations as shown below.

$$SEM = 14.327 \sqrt{1 - .91}$$

$$SEM = 4.2981 \text{ or } 4.3$$

Calculating a 95% Confidence Interval

The formula for calculating a 95% confidence interval *(CI)* around a score is:

$$95\% \; CI = X + 1.96 \; (SEM)$$

where

95% *CI* = the 95 percent confidence interval
X = an individual's observed test score
SEM = the standard error of measurement for the test

1.96 represents the two points on the normal curve that include 95% of the scores

Therefore, if the observed test score is 90 and the standard error of measurement (SEM) is 4.3, then we can be 95% confident that the true test score *(T)* falls between (90 − 8.428) or 81.572 and (90 + 8.428) or 98.428.

$$95\% \; CI = 81.572 \; \text{to} \; 98.428$$

how much error exists in an individual's score. The confidence interval in In Greater Depth 6.5 was calculated using the data in Table 6.3, where the test scores fall at 5-point intervals. Although the reliability estimate was high (+.91), the confidence intervals still overlap adjacent scores. A person who scores 75 could have the same true score as the person who scored 70. Therefore, it is possible that the person who scored 75 and the person who scored 70 have the same true score.

Using the SEM to calculate confidence intervals and overlap between adjacent confidence intervals can be less accurate for extremely high or extremely low scores. As Embretson (1996) has demonstrated, SEMs are not constant across the entire set of scores. In other words, SEMs tend to be lower for scores near the mean (or average) scores and higher for extreme scores (the highest and lowest scores).

When test reliability is high, the standard error of measurement is small. As test reliability decreases, the standard error of measurement increases. Although high reliability is always important, it is especially so when test scores are used to distinguish among individuals.

TABLE 6.3. Test Scores for Two Candidates on Two Administrations

Test Taker	Score	
	First Administration	Second Administration
Adams	90	95
Butler	70	75
Chavez	50	65
Davis	100	95
Ellis	90	80
Franks	70	75
Garrison	60	65
Hartmann	75	80
Isaacs	75	80
Jones	85	80

For instance, many government agencies interview and hire people from a list that ranks candidates using scores from employment tests. The person with the highest score is ranked first, the person with the second highest score is ranked second, and so on. Managers interview the top three people instead of simply hiring the person with the highest score. Sometimes the person who is hired has a lower score than others on the list. Does this mean that he or she is less qualified?

Although factors other than test scores might be taken into account for hiring, the answer to whether the candidate really had a lower test score can be found by using the standard error of measurement to calculate a 95% confidence interval around each candidate's score. Often, there will be a substantial overlap of confidence intervals suggesting that, although there is a difference in observed scores, there might not be a difference in true scores of candidates.

Next we will discuss how the reliability estimate, and thus the reliability of the test, can be increased or decreased.

Summary Box 6.2
Calculating and Interpreting the Reliability Coefficient

- A reliability coefficient (r_{xx}) is calculated by correlating the scores of test takers on two administrations of the test.
- A reliability coefficient is interpreted by examining its sign (positive or negative) and its proximity to 1.00. Reliability coefficients should be positive and very close to 1.00.

- The standard error of measurement (SEM) provides a measure of how much an individual's score is likely to differ from the individual's true score.
- Using the standard error of measurement, we can calculate a confidence interval that is likely to contain the true score.

FACTORS THAT INFLUENCE RELIABILITY

Because reliability is so important to accurate measurement, we need to consider several factors that can increase or decrease test reliability. Error that can increase or decrease individual scores and thereby decrease reliability comes from four sources:

- *The test itself.* The test can generate error by being poorly designed or by containing trick questions, ambiguous questions, or poorly written questions, or by requiring a reading level higher than the reading level of people in the target population. (Chapter 10 provides information for designing tests that yield a minimal amount of error.)
- *The test administration.* Test administration can generate error when administrators do not follow instructions for administration in the test manual or allow disturbances to occur during the test period. For example, the test administrator might misread the instructions for the length of the test period, answer test takers' questions inappropriately, allow the room to be too hot, cold, or noisy, or display attitudes that suggest the test is too difficult or unimportant.
- *The test scoring.* Test scoring must be conducted accurately and according to the directions in the test manual. Scorers might make errors in judgment or in

calculating test scores. Although computer scoring is likely to decrease scoring errors, it is important that the correct scoring scheme be entered in the computer.

- *Test takers.* The test takers themselves also can contribute to test error. Fatigue and illness or exposure to test questions before the test can change test scores. In addition, test takers who do not provide truthful and honest answers introduce error into their test scores.

Table 6.4 shows how these sources of error affect the three strategies for estimating reliability related to the test itself. There are six particularly important factors related to the sources of error in Table 6.4—test length, homogeneity of questions, the test-retest interval, test administration, scoring, and cooperation of test takers. These are factors on which test developers and administrators can focus in order to increase test reliability and accuracy, and we discuss each in turn.

Test Length

As a rule, adding more questions that measure the same trait or attribute can increase a test's reliability. Each question on a test serves as an observation that indicates the test taker's knowledge, skill, ability, or other trait that is being measured. The more observations there are, the more accurate the measure is likely to be.

Adding more questions to a test would be similar to adding finer distinctions to a measuring tape—such as adding indications for each sixteenth of an inch to a tape that only had marks for each eighth of an inch. Likewise, shortening a test by skipping or dropping questions diminishes the test's reliability. An extreme exam-

TABLE 6.4. Effects of Error on the Reliability Coefficient

Method of Estimating Reliability	Source of Error			
	Test Itself	Test Administration	Test Scoring	Test Taker
Test-retest (short interval)	Minimal effect	Minimal if test is standardized Moderate if test is teacher made	Minimal if test is objective Moderate if test is subjective	Minimal effect
Test-retest (long interval)	Minimal effect	Minimal if test is standardized Moderate if test is teacher made	Minimal if test is objective Moderate if test is subjective	Extensive effect
Alternate forms (short interval)	Moderate if test is standardized Extensive if test is teacher made	Minimal if test is standardized Moderate if tests is teacher made	Minimal if test is objective Moderate if test is subjective	Minimal effect
Alternate forms (long interval)	Moderate if test is standardized Extensive if test is teacher made	Minimal if test is standardized Moderate if test is teacher made	Minimal if test is objective Moderate if test is subjective	Extensive effect
Internal consistency	Minimal effect	Minimal effect	Minimal effect	Minimal effect

ple is the test that is made up of only one question—a most unreliable way to measure any trait or attitude.

As you recall, the Spearman-Brown formula adjusts the reliability estimate for test length. Test developers can also use the Spearman-Brown formula to estimate the number of questions to add to a test to increase its reliability to the desired level.

There is an important exception to this rule pointed out by Embretson (1996): When using adaptive tests (such as the computer-based version of the GRE), a short test can be more reliable than a longer version. In an adaptive test, the test taker responds to questions selected based on her or his skill or aptitude level, and therefore the standard error of measure (SEM) decreases. As a result, the test taker answers fewer questions without sacrificing reliability. This circumstance, however, does not suggest that a test made up of one or only a few questions would be reliable.

Homogeneity of Questions

There is one important exception to the rule that adding questions increases reliability. A test will increase in reliability only if the questions on the test are homogeneous. That is, in order to increase reliability, the added questions must measure the same factor. Heterogeneous tests can be expected to have lower reliability coefficients. As you may recall, estimating reliability by calculating internal consistency is not appropriate for heterogeneous tests. If you have ever taken a test in which it seemed you were asked the same questions a number of times in slightly different ways, you have experienced a test that is homogeneous and probably very reliable.

Test-Retest Interval

The longer the interval between administrations of a test, the lower the reliability coefficient is likely to be. A long interval between test administrations provides more opportunity for test takers to change on the factor being measured. Such changes cause a change in individuals' true scores. In addition, the longer time increases the possibility of error through changes in test administration, environment, or personal circumstances.

Test Administration

Proper test administration affects the reliability estimate in three ways. First, carefully following all the instructions for administering a test ensures that all test takers experience the same testing situation each time the test is given. In other words, test takers hear the same instructions and take the test under the same physical conditions each time. Treating all test takers in the same way decreases error that arises from creating differences in the way individuals respond. Second, constancy between two administrations decreases error that arises when testing conditions differ. Third, effective testing practices (discussed in detail in Chapter 11) decrease the chance that test takers' scores will be contaminated with error due to poor testing conditions or poor test instructions.

Scoring

Even tests scored by computer are subject to being scored incorrectly. Test users must be careful to use the correct scoring key, to check questions that have unusually high numbers of correct or incorrect answers for mistakes in scoring, and to exercise considerable care when scoring tests that require judgments about whether an answer is right or wrong. Frequent checks of computations, including those made by computers, also decrease the chance of scoring errors.

Cooperation of Test Takers

Some tests such as the PAI have a built-in method for determining whether test takers guessed, faked, cheated, or in some other way neglected to answer questions truthfully or to the best of their ability. Many times, however, it is up to the test administrator to observe and motivate respondents to cooperate with the testing process. For instance, test administrators need to be aware of individuals who complete the test in an unusually short amount of time. These individuals might have checked off answers without reading the questions or skipped whole pages deliberately or by mistake. Although respondents cannot be forced to participate honestly, their tests can be dropped from the group of tests used to calculate reliability when there are doubts about the truthfulness of their answers.

Summary Box 6.3
Factors That Influence Reliability

- Errors that increase or decrease individual scores and change the reliability estimate come from four sources: the test itself, test administration, test scoring, and test takers.
- Errors resulting from poor test design include "trick," ambiguous, or poorly worded questions and reading levels that are too high for the target audience.
- Test administration can generate error when administrators do not follow instructions for test ad-

ministration or when the testing environment is uncomfortable or distracting.
- Tests must be scored accurately and according to the instructions in the test manual.
- Test takers can contribute to test error by being fatigued, ill, or by cheating or providing dishonest answers to questions.
- Reliability is related to test length—the longer the test, the more reliable it is likely to be—provided that the questions on the test are homogeneous.

SUMMARY

Psychological tests are measurement instruments. An important attribute of a measurement instrument is its reliability or consistency. We need evidence that the test yields the same score each time a person takes the test, unless he or she has actually changed. When we know a test is reliable, we can conclude that changes in a person's score really are due to changes in that person. Also, we can compare the scores of two or more people on a reliable test.

There are four methods for checking reliability. Each takes into account various conditions that could produce differences in test scores. Using the test-retest method, a test developer gives the same test to the same group of test takers on two different occasions. The scores from the first and second administrations are then correlated to obtain the reliability coefficient. The greatest danger in using the test-retest method of estimating reliability is that the test takers will score differently (usually higher) on the test because of practice effects.

To overcome such problems as practice effects and differences in persons and the test administration from one time to the next, psychologists often give two forms of the test—that follow the same test plan but have different content—to the same people at the same time. This method is called alternate or parallel forms.

When alternate forms are not available or feasible to use, psychologists measure the internal reliability or consistency of a test by giving the test once to one group of people. They do so by dividing the test into halves, then they correlate the scores on the first half with the scores on the second half. This method, called split-halves reliability, includes using the Spearman-Brown formula to adjust the correlation coefficient for test length. An even better way to measure internal consistency is to compare individuals' scores on all possible ways of splitting the test in using the KR-20 or coefficient alpha formulas.

The reliability of the method of scoring is also important. Tests that require the scorer to make judgments about the test taker's answers or tests that require observation of the test taker's behavior can have error contributed by the scorer. Scorer reliability—also known as inter-rater reliability—is estimated by having the test scored by two or more persons, then correlating their judgments.

No measurement instrument is perfectly reliable or consistent. We express this idea by saying that each observed test score *(X)* contains two parts—a true score *(T)* and error *(E)*. There are two types of error that appear in test scores—random error and systematic error.

To quantify a test's reliability estimate, we use a reliability coefficient—another name for the correlation coefficient when it estimates reliability. This statistic quantifies the estimated relationship between two forms of the test. The statistical procedure we use to calculate the reliability coefficient is the Pearson product-moment correlation. All statistical software programs and many spreadsheet programs will calculate the Pearson product-moment correlation. Coefficient alpha and KR-20 are available on statistical packages only.

To interpret the meaning of the reliability coefficient, we look at its sign and the number itself. Correlation coefficients range from −1 (a perfect negative correlation) to +1 (a perfect positive correlation). Psychologists have not set a fixed value at which reliability can be interpreted as satisfactory or unsatisfactory.

Psychologists use the standard error of measurement (SEM) as an index of the amount of inconsistency or error expected in an individual's test score. We can then use the SEM to construct a confidence interval—a range of scores that most likely includes the true score. Confidence intervals provide information about whether individuals' scores are truly different.

Finally, six factors—test length, homogeneity of questions, the test-retest interval, test administration, scoring, and cooperation of test takers—are important factors that influence test reliability.

KEY CONCEPTS

alternate forms
confidence interval
correlation
heterogeneous
homogeneous
internal consistency
internal reliability
inter-rater reliability

intrascorer consistency
measurement error
order effects
parallel forms
power test
practice effects
random error

reliability
scorer reliability
speed test
split-half method
standard error of
   measurement (SEM)
systematic error
test-retest method

LEARNING ACTIVITIES

1. Estimating Reliability

A. Below are the data for a test that was administered on two occasions to the same people to estimate its reliability. Answer the questions below regarding these data.

| | *Score* | |
Test Taker	First Administration	Second Administration
Tony	6	6
Meg	5	4
Chris	8	7
Sam	4	2
Tina	5	5
Ted	2	1
Abe	9	10
Ricardo	3	3

1. What type of reliability is being estimated?
2. What is the reliability coefficient for the test?
3. What is the standard error of measurement (SEM)?
4. What is the confidence interval that we can be 95% certain contains Tony's true score?
5. Would you say that Tony definitely scored higher than Meg did?

B. The data on the first administration of this test were also divided by randomly assigning each of the 10 questions to one of two halves. The results are shown below:

	Score	
Test Taker	First Half	Second Half
Tony	3	3
Meg	3	2
Chris	4	4
Sam	2	2
Tina	3	2
Ted	1	1
Abe	4	5
Ricardo	1	2

1. What type of reliability is being estimated in this instance?
2. What is the reliability coefficient for the test using these data?
3. Can you explain the difference in the two estimates of reliability?

2. Estimating Reliability Appropriately

Following are descriptions of situations in which the researcher needs to identify one or more ways to estimate reliability. In each instance, choose one or more methods for estimating reliability, tell why you chose the method(s), and describe the steps necessary for gathering the data needed to calculate your reliability coefficient.

1. An instructor has designed a comprehensive math exam for students entering community college. The exam is made up of multiple-choice questions that measure each of the following dimensions: reading formulas, carrying out math calculations, and solving word problems. He can only give his exam once, but he needs to know how reliable the test scores are. What should he do?
2. A researcher wants to assess attitudes about quality of work life. She wants to be sure her instrument is reliable. Her instrument contains 20 statements that respondents rate from 1 to 5. She has designed her instrument to be homogeneous. What method(s) should she use?
3. A promotion test for firefighters requires them to be rated by two experts on their knowledge, use, and maintenance of safety equipment. How can their scores be checked for reliability?
4. A test developer is constructing a measure of critical thinking. The instrument consists of a number of anagrams and riddles—problems whose answers are not readily apparent until solved. The test score depends on the length of time required to solve each problem. How should the test developer estimate reliability?

3. *Explaining Various Reports of Reliability*

In 1966, Julian Rotter published a monograph describing a personality construct he called *locus of control*—the extent to which a person believes that the reinforcements received in life are due to his or her own effort and ability. The monograph also contains a personality test to measure the extent of this belief in individuals. Table 6.5 contains the reliability information Rotter published for his test. Identify the types of reliability measured and explain why the reliability coefficients differ.

TABLE 6.5. Internal-External Control Test Data: Reliability Information From Rotter (1966) Reprinted by Permission

	INTERNAL CONSISTENCY			
Sample	Type	N	Sex	r
Ohio State University	Split half	50	M	.65
Elementary psychology students	Spearman-Brown	50	F	.79
Sample 1		100	Combined	.73
	Kuder-Richardson	50	M	.70
		50	F	.76
		100	Combined	.73
Ohio State University	Kuder-Richardson	200	M	.70
Elementary psychology students		200	F	.70
		400	Combined	.70
National stratified sample	Kuder-Richardson	1,000	Combined	.69
Purdue opinion poll			M & F approximately equal N's	

	TEST-RETEST RELIABILITY			
Sample	Type	N	Sex	r
Ohio State University	1 month	30	M	.60
Elementary psychology students	Group administration	30	F	.80
		60	Combined	.72
Prisoners Colorado Reformatory	1 month	28	M	.78
Ohio State University	1st group administration	54	F	.61
	2nd individual administration	117	Combined	.55

Evaluating What a Test Really Measures

"I purchased an intelligence test at the bookstore. I showed it to my psychology professor and he told me to be careful. He said that just because the test is called an intelligence test doesn't necessarily mean that it measures intelligence. How do you know whether a test measures what it says it measures?"

"I took the driving portion of my driving test yesterday. It took about an hour. I had to show them how to use the blinkers, flashers, and lights. I also had to make a right turn, left turn, parallel park, merge into traffic, and drive in the city and on the highway. Why did they make me do so many things?"

"We have a psychology midterm exam next week. The psychology professor showed us what he called a test plan. He said that the test would cover five chapters. He said we would need to know the terms and be able to apply the principles. He also said that there would be 50 questions on the test. Why would he give us this information?"

"I applied for a secretarial job last week. The written test they gave me didn't look very professional. The test form was dirty and crumpled, the questions were confusing, and they asked me questions that were totally unrelated to secretarial work. What is the deal?"

Many people believe that the title of a test tells them what the test measures. The title of a test actually tells us very little. A test might measure some broader, narrower, or even different attribute than implied by the title. A test titled "The Math Achievement Test" might measure academic achievement (which is broader), achievement in geometry (which is narrower), or general intelligence (which is a different attribute altogether). Measures of reliability tell us whether a test measures whatever it measures consistently, but only measures of **validity** can provide us with information about what a test actually measures.

This chapter introduces three measures of validity—content validity, criterion-related validity, and construct validity. It provides an overview of these types of validity and provides some guidelines for determining when each type of validity is appropriate. We focus most of our attention on defining content validity and discussing two methods for evaluating the content validity of a test. Chapters 8 and 9 provide detailed discussions of criterion-related validity and construct validity. This chapter ends with another, although less important, type of validity—face validity.

THE DIFFERENT FORMS OF VALIDITY

Validity in General

When we ask whether a test is valid, we are asking "Does the test measure what it claims to measure?" It is crucial to know the answer to this question because, as you recall, psychological tests are used to make important decisions. In education, classroom tests are used to test a student's knowledge of the material presented and to determine grades. In organizations, tests are used to make decisions about hiring, promotion, and salary, and to determine training effectiveness. In clinical settings, tests are used to make diagnoses and treatment decisions. If we don't know whether a test really measures what it claims to measure, then we cannot know whether the decisions we make using the test are right. You wouldn't want to place faith in the score you obtained on a store-bought intelligence test if there was no evidence that it really measured intelligence, would you?

Major Types of Validity

The American Psychological Association's *Standards for Educational and Psychological Testing* (1985) and psychological testing specialists generally recognize three ways of deciding whether a test is sufficiently valid to be useful. These are strategies for obtaining evidence of content validity, criterion-related validity, and construct validity.

Content Validity

We determine **content validity** by carefully examining a test to determine whether the questions on the test are representative of the material that should be covered by the test. If a test is made up of questions that represent all aspects of the attribute being measured, then the test is said to show evidence of content validity. For example, there are many different behaviors one must perform when driving an automobile. If the road portion of a driving test requires the test taker to perform a representative sample of these driving activities (for example, turning left and right, merging into traffic, parallel parking), then there is evidence the test has content validity.

Criterion-Related Validity

We determine the **criterion-related validity** of a test by correlating the scores on a test with scores on another measure of performance or behavior. If the scores on a test correlate with the other measure of performance, the test shows evidence of criterion-related validity. For example, if applicants' scores on an employment test correlate with their scores on a measure of their job performance, the test shows evidence of criterion-related validity.

There are two types of criterion-related validity, predictive and concurrent. An employment test has predictive validity if high scores are achieved by those who later do well on the job. For example, if a number of people score high on an employment test and then they later perform well on the job, as measured by a performance appraisal, peer evaluations, and so on, (and people who score low perform poorly on the job) the test shows evidence of predictive validity. On the other hand, an employment test has concurrent validity if the scores on the test correlate closely, at the same point in time, with the scores on some other well-established measure of job performance. For example, if a performance appraisal indicates that some current employees are doing well on the job and these employees also do well on the employment test, while poorly performing employees do poorly on the test, the test shows evidence of concurrent validity. Chapter 8 explains criterion-related validity in detail.

Construct Validity

Last, we determine the **construct validity** of a test by examining whether the test's relationship to other information coincides with some theory. There are several different ways of providing evidence of construct validity, and we discuss these in more detail in Chapter 9. One way to evaluate construct validity is to examine whether the scores on a test coincide with some expected behavior. For example, if a test were supposed to measure marital satisfaction, we would expect unhappy couples who have attended marital therapy to score higher than unhappy couples who have not attended marital therapy. We might also expect that marital satisfaction scores would be unrelated to a test of mechanical aptitude, because marital satisfaction and mechanical ability are unrelated.

Face Validity

Although it is not recognized as one of the primary types of validity, test developers and users often speak of **face validity**—the extent to which the test taker perceives that the test measures what it is supposed to measure.

Summary Box 7.1
The Different Forms of Validity

- When we ask whether a test is valid, we are asking "Does the test measure what it claims to measure?" We can answer this question by evaluating a test's content validity, criterion-related validity, or construct validity.
- *Content validity* is a validation strategy that involves scrutinizing the content of a test to determine whether the sample of questions in the test is representative of all the relevant questions that might have been asked.
- *Criterion-related validity* is a validation strategy that involves determining whether scores on a psychological test are correlated with some external criterion. There are two types of criterion-related validity. Predictive validity is a valida-

tion procedure that involves correlating scores on a test with scores on future performance or behavior. Concurrent validity is a validation procedure that involves correlating scores on a test to the scores on a measure of current performance or behavior.
- *Construct validity* is a validation strategy that involves accumulating evidence that the expected behavior of high scorers and low scorers on the test is related to the test scores.
- *Face validity* is concerned with the extent to which the test taker *perceives* that the test measures what it is supposed to measure, unlike the other forms of validity, which are concerned with whether a test measures what it says it measures.

THE APPROPRIATE USE
OF VALIDATION STRATEGIES

A valid test is a test that does the job it is intended to do: It measures the construct it is supposed to measure or predicts the outcome it claims to predict. Achievement tests are supposed to measure how well the test taker has mastered the content of a course or training program. Aptitude tests are supposed to measure a person's ability to perform a task or activity. Some employment tests are supposed to predict future performance on the job. Measures of validity help us determine whether the test does what it is supposed to or measures what it says it measures.

Another attribute of test validity is that the test must be used for its intended purpose. A reading test that is valid and appropriate for determining how well the test taker can read and comprehend written material would not be a valid measure of intelligence.

It is sometimes possible, but not always necessary, to gather evidence of content validity, criterion-related validity, and construct validity for a single test. Usually, the appropriate strategy for gathering validity evidence depends on the purpose of the test.

Some tests measure **concrete attributes** like the ability to play the piano. Concrete attributes are attributes that can be described in terms of specific behaviors. Most people would agree that there are specific behaviors associated with being able to play the piano. Other tests measure **abstract attributes** such as personality, intelligence, creativity, and aggressiveness. These attributes are more difficult to describe in terms of behaviors because people might disagree on what these behaviors represent. (Try this yourself. What does it mean to be intelligent? Is the person a high academic achiever? Does the person demonstrate common sense? Is creativity part of intelligence?)

Content validity is most appropriate for tests like achievement tests that measure concrete attributes, because the job of an achievement test is to measure how well someone has mastered the content of a course or training program. To determine whether the test measures what it says it measures, we can compare the content of the test to the content of the course. If the test is content valid, the questions on the test should be representative of all the relevant information covered in the course. They should also match the instructional objectives of the course.

Gathering evidence of content validity is more difficult (but not necessarily less appropriate) when the attribute being measured (like personality or intelligence) is abstract, because such attributes have to be carefully defined and linked to observable behaviors.

Criterion-related validity is most appropriate for tests that claim to predict outcomes, such as success on the job. If an employment test needs to forecast who is likely to be successful on the job, then its purpose is to predict future job performance, not to determine how well certain concepts have been mastered. Criterion-related validity is therefore most appropriate for employment tests.

Construct validity is appropriate when a test measures an abstract construct like marital satisfaction. Construct validity involves accumulating evidence of reliability and a number of types of validity. Rather than thinking of construct validity as a distinct and different type of validity, it is best to think of it as a larger category that can overlap content validity and criterion-related validity.

CONTENT VALIDITY

Content validity is the extent to which the questions on a test are representative of the trait, behavior, or attribute being measured. Content validity is similar to criterion-related and construct validity in that it helps us answer the question about whether a test measures what it says it measures. However, as you will see in Chapters 8 and 9, content validity differs from criterion-related and construct validity because it involves examining the questions on the test rather than correlating the test scores to a measure of performance or another test. Furthermore, gathering evidence of content validity need not involve a statistical analysis.

Content validity is important to all types of psychological tests. Here are some examples:

- A content-valid paper-and-pencil test of "attitude toward life" has questions that adequately represent the wide-ranging situations in which people can demonstrate their attitudes toward life—in the home, on the job, and in social situations.
- A content-valid employment test intended to measure mechanical aptitude contains test questions that represent the many tasks a mechanic must perform.
- A classroom math achievement test shows evidence of content validity if the proportion and type of math questions on the exam approximate the proportion and type of material read and/or covered in the class.

How do you obtain evidence of content validity? Content validity is demonstrated in two ways. The first involves performing a series of systematic steps, beginning with defining a testing universe—the attribute, behavior, or trait being measured (for example, math achievement or personality)—and ending with the administration of the test. This method does not result in any final number by which to evaluate the content validity of the test; rather, it gives the test developer and user confidence that the test includes a representative sample of behaviors.

The second method for demonstrating content validity occurs after the test has been developed and involves having experts rate how essential each test question is to what is being measured. This method does result in a final number that can be used to quantify the content validity of the test. In other words, the experts' rating provides a measure of how relevant the questions are to the attribute being measured.

Defining the Testing Universe and Developing a Test Plan

To ensure that a test is content valid, test developers perform the following steps when designing written tests or tests of performance.

Define the Testing Universe

The first step is to define carefully the **testing universe**—the body of knowledge or behaviors that the test represents. Is the test developer interested in developing a test to measure knowledge of psychology, life satisfaction, personality, or intelligence, or some other concrete or abstract attribute, skill, or knowledge area? This step usually involves locating theoretical or empirical research on the attribute, reviewing other instruments that measure the attribute, and interviewing experts who are familiar with the attribute. A content-valid test covers all major aspects of the testing universe in the correct proportion (Groth-Marnat, 1997).

For example, if the attribute being measured is self-esteem, the test developer would review various theories of self-esteem, studies in which self-esteem has been investigated, and other tests of self-esteem. If the attribute is more concrete, such as computational math skills, the test developer would review research, including other tests, on computational math skills as well as interview those who teach computational math skills to the target audience.

Develop Test Specifications

After the universe has been defined, test developers develop **test specifications** that document the plan for the written test or practical exam. These are similar to the specifications for building a building or a piece of equipment. The specifications can vary depending on whether the test developer is developing a test to measure an attribute, skill, or knowledge. Most test specifications for tests of knowledge identify the **content areas** (the topics that are to be covered in the test), the **instructional objectives** (what one should be able to do with those topics), and the number of questions to be asked within each content area and instructional objective. In Greater Depth 7.1 presents the test specifications for a 70-item exam for students studying psychological tests and measurements. For Your Information 7.1 discusses training, competency exams, and content validity.

Establish a Test Format

Once the test plan has been developed, test developers decide on the test format. They decide whether the test will be a written test, in which a test taker must answer a series of questions, or a practical test, in which a test taker must actively

---

IN GREATER DEPTH 7.1

Specification Table of a 70-Item Exam on Tests and Measurements

To design a test, test developers begin with a defined testing universe. A specification table or test plan for a test of knowledge further defines the testing universe and identifies the content areas and the instructional objectives covered on the test. The specification table also includes the number of questions to be asked in each content area and for each instructional objective.

Below is a test specification table similar to ones that the authors of this text use to write questions for an exam on psychological tests and measurements. The content areas are test-retest reliability, alternate forms reliability, split-half reliability, inter-rater reliability, content validity, criterion-related validity, and construct validity. The instructional objectives are to teach students the terms and concepts of reliability and validity and to teach them to apply these concepts. As you can see, the specification table indicates that the same number of questions will be asked to measure students' knowledge of each of the content areas and each of the instructional objectives.

INSTRUCTIONAL OBJECTIVES

Content Area	Knowledge of Terms and Concepts	Application of Concepts	Number of Questions
Test-retest reliability	5	5	10
Alternate forms reliability	5	5	10
Split-half reliability	5	5	10
Inter-rater reliability	5	5	10
Content validity	5	5	10
Criterion-related validity	5	5	10
Construct validity	5	5	10
Total questions	35	35	70

Organizations invest money, time, and energy in developing, administering, and evaluating training programs. Organizations also evaluate training programs so they can systematically collect information and make informed decisions about selecting, adopting, and modifying training programs (Goldstein, 1993).

Many organizations administer a competency exam at the completion of a training program to determine whether the training program was effective (Smith & Merchant, 1990). Competency exams attempt to measure how well individuals learned the knowledge and skills taught during training. Competency exams can be paper-and-pencil exams or practical "hands-on" exams. (Paper-and-pencil exams require test takers to answer questions on paper; practical exams require individuals to demonstrate their knowledge or display their new skills in a real-life situation.)

When properly developed and administered, competency exams help organizations in a variety of ways. For example, they can determine whether

- employees can use the new computer software they have been trained to use,
- customer service representatives can provide the correct information to customers, or
- telephone operators can properly use the switchboard.

If a competency exam suggests that employees do not have the necessary knowledge or skills, then the organization needs to reevaluate the content and delivery of its training program. Like other types of tests, competency-based tests are only as useful as they are content valid. Therefore, the developers of competency-based training programs must ensure that their exams are valid—that they adequately measure a trainee's knowledge, skills, and behaviors (Smith & Merchant, 1990). To develop and administer a valid competency exam, test developers perform the following steps:

1. Determine the learning objectives of the training program. These objectives come from an indepth analysis of the knowledge, skills, and abilities required for a particular job. The requirements of a job can be determined by conducting a job analysis, by reviewing job descriptions, or by interviewing job incumbents.
2. Outline the content areas of the exam. An outline ensures that relevant subject matter is neither omitted nor inappropriately emphasized on an exam. Table 7.1 shows a sample outline of the content for a generated manufacturing orders training module competency exam.
3. Establish the format for the exam. They must decide whether the exam will be a written exam or a practical exam, and what types of items will be included on the exam (e.g., multiple-choice and true/false).
4. Construct the exam items.
5. Put the exam in writing.

When they have finished writing the exam, they reevaluate the content validity of the exam by asking the following questions (Smith & Merchant, 1990):

1. Are all exam items job-related? (Knowledge or skills that are not needed on the job should not be included on the competency exam.)
2. Are the knowledge and skills being tested adequately covered in the training program?
3. Is the exam comprehensive and does it weigh areas appropriately?

Competency exams can provide organizations with valuable information about whether their training programs are teaching the knowledge, skills, and abilities necessary to be successful on a job. However, the usefulness of competency exams, like all psychological tests, depends on showing evidence that the test is valid—that it measures what it claims to measure—and using the test for its correct purpose.

TABLE 7.1. Examination Content Outline

Content	Areas	Weight	Question Number	Question Number
General categories	Subcategories	(Percentage of total score)	**Written questions** (paper and pencil)	**Practical questions** (work samples and simulations)
Manufacturing repair process		25	1, 2, 3, 4, 5	
Manufacturing repair process	A. Concepts	50	9, 10, 11, 13	1, 2, 4
	B. Netting logic and Application		8, 12, 14, 15, 16, 18, 19, 25, 26, 27	3, 5, 6, 7, 11, 13 8, 9, 10, 12, 14, 15,
	C. BOM		6, 7, 17, 28	16
Maintenance transactions	A. Creating an order	25	20, 21, 22	17, 18, 21
	B. Allocating material		23, 24, 29	19, 20
	C. Releasing order		30, 31	22, 23, 24, 25, 26

Source: Adapted from Smith & Merchant, 1990.

demonstrate skills in specific situations. The test developers also decide what types of questions (multiple-choice, true/false, matching, etc.) to use.

Construct Test Questions

After the test format has been decided, test developers write the test questions, being careful that each represents the content area and objective it is intended to measure. We will discuss test development and item writing (steps 3 and 4) in great detail in Chapters 10 and 11. In Greater Depth 7.2 describes the assessment center method, which is based on content validity.

Summary Box 7.2
Content Validity and Test Specification Tables

- Content validity is the extent to which the questions on a test are representative of the construct, trait, or attribute being measured.
- Content validity is similar to criterion-related and construct validity in that it helps us answer the question about how adequately a test measures what it says it measures.
- Content validity differs from criterion-related and construct validity because it involves examining the questions on a test rather than correlating the test scores to a criterion or another test.
- Content validity is established during the construction of a test by defining a testing universe, constructing a test specification table that defines the content of the test, establishing a test format, and carefully writing test questions.

Evaluating Content Validity After Test Development

When purchasing a test, users should not *assume* that a test is content valid or shows evidence of any form of validity. Evidence of validity should be provided by the publisher in the test manual that accompanies the test. Chapter 11 describes

The Assessment Center Method

The Assessment Center Orientation

An **assessment center** is a method—not a place—that organizations use for assessing job-related dimensions, such as leadership, decision-making, planning and organizing. Employers use assessment center results to make decisions regarding hiring, promoting, or training. A typical assessment center contains job simulations that engage the test taker in role-play activities. Trained assessors observe and document the test takers' behaviors during the simulations and rate the test takers' demonstration of expertise on well-defined dimensions of job performance.

Common simulations known as "exercises" are:

- *The in-basket exercise.* This simulation provides the test taker with simulated incoming mail. Other materials include a calendar and an organizational chart identifying key persons in the fictional organization. The test taker must take appropriate action on each piece of mail. Those actions are then evaluated and rated by the assessors.
- *Role plays.* These exercises are detailed role-playing activities in which the test taker interacts with one or more persons (trained role players) to solve problems. Typical themes include handling a difficult employee or customer. Assessors observe and rate test takers' behaviors in these exercises.
- *Leaderless discussion groups.* In this exercise, test takers are assigned to small groups with in-

structions to discuss or solve a job-related issue. Again, the assessors observe and rate test takers' behaviors.

A selection program used by the U.S. Office of Strategic Services (OSS) during World War II is credited as beginning the assessment center movement (Smither, 1994). The OSS—forerunner of the Central Intelligence Agency (CIA)—developed a 3-day psychological screening program for potential agents that was used to predict how an individual would perform (and succeed!) as a spy. What was different about this screening program was that candidates for the job of spy were observed and evaluated on behavioral simulations.

One role-play required the candidate to devise a cover story in 12 minutes that would explain why he was carrying secret government files. Three examiners then relentlessly questioned the candidate in a manner that became progressively more hostile and abusive. After the questioning, all candidates were told they had "failed" the exercise, then they were directed to another office where a friendly colleague encouraged them to discuss the exercise. When the candidates relaxed and openly discussed their interrogation, they found they had made a fateful misjudgment. They had just confided important information—not to a friend—but to another examiner! (Smither, 1994).

After the war, large industrial organizations began to use the assessment center method to hire managers. Gatewood and Feild (1994) cite the Management Progress Study of AT&T begun in 1956 as the first industrial application of the assessment center method. Other early users included Michigan Bell, Sears Roebuck, and General Electric. Such programs provided information that was used for hiring and promoting of managers.

In the next two decades, assessment centers continued to achieve growing acceptance. One expert (Cohen, 1978) estimated that in the early 1970's the number of organizations using assessment centers grew from 100 to 1,000. Assessment centers also became important in the public sector as state and local governments discovered that this method was fair and accurate for hiring police officers and fire fighters.

Today, assessment centers are still a popular method for hiring and promoting police and fire personnel. A number of Fortune 500 corporations continue to evaluate managers in assessment centers. A major barrier to the use of assessment centers in the 1990s is the labor cost associated with an assessment procedure that requires a number of professionally trained assessors and role players. Since untrained assessors are not likely to provide accurate judgments or ratings, assessors should receive training on observing, documenting and rating behaviors.

Interscorer reliability is a major concern for assessment centers, because all scores are based on the subjective ratings of assessors. Usually, assessors meet to discuss their observations and arrive at consensual ratings for each individual in a process that ensures interrater consistency. When Brostoff and Meyer (1984) required assessors to make independent ratings, they obtained interrater reliability ranging from .84 to .91.

Most assessment centers rely on a content validity strategy. *The Uniform Guidelines on Employee Selection Procedures* (1978) requires organizations to link the test with a thorough job analysis to provide evidence of content validity. In 1982, Haymaker and Grant presented a model for the content validation of assessment centers that specified nine steps:

1. *Identification of job task domain:* In this step, job analysts compile a list of tasks performed by job incumbents.

2. *Refinement of job task content domain:* Incumbents rate each task for its importance, frequency, and whether they learned to perform the task on the job.

3. *Identification of content domain of knowledge, skills, and abilities (KSAs):* Experts determine the KSAs needed to perform each task.

4. *Refinement of content domain of KSAs:* Incumbents rate each KSA on its importance for successful performance of the job.

5. *Deviation and definition of assessment center dimensions:* Test developers analyze the KSA ratings to determine the dimensions on which individuals will be tested.

6. *Affirmation of assessment center dimensions:* Test dimensions are reviewed by job experts for suitability.

7. *Development of assessment center exercises:* Simulations are written that directly reflect job tasks.

8. *Affirmation of the adequacy of dimension behavior sampling:* An independent panel rates each simulation on the extent to which appropriate behaviors are elicited by the exercise.

9. *Standardization and assessor training:* Preparation of a test manual containing instructions for assessors, assessor trainers, and administrators assures that the assessment center will be properly conducted. (Haymaker and Grant, 1982)

Research suggests that assessment centers provide one of the best predictors of job performance. A meta-analysis of validation studies estimated validity for assessment centers at .53 for job potential and .36 for job performance (Gaugler, Rosenthal, Thornton & Bentson, 1987). Chapter 8 provides a thorough discussion of validity coefficients and their interpretation.

A related advantage for the assessment center method is its lack of sex and race bias. The results of a validation study (Knowles and Bean, 1981) for an assessment center used by the City of St. Louis for selecting Captains in their fire department is typical. This examination contained a written test and an assessment center. On the written test, the average score for Blacks was over 8 points lower (statistically different at $p < .05$); however, on the assessment center, the average score for Blacks was less than one point different from that of Whites (not statistically different).

the test manual and its contents in more detail. In addition, test users may wish to evaluate a test after purchase. Validation by the test user is particularly important when the test is used for a group of people other than those for whom it was developed. For instance, one organization might purchase a test that was developed for another organization. In this case, a panel of experts can rate whether each question on the test measures the attribute, knowledge, or skill the test assesses as defined by their organization.

Experts rate each question on the test as (1) essential, (2) useful but not essential, or (3) not necessary. The number of experts who state that a question is essential is noted for each question. The question is considered content valid if more than half of the experts indicate that the question is essential for measuring a portion of the test domain. The more "essential" ratings a question has, the more content valid the question is (Lawshe, 1975).

Content validity ratios have been used to determine the content validity of employment tests (Ford & Wroten, 1984), measures of the work behavior of psychiatric aides (Distefano, Pryer, & Erffmeyer, 1983), mathematics achievement tests (Crocker, Llabre, & Miller, 1988), and assessment centers.

Content Validity Summary

It is important that psychological tests show evidence of content validity. The usefulness of content validity is clear in educational and organizational settings. In educational settings, content validation plays an important role in validating educational achievement tests that assess how well a student has learned the content of a course. In organizational settings, content validation is essential for tests used in personnel selection to establish that a test is job-related. Content validation is also playing a somewhat larger role in clinical and personality assessment, because test developers are constantly working to define their constructs (Butcher, Graham, Williams, & Ben-Porath, 1990; Haynes, Richard, & Kubany, 1995; Millon, 1994). Chapter 9 discusses the role that content validity plays in establishing construct validity and the distinction between content and construct validity.

FACE VALIDITY

Sometimes test users and test developers discuss face validity. Unlike the other forms of validity, *face validity tells us nothing about what a test actually measures.* Instead, face validity refers to how test takers *perceive* the attractiveness and appropriateness of a test. Face validity is important, for it can influence how test takers approach the test. If test takers believe that a test has face validity, they will often make a more conscientious effort to complete the test. If a test taker believes that a test does not have face validity, they might hurry through the test and take it less seriously (Rogers, 1995).

Imagine that you applied for a secretarial job and were asked to take a paper-and-pencil employment test designed to measure secretarial ability. When you sat down to take the test, you noticed that it contained questions about your communication skills and your knowledge of office equipment. You would probably perceive this test as being appropriate or face valid because being a secretary requires good communication skills and familiarity with office equipment.

Now imagine that you applied for a secretarial position and when you sat down to take the test, you noticed that it contained questions that asked you about your knowledge of engineering. You would probably wonder whether engineering has anything to do with your secretarial skills. You might perceive this test as inappropriate (or having low face validity) and devote less effort to completing the test carefully and honestly.

So, even though a psychological test might show evidence of content validity (and criterion-related or construct validity as we will discuss in the next two chapters), if it does not appear to be face valid to the test takers, the test might not provide an accurate measurement due to decreased effort or cooperation on the part of the test taker. Chapter 8 discusses research on the use of "subtle" questions (which lack face validity) on the Minnesota Multiphasic Personality Inventory (MMPI).

Some researchers take face validity seriously, and they have proposed a quantitative way of assessing the face validity of a psychological test (Nevo, 1985, 1993; Nevo & Sfez, 1985). In their study, test takers and other "psychometrically naive" persons complete a questionnaire that requires them to answer questions about the suitability of a test for its intended use. Research on the value of such a procedure shows promising inter-rater agreement and test-retest reliability. These researchers recommend that test manuals include both qualitative and quantitative information about the face validity of tests.

Although it is helpful for a test to have face validity, face validity alone is not an acceptable means of determining the true validity of a test. The next chapter discusses criterion-related validity and also points out how face validity can decrease validity by allowing respondents to fake or lie about their responses.

Summary Box 7.3
Evaluating Content Validity and Face Validity

- Test users should not assume that a test is content valid.
- The test publisher should provide evidence of validity in a test manual.
- Test users may evaluate the content validity of a test using a panel of experts who rate whether each question on the test measures an attribute, knowledge, or skill defined by their organization.

- Face validity—unlike other forms of validity—tells nothing about what the test actually measures. Rather face validity refers to whether test takers perceive the test to be appropriate.
- Although it is helpful for a test to have face validity, face validity alone is not an acceptable means of determining the true validity of a test.

SUMMARY

Because decisions are made using psychological tests, it is important that psychological tests measure what they say they measure and that test users administer the test only for its intended purpose. The validity of a test helps us understand how adequately a test measures what it is designed to measure. There are three primary measures of validity—content validity, criterion-related validity, and construct va-lidity. It is usually not appropriate or possible to estimate the validity of a test us-ing all of these validation procedures. The strategy chosen to provide evidence of validity depends on the nature and purpose of the psychological test.

The content validity of a test is determined by scrutinizing the content of a test to ensure that the test includes a representative sample of behaviors. There are two methods for determining the content validity of a test. The first method involves developing a test plan during test development, and the second involves calculat-ing agreements among raters after the test has been developed. Though different from other types of validity, face validity—the perception of the test taker that the test questions are appropriate—is also important.

KEY CONCEPTS

abstract attributes	**content areas**	**instructional objectives**
assessment center	**content validity**	**test specifications**
concrete attributes	**criterion-related validity**	**testing universe**
construct validity	**face validity**	**validity**

LEARNING ACTIVITIES

1. Constructing Test Specifications for an Exam

A. Review the material in this chapter, then construct a test specification table for an exam on this chapter. Include both knowledge and practical questions.
B. Compare your test specification table with those of two or three other students, and identify areas where you agree and disagree. Discuss your disagreements and come to a consensus about what test specifications would lead to a con-tent-valid exam.

2. Defining the Testing Universe for an Abstract Concept

A. Select an abstract attribute, such as self-esteem, intelligence, or job satisfaction. How would you go about defining the testing universe? Write your definition of the construct and describe what should be included in the testing universe.
B. Be prepared to explain your testing universe to the class and get their reactions.

Using Tests
to Make Decisions

"The graduate school I'm applying to says they won't accept anyone who scores less than 1,000 on the GRE. How did they decide that 1,000 is the magic number?"

"When I applied for my job, I had to take an honesty test. Can a few questions on a piece of paper predict how honest someone will be on the job?"

"My company uses a test for hiring salespeople to work as telemarketers. The test is designed for people selling life insurance and automobiles. Is this a good test for hiring telemarketers?"

Have you ever wondered how psychological tests really work? How can we be comfortable using people's answers to test questions to make decisions about hiring them for a job or admitting them to college? Can mental disorders really be diagnosed using scores on standard questionnaires?

Psychologists who use tests for decision making are constantly asking these questions and others like them. When tests are used for making decisions that affect individual lives, psychologists as well as the public want substantial evidence that the decisions being made are the correct ones.

This chapter describes the processes that psychologists use to assure that tests perform properly when they are used for making predictions and decisions. We begin by discussing the concept of criterion-related validity. We also discuss the importance of selecting a valid criterion measure, how to evaluate validity coefficients, and the statistical processes that provide evidence that a test can be used for making predictions.

WHAT IS CRITERION-RELATED VALIDITY?

In this chapter, we examine how tests are used to make predictions. An important standard for determining validity (whether the test measures what it is supposed to measure) is how strongly the test predicts behaviors or events. When test scores correlate with independent behaviors, attitudes, or events, we say the test has **criterion-related validity.**

For example, when you apply for a job, you might be asked to take a test that predicts how well you will perform the job. If the job is clerical, the test score should be related to your skill in performing clerical duties, such as word processing and filing. To provide evidence that the test predicts clerical performance, psychologists correlate test scores for a large number of people with a measure of their performance on clerical tasks. Often supervisors rate employees' performance, and these ratings are correlated with test scores. The measure of performance that is correlated with test scores is called the **criterion.**

Tests are often used in a clinical setting to diagnose mental disorders. A diagnosis made by a psychologist or psychiatrist independent of the test becomes the criterion. Test scores are then correlated with clinical diagnoses to establish evidence of criterion-related validity.

Educators use admissions tests to forecast how successful an applicant will be in college or graduate school. The Scholastic Assessment Test (SAT) and the

Graduate Record Exam (GRE) are examples of admissions tests used by colleges. The criterion of success in college is often the student's grade point average (GPA).

149

CHAPTER 8
Using Tests to Make Decisions

METHODS FOR DEMONSTRATING CRITERION-RELATED VALIDITY

There are two methods for demonstrating criterion-related validity: the predictive method and the concurrent method. This section defines and gives examples of each method.

The Predictive Method

When it is important to show a relationship between test scores and a future behavior, the predictive method is used to establish validity. In this case, a large group of people takes the test, and their scores are held for a preestablished time interval. When the time interval has elapsed, a measure of some behavior (the criterion) is taken. Then the test scores are correlated with the criterion scores. If the test scores and the criterion scores correlate, we say the test has **predictive validity.**

The predictive method was chosen by the researchers at Brigham Young University to demonstrate the criterion-related validity of the PREParation for Marriage Questionnaire. For Your Information 8.1 describes the study they conducted.

Psychologists might use the predictive method in an organizational setting to establish predictive validity for an employment test. To do so, they administer an employment test (predictor) to candidates for a job. Researchers file test scores in a secure place, and the scores are not used for making hiring decisions. All, or most, of the candidates are hired—often on the basis of some other criterion. After a predetermined time interval, usually 3 to 6 months, supervisors evaluate the new hires on how well they perform the job (the criterion). To determine whether the test scores predict the candidates who were successful and unsuccessful, researchers correlate the test scores with the ratings of job performance. The resulting correlation coefficient is called the **validity coefficient.** We use it to infer the extent of criterion-related validity that the test may have.

It is important when using the predictive method that everyone who took the test is also measured on the criterion. For organizations this requirement presents problems, because there are rarely as many job openings as candidates, and managers do not wish to hire everyone regardless of their qualifications. Therefore, predictive studies in organizations often use only some candidates for the job. Usually another method, such as an interview, determines who will be hired and thus included in the study. Because the majority of those hired are likely to be high performers, a **restriction of range** in the distribution of test scores is created. In other words, the low performers are usually not hired. This causes the range of test scores to be reduced or restricted. Having a restriction of range in test scores means that the validity coefficient calculated is likely to be lower than if all candidates had been hired and included in the study. Fortunately, the correlation coefficient can be adjusted for restriction of range to get a better estimate of the predictive validity of the employment test.

These problems exist in educational and clinical settings as well, because people might not be admitted to an institution or they might leave during the predictive validity study. For Your Information 8.2 describes a validation study that might have failed to find evidence of validity because of a flawed design.

The Concurrent Method

Concurrent validity is another form of criterion-related validity. In this method, test administration and criterion measurement happen at approximately the same time. This method does not involve prediction. Instead, it provides information about the present and the status quo (Cascio, 1991). The concurrent method is appropriate for validating clinical tests that diagnose behavioral, emotional, or mental disorders. The study described in For Your Information 8.3 provides a good example of a concurrent validity study.

For Your Information   8.1
The Criterion-Related Validity of a Premarital Assessment Instrument

In 1991, researchers (Holman, Larson, & Harmer, 1994) at Brigham Young University conducted a study to determine the criterion-related validity of the PREParation for Marriage Questionnaire (PREP-M; Holman, Busby, & Larson, 1989). Counselors use the PREP-M with engaged couples who are participating in premarital courses or counseling. The PREP-M has 206 questions that provide information on couples' shared values, readiness for marriage, background, and home environment. The researchers contacted 103 married couples who had taken the PREP-M one year earlier as engaged couples and asked them about their marital satisfaction and stability.

The researchers predicted that those who had high scores on the PREP-M would express high satisfaction with their marriage. They used two criteria to test their hypothesis. First, they drew questions from the Marital Comparison Level Index (Sabatelli, 1984) and the Marital Instability Scale (Booth, Johnson, & Edwards, 1983) to construct a criterion that measured each couple's level of marital satisfaction and marital stability. The questionnaire showed an internal consistency of .83. They also classified each couple as either "married satisfied," "married dissatisfied," or "canceled/delayed" and as either "married stable," "married unstable,"

or "canceled/delayed." These classifications provided a second criterion.

The researchers correlated the couples' scores on the PREP-M with their scores on the criterion questionnaire. Husbands' scores on the PREP-M correlated at .44 ($p < .01$) with questions on marital satisfaction and at .34 ($p < .01$) with the questions on marital stability. The wives' scores on the PREP-M were correlated with the same questions at .25 ($p < .01$) and at .20 ($p < .05$) respectively. These correlations show that PREP-M is a moderate to strong predictor of marital satisfaction and stability—good evidence for criterion-related validity of the PREP-M. (Later in this chapter, we discuss the size of correlation coefficients needed to establish criterion-related validity.)

In addition, the researchers compared the mean scores of those husbands and wives classified as "married satisfied," "married dissatisfied" or "canceled/delayed" and those classified as "married stable," "married unstable" or "canceled/delayed." As predicted, those who were "married satisfied" or "married stable" scored higher on the PREP-M than those in the other two categories. In practical terms, these analyses show that counselors can use scores on the PREP-M to make predictions about how satisfying and stable a marriage will be.

Does students' academic self-concept—how they view themselves in the role of a student—affect their academic performance? In 1976, Michael and Smith developed a self-concept measure, Dimensions of Self-Concept (DOSC), that emphasizes school-related activities. The DOSC has five subscales that measure level of aspiration, anxiety, academic interest and satisfaction, leadership and initiative, and identification versus alienation.

Researchers (Gribbons, Tobey, & Michael, 1995) at the University of Southern California examined the criterion-related validity of the DOSC by correlating DOSC test scores with grade point average (GPA). They selected 176 new undergraduates from two programs for students considered at risk for academic difficulties. The students came from a variety of ethnic backgrounds, and 57% were men.

At the beginning of the semester, the researchers administered the DOSC to the students following the guidelines described in the DOSC manual (Michael, Smith, & Michael, 1989). At the end of the semester, they obtained each student's first-semester GPA from university records. When they analyzed the data for evidence of reliability and validity, the DOSC showed high internal consistency, but scores on the DOSC did not predict GPA.

Did something go wrong? One conclusion is that self-concept as measured by the DOSC is unrelated to GPA. But if the study or the measures were somehow flawed, the predictive validity of the DOSC might have gone undetected. The researchers suggested that perhaps academic self-concept lacks stability during students' first semester. Although the internal reliability of the DOSC was established, the test-retest method of reliability was not used, so this possibility cannot be ruled out. The researchers also suggested that GPA could be an unreliable criterion.

Could restriction of range have caused the validity of the DOSC to go undetected? This is a distinct possibility, for two reasons: First, the researchers chose students for the study who were all at risk for experiencing academic difficulties. The population of students also includes those who are expected to succeed, so the researchers might have restricted the range of both the test and the criterion. Second, the students in the study were enrolled in programs to help them become academically successful, and participating in the programs might have enhanced their academic self-concept.

This study demonstrates two pitfalls that researchers designing predictive validity studies must avoid. Researchers must be careful to include participants in their studies who represent the entire possible range of performance on both the test and the criterion. In addition, they must design predictive validity studies so that participants are unlikely to change over the course of the study in ways that affect the abilities or traits they are measuring.

The concurrent method involves administering two tests (or one test and a second measure of the attribute) to the same group of individuals at approximately the same point in time. One test is the one to be validated, and the other test (or measure) is the criterion that is thought to measure the same attribute. It is very important that the criterion test be reliable and valid itself (we will discuss this further later in this chapter). The scores on the two tests are then correlated. If the scores are correlated, then the test is said to have concurrent validity.

In practice, concurrent studies are often used as alternatives to predictive studies, because employers do not want to hire applicants with low test scores. Researchers (Barrett, Phillips, & Alexander, 1981) have compared the two methods for determining criterion-related validity in an organizational setting using cognitive ability tests. They found that the two methods provide similar results.

A study by Watson, Detra, Kurt, Ewing, Gearhart, and DeMotts (1996) is a good example of a concurrent validity study. These researchers administered two self-report alcoholism measures to 118 volunteers recruited from chemical dependency or psychiatric wards at a Veterans Administration medical center. At approximately the same time, the volunteers were asked to complete the criterion measure, a computerized version of the Diagnostic Interview Schedule (C-DIS; Blouin, 1987). The C-DIS asks questions that reflect the *Diagnostic and Statistical Manual of Mental Disorders Third Edition–Revised* (*DSM-III-R;* American Psychiatric Association,

1987), a reference book for psychologists and psychiatrists that lists symptoms of various mental disorders. The researchers chose the C-DIS as a criterion because it has shown high test-retest reliability and good content validity.

Correlations of the self-report tests with the criterion, the C-DIS, were .75 and .60 respectively. These data suggest that the self-report measures of alcoholism have high concurrent validity and that they are appropriate tools for diagnosis of alcohol dependency. (Later in this chapter, we describe how to interpret validity coefficients to provide evidence of criterion-related validity.)

Summary Box 8.1
Demonstrating Criterion-Related Validity

There are two basic methods for showing a relation between a test and independent events or behaviors (the criterion).

- *Predictive validity* is established by correlating test scores taken at one time with scores on a criterion measure obtained at a later date, usually months later. This method establishes that the

test provides information about events in the future.
- Concurrent validity is established by correlating test scores and criterion scores obtained at about the same time, usually within a week. This method establishes that the test can provide information about independent events or behaviors in the present.

How Criterion-Related Validity Differs From Content Validity and Reliability

As you recall from Chapter 7, the purpose of content validation is to provide detailed evidence that the content of the test matches the testing universe. The test plan used to develop a content-valid test clearly defines what the test is supposed to measure. The test questions originate from the test plan.

For criterion-related validity, test developers use questions that predict the criterion. The questions on the test might appear to have no relation to the test's purpose or the criterion. Evidence of criterion-related validity depends on empirical or quantitative methods of data analysis.

For a similar discussion, see In Greater Depth 8.1 on the differences between reliability (described in Chapter 7) and criterion-related validity.

Differences Between Reliability and Validity

As you recall from Chapter 6, the reliability coefficient provides a quantitative estimate of a test's consistency of measurement. A yardstick, for example, is a reliable or consistent measuring instrument because each time it measures an article it gives the same answer. In addition, a yardstick is an appropriate measure for measuring distance. Therefore, we can say the yardstick has validity as a distance measure. If you know how long it takes you to ride a mile on your bicycle, we can use our distance measure to predict the time it will take you to ride five miles.

On the other hand, a yardstick is not a valid measure of intelligence. There is no relation between height and intelligence, therefore we would not use a yardstick to predict IQ. This example demonstrates the principle that reliability and validity are two separate issues. A psychological test might be reliable, but not valid—as in the case of trying to use the yardstick to predict intelligence. *Reliability is a characteristic of the test itself; validity depends on how the test is used.* When a test is used inappropriately, such as using a yardstick to predict intelligence, we can no longer say it is valid.

SELECTING A CRITERION

A criterion is an evaluative standard that can be used to measure a person's performance, attitude, or motivation. Criterion-related validity provides evidence that the test is related to some behavior or event that is independent of the psychological test. As you recall, researchers at Brigham Young University (Holman, et al., 1994) constructed two criteria for their study—a questionnaire and classifications on marital satisfaction and marital stability—to demonstrate the criterion-related validity of the PREP-M.

In a business setting, preemployment tests are often used to predict how well an applicant is likely to perform a job. In this case, supervisors' ratings of job performance can serve as a criterion that represents performance on the job. Other criteria that represent job performance include accidents on the job, attendance or absenteeism, disciplinary problems, training performance, and ratings by **peers**— other employees at the work site. None of these measures can perfectly represent job performance, but each provides information on important characteristics of job performance.

Objective and Subjective Criteria

Criteria for job performance fall into two categories, objective criteria and subjective criteria. An **objective criterion** is one that is observable and measurable, such as the number of accidents on the job, days absent, or disciplinary problems in a month. A **subjective criterion** is based on a person's judgment. Supervisor and peer ratings are examples of subjective criteria.

Each has advantages and disadvantages. Well-defined objective criteria contain less error, because they are usually tallies of observable events or outcomes. Their scope, however, is often quite narrow. For instance, dollar volume of sales is an objective criterion that might be used to measure a person's sales ability. This

153

number is easily calculated and there is little chance of disagreement on its numerical value. It does not, however, take into account a person's motivation or the availability of customers. On the other hand, a supervisor's ratings of a person's sales ability are based on judgment and can be biased or based on information not related to sales ability, such as expectations about race or gender. Table 8.1 lists a number of criteria used in education, clinical, and organizational settings.

Does the Criterion Measure What It Is Supposed to Measure?

The concept of content validity (addressed in Chapter 7) also applies to criteria. Criteria must be representative of the events they are supposed to measure. They are said to be valid to the extent that they match or represent the events in question. Therefore, a criterion of sales ability must be representative of the entire testing universe of sales ability. There is more to selling than just having the highest dollar volume of sales, so several objective criteria might be used to represent the entire testing universe of sales ability. For instance, we might need to add the number of sales calls made each month to measure motivation and the size of the target population to measure customer availability.

Subjective measures, such as ratings, are often more content valid, because the rater can provide judgments for a number of dimensions. Rating forms are psychological measures, and we expect them to be reliable and valid, as we do any measure. We estimate their reliability using the test-retest or internal consistency methods, and we estimate their content validity by matching them to the testing universe. Chapter 15 contains more information on various types of rating scales and their uses in organizations.

By reporting the reliability of their criteria, researchers provide us with information on how accurate the outcome measure is. As you may have noticed, the researchers at Brigham Young University (Holman, et al., 1994) who conducted the study on the predictive validity of the PREP-M reported high reliability for their criterion measure. Likewise, the researchers (Watson et al., 1996) at the Veterans

TABLE 8.1. Common Criteria

	Objective	Subjective
Educational setting		
Grade point average	x	
Withdrawal or dismissal	x	
Teacher's recommendations		x
Clinical setting		
Diagnosis		x
Behavioral observation	x	
Self-report		x
Organizational setting		
Units produced	x	
Number of errors	x	
Ratings of performance		x

Administration medical center chose the C-DIS as a criterion because it reflected the *DSM-III* diagnosis of alcohol dependency—evidence that the C-DIS showed content validity.

Sometimes criteria do not represent all the dimensions in the behavior, attitude, or event being measured. When this happens, we say the criterion lacks content validity. If the criterion measures more dimensions than those measured by the test, we say there is **criterion contamination.** For instance, the dollar volume of sales could be high for a new salesperson. If that dollar volume of sales reflects the filling of back orders sold by another person, however, the criterion might be contaminated.

For Your Information 8.4 describes the issues associated with identifying an appropriate criterion to represent success in graduate school.

As you can see, when evaluating a validation study, it is important to think about the criterion in the study as well as the predictor. When unreliable or inappropriate criteria are used for validation, the true validity coefficient can be under- or overestimated.

CALCULATING AND EVALUATING VALIDITY COEFFICIENTS

As you recall from Chapter 5, the correlation coefficient is a quantitative estimate of the relationship between two variables. Predictive and concurrent validity are also represented by correlation coefficients. In validity studies, we refer to the correlation coefficient as the validity coefficient. The validity coefficient represents the amount or strength of criterion-related validity that can be attributed to a test.

Validity coefficients must be evaluated to determine whether they represent a level of validity that makes the test useful and meaningful. This section describes two methods for evaluating validity coefficients and how criterion-related validity information is used to make predictions about future behavior or performance.

For Your Information 8.4
Choosing a Criterion to Represent Success in Graduate School

Choosing an appropriate criterion is often difficult. For example, how do you measure success in graduate school? In 1980, two psychologists at the Educational Testing Service (Hartnett & Willingham, 1980) described the "criterion problem" as an important issue in validation studies of graduate school admissions tests. Grades in graduate school, they said, are often used as a criterion of success; however, grades have low consistency. Furthermore, graduate school students receive only A's and B's—causing restriction of range—and, as you know, grading standards vary from professor to professor.

Whether or not a student graduates is certainly an important measure of success, but this criterion also has disadvantages. Students drop out of graduate school for many reasons, some of which have nothing to do with academic success. The time students spend in graduate school has also been used as a criterion, but it has the same drawback. Students can be delayed in completing their graduate programs for reasons not related to academic achievement, such as a family tragedy, illness, or financial problems.

Tests of Significance

A validity coefficient is interpreted much the same as a reliability coefficient, except our expectations are not as great. We cannot expect a validity coefficient to have as strong a relationship with another variable (criterion-related validity) as it does with itself (reliability). Therefore, we must evaluate the validity coefficient by using a test of significance and by examining the coefficient of determination.

The first question to ask about a validity coefficient is this: How likely is it that the correlation between the test and the criterion resulted from chance or sampling error? In other words, if the test scores (for example, SAT scores) and the criterion (for example, college grade point average) are not related, then their true correlation is zero. What is the probability that our study would have yielded the validity coefficient we are evaluating by chance alone? If the probability is low—less than 5 chances out of 100 ($p < .05$)—then we can be reasonably sure that the test and its criterion are truly related. This process is called a **test of significance.** In statistical terms, we refer to the validity coefficient as "significant at the .05 level."

Because larger sample sizes reduce sampling error, this test of significance requires that we take into account the size of the group *(N)* from whom we obtained our data. Appendix D (at the back of this book) can be used to determine whether a correlation is significant at varying levels of significance. To use this table, calculate the degrees of freedom *(df)* for your correlation *(df = N − 2)*, then determine the probability that the correlation occurred by chance by looking across the row associated with that degree of freedom. The correlation coefficient you are evaluating should be larger than the critical value shown in the table. You can determine the level of significance by looking at the column headings. At the level where your correlation coefficient is smaller than the value shown, the correlation can no longer be considered significantly different from zero. In Greater Depth 8.2 provides an example of this process.

When researchers or test developers report a validity coefficient, they should also report its level of significance. You might have noted that the validity coefficients of the PREP-M (reported earlier in this chapter) are followed by the statements ($p < .01$) and ($p < .05$). This information tells the test user the likelihood that a relationship was found by chance or as a result of sampling error was either 5 chances out of 100 ($p < .05$) or one chance out of 100 ($p < .01$).

If the correlation between the test and the predictor is not as high as the critical value shown in the table, we can say that the chance of error associated with the test is above generally accepted levels. In such a case, we would conclude that the validity coefficient does not provide sufficient evidence of criterion-related validity.

The Coefficient of Determination

Another way to evaluate the validity coefficient is to determine the amount of variance that the test and the criterion share. We can determine the amount of shared variance by squaring the validity coefficient to obtain r^2—called the **coefficient of determination.** For example, if the correlation *(r)* between a test and a criterion is .30, then the coefficient of determination (r^2) is .09. This means that the test and the criterion have 9% of their variance in common. Larger validity coefficients

Test of Significance for a Correlation Coefficient

In this box, we illustrate how to determine whether a correlation coefficient is "significant" (evidence of a true relationship) or "not significant" (no relationship). Let us say that we have collected data from 20 students. We have given them a test of verbal achievement, and we have correlated those scores with the students' grades from a course on creative writing. The resulting correlation coefficient is .45.

We now go to the table of critical values for Pearson product-moment correlation coefficients, Appendix D in this text. The table shows the *df* (degrees of freedom) and alpha *(α)* levels for two-tailed and one-tailed tests. Psychologists usually set their alpha level at 5 chances out of 100 ($p < .05$) using a two-tailed test, so we will use that standard for our example.

Because we used the data from 20 students in our sample, we substitute 20 for *N* in the formula for

degrees of freedom ($df = N - 2$). Therefore, $df = 20 - 2$ or 18. We then go to the table and find 18 in the column marked "*df.*" Finally, we locate the critical value in that row under the column marked ".05."

The portion of the table reproduced here as Table 8.2 shows the alpha level for a two-tailed test. The critical value of .4438 is the one we will use to test our correlation. Our correlation (.45) is *greater* than the critical value (.4438), so we can infer that the probability of finding our correlation by chance is less than 5 chance out of 100. Therefore, we assume that there is a true relationship, and we refer to the correlation coefficient as "significant." Note that if we had set our alpha level at more stringent standard of .01 (1 chance out of 100), our correlation coefficient would have been interpreted as "not significant."

TABLE 8.2. Critical Values for Pearson Product-Moment Correlation Coefficients

df	.10	.05	.02	.01	.001
16	.4000	.4683	.5425	.5897	.7084
17	.3887	.4555	.5285	.5751	.6932
18	.3783	*.4438*	.5155	.5614	.6787
19	.3687	.4329	.5034	.5487	.6652
20	.3598	.4227	.4921	.5368	.6524

Source: Adapted from Table VII of Fisher & Yates (1963), *Statistical Tables for Biological, Agricultural and Medical Research,* published by Longman Group Ltd., London (previously published by Oliver & Boyd, Edinburgh), and by permission of the publishers.

represent stronger relationships with greater overlap between the test and the criterion. Therefore, when $r = .50$, then $r^2 = .25$—or 25% shared variance.

We can calculate the coefficient of determination for the correlation of husbands' scores on the PREP-M and the questionnaire on marital satisfaction and stability. By squaring the original coefficient, .44, we obtain the coefficient of determination, $r^2 = .1936$. This means that approximately 19% of the variance between the predictor, the PREP-M, and the criterion, the questionnaire, was shared.

Unadjusted validity coefficients rarely exceed .50. You can see, therefore, that even when a validity coefficient is statistically significant, the test can account for only a small portion of the variability in the criterion. The coefficient of determination is important to calculate and remember when using the correlation between the test and the criterion to make predictions about future behavior or performance.

How Confident Can We Be About Estimates of Validity?

Conducting one validity study that demonstrates a strong relationship between the test and the criterion is not the final step, but the first step in a process of validation that might continue for as long as the test is being used. No matter how well designed the validation study, elements of chance, error, and situation-specific factors are always present that can over- or underinflate the estimate of validity. Ongoing investigations of validity include cross-validation and meta-analyses. Psychologists also inquire whether validity estimates are stable from one situation to another—a question of validity generalization. Chapter 11 addresses these issues in more detail.

Summary Box 8.2
Evaluating Validity Coefficients

- Tests of significance establish how likely it is that a correlation between the test and the criterion was obtained by chance.
- The coefficient of determination describes how much variance the test and the criterion share.

- Ongoing investigations of validity include cross-validation and meta-analyses.
- Psychologists also inquire whether validity estimates are stable from one situation to another—a question of validity generalization.

USING VALIDITY INFORMATION TO MAKE PREDICTIONS

When a relationship can be established between a test and a criterion, then the test scores from other individuals can be used to predict how well those individuals will perform on the criterion measure. For example, students' scores on the SAT can be used to predict their success in college. In organizations, job candidates' scores on pre-employment tests that have criterion-related validity can be used to predict those candidates' scores on criteria of job performance.

Linear Regression

We use the statistical process called **linear regression** when we use one set of test scores *(X)* to predict one set of criterion scores *(Y')*. To do this we construct the linear regression equation shown below.

$$Y' = a + bX$$

where

Y' = the predicted score on the criterion
a = the intercept
b = the slope
X = the score the individual made on the predictor test

This equation actually provides a predicted score on the criterion *(Y′)* for each test score *(X)*. When the *Y′*s are plotted, they form the linear regression line associated with the correlation between the test and the criterion.

We can calculate the **slope** *(b)* of the regression line—the expected change in one unit of *Y* for every change in *X*—using the formula shown below:

$$b = r\left(\frac{S_y}{S_x}\right)$$

where

r = the correlation coefficient
S_x = the standard deviation of the distribution of *X*
S_y = the standard deviation of the distribution of *Y*

The **intercept** is the place where the regression line crosses the *Y* axis. *a* designates the intercept and is calculated using the formula

$$a = \overline{Y} + b\overline{X}$$

where

$\overline{Y}$ = the mean of the distribution of *Y*
b = the slope
$\overline{X}$ = the mean of the distribution of *X*

In Greater Depth 8.3 shows the calculation of a linear regression equation and how it is used to predict scores on a criterion.

The process of using correlated data to make predictions is also important in clinical settings. For Your Information 8.5 describes how test scores were used to identify adolescents being at risk for committing suicide.

Multiple Regression

Often it is difficult to predict complex criteria, such as job performance or success in graduate school, with a single test. In these situations, more than one test is needed to make an accurate prediction. An expansion of the linear regression equation helps in this situation.

We use the statistical process called **multiple regression** when we use *more* than one set of test scores $(X_1, X_2, \ldots X_n)$ to predict one set of criterion scores *(Y′)*. The multiple-regression equation, which incorporates information from more than one predictor or test, is shown below:

$$Y' = a + b_1X_1 + b_2X_2 + b_3X_3 \ldots b_nX_n.$$

where

Y' = the predicted score on the criterion
a = the intercept
b = the slope
X = the predictor

Because each combination of $a + bX$ in the equation above indicates the presence of a different line, the multiple-regression equation is difficult to plot. It

Making Predictions With a Linear Regression Equation

Research suggests that academic self-efficacy (ASE) and class grades are related. We have made up the following data to show how we could use the scores on an ASE test to predict a student's grade. (Note: Our fake dataset is small to facilitate this illustration.)

For instance, we can ask the question: If a student scores 65 on the ASE test, what course grade would we expect the student to receive?

Student	TSSE (X)	GRADE (Y)*
1	80	2
2	62	2
3	90	3
4	40	2
5	55	3
6	85	2
7	70	4
8	75	3
9	25	2
10	50	3

*A = 4; B = 3; C = 2; D = 1

Step 1: Calculate the mean and standard deviations for X and Y.

$\bar{X} = 63.2$
$\bar{Y} = 2.6$
$S_x = 19.8$
$S_y = .7$

Step 2: Calculate the correlation coefficient (r_{xy}) for X and Y.

$r_{xy} = .24$

Step 3: Calculate the slope and intercept.

$b = r \dfrac{S_y}{S_x}$, so $b = .33 \, (.7/19.8)$, so $b = .008$

$a = \bar{Y} + b\bar{X}$, so $a = 2.6 - (.008)(63.2)$, so
$a = 2.09$

Step 4: Calculate Y′ when X = 65.

$Y' = a + bX$
$Y' = 2.09 - (.008)(65)$
$Y' = 2.61$

The best answer we can give is that a person who scored 65 on a ASE test would be expected to make a course grade somewhere between a B and C. Note that by substituting any test score for X, we will receive a corresponding prediction for a score on Y.

works in theory, however, much the same as the linear regression equation. The value of each b (partial regression coefficient) indicates how many units Y increases for every increase in X. Therefore each b indicates the unique contribution that each predictor makes in determining a predicted score on the criterion (Y').

In multiple regression, there is one criterion (Y) but there are several predictors (X). To describe this relationship, we use a multiple correlation (R). We can evaluate this R by calculating the coefficient of multiple determination (R^2), which indicates the proportion of variance in the criterion accounted for by all the predictors. The R can also be subjected to a test of significance to determine whether it is significantly different from zero.

A study by Meyer, Woodard, and Suddick (1994) illustrates the usefulness of multiple regression in criterion-related validity studies. Meyer and colleagues conducted a predictive validity study of two of the Descriptive Tests of Mathematics Skills (DTMS) of the College Entrance Examination Board (Educational Testing Service, 1979). At their university, elementary education majors are required to pass the Arithmetic Skills and Elementary Algebra Skills tests of the DTMS. They are also required to take an upper-division mathematics concepts and structures

The suicide rates for 15- through 19-year olds quadrupled from 1957 to 1987 (Berman & Jobes, 1991). If adolescents who are at risk for suicide and suicide attempts can be identified, then greater vigilance is likely to prevent such actions. Researchers (Larzelere, Smith, Batenhorst, & Kelly, 1996) at Father Flanagan's Boys' Home in Nebraska conducted a predictive validity study for the Suicide Probability Scale (SPS) that provided encouraging results for predicting suicidal behaviors in adolescents.

The SPS has 36 questions that assess suicide risk, including suicide thoughts, depression, and isolation. This measure was administered to 840 boys and girls when they were admitted to Boys Town's residential treatment program from 1988 through 1993. The criteria for this study were the number of suicide attempts, suicide verbalizations, and self-destructive behaviors recorded in the program's Daily Incident Report completed by supervisors of the group homes. (The inter-rater reliability for reports of verbalizations and self-destructive behaviors was very high—.97 and .89, respectively. The researchers were unable to calculate a reliability estimate for suicide attempts, because only one attempt was recorded in the reports they selected for the reliability analysis.)

After controlling for a number of confounding variables such as gender, age, and prior attempts of suicide, the researchers determined that the total SPS score and each of its subscales differentiated ($p < .05$) between those who attempted suicide and those who did not. In other words, the mean SPS scores of those attempting suicide were significantly higher than the scores for those who did not attempt suicide. The mean SPS scores of those who displayed self-destructive behavior were also significantly higher ($p < .01$) than for those who did not attempt self-destructive behavior. Finally, the total SPS score correlated .25 ($p < .001$) with the suicide verbalization rate. Predictions made by the SPS for those at risk for attempting suicide showed that each 1-point increase in the total SPS predicted a 2.4% greater likelihood of a subsequent suicide attempt.

The researchers suggested a cutoff score of 74 for those without prior attempts of suicide and 53 for those who have previously attempted suicide. In other words, if an adolescent who has no previous history of suicide attempts scores above 74 on the SPS, the adolescent would be classified as "at risk for suicide" and treated accordingly. If a youth who has a previous history of a suicide attempts scores below 53, that person would be classified as "not at risk for suicide."

The researchers emphasize, however, that although the SPS demonstrated statistically significant validity in predicting suicide attempts, it is not a perfect predictor. A number of suicide attempts were also recorded for those with low scores. Therefore, a low SPS score does not ensure that an adolescent will not attempt suicide. The SPS does, however, provide an objective instrument for accurately identifying adolescents at risk of committing suicide.

---

course. In this study, the Arithmetic Skills and Elementary Algebra Skills tests were the predictors and the grade received in the upper-division math course became the criterion. The participants were 60 elementary education majors.

In their data analysis, the researchers found evidence of internal consistency for the two tests—Arithmetic Skills (.72) and Elementary Algebra Skills (.77). Course grades (the criterion) correlated with Arithmetic Skills at .48 ($p < .001$) and Elementary Algebra Skills at .49 ($p < .001$).

Next the researchers used both tests in a multiple-regression equation to predict course grades. They found a multiple R of .54, which accounted for approximately 29% of the variance in the two tests and course grades ($R^2 = .286$). Most of the variance, however, was predicted by one test, Elementary Algebra, which accounted for 24% of the variance ($R^2 = .241$). The multiple R for Elementary Algebra alone and the R for both tests together were not significantly different.

Meyer and colleagues (1994) concluded that each test showed evidence of predictive validity and could be used as a predictor of math performance for elementary education majors. In addition, they suggested simplifying the assessment program by using one test instead of two because the tests supplied redundant information about the criterion (course grades).

Summary Box 8.3
Using Validity Information to Make Predictions

- When a relationship can be established between a test and a criterion, the test scores can be used to predict how well individuals are likely to perform on the criterion.
- *Linear regression* is used to make predictions from scores from one test.

- The *slope* (the expected change in one unit of *Y* for every change in *X*) and the *intercept* (the point where the regression line crosses the *Y* axis) are important for plotting a regression line.
- *Multiple regression* is used to make predictions from two or more different tests.

ETHICAL ISSUES ASSOCIATED WITH TEST VALIDATION

Criterion-related validation is a cornerstone of test use. Decisions based on test predictions have far-reaching consequences. Each day in the United States and other industrialized nations, individuals are hired or rejected by organizations based on employment tests. Educators also use test results to admit or refuse admittance to programs based on predictions made by educational ability tests, and clinicians use tests to screen clients for residential or outpatient treatment and to admit them to specific treatment programs based on diagnoses made by tests.

With each decision, the test user is ethically and morally responsible for ascertaining that the test instrument shows acceptable evidence of reliability and validity. In some cases, such as employment decisions in which there is discrimination against protected classes, test users can be held legally liable for improper test use. Test users rely on researchers and test publishers to provide full information about tests. Test publishers have a particular responsibility to prevent test misuse by making test manuals and validity information available and accessible *before* purchase and to refuse to provide test materials to persons who are likely to misuse them. Finally, psychologists in general have a responsibility to increase public awareness about the importance of test reliability and validity, so the public can understand the role that tests play in decisions that affect their lives.

SUMMARY

Criterion-related validity—the extent to which a test is related to independent behavior or events—is one of the major methods for obtaining evidence of test validity. The usual method for demonstrating criterion-related validity is to correlate scores on the test with a measure of the behavior we wish to predict. This measure of independent behavior or performance is called the criterion.

Criterion-related validity depends upon evidence that the scores on the test correlate significantly with an independent criterion—a standard used to measure a person's performance, attitude, or motivation. Criteria can be objective or subjective, but they must be reliable and content valid. There are two methods for demonstrating criterion-related validity—the predictive method and the concurrent method.

We use correlation to describe the relationship between a psychological test and a criterion. In this case, the correlation coefficient is referred to as the validity coefficient. Psychologists interpret validity coefficients using tests of significance and the coefficient of determination.

Either a linear or a multiple regression equation can be used to predict criterion scores from test scores. Predictions of success or failure on the criterion enable test users to use test scores for making decisions about hiring in an organization, admission to educational programs, or diagnosis and treatment in clinical settings.

Finally, decisions based on test predictions have far reaching consequences. Researchers, test developers, test publishers, and test users are ethically and morally responsible for ascertaining that any psychological test used for making predictions and decisions shows acceptable evidence of reliability and validity. It is also their responsibility to guard against test misuse and to increase public awareness about the important role that tests play in their lives.

KEY CONCEPTS

coefficient of
    determination
concurrent validity
criterion
criterion contamination
criterion-related validity

intercept
linear regression
multiple regression
objective criterion
peers

predictive validity
restriction of range
slope
subjective criterion
test of significance
validity coefficient

LEARNING ACTIVITIES

1. Interpreting Validity Studies

This exercise contains summaries of published criterion-related validation studies. Identify the following elements in each summary:

1. Predictor(s)
2. Criterion
3. Type of validity examined
4. Validity coefficient and its strength
5. Reliability of the test (where given)

A. *College Students' Recent Life Experiences.* Researchers administered to 216 undergraduate students (in the same time period) the Inventory of College Students' Experiences and a measure of daily hassles. The total coefficient alpha was .92 for the inventory and .96 for the measure of daily hassles. The inventory correlated with daily hassles at .76 ($p < .001$). (Adapted from Osman, Barrio, Longnecker, & Osman, 1994)

B. *The Pilot Personality.* Test scores for the Eysenck Personality Inventory and Cattell's 16 Personality Factor Questionnaire (16PF) were obtained for male army applicants for flyer training. Forms A and B were used for each test, and the correlations between forms for the same test ranged from .39 to .85. Some of the men entered flying school several years after taking the tests. The correlations of the subscales on the two tests with training outcome (pass or fail) averaged about .20. (Adapted from Bartram, 1995)

C. *Computer Aptitude and Computer Anxiety.* Researchers gave 162 students enrolled in computer courses a test that measured computer anxiety and another that measured computer aptitude. Both were given at the beginning of the course. Student performance in the course was measured by the grades they earned in the course. Computer aptitude was correlated with course grade at .41 ($p < .01$) for one course and .13 ($p < ns$) for the other. Correlations of computer anxiety and course grade were .01 and .16 ($p < ns$) (*ns* indicates "not significant"). (Adapted from Szajna, 1994)

2. Objective and Subjective Criteria

A number of criteria are listed in the table below. Decide what type of criterion each is and mark "O" if objective or "S" if subjective. Discuss the advantages and disadvantages you think might be associated with using each of the criteria.

Criterion	Type
Ratings of training success	
Letters of reference	
Completion of a work sample (pass/fail)	
Ratings based on a work sample	
Annual salary	
Number of alcoholic drinks	
Self-ratings of drug use	
Course grade	
Number of weeks in therapy	
Therapist's estimate of weekly progress	

3. Interpreting Statistics

The table below contains symbols that stand for statistics used in validation studies. Identify each and explain when to use it and what it means.

r _____

_____

r^2 _____

_____

R _____

_____

R^2 _____

_____

Y' _____

_____

a _____

_____

b _____

_____

X _____

_____

p _____

_____

Consolidating Evidence of Validity

"What does it mean when a person has a dependency on alcohol? Does that mean they drink every day? Or that when they drink they get very drunk? Do you have to lose your job, your house, and your family to be classified as an alcoholic?"

"My professor says that spanking can be classified as child abuse. I disagree! Child abusers are people who torture children and use them for their sexual pleasure. Discipline is something else!"

"My 8-year-old has an IQ of 130. She makes good grades, but sometimes she says and does really silly things. I thought she was supposed to be smart!"

Another chapter on validity? How many kinds of validity can there be? Validity is such an important issue in psychological testing that measurement experts have identified numerous ways to show that tests measure what they are supposed to measure.

In the last two chapters, we discussed content validity, face validity, criterion-related validity, predictive validity, and concurrent validity. In this chapter, we introduce the concept of construct validity, which establishes that the test is based in sound psychological theory.

This chapter defines and illustrates the terms *psychological construct, theory,* and *nomological network.* Because establishing evidence of construct validity involves accumulating and relating all the psychometric information known about a test, we will show how familiar concepts—such as reliability, content validity, and criterion-related validity—are linked to construct validity. In addition, convergent validity and discriminant validity are two new strategies for establishing construct validity.

Finally, we discuss experimental methods used to establish construct validity for a test, including a procedure called confirmatory factor analysis.

WHAT IS CONSTRUCT VALIDITY?

Prior to 1954, psychologists had gathered evidence for the validity of tests by pursuing the two methods we discussed in Chapters 7 and 8—content validity and criterion-related validity. However, a number of theorists challenged these strategies because they failed to link the testing instrument to an accepted theory of psychological behavior (Rogers, 1995). In 1954, the American Psychological Association published recommendations that established a new method for establishing validity in which the researcher provides evidence that the testing instrument measures behavior predicted by a psychological theory. The American Psychological Association called this evidence construct validity.

Therefore, **construct validity** is defined as the extent to which the test measures a theoretical construct. The process of establishing construct validity for a test is a gradual accumulation of evidence that the scores on the test relate to observable behaviors in the ways predicted by the underlying theory.

Such a methodology implies one important consideration pointed out by Cronbach and Meehl (1955). When test users accept evidence of construct validity, they must accept the underlying definition of the construct used in the validation process. In other words, the test user accepts the definition of the construct used by those who developed and validated the test.

At first glance, this consideration does not seem a problem. Recall, however, that definitions of a construct can vary from theorist to theorist. The best example of this variation is the numerous definitions given to the construct of intelligence. Who is highly intelligent? Is it someone who always makes perfect grades? Is it someone who is highly creative and farsighted? Is it someone who is perfectly rational and logical? Is it someone who displays knowledge and skills greater than those of others of the same chronological age? Is intelligence inherited? Is it a series of learned behaviors? Is it a combination of some or all of these traits? As you can see, choosing a test to measure intelligence means choosing a test that matches your definition of intelligence. Without this consideration, the test scores would be confusing or meaningless.

What Is a Construct?

Before discussing how to establish evidence of construct validity, we need to define what we mean by a theoretical or psychological **construct.** As you remember from Chapter 7, psychologists gain their understanding of people and other organisms by focusing their attention on concrete and abstract constructs. Behaviors—activities that are observable and measurable—are concrete constructs. Underlying attitudes or attributes that exist in our imaginations are abstract constructs. Intelligence, beauty, love, and self-esteem are all psychological constructs, but your instructor cannot bring a bucket of intelligence or a big box of self-esteem to class. These constructs exist in theory. We cannot directly observe or measure them.

We can, however, observe and measure the behaviors that show evidence of these constructs. Psychological theories propose the presence of constructs, such as intelligence, beauty, love, and self-esteem, and make predictions about behaviors that are related to them. By observing and measuring those behaviors, we assume that we have measured the abstract construct. As an example of this process, Murphy and Davidshofer (1994) use the theoretical construct of gravity. Before Isaac Newton, the notion of gravity did not exist. Newton theorized that apples fall to earth because of a concept he called gravity. We cannot see gravity, but we see what we assume to be its result—falling apples!

As you can see from the statements at the beginning of this chapter, definitions of constructs can vary from person to person. Many times the definitions that professionals use for constructs, such as alcoholism, child abuse, and intelligence, differ from those used by the general population. Psychologists even disagree among themselves, so they must clearly define constructs before they can measure them.

To illustrate this process in terms of testing, let's consider an abstract construct proposed by Albert Bandura, a well-known cognitive psychologist. In 1977, Bandura suggested that a construct exists that he called *self-efficacy*—a person's expectations and beliefs about his or her own competence and ability to accomplish an activity or task. Bandura (1977) proposed that

> expectations of personal efficacy determine whether coping behavior will be initiated, how much effort will be expended, and how long it will be sustained in the face of obstacles and aversive experiences. (p. 191)

Major Sources of Efficacy Information

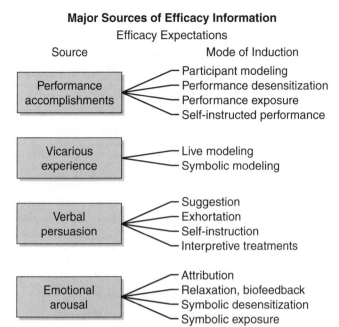

FIGURE 9.1. Illustration of Bandura's theory of self-efficacy

Figure 9.1 illustrates the sources of self-efficacy. People form their opinion about their own self-efficacy from their own performance accomplishments, their experience from watching others perform (vicarious experience), the messages they receive from others about their performance (verbal persuasion), and their emotional arousal. Modes of induction in the model show the various ways that information is received. The test developer can use this model as a test plan for constructing an instrument that measures self-efficacy. For instance, the instrument may ask the test taker questions about his or her experience with each source of self-efficacy.

Since Bandura published his self-efficacy theory, numerous tests have been developed that measure general self-efficacy—individuals' expectations of competency and resulting coping behaviors, and extended effort in general (Lee & Bobco, 1994; Sherer et al., Maddux, Mercandante, Prentice-Dunn, Jacobs, & Rogers, 1982; Tipton & Worthington, 1984). In addition to general measures, researchers have developed tests that measure self-efficacy for mathematics (Pajares & Miller, 1995), computer skills (Murphy, Coover, & Owen, 1989), social interactions (Wheeler & Ladd, 1982), and career choice (Betz & Hackett, 1986), to name only a few. Most research using tests of self-efficacy have borne out Bandura's predictions (Bandura, Barbaranelli, Caprara & Pastorelli, 1996) about coping behavior. In addition, researchers have found self-efficacy to be a good predictor of performance (Sharpley & Ridgway, 1993; Tam, 1996; Weinberg, Gould, & Jackson, 1980).

Construct Explication

Measurement of an abstract construct depends on our ability to observe and measure related behavior. Murphy and Davidshofer (1994) describe three steps for defining or explaining a psychological construct, referred to as **construct explication.**

1. Identify the behaviors that relate to the construct.
2. Identify other constructs that may be related to the construct being explained.
3. Identify behaviors related to similar constructs and determine whether these behaviors are related to the original construct.

A construct validation study of The Self-Efficacy Scale conducted by Mark Sherer and his associates (Sherer et al., 1982) illustrates these principles of construct explication. These researchers were interested in validating a scale that measures self-efficacy. They reviewed the research of Bandura and others and determined that positive correlations exist between therapeutic changes in behaviors and changes in self-efficacy. In other words, as an individual's self-efficacy increases, her or his behavior in treatment is likely to improve also (Step 1). Sherer and colleagues also noted that expectations or past performance are related to self-efficacy (Step 2). In addition, individuals who have experienced numerous successes in the past are likely to have developed high self-efficacy, demonstrated by their persistence in pursuing goals with which they have limited experience (Step 3). Figure 9.2 provides an illustration of this explication process.

As theorists identify more constructs and behaviors that are interrelated, they construct what psychologists Cronbach and Meehl (1955) referred to as a **nomological network**—a method for defining a construct by illustrating its relation to as many other constructs and behaviors as possible. This nomological network then provides the basis for establishing a test's construct validity by providing a number of **hypotheses**—educated guesses or predictions—about the behaviors that people who have small or large quantities of the construct should display. For instance, based on the research on self-efficacy, we expect people with high self-efficacy to express positive attitudes regarding their own competence and to dis-

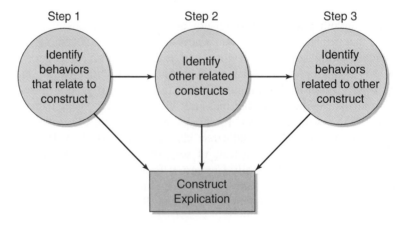

FIGURE 9.2. The process of construct explication

play persistence in accomplishing a new and difficult task. Establishing evidence of construct validity then is the process of testing the predictions made by the nomological network.

Summary Box 9.1
Defining a Construct

- Construct validity is the extent to which a test measures a theoretical construct.
- Behaviors—activities that are observable and measurable—are concrete constructs.
- Underlying attitudes or attributes are abstract concepts that exist only in our imaginations.
- Definitions of abstract constructs can vary from person to person.

- Construct explication is the basis for establishing a test's construct validity. A construct must be part of a theory that defines the construct in observable and measurable terms.
- A nomological network defines a construct by illustrating its relation to other constructs and behaviors.

GATHERING EVIDENCE OF CONSTRUCT VALIDITY

To understand the process of establishing construct validity, we apply the scientific method for testing the hypotheses proposed by theories. We can divide this process in two parts: gathering theoretical evidence and gathering psychometric evidence. Figure 9.3 provides an overview of this methodology.

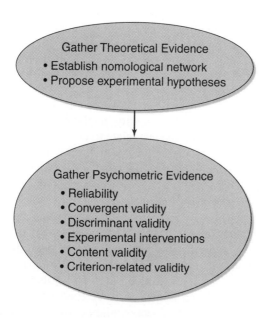

FIGURE 9.3. Methodology for establishing construct validity

Gathering Theoretical Evidence

The first step in the validation process is establishing a nomological network. As we illustrated with the example of self-efficacy, researchers first review as many studies of the construct as possible to establish the construct's relation to observable and measurable behaviors. They also seek to find relationships with other constructs and the behaviors associated with them. Establishing construct validity requires a thorough understanding of the construct in question, and there is no substitute for careful reading of all available literature, both theoretical observations and empirical studies. The researcher then develops the nomological network—a definition or model of the construct that links it to other constructs and observable behaviors.

Second, using the nomological network, the researcher proposes one or more experimental hypotheses using the test as an instrument for measuring the construct. If the test is a valid measure of the construct, then scores on the test should perform in accordance with the predictions made for the construct.

Let's return to Mark Sherer's (Sherer et al., 1982) validation of a test called The Self-Efficacy Scale to examine how this process works. A review of theoretical and empirical studies of self-efficacy revealed that self-efficacy is linked to a number of personality characteristics: locus of control, social desirability, ego strength, interpersonal competency, and self-esteem. Sherer and his associates hypothesized that scores on The Self-Efficacy Scale would be significantly correlated with personality tests measuring each of these constructs but the correlation would not be strong enough to suggest that the scales were measuring the same construct. The researchers designed a study to test this hypothesis.

It is important to note that Sherer and his associates proposed a specific hypothesis based on the accepted definition of self-efficacy and the nomological network they constructed. According to Cronbach (1988, 1989), the preferred method for establishing construct validity is to propose a hypothesis based on the nomological network and test it. The alternative he referred to as "dragnet empiricism," which involves collecting evidence based on convenience rather than on a specific hypothesis. Using dragnet empiricism, the researcher collects evidence without regard to whether it provides evidence for or against the underlying theory.

Gathering Psychometric Evidence

As you recall, establishing construct validity involves an ongoing process of gathering evidence that the scores on the test relate to observable behaviors in the ways predicted by the underlying theory and the nomological network. There are a number of ways to establish quantitative evidence to suggest that the test has construct validity.

Reliability

As you recall from Chapter 5, reliability is an essential characteristic for a psychological test. To show that the test measures a single theoretical construct, there should be evidence of *internal consistency* or *homogeneity*. If the test measures more than one construct, it is difficult to establish that scores on the test represent the behaviors related to a single construct. Evidence of test-retest reliability is also important, otherwise the test scores might correspond to theoretical predictions one time but not another time.

In addition, the theory underlying psychological testing suggests that a test cannot have a stronger correlation with any other variable than it does with itself. Estimates of reliability can therefore be used to evaluate the strength of correlations with other variables that are related to the theoretical construct.

Convergent Validity

If the test is construct valid, we would expect the scores on the test to correlate strongly with scores on other tests that measure the same construct. We refer to this correlation as **convergent validity.** For example, researchers have developed a number of tests to measure general self-efficacy as well as self-efficacy related to a specific task. We would expect two measures of general self-efficacy to yield strong, positive, and statistically significant correlations. They might also correlate with scores from task-specific tests, but not to as great an extent.

This concept always raises a very good question: If there is already a test that measures the construct, why develop another? One might develop another test in order to create parallel forms, create tests for specific populations (such as children or people who speak another language), revise the test to increase reliability and validity, reproduce the test in another format (for example, for administration by computer or in a shortened version), develop a test that represents an altered definition of the underlying construct, and so forth. In each of these cases, the new test would yield different scores than the original test, but we would expect the two sets of scores to be highly correlated.

If the test scores are correlated with measures of constructs that the underlying theory says are related, then we would also describe those correlations as evidence of convergent validity. For example, Bandura's (1977) theory of self-efficacy suggests that self-efficacy is related to measures of competency. Sherer and colleagues (1982) administered their measure of self-efficacy and a measure of interpersonal competency to 376 students. They found a moderate correlation ($r = .45$) between the two tests. This correlation provides evidence of convergent validity for the measure of general self-efficacy used by Sherer and colleagues.

Discriminant Validity

Just as the test would be expected to correlate with some tests, there are other tests with which there should be no correlation. When the test scores are not correlated with unrelated constructs, there is evidence of **discriminant validity.** For example, a test that measures skill at performing numerical calculations would not be expected to be related to reading comprehension. If the correlation between the numerical calculations test and a test of reading comprehension is zero (or not statistically significant), then there is evidence of discriminant validity for the numerical calculations test.

Multitrait-Multimethod Method

In 1959, Campbell and Fiske cleverly combined the need to collect evidence of reliability, convergent validity, and discriminant validity in one study. They called it the **multitrait-multimethod design** for investigating construct validity. Using this approach, investigators test for "*convergence* across *different* measures . . . of the same 'thing' . . . and for *divergence* between measures . . . of related but conceptually distinct 'things' (Cook & Campbell, 1979, p. 61). In other words, the researcher chooses three constructs that are unrelated in theory and three types of tests—such as objective, projective, and a peer rating—to measure each of the constructs. Data are collected on each participant in the study on each construct using each method.

Figure 9.4 shows a multitrait-multimethod correlation matrix from Campbell and Fiske's (1959) article. In a **correlation matrix,** the same tests and measures are listed in the horizontal and vertical headings, and correlations are in the body of the table. In this multitrait-multimethod matrix, three methods are used for measuring each of three constructs (A, B, and C). The reliability estimate for each measure is shown in parentheses in the diagonal. The correlation coefficients arranged diagonally between the broken line triangles represent convergent validity coefficients—correlations between tests that measure the same construct but have different methods or formats. The triangles in solid lines are correlations of different tests that have the same format or method of measurement. These provide an idea of bias that might be associated with the method or format of the test. The triangles shown in broken lines are estimates of discriminant validity—correlations of tests using different methods and measuring different constructs.

To interpret the multitrait-multimethod study, one would expect high reliability estimates for each measure, high validity coefficients for tests with different formats measuring the same construct, and low correlation coefficients for tests

A Synthetic Multitrait-Multimethod Matrix

	Traits	Method 1			Method 2			Method 3		
		A_1	B_1	C_1	A_2	B_2	C_2	A_3	B_3	C_3
Method 1	A_1	(.89)								
	B_1	.51	(.89)							
	C_1	.38	.37	(.76)						
Method 2	A_2	.57	.22	.09	(.93)					
	B_2	.22	.57	.10	.68	(.94)				
	C_2	.11	.11	.46	.59	.58	(.84)			
Method 3	A_3	.56	.22	.11	.67	.42	.33	(.94)		
	B_3	.23	.58	.12	.43	.66	.34	.67	(.92)	
	C_3	.11	.11	.45	.34	.32	.58	.58	.60	(.85)

Note: The validity diagonals are the three sets of italicized values. The reliability diagonals are the three sets of values in parentheses. Each heterotrait-monomethod triangle is enclosed by a solid line. Each heterotrait-heteromethod triangle is enclosed by a broken line.

FIGURE 9.4. A multitrait-multimethod correlation matrix from Campbell and Fiske (1959)

with different formats measuring different constructs. If correlations of tests with the same format measuring different constructs are high, then one can assume that there is bias associated with the format of the test. In other words, a certain format, such as projective tests, elicits similar responses from test takers regardless of the construct being measured.

Experimental Interventions

Experimental interventions in which the test is used as an independent or dependent variable make a substantial contribution to the argument for construct validity. For instance, if the underlying theory predicts that a course of treatment or training will increase or decrease the psychological construct, then a significant difference between pretest and posttest scores would be evidence of construct validity.

Another study that provides evidence of construct validity would be one that verifies a prediction that group membership affects the construct. For instance, if the underlying theory predicts that one group will have higher or lower mean test scores than another and the data yield such a result, then the study provides evidence of construct validity.

For example, Melchert, Hays, Wiljanen, and Kolochek, (1996) administered the Counselor Self-Efficacy Scale (CSES) to 138 participants who were either students enrolled in graduate counseling courses or licensed professional psychologists. Because Bandura's theory states that experience with a particular activity is likely to raise self-efficacy for that activity, the researchers hypothesized that those who had higher levels of training and experience would score higher on the CSES. Their data yielded four groups—first-year master's students, second-year master's students, postmaster's doctoral students, and professional psychologists—who were differentiated by scores on the CSES that increased as levels of training and experience increased. These data provide evidence of construct validity for the CSES.

Content Validity

As you recall from Chapter 7, a test is content valid when its questions are a representative sample of a well-defined test domain. Content validity is usually the appropriate approach for providing evidence of validity for math, reading, or other test domains with known boundaries. Because psychological constructs exist primarily in our imagination and are not observable, it is more difficult to define a test domain well enough to construct a test that contains a representative sample from the test domain. However, some psychological constructs do lend themselves to content validation, and when evidence of content validity can be provided, it greatly strengthens the case for construct validity.

Cronbach (1989) distinguishes between content validity and construct validity in this way:

> Content validation stops with a demonstration that the test conforms to a specification; however, the claim that the *specification* is well chosen embodies a CV [construct validity] claim. . . . Any interpretation invokes constructs if it reaches beyond the specific, local, concrete situation that was observed. (p. 151)

Bandura's construct of self-efficacy lends itself to content validation because Bandura (1977) specified four sources of self-efficacy (performance accomplishments, vicarious experience, verbal persuasion, and emotional arousal). To develop a test plan for an instrument that measures self-efficacy, the test developer would stipulate that an equal number of questions would represent a connection to each source of self-effi-cacy (Fritzsche & McIntire, 1997). Showing that the test questions do indeed reflect the four sources of self-efficacy, however, is a matter of construct validity. Such infor-mation, in addition to evidence of reliability and convergent and discriminant validity, substantially strengthens the argument that the test measures the theoretical construct and thus has construct validity.

Criterion-Related Validity

Likewise, although criterion-related validity relies solely on the statistical re-lationship between the test and a criterion, it too can provide evidence of construct validity. If the underlying theory predicts that a psychological construct is related to observable behaviors, such as job performance or a cluster of behaviors that de-note a mental disorder, then evidence of that relationship (criterion-related valid-ity) adds to the evidence for construct validity also. In other words, when an un-derlying theory *explains* the relation between a predictor and a criterion, there is evidence of construct validity.

There are numerous examples of this validation strategy for tests of self-effi-cacy. Bandura's theory predicts that persons who have high self-efficacy will per-form better than persons with low self-efficacy, and many validation studies of measures of self-efficacy include evidence of criterion-related validity as well as convergent validity and reliability. For instance, Sherer and colleagues (1982)—in addition to demonstrating convergent validity for their measure of general self-efficacy—demonstrated criterion-related validity by finding significant correla-tions between self-efficacy scores (predictor) and current employment, number of jobs quit, and number of times fired (criteria). Because Bandura's theory predicts these relationships, evidence of criterion-related validity strengthens the argument that the instrument is construct valid.

Summary Box 9.2
Gathering Evidence of Construct Validity

- We gather theoretical evidence by establishing a nomological network and proposing experimental hypotheses using the test to measure the construct.
- We gather psychometric evidence of construct valid-ity by conducting empirical studies of the following:
  - To show reliability, test developers and re-searchers should provide evidence of internal consistency or homogeneity. Evidence of test-retest reliability is also appropriate.
  - Convergent validity, a strong correlation be-tween the test and other tests measuring the same or similar constructs, is necessary.
  - Discriminant validity, a lack of correlation be-tween the test and unrelated constructs, is also valuable.
- Designing a study that yields a multitrait-multi-method matrix of data is an elegant way to demonstrate the first three of these strategies—reliability, convergent, and discriminant validity.
- Experimental interventions in which the test is used as an independent or dependent variable make a substantial contribution to the argument for construct validity.
- Content validity or criterion-related validity, when available and appropriate, strengthen the argument for construct validity.

Multiple Studies

177

CHAPTER 9
Consolidating
Evidence
of Validity

Gathering evidence of construct validity is an ongoing process, so the argument that a test is construct valid is strengthened when the test demonstrates one or all of these characteristics in a number of studies conducted on different samples of participants by different researchers. Cross-referencing of such studies suggests that individual studies were not unduly affected by biases related to the experimenter or special characteristics of the sample. Therefore, test users can conclude that the test faithfully represents and measures the underlying construct.

CONFIRMATORY FACTOR ANALYSIS

Over the last two decades, the introduction and availability of computer software to psychological researchers and test developers has allowed them to broaden studies of construct validity into investigations of the underlying factors that a test measures. To investigate underlying aspects of constructs, researchers use **factor analysis**—an advanced statistical procedure based on the concept of correlation that helps investigators explain why two tests are correlated (Murphy & Davidshofer, 1994). In Greater Depth 9.1 provides a brief overview of the statistical procedure of factor analysis.

Using factor analysis, researchers and test developers consider the theory associated with a test and propose a set of underlying factors they expect the test to contain. Then they conduct a factor analysis to see whether the factors they proposed do indeed exist. Such a study is called a **confirmatory factor analysis** and provides an excellent method for obtaining evidence of construct validity. Evidence that the factors obtained empirically are similar to those proposed theoretically is provided by a statistical procedure call the **goodness-of-fit test.** A number of statistical analyses can be used to check goodness of fit, such as the chi square procedure.

A good example of the process of confirmatory factor analysis is provided by Longshore, Turner, and Stein (1996). They tested the construct validity of a scale developed to measure self-control in a population of offenders in the criminal justice system (Grasmick, Tittle, Bursick, & Arnekliv, 1993). A general theory of crime (Gottfredson & Hirschi, 1990) suggests that self-control—the degree that a person is vulnerable to momentary temptation—is important in predicting whether a person will commit a crime. This theory has been challenged by others who argue that there is a lack of empirical evidence that self-control is a stable trait. To answer these charges, a scale measuring self-control as defined by Gottfredson and Hirschi was developed by Grasmick and colleagues (1993). The scale contains 23 statements about noncriminal predispositions, such as impulsiveness and risk seeking, to which test takers agree or disagree. Studies of the scale by the test developers suggest it is reliable and valid (Grasmick et al., 1993).

Longshore and colleagues used data collected during an evaluation of a program to treat offenders to conduct their confirmatory factor analysis. They hypothesized (based on the Gottfredson and Hirschi theory and previous research conducted by the test developers [Grasmick et al., 1993]) that the measure of self-control would have six underlying factors:

Factor analysis is a statistical procedure whose purpose is to identify underlying variables or factors that contribute to an overall test score. These factors may be thought of as subordinate or contributing variables that contribute information to the more complex construct that is being measured. Not all constructs have underlying factors. Some constructs are referred to as univariate because there are no underlying factors. In other words, univariate constructs are homogeneous. On the other hand, complex constructs have a number of underlying factors and they are heterogeneous.

Although factor analyses were originally calculated laboriously by hand or with the help of calculators, we can now conduct factor analyses using statistical software such as SPSS or SAS. The researcher enters a matrix of raw data (usually individual answers to test questions), and the software program calculates a correlation matrix of all variables or test questions. The software program then uses the correlation matrix to calculate a factor solution based on a geographic representation of each test question's relationship to the others. As the test questions group together, they form factors—underlying dimensions of questions that measure the same trait or attribute. Researchers then examine the questions in each factor and name the factor based on the content of the questions that are most highly correlated with that factor. Figure 9.5 shows a plot of a factor solution.

There are a number of ways of calculating a factor matrix that depend on basic assumptions, such

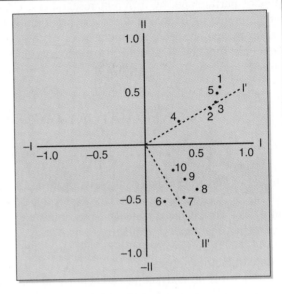

FIGURE 9.5. A hypothetical factor pattern, showing weights of two group factors in each of 10 tests

as whether the underlying factors are independent (not correlated) or dependent (correlated). A full explanation of this procedure is beyond the intended scope of this text. For a more complete explanation of factor analysis, we suggest you consult a textbook on multivariate statistical techniques.

1. *Impulsiveness:* Low self-control people seek immediate gratification.
2. *Simple tasks:* Low self-control people prefer simple tasks and lack the diligence and tenacity needed for benefiting from more complex tasks.
3. *Risk seeking:* Low self-control people are drawn to excitement and adventure.
4. *Physical activity:* Low self-control people prefer physical activity to contemplation and conversation.
5. *Self-centeredness:* Low self-control people tend to be indifferent to the needs of others.
6. *Temper:* Low self-control people have low tolerance for frustration and are likely to handle conflict with confrontation. (Longshore, Turner, & Stein, 1990)

Their factor analysis provided support for the hypothesis. The data yielded the factors predicted. However, the factors of impulsiveness and self-centeredness were combined, resulting in five factors instead of six. Based on these data, the researchers concluded that there was good evidence of construct validity for the measure of self-control.

Summary Box 9.3
Confirmatory Factor Analysis

- Researchers use factor analysis to identify underlying variables or factors that contribute to a construct or an overall test score.
- A confirmatory factor analysis is a study in which researchers hypothesize the underlying variables, then test to see if they are there.

- Confirmatory factor analyses that confirm predicted underlying variables provide evidence of construct validity.

In conclusion, it is important to remember Cronbach's (1989) advice about construct validation:

> To call Test A valid or Test B invalid is illogical. Particular interpretations are what we validate. . . . Validation is a lengthy, even endless process. (p. 151)

Section Two has discussed the basic psychometric principles associated with establishing test reliability and validity. As you can see, these are research-based activities that provide cumulative evidence regarding a test's usefulness and interpretation. The next section discusses the process of developing psychological tests and surveys. It also describes in more detail how validation studies are conducted.

SUMMARY

Psychologists measure behaviors (activities that are observable and measurable) and constructs (underlying attitudes or attributes that exist only in our imaginations.) Although we cannot directly observe or measure constructs themselves, we can predict behaviors that they influence and measure those behaviors. Construct validity is the extent to which a test measures the theoretical construct it is supposed to measure.

Because definitions of constructs vary from person to person, psychologists define and explain constructs carefully. Construct explication is the process of relating a construct to a psychological theory and proposing a nomological network of the constructs and behaviors to which the construct is related.

We gather theoretical evidence of construct validity by proposing the nomological network and experimental hypotheses. We then gather psychometric evidence of construct validity by establishing evidence that the test is reliable, that it correlates with other tests measuring constructs in the nomological network (convergent validity), and by confirming that it is not correlated with constructs to which it is theoretically unrelated (discriminant validity). In addition, evidence of content validity and criterion-related validity also bolsters the argument that the test is construct valid. Finally, researchers can propose and conduct experiments using the test to measure the construct.

Confirmatory factor analysis is a method that tests theoretical predictions about underlying variables or factors that make up a construct. Although some constructs are univariate or homogeneous, many constructs are made up of subordinate variables. The process of confirmatory analysis involves proposing underlying factors then verifying their existence using the statistical procedure of factor analysis.

KEY CONCEPTS

confirmatory factor analysis	**convergent validity**	**hypothesis**
construct	**correlation matrix**	**multitrait-multimethod design**
construct explication	**discriminant validity**	**nomological network**
construct validity	**factor analysis**	
	goodness-of-fit test	

LEARNING ACTIVITIES

1. Defining Various Types of Validity

In Section II, we have discussed the eight types of validity listed below. Find the definition in Column III that matches each type of validity shown in Column II. Place the letter that corresponds to your answer in Column I.

I	II	III
	discriminant validity	A. The test provides a representative sample of the behaviors in the testing universe.
	face validity	B. The test scores are related to independent behaviors, attitudes, or events.
	content validity	C. Questions on the test appear to measure what the test is supposed to measure.
	validity	D. Test demonstrates a relationship between a test and a future behavior or outcome.
	criterion-related validity	E. Test measures what it is supposed to measure.
	convergent validity	F. Test is correlated with measures of constructs that are theoretically related to the test's construct.
	predictive validity	G. Test is highly correlated with itself.
	concurrent validity	H. Test is related to behaviors or events in the present.
		I. Test is not correlated with measures of constructs with which the test has no theoretical relationship.

2. Validating a Measure of Self-Esteem

Students in the tests and measures class at Northwest Random College have been given the assignment to design a validation study for a test that measures self-esteem in preadolescents. The test contains 30 statements to which the test taker responds "True of me" or "Not true of me." In general, the statements reflect the test taker's satisfaction with her or his academic and athletic skills, physical attractiveness, and relationships to friends and family. The elementary school across the street from the college has agreed to participate in an empirical study by administering the test to its students.

1. What psychometric information would you like to get about the test in order to gather evidence of its validity?
2. Would you need to administer to the participants measures other than the test you are validating? If so, what other measures would you like to administer?
3. Can you gather all the information you need in one administration? Explain why or why not.
4. What statistical procedures will you use to analyze your data?
5. Describe the types of judgments or decisions your study will allow you to make. What types of judgment or decisions will you not be able to make?
6. Describe any follow-up studies your validation study will require.

3. Interpreting a Multitrait-Multimethod Design

In 1995, psychologists at Pennsylvania State University (Conte, Landy, & Mathieu, 1995) conducted a multitrait-multimethod study to examine the construct validity of seven behaviorally anchored rating scales (BARS) that measure a construct called "time urgency." Time urgency is believed by some to be a core element of Type A behavior pattern (behaviors associated with coronary heart disease). Seven rating scales measuring (1) time awareness, (2) eating behavior, (3) scheduling, (4) nervous energy, (5) list making, (6) speech patterns, and (7) deadline control make up the overall measure of time urgency.

The researchers recruited students in introductory psychology classes to serve as participants in the validation study. In addition to rating themselves on the seven BARS, students were asked to enlist a friend or parent to rate them as well. The data obtained for 95 participants is shown in Table 9.1.

1. Which figures in Table 9.1 represent test-retest reliability? Which rater/dimension had the highest reliability? lowest reliability?
2. Which figures represent convergent validity? Which BAR had the greatest convergent validity? Which had the lowest?
3. Which figures represent discriminant validity?
4. Do these data indicate evidence of construct validity for the seven BARS? Explain your answer.

TABLE 9.1.   Multitrait, Multirater Matrix (Conte, Landy, & Mathieu, 1995)

(Multitrait-multimethod intercorrelation matrix for time urgency bars: seven dimensions × four raters)

Variable	1	2	3	4	5	6	7	8	9	10	11	12	13
1. S1	(.42)	.00	.38	.06	.16	−.38	.24	.40	−.07	.33	.00	.20	−.05
2. S2	−.02	(.52)	.00	.23	.00	.20	−.29	.04	.41	−.04	.01	.02	−.01
3. S3	.25	−.19	(.42)	.05	.39	−.06	.37	.36	−.13	.41	−.06	.28	.04
4. S4	.06	.11	−.01	(.53)	.11	−.06	.00	.29	.24	.14	.36	.16	.06
5. S5	.29	−.11	.47	.00	(.57)	.18	.25	.11	−.21	.19	−.13	.46	−.02
6. S6	.08	.01	.09	.08	.00	(.68)	.22	−.04	−.05	−.04	−.04	−.03	.38
7. S7	.32	−.08	.45	.03	.35	.08	(.65)	.16	−.31	.36	−.20	.20	.16
8. P1	.25	−.19	.21	.07	.27	.03	.22	(.44)	−.05	.48	−.04	.33	−.02
9. P2	.02	.21	.01	.04	−.04	−.08	.06	−.09	(.41)	−.11	.35	−.11	.22
10. P3	.20	−.04	.35	.01	.24	−.02	.36	.42	.12	(.54)	.09	.49	−.02
11. P4	.05	.07	.03	.27	−.03	.02	.03	−.02	.30	.14	(.40)	−.12	.30
12. P5	.14	−.10	.33	.09	.39	.08	.29	.43	−.08	.50	.08	(.63)	−.15
13. P6	.03	−.09	.08	.08	−.04	.26	.05	.19	.18	.19	.21	.10	(.54)
14. P7	.20	−.12	.42	−.04	.26	−.04	.45	.41	.00	.56	.17	.43	.09
15. M1	−.05	−.10	.21	−.03	.17	.04	.15	.14	.02	.08	−.04	.13	.14
16. M2	.00	.12	−.05	.10	.01	−.06	.07	.04	.17	−.09	.05	−.04	.01
17. M3	.06	−.04	.30	−.05	.26	.05	.39	.19	.06	.07	−.04	.23	.05
18. M4	−.01	.01	.10	.18	.04	−.07	.05	.02	.19	−.02	.11	.10	−.01
19. M5	.09	−.08	.31	.03	.42	.08	.35	.24	−.06	.15	−.06	.34	.03
20. M6	.05	−.08	.05	−.04	−.12	.34	−.01	.11	.01	−.07	−.09	.01	.17
21. M7	.04	−.06	.41	−.12	.24	.04	.45	.16	−.05	.23	−.05	.29	.04
22. F1	.18	−.08	.34	.08	.16	.08	.35	.24	.00	.19	−.03	.27	.06
23. F2	.00	.08	−.20	.10	−.03	.01	.01	.04	.12	.08	−.04	.03	−.01
24. F3	.01	−.10	.28	.08	.22	.01	.33	.17	.02	.15	−.01	.29	.02
25. F4	−.05	.08	−.02	.03	.08	−.03	−.01	.02	.28	.03	.10	.03	−.05
26. F5	.12	−.06	.28	.18	.33	.03	.35	.33	−.02	.22	.01	.40	.10
27. F6	−.03	−.12	−.10	−.01	−.12	.11	−.08	.07	.12	−.06	−.11	−.11	.16
28. F7	.02	−.05	.40	.04	.23	.05	.37	.21	.01	.21	.09	.24	.03
Time 1													
M	5.22	4.93	4.57	5.03	5.40	4.41	4.80	4.75	4.30	4.54	4.50	4.83	4.03
SD	1.17	1.12	1.30	1.32	1.31	1.34	1.31	1.28	1.35	1.36	1.51	1.43	1.33
Time 2													
M	5.31	4.98	4.65	5.07	5.32	4.23	4.76	4.77	4.33	4.48	4.51	4.96	4.07
SD	1.16	1.01	1.16	1.23	1.34	1.18	1.18	1.18	1.06	1.33	1.50	1.43	1.40

14	15	16	17	18	19	20	21	22	23	24	25	26	27	28
.24	.22	.17	.18	.12	.14	.02	.15	.25	.07	.14	.00	.18	-.13	.06
.02	-.06	.17	-.27	.02	-.16	.12	-.18	.09	.14	-.13	.18	-.10	.28	-.12
.43	.20	.24	.24	.12	.24	.19	.15	.19	.27	.09	.20	.20	.04	.19
.27	.17	.15	.29	.32	.14	.03	.12	.07	.14	.08	.46	.08	.04	.19
.20	-.09	.02	.27	.07	.33	.02	.15	.12	.12	.12	.10	.31	-.15	.19
-.02	-.04	.09	-.07	-.18	.03	.30	.04	.01	-.08	-.18	-.14	-.22	.20	-.09
.41	.21	.04	.25	.01	.36	.14	.41	.07	-.01	.09	-.01	.11	.00	.34
.43	.21	.25	.31	.19	.11	.02	.11	.13	.14	.17	.22	.18	-.01	.16
-.11	.00	.11	-.16	.22	-.04	-.03	-.25	-.03	.21	-.05	.16	.04	.01	-.09
.68	.20	.26	.31	.11	.13	.11	.10	.21	.04	.19	.28	.27	.03	.25
-.01	.19	.19	-.05	.13	-.14	.03	-.13	.21	.11	.01	.15	-.07	.06	-.17
.44	.15	.19	.46	.10	.34	.13	.24	.11	.16	.45	.08	.52	-.12	.27
-.14	.28	.11	-.01	.12	.18	.33	.10	.30	-.02	.12	.06	.04	.25	.26
(.61)	.14	.17	.29	.19	.22	.18	.17	.14	.02	.11	.23	.21	.00	.20
.05	(.63)	.26	.41	.26	.39	.31	.36	.51	.10	.26	.06	.20	.03	.25
.07	.04	(.43)	.10	.46	.14	.20	.12	.18	.40	.05	.31	-.04	.17	.16
.10	.52	.09	(.56)	.17	.71	.13	.51	.20	-.15	.53	.06	.46	-.18	.45
.05	.09	.33	.19	(.46)	.30	.14	.23	.03	.27	.07	.58	.20	.07	.20
.11	.46	.05	.43	.09	(.81)	.27	.57	.15	-.14	.47	.15	.46	-.05	.54
-.10	-.07	.05	.04	.09	.12	(.61)	.31	.27	.11	.16	.09	.09	.52	.26
.29	.28	-.03	.48	.11	.53	.18	(.58)	.14	-.04	.32	.10	.28	.10	.54
.15	.49	.09	.41	.14	.41	-.04	.35	(.58)	.03	.38	.05	.35	.25	.29
.00	.01	.48	.08	.16	.08	.00	-.11	.05	(.53)	-.06	.12	.02	.19	-.04
.15	.39	.02	.50	.07	.37	-.02	.39	.52	.07	(.48)	.08	.66	.00	.53
.09	.09	.29	.17	.55	.02	.02	-.01	.06	.39	.18	(.67)	.15	.22	.19
.16	.36	-.01	.45	.04	.61	.13	.42	.53	.02	.56	.05	(.76)	-.02	.50
-.06	.04	.08	.02	.09	.04	.36	.02	-.04	.21	.11	.09	.01	(.50)	.21
.26	.30	-.08	.40	.13	.31	.10	.57	.48	-.11	.60	.11	.54	-.03	(.63)
4.57	5.01	4.37	4.73	4.35	5.38	4.36	4.90	5.01	4.39	4.70	4.20	4.78	4.35	4.65
1.36	1.25	1.17	1.17	1.43	1.40	1.08	1.17	1.18	1.19	1.22	1.37	1.41	1.10	1.33
4.53	4.79	4.45	4.65	4.35	5.18	4.32	4.74	4.88	4.22	4.67	4.27	5.09	4.17	4.69
1.38	1.20	1.03	1.07	1.38	1.47	1.17	1.02	1.07	1.04	1.19	1.35	1.26	1.05	1.07

Source: J. J. Conte, F. J. Landy, J. E. Mathieu, "Time Urgency: Conceptual and Construct Development," *Journal of Applied Psychology, 80* (1995), 178–185, Table 1, pp. 180–181. Reprinted with permission.

Note. Correlations from Time 1 are shown below the diagonal ($n = 183$); $|r| \geq .15, p < .05$; $|r| \geq .20, p < .01$. Correlations from Time 2 are shown above the diagonal ($n = 70$); $|r| \geq .23, p < .05$; $|r| \geq .31, p < .01$. Diagonal entries within parentheses are test–retest correlations ($n = 95$). BARS = behaviorally anchored rating scales; S = subject; P = peer; M = mother; F = father; 1 = time awareness; 2 = speech patterns; 3 = scheduling; 4 = nervous energy; 5 = list making; 6 = rating behavior; 7 = deadline control.

Developing and Piloting Psychological Tests and Surveys

The third section of this text consists of three chapters that introduce you to how psychological tests and surveys are designed.

- **CHAPTER 10—DEVELOPING PSYCHOLOGICAL TESTS** In Chapter 10, we describe the process of designing a psychological test. We discuss the importance of having a test plan as well as the strengths and weaknesess of various test formats (for example, multiple-choice). After discussing some guidelines on how to write good test questions, we discuss the importance of the instructions that accompany a test.

- **CHAPTER 11—PILOTING AND REVISING TESTS** In Chapter 11 we continue to discuss test development but focus on the importance of pilot testing. We discuss how pilot testing allows us to analyze how difficult test items are, how well test items discriminate among respondents, and how likely it is that test items will introduce error into the test results. We discuss how tests are revised and how we gather information about the reliability and validity of a test. Lastly, we discuss the contents of the test manual.

- **CHAPTER 12—CONSTRUCTING AND ADMINISTERING SURVEYS AND USING SURVEY DATA** In Chapter 12 we discuss how to design, administer, and analyze survey data. We begin with an overview of the different ways we acquire knowledge, focusing on one approach, the scientific method. We focus our attention on a detailed discussion of a five-phase approach to constructing, administering, and analyzing survey data: presurvey issues, constructing the survey, administering the survey, entering and analyzing the data, and presenting the findings.

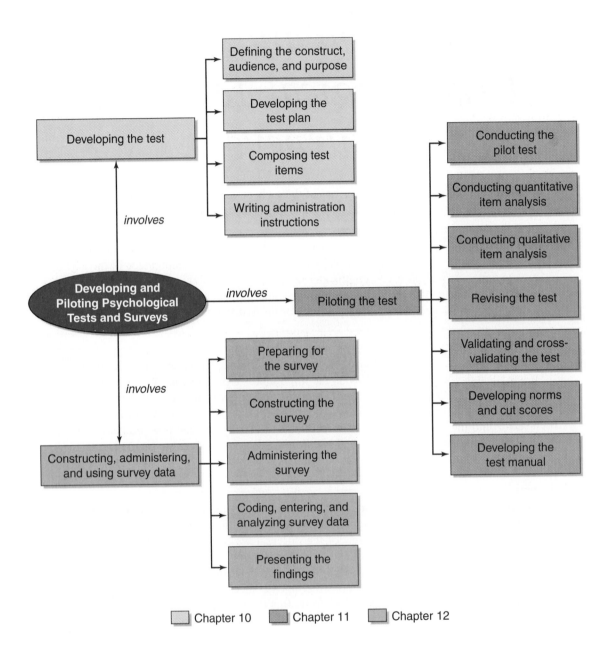

Developing Psychological Tests

188

SECTION THREE
Developing
and Piloting
Psychological Tests
and Surveys

"Some of my professors use a test bank supplied by the publisher of our textbook to make up their tests. I don't think that's right, since those questions are much harder than the questions that professors make up themselves."

"The concept of self-esteem really interests me, so I made up a self-esteem test and gave it to my friends. All my friends had high scores, so I know they all have high self-esteem."

"My supervisor at work has a test she put together herself that she gives to everyone who applies for a job in her unit. She won't hire anyone who doesn't pass the test. When I looked at the test, I could tell right away what the right answers were even though I don't know anything about the job!"

"I spent eight hours studying for my psychology final. Nothing that I studied was on the test! What gives?"

Why develop a new test? Thousands of psychological tests are available from commercial marketers and research journals. Most academic textbook publishers provide test questions—called **test banks**—for instructors to use when they develop classroom tests. It would seem that there are plenty of psychological tests from which the user can choose, and in many cases, this is so.

As we discussed in Section Two, however, test validity depends on the suitability of a test for a particular audience of test takers, adequate sampling of behaviors from a specific test domain, and the purpose for which test scores are used. Therefore, new tests are usually developed to meet the needs of a special group of test takers, to sample behaviors from a newly defined test domain, or to improve the accuracy of test scores for their intended purpose. For instance, an achievement test might be needed for a special population of respondents with a disability that affects how they perceive or answer the test questions. A new theory might suggest fresh definitions of constructs and require a new test to assess them. Finally, a better-defined test domain might generate test scores that more accurately predict a critical criterion.

In this chapter and the next, we discuss the steps for developing psychological tests. This chapter looks at the process of constructing a test plan. We examine various formats for writing questions (such as multiple-choice or true/false), discuss their strengths and weaknesses, and explain how test takers' perceptions and preconceptions can influence test scores. Finally, we present guidelines on how to write test questions and talk about the importance of the instructions that accompany a test.

This chapter discusses the first four steps in the process:

1. Defining the test universe, audience, and purpose
2. Developing a test plan
3. Composing the test items
4. Writing the administration instructions

Chapter 11 covers the last six steps:

5. Conducting the pilot test(s)
6. Conducting the item analysis

7. Revising the test
8. Validating the test
9. Developing the norms
10. Compiling the test manual

Figure 10.1 shows a flowchart of the test development process. As you can see, the information for the test manual is gathered throughout the process.

DEFINING THE TEST UNIVERSE, AUDIENCE, AND PURPOSE

The first step in test development is to define the test domain or universe, the target audience, and purpose of the test. This stage provides the foundation for all other development activities, so it is important to put ample time and thought into these issues.

- *Defining the test universe.* To do this, the developer prepares a working definition of the construct the test will measure. If the test is going to measure an abstract construct, the developer then conducts a thorough review of the psychological literature to locate studies that explain the construct and any current

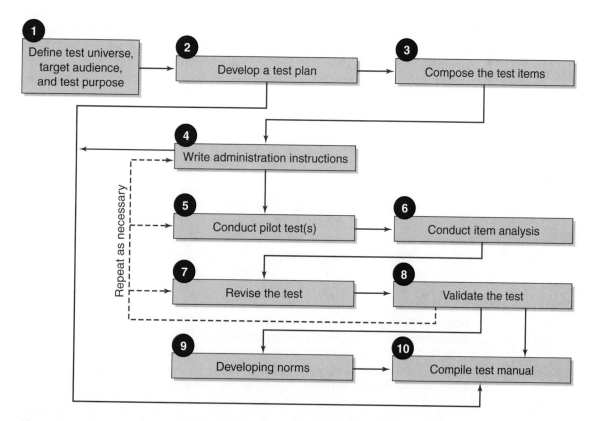

FIGURE 10.1. Flowchart of the test development process

190

*SECTION THREE
Developing
and Piloting
Psychological Tests
and Surveys*

tests that measure the construct. As we have discussed before, constructs must be defined operationally in terms of behaviors that are associated with the construct.

- *Defining the target audience.* The developer also needs to make a list of the characteristics of the persons who will take the test—particularly those characteristics that affect how test takers will respond to the test questions. For instance, what reading level is appropriate for the target audience? Do they have any disability or characteristic that would require a special test format? Will test takers be motivated to answer the test questions honestly? What language is appropriate for this audience?

- *Defining the purpose.* The purpose includes not only what the test will measure—for instance, self-esteem—but also how the outcomes of the test will be used. Will the scores be used to compare test takers (a normative approach) or will they be used to indicate achievement (criterion approach)? Will the test scores be used to predict a performance criterion (as in an employment test) or to make a diagnosis (as in a clinical setting)? Will the scores be used cumulatively to test a theory (for instance, to identify a correlation between intelligence and another variable) or individually to provide information about the individual (such as his or her IQ)?

Information about the test domain/universe, target audience, and purpose provide the basis for making other decisions about the test. For instance, information about the intended test takers and how test scores will be used determines whether the test can be administered to groups, individuals, or both. As we discussed in Chapter 4, special populations might require special types of administration by computer or in a one-on-one test setting. Characteristics such as reading level determine whether the construct can be measured in a group setting using a paper-and-pencil format or whether the test should be administered orally in a one-on-one setting.

DEVELOPING A TEST PLAN

The next step in test development is to write out a test plan. A **test plan,** as you recall from Chapter 6, specifies the characteristics of the test, including a definition of the construct, the content to be measured (the test domain), the format for the questions, and how the test will be administered and scored. Let us consider each part of the test plan in more detail.

Defining the Construct

After reviewing the literature about the construct and any available tests, the test developer is ready to write a concise definition of the construct. Such a definition includes operationalizing the construct in terms of observable and measurable behaviors. The definition also provides boundaries for the test domain by specifying what content should be tested and excluding content that is not appropriate for testing.

The test plans for clinical tests are based on carefully researched constructs. For example, For Your Information 10.1 contains operational definitions of the

Anxiety

Definition: A measure of clinical anxiety, focusing on common affective, cognitive, and physiological symptoms.

Behaviors: High anxiety is indicated by muscle tension, increased vigilance and scanning of the environment, rapid and shallow respiration, excessive concerns and worries about real or expected life events, which might be experienced as intrusive and unwanted thoughts.

Depression

Definition: A measure of clinical depression, focusing on common affective, cognitive, and physiological symptoms.

Behaviors: Depression is indicated by easy or chronic fatigue, loss of interest or pleasure in normally enjoyable activities, feelings of sadness and hopelessness, social withdrawal or isolation from friends and peers.

Suicidal Ideation

Definition: A measure of the extent of recent ideation (ideas) reflecting suicide, including hopelessness, and resignation.

Behaviors: Suicidal ideation is indicated by reports of thinking about suicide or behaviors associated with suicide attempts, including formulating a suicide plan.

Substance Abuse

Definition: A measure of disruption in interpersonal, social, academic, and vocational function as a result of substance use and abuse.

Behaviors: Substance abuse is indicated by difficulties in interpersonal, social, academic, and vocational functioning as a result of substance abuse or reporting guilt or shame about substance use, including embarrassment about behaviors displayed while abusing drugs or alcohol.

Self-Esteem Problems

Definition: A measure of global self-esteem that taps negative self-evaluations and dissatisfaction with personal achievement.

Behaviors: Self-esteem problems are indicated by self-criticism and dissatisfaction with perceived skills, abilities, or achievement in comparison to peers, including seeing oneself as unassertive, excessively sensitive to criticism from others, or physically or sexually unattractive.

Interpersonal Problems

Definition: A measure of the extent of problems in relating to others in the campus environment.

Behaviors: Interpersonal problems are indicated by difficulty in relating to others, including excessive dependence or increased vulnerability, and/or a distrustful, argumentative style of relating to others.

Family Problems

Definition: A measure of difficulties experienced in relationships with family members.

Behaviors: Family problems are indicated by difficulty achieving emotional separation from family and learning to live independently, including worry or concern over problems occurring in a conflicted or tumultuous family.

Academic Problems

Definition: A measure of the extent of problems related to academic performance.

Behaviors: Academic problems are indicated by poor study skills, inefficient use of time, poor concentration ability, or test anxiety.

Career Problems

Definition: A measure of the extent of problems related to career choice.

Behaviors: Career problems are indicated by difficulty in setting career goals and making decisions important for career goal attainment, including anxiety or worry about selecting an academic major or future career.

Source: Adapted from Anton & Reed (1991).

192

SECTION THREE
*Developing
and Piloting
Psychological Tests
and Surveys*

constructs measured by the College Adjustment Scales (CAS; Anton & Reed, 1991), a test designed to measure common developmental and psychological problems experienced by college students.

In organizations, test developers base their test plan on a job analysis that defines the knowledge, skills, abilities and other characteristics (KSAOs) required to perform the job successfully. These KSAOs are the constructs the test measures. The job analysis also describes the tasks performed on the job. These tasks are the observable and measurable behaviors associated with each KSAO. Chapter 15 discusses job analysis in more detail.

In educational settings, the curriculum (assigned readings, handouts, lectures, and so on) provides the basis for developing a test plan, and the constructs being measured are operationalized as learning objectives. As you recall, Chapter 7 describes test plans and their relation to content validity.

In addition to defining and operationalizing the construct being measured, the test plan specifies the approximate number of questions needed to sample the test domain. Should the test developer write 5 questions or 50 questions to measure this construct? This decision also depends in part on the test format that the test developer chooses.

Choosing the Test Format

The **test format** refers to the type of questions that the test will contain. For ease of response by the test taker and ease of administration and scoring, most test developers prefer to use one type of format throughout the test. Sometimes test inventories or batteries that measure several different constructs use different formats in different sections. In such cases, it is important to provide administration instructions for each section and administer each section separately.

Test formats provide two elements: a *stimulus* to which the test taker responds and a *mechanism for response*. For instance, a multiple-choice question might provide a question (stimulus) following by four or five possible answers (mechanisms for response). A multiple-choice format is also defined as an **objective test format,** because objective test formats have one response that is designated as correct or that provides evidence of a specific construct. (In other words, the test taker receives credit for choosing this response.) Other types of objective test formats include true/false questions and "fill in the blank" questions. Most test developers prefer objective test formats because they can be readily and reliably scored. Objective test formats also can be directly related to the test plan and the construct designated for measurement. These attributes facilitate documentation of the test's reliability and validity.

Subjective test formats, on the other hand, do not have a response that is designated as correct. Interpretation of the response as correct or providing evidence of a specific construct is left to the judgment of the person who scores or interprets the test taker's responses. **Projective tests** (such as the Rorschach Inkblot Test and the Thematic Apperception Test, described in detail in Chapter 14) are subjective test formats, because the stimuli for these tests are ambiguous pictures. The test taker provides a story or explanation (mechanism for response) of the picture, which is interpreted subjectively by the person scoring the test. Other examples of subjective test formats are "open-ended" or essay questions and the traditional employment interview. In each of these, the test taker or interviewee responds with any answer she or he thinks appropriate. Documenting the reliability and validity of tests based on subjective test formats is more difficult than for objective tests. For this reason, many test developers prefer objective test formats. We will discuss these formats in more detail in this chapter.

Specifying Administration and Scoring Methods

After choosing a test format (objective or subjective) and the appropriate type of question (true/false, multiple-choice, open-ended), the test developer needs to specify how to administer and score the test. This information is an important part of the test plan and can also affect how some of the test questions are written. For example, will the test be administered in writing, orally, or by computer? How long will the test taker have to complete the test? Will the test be administered to groups or individuals? Will the test be scored by the test publisher, the test administrator, or the test taker? Finally, what type of data is the test expected to yield—in other words, will the test scores provide the information required by the purpose of the test?

Scoring Methods

The test plan must also specify the method for scoring the test. The **cumulative model of scoring** is probably the most common method for determining an individual's final test score. This model assumes that the more the test taker responds in a particular fashion (either with "correct" answers or ones that are consistent with a particular attribute), the more the test taker exhibits the attribute being measured. To score a test using the cumulative model, the test taker receives one point for each correct answer. Therefore, the total number of correct answers becomes the raw score. Assuming that the test questions are comparable, the cumulative model of scoring can yield interval-level data. In any case, psychologists traditionally assume that such tests produce interval-level data that can then be interpreted using the norming procedures described in Chapter 5.

The **categorical model of scoring** is used to place test takers in a particular group or class. For instance, the test taker must display a pattern of responses that indicates diagnosis of a certain psychological disorder or behavioral trait. This model typically yields nominal data because it places test takers in categories.

The **ipsative model of scoring** differs from the cumulative and categorical models because the test taker's responses are not compared to those of other test takers. Instead, using the ipsative model, the test taker's scores on various scales within the inventory are compared to each other to yield a profile. This relative standing on various traits provides information on the test taker's overall performance or attributes. Using the ipsative method, test outcomes for individuals should not be compared or grouped with those of others, because the ipsative model assumes that individuals are themselves unique and incomparable.

The cumulative model may be combined with either the categorical model or the ipsative model. For instance, using the categorical model, scale scores are usually obtained using the cumulative method, then the categorical model is applied to obtain an overall interpretation or diagnosis of the individual test taker's performance.

After completing the test plan, the test developer is ready to begin writing the test questions and instructions. Composing the actual testing stimuli is an important and time-consuming activity, and we devote the remainder of this chapter to the art of writing the test itself.

After the initial test questions are written, the test developer conducts a pilot test, a scientific evaluation of the test's performance, followed by revisions to determine the final form the test will take. The test developer then follows up the pilot test with other studies that provide the necessary data for validation and norming. Conducting the pilot test and analyzing its data are an integral part of the test development process. We address these issues in Chapter 11.

Summary Box 10.1
Steps in Test Construction

- The first step in test development involves defining the test universe, the target audience, and purpose of the test.
- The next step in test development is to write out a test plan that includes the definition of the construct(s), the test format, the administration method, and the scoring method.
- After a review of the literature, the test developer writes a concise definition of the construct operationalizing the construct in terms of observable and measurable behaviors.
- The test developer chooses an objective or subjective format the type of test question (e.g., multiple-choice, true/false, open-ended, or essay).

- Next the test developer specifies how the test is to be administered and scored. The test might yield nominal, ordinal, interval, or ratio data. Three models for scoring are the cumulative model, the categorical model, and the ipsative model.
- After completing the test plan, the test developer is ready to begin writing the actual test questions and administration instructions.
- After writing the test, the developer conducts a pilot test followed by other studies that provide the necessary data for validation and norming.

COMPOSING THE TEST ITEMS

As you can see, test developers have much to do before they begin to write the test itself. Careful definition and review of the construct being assessed, however, makes development much easier and yields more successful questions. Many decisions, such as method of administration, have been considered and resolved while developing the test plan. Therefore, the test plan becomes the blueprint for proceeding with development.

Throughout this book, we have referred to the stimulus to which the test taker responds as a "test question." In reality, test questions are not always questions. Stimuli are frequently presented on tests in the form of statements, pictures, or incomplete sentences as well as other less common forms. Therefore, psychologists and test developers refer to these stimuli or test questions as **test items,** and we will refer to them as such for the remainder of this chapter and the next.

The test developer chooses the item format based on information in the test plan, such as the target audience, method of administration, and requirements for scoring. Following is a discussion of some standard item formats, including strengths or weaknesses that can cause test developers to choose or reject them as appropriate formats in various situations.

Objective Items

Multiple Choice

The item format used most often for tests in educational settings is **multiple choice.** Because this format is familiar to many people, it is also used for personality inventories and preemployment tests. The multiple-choice format consists of a question or partial sentence, called a **stem,** followed by a number of responses (usually four or five) of which only one is correct. The responses that are incorrect are called **distracters,** because they are designed to appear correct to someone who does not know the correct answer.

When writing a multiple-choice item, the developer must clearly differentiate the correct response from the distracters. Distracters that are "almost right" can be tricky and confusing to the respondent, and they rarely yield accurate assessment information. On the other hand, the distracters must be realistic enough to appeal to the uninformed test taker. Therefore, funny or unrealistic distracters decrease accurate assessment.

Multiple-choice items are popular because having one right answer eliminates confusion or controversy in scoring a correct response. Scoring is also easily accomplished by a nonprofessional aide or by a computer. One problem, however, is that test takers who do not know the correct answer can obtain credit by guessing. A test taker who does not know the correct answer for a multiple-choice item with four responses has a 1-in-4 (25 percent) chance of guessing the correct answer. These odds can be improved if the test taker can eliminate one or two of the distracters, yielding a 1-in-3 or 1-in-2 chance of guessing the correct answer. This disadvantage is offset by presenting a large number of items. For instance, compared to the 1-in-4 chance of guessing the correct answer on one item, the odds that an uninformed test taker will guess the correct response (when there are four responses) to each of 10 multiple-choice questions are 1 in 1,048,576!

True/False

The stem of the **true/false item** asks "Which of the following is True?" Usually this question is followed by two statements—one true and one false. If an entire test is made up of true/false items, the instructions contain the stem and direct the test takers to mark each statement "true" or "false." Again, test takers can gain some advantage by guessing. The true/false format can be translated into a multiple-choice format by presenting four or five statements from which the test taker chooses the one that is true.

Forced Choice

The **forced-choice** format is similar to the multiple-choice format. It is used, however, for personality and attitude tests rather than knowledge tests. This format requires the test taker to choose one of two or more words or phrases that appear to be unrelated but equally acceptable. The stem of the forced-choice question (often

196

SECTION THREE
Developing
and Piloting
Psychological Tests
and Surveys

included in the test instructions) might ask the respondent, "Which of each pair is most descriptive of you?" Although the words or phrases appear unrelated, there should be empirical evidence that they yield significantly different responses from different types of people. In other words, people with similar personality traits usually prefer one response to the other.

Test developers use forced-choice items because they are more difficult for respondents to guess or fake. Because the paired words or phrases appear to have little in common, the test taker cannot guess what the best response should be. On the other hand, the forced-choice format has little face validity—that is, no apparent connection with the stated purpose of the test. As you may recall from Chapter 6, lack of face validity can produce poor test taker responses. Making a number of decisions between apparently unrelated words or phrases can become distressing, and test takers who want to answer honestly and accurately often become frustrated with forced-choice questions.

For Your Information 10.2 shows an example of each of these objective item formats.

Subjective Items

Sometimes test developers prefer subjective items to objective items. Although objective items are easily scored and interpreted, they also rely on cues provided by the test. Subjective items, on the other hand, give the test taker fewer cues and open wider areas for response.

Essay questions are popular subjective items in educational settings. Such questions are usually general in scope and require lengthy written responses by test takers. Essays provide a freedom of response that facilitates assessing higher

---

For Your Information   10.2
Examples of Objective Item Formats

Multiple-choice format:
1. Which of the following levels of measurement involves ranking from lowest to highest?
    a. Nominal
    b. Ordinal
    c. Equal interval
    d. Ratio

True/false format:
Indicate whether the following statements are true or false by placing a "T" for true or "F" for false in the space to the left of the statement.
    1.___ Proportions can be calculated only from data obtained using a ratio scale.
    2.___ Equal-interval scales do not have a true zero point.

Forced-choice format:
Place an "X" in space to the left of the word in each pair that best describes your personality.
    1. ____ sunny   2. ____ outgoing
       ____ friendly   ____ loyal

cognitive behaviors such as analysis, synthesis, and evaluation (Hopkins & Antes, 1979). The responses generated can vary in terms of width and depth of topic, so the scorer must make a judgment regarding whether the response is correct. Often the scorer awards points based on how closely the test taker's response matches a predetermined correct response.

Many students prefer essay questions because this format allows them to focus on demonstrating what they have learned and does not limit them to specific questions. Others point out, however, that scorer judgments can be influenced by writing skills ranging from legibility to graceful phrasing. Unless writing skills are part of the testing domain, such considerations can lead to inaccurate test scores.

In organizational settings, the traditional subjective test is the employment interview. **Interview questions,** like essay questions, are general in scope. It is up to the interviewer to decide what is a "good" or "poor" answer. The test plan for an employment interview should be based on the knowledge, skills, abilities, and other characteristics (KSAOs) required to perform the job. This information can be obtained from a job description or job analysis, current job incumbent, supervisor, training objectives, and other job resources. In other words, the interview questions should assess the qualities necessary to perform the job. Chapter 15 provides more discussion on employment interviewing.

In clinical settings, test developers have developed a number of **projective techniques.** This type of subject format uses a highly ambiguous stimulus to elicit an unstructured response from the test taker. In other words, the test taker "projects" his or her perspective and perceptions onto a neutral stimulus. There are a variety of types of projective stimuli, including pictures and written or spoken words. Test takers may respond verbally or by drawing pictures. Interpretation of children's play also can be categorized as a projective technique (Krall, 1986). Chapter 14 describes projective techniques in more detail.

Another subjective format often used in attitude or personality scales is the **sentence completion** format. This format presents an incomplete sentence such as *I feel happiest when I am _____.* The respondents then complete the sentence in any way that makes sense to them. One person might say, "I feel happiest when I am *playing the piano.*" Another might respond, "I feel happiest when I am *studying for an important exam.*" The person scoring the test will then compare test takers' response with responses supplied by the test developer to award points or identify a trait or type.

For Your Information 10.3 shows an example of each of these subjective item formats.

By their nature, subjective tests, including projective tests, are at risk for introducing judgment error into test scores. Therefore, evidence of inter-rater reliability is of particular importance for subjective tests. Test developers can reduce scoring errors by providing clear and specific scoring keys that illustrate how various types of responses should be scored. Test users can increase the reliability of scoring essays, interviews, and projective tests by providing training for scorers and having two scorers who make independent evaluations.

Response Bias

If not carefully constructed, both objective and subjective test item formats are likely to introduce error into test scores. Even when carefully constructed, some formats are more likely than others to introduce error.

Another source of error in test scores comes from test takers. Researchers have found that some people have response sets (also known as response styles) for choosing test answers. **Response sets** are patterns of responding that result in false or misleading information. These sources of error limit the accuracy and usefulness of test scores, so test developers need to consider the possible effects of response bias when they develop a test.

Social Desirability

One problem for test developers is the tendency of some test takers to provide or choose answers that are socially acceptable or present them in a favorable light. This response set is known as **social desirability.** When developing a test, it is important to take social desirability into account. For instance, when providing responses for multiple-choice questions, developers try to balance the social desirability of the correct response and the distracters. When using the forced-choice format, responses can be paired on the basis of their desirability. When social desirability is likely to cause error, test developers might conduct a study to determine how socially desirable each proposed response is to a sample of people who resemble the test's target audience. Responses that are shown to be highly desirable are discarded.

Acquiescence

Another response set familiar to test developers is called **acquiescence.** This style refers to the tendency to agree with any ideas or behaviors presented. For instance, someone who labels each statement on a true/false test as "true" would be demonstrating a response set of acquiescence. For this reason, test developers often balance items for which the correct response would be positive with an equal number of items for which the correct response would be negative. In Greater Depth 10.1 illustrates this strategy and describes how balancing positive and negative items affects cumulative scoring.

Random Responding

Sometimes test takers are unwilling or unable to respond to test items accurately. In this case, they might respond to items in a random fashion by marking

Using "Reverse Scoring" to Balance Positive and Negative Items

Some test takers are inclined to give mostly positive responses to questions, regardless of the question's content. The test developer tries to offset the effects of this response set, known as acquiescence, by balancing positive statements with negative statements. Because scoring is usually a cumulative estimate of how much the test taker exhibits or agrees with the test's construct, it then becomes necessary to "reverse" the responses to negative items. For example, a test assessing a student's attitude toward studying might ask the test taker to respond using the following five-point scale:

1—Rarely true
2—Sometimes true
3—Neither true or false
4—Very often true
5—Almost always true

High (4 or 5) responses to positive statements, such as "I enjoy memorizing vocabulary words," would reflect a positive attitude toward studying. However, high responses to negative items, such as "When I sit down to study I get depressed," would indicate the opposite—a negative attitude toward studying. Therefore, the test scorer reverses the response numbers of negative items. A "5" answer to a negative item would be changed to a "1," a "4" answer to a "2," and so on. Neutral responses "3" would remain the same.

After reversing the responses on the negative items, the test scorer then uses the cumulative model of scoring in which the numbers indicated for each response are added to arrive at the overall score.

answers without reading or considering them. This response set is likely to occur when test takers lack necessary skills (such as reading) to take the test, do not wish to be evaluated, or lack the attention span necessary to complete the task. Some tests contain a scale that records a high score for test takers who are uncooperative. Such scales usually contain a number of items that have obvious responses for most of the population. In other words, they will be either true or false for almost everyone in the target audience. Test takers who respond randomly are likely to answer differently from most people on a number of these items, thereby tipping off the scorer that they were not cooperating.

Faking

A similar response set is called **faking** and refers to the inclination of some test takers to try to answer items in a way that will cause a desired outcome or diagnosis. For instance, a test taker completing a personality test for a prospective employer might try to answer items in a way that makes her appear friendly and cooperative (faking "good"). On the other hand, a test taker who has been charged with a serious crime might wish to appear mentally disturbed (faking "bad"). Again, a number of personality and clinical tests, such as the MMPI-2, contain scales designed to detect faking.

Questions that have no apparent relation to the test purpose or criterion are referred to as **subtle questions.** Not only are these questions difficult to fake, but researchers themselves often cannot explain what the question measures or how it relates to the criterion (Duckworth, 1990). For Your Information 10.4 describes the results of two studies on the validity of the subtle questions on the MMPI-2.

Lately, a number of researchers have questioned the usefulness of the MMPI's subtle questions. Brems and Harris (1996) explored the effect on profiles generated by the MMPI-2 (a revised version of the MMPI) by asking college students to fake "good" responses, fake "bad" responses, or answer truthfully. In their study, students were able to raise or lower their scale scores on the obvious scales. The scores for both groups who faked answers were higher than those who answered truthfully, although only the scores of those who faked "good" were significantly higher. They concluded that the scales made up of subtle questions on the MMPI-2 are useful for detecting faking.

Another researcher (Boone, 1995) conducted a similar study using patients diagnosed as (1) "at risk" or "not at risk" for suicide and (2) and depressed or nondepressed. He compared these patients scores on the full scale and a scale made up of only the obvious questions. The subtle questions differentiated between those assessed "at risk" and "not at risk" for suicide, but in the opposite direc-

tion of the other scales. In other words, "not at risk" patients scored significantly higher ($p < .01$) than the "at risk" patients on the subtle questions. The subtle items were not able to differentiate between the depressed and the nondepressed patients. Based on his study, Boone suggests that the subtle questions on the MMPI-2 might weaken estimates of its validity. He suggests that the MMPI-2 might be a better predictor of some problems, such as depression, if the subtle items are disregarded.

Not all tests that predict independent criteria have questions that are subtle. Today, many test developers show evidence of both content validity and criterion-related validity for their tests. Test takers—particularly those in educational and organizational settings—resent tests that ask questions about personal feelings and activities that appear to have no relation to the purpose of the test. As you may recall from Chapter 7, *face validity*—what the test appears to measure—is not essential for a test to be valid, but it can enhance the test taker's willingness to cooperate with the testing process.

Writing Good Items

As you can see, a lot of thought goes into writing test items that will elicit accurate and honest information. Most developers consider item writing an art that depends on originality and creativity combined with knowledge of the test domain and good item-writing practices. After the test items are written, they should be administered to a sample of the target audience to determine whether they yield the desired information. (This process, called pilot testing, is discussed in Chapter 11.) Experienced item writers know that not all items will perform as expected. Test takers will misinterpret some items. Other items will be too easy or too difficult, and a few items might be answered differently by women and men. Therefore, developers follow a general rule of thumb: "Write twice as many items as you expect to use in the final test." Doing so allows developers to discard poor items after the pilot test.

Although there is no set of rules that guarantees that items will perform as expected, we can pass along some suggestions from the test development literature. Here are some general suggestions for constructing both objective and subjective items:

- *Identify item topics by consulting the test plan.* In this way, the test developer maximizes the relation between the test plan and the test itself, thereby increasing content validity.

- *Be sure that each item is based on an important learning objective or topic.* Structure the item around one central idea or problem. Do not test for trivial or peripheral information or skills.
- *Write items that assess information or skills drawn only from the testing universe.* This guideline is important for education and training programs. If the test's purpose is to measure how much the test taker learned in a training class, the test developer needs to write items from the course material. Such items should ask questions that respondents are unlikely to be able to answer from general knowledge.
- *Write each item in a clear, direct manner.* Precise words and simple sentence structure, as well as correct grammar and punctuation, should be used to describe the problem or ask the intended question.
- *Use vocabulary and language appropriate for the target audience.* Do not make an item a test of reading ability unless you are constructing a test of reading skill.
- *Make all items independent.* Developers need to check all items to be sure that cues for the correct response to one item are not found elsewhere in the test.
- *Ask someone else, preferably a subject matter expert, to review items to reduce unintended ambiguity and inaccuracies.* This step assures that the test items convey clear information and questions. Questions that have multiple interpretations should be revised or discarded.

Multiple Choice

Here are some specific guidelines for writing true/false and multiple-choice questions:

- *Avoid using negative stems and responses.* Instead of asking, "Which of the following is *not* true?" it is better to ask, "Which of the following is *false?*" Likewise, a response that reads, "Confidentiality means that individuals are assured that all personal information they disclose will be kept private" is preferable to a negatively worded response, such as "Individuals that are *not* assured that all personal information they disclose will be kept private are *not* assured of confidentiality."
- *Make all responses similar in detail and length.* The tendency to make the correct response more detailed can be avoided by making sure that all responses are similar in detail and length.
- *Make sure the item has only one answer that is definitely correct or "best."* To assure there is only one correct answer, construct an answer key that contains a brief rationale for the correct answer for each item.
- *Avoid determining words such as "always" or "never."* Instead use "sometimes" or "often" as qualifiers.
- *Avoid overlapping responses.* For instance, quantitative responses such as "10 to 20" and "20 to 30" overlap and leave the test taker who wishes to answer "20" confused about how to respond.
- *Avoid using inclusive distracters.* "All or the above," "None of the above," and "Both a and c" are called inclusive distracters. This type of response usually makes items very easy or difficult. If you choose to use them, be sure to balance the number of times they are used as the correct and incorrect response.

202

SECTION THREE
Developing
and Piloting
Psychological Tests
and Surveys

- *Use random assignment to position the correct response.* Research suggests that test takers often assign the correct response to "c" or "b." Random assignment of the correct response assures uniformity of response probability and decreases test takers' ability to guess the correct response.

Essay and Interview Questions

The following tips provide some guidance in developing and scoring effective essay and interview questions.

- *Use essay items appropriately.* Essays are most effective for assessing higher-order skills, such as analysis, synthesis, and evaluation. If the developer wishes to measure simple recall, an objective format might be more efficient.
- *Consider the time necessary for response.* Frame instructions and items in a way that lets the test taker know the expected length of response. In this way, the developer can provide the appropriate number of essay questions for the time allotted for testing. Remember that some test takers will take longer to complete the test than others because of variation in writing skills. Ample time should be allotted for all test takers to respond to their satisfaction.
- *Prepare an answer key.* The key for open-ended essays and interviews should outline the expected correct response. In addition, it should list other possible responses along with scores based on the appropriateness of the response. For example, a response that matches the desired response might receive full credit and others might receive partial credit. Remember that in subjective testing it is possible for a test taker to submit a totally unexpected solution or response that is as correct as or better than the expected response!
- *Score essays anonymously.* Anonymous scoring, when possible, decreases the possibility of bias associated with personal knowledge of the respondent or the respondent's characteristics, such as sex, race, and age.
- *Use multiple, independent scorers.* Having two or more scorers who read essays or conduct interviews provides an opportunity to detect and decrease bias as well as establish scorer reliability.

A Comparison of Objective and Subjective Formats

In this section, we draw from the work of Kryspin and Feldhusen (1974) to summarize the strengths and weaknesses associated with objective and subjective item formats. We consider how thoroughly the test developer can sample the test domain, ease of construction, the process of scoring, and how the test taker prepares for the test.

Sampling

Objective formats with structured responses, such as multiple-choice and true/false items, provide ample opportunity to sample the test universe. Because test takers expend less time and effort to answer these items, the test developer can cover a wider array of topics, thus increasing content validity. With subjective formats, such as the essay or interview question, the test developer is limited to the number of questions or topics to which the test taker can respond in one session. When the test universe covers a wide range of topics, content validity for the test usually suffers.

Construction

Objective items, especially multiple-choice, require extensive thought and development time, because the test developer needs to balance responses in terms of content depth, length, and appeal to the test taker. Novice developers are quick to note that supplying three or four distracters that resemble the correct response is not an easy task. On the other hand, subjective tests require fewer items and those items are easier to construct and revise. Furthermore, some measurement experts suggest that essay and interview questions are better suited for testing higher-order skills such as creativity and organization.

Scoring

Scoring of objective items is simple and can be done with a high degree of reliability or accuracy by an aide or a computer. Scoring subjective items, however, requires time-consuming judgments by an expert. Essay and interview scoring is most reliable and accurate when there are two independent scorers who have been trained to avoid biased judgments. Scoring keys are important for subjective items, but these are more difficult to construct because they must address as many likely responses as possible.

Response Sets

Test takers have the option of guessing the correct response on objective tests. They also might choose socially desirable responses or acquiesce to positive statements. Even though subjective items do not elicit this type of response bias, respondents might bluff or pad answers with superfluous or excessive information. Scorers might be influenced by irrelevant factors such as poor verbal or writing skills.

As you can see, each format has advantages and drawbacks. Objective items require more time and thought during the development phase. When objective questions are properly developed, they have high content validity and provide reliable and accurate scores. On the other hand, subjective items, such as essays and interviews, can be more appropriate for assessing higher-order skills. In addition, subjective items require less time to develop. These advantages, however, are offset by the time and expertise required to score or interpret responses and their greater susceptibility to scorer bias.

WRITING THE ADMINISTRATION INSTRUCTIONS

Although the test items make up the bulk of the new test, they are meaningless without specific instructions on how the test is to be administered. The test developer needs to write two sets of instructions. One set of instructions is for the person administering the test, and the other is for the test taker.

Administrator Instructions

The circumstances under which the test is administered—called the **testing environment**—can affect how test takers respond. A standardized testing environment, as you may recall, decreases variation or error in scores that can be attributed to factors other than the attribute being measured. Specific and concise instructions

---

Summary Box 10.2
Composing Test Items

- The test developer chooses the item format based on information in the test plan, such as the target audience, method of administration, and requirements for scoring.
- *Objective formats* include multiple-choice, true/false, and forced-choice items.
- *Subject formats* include essay and interview questions.
- *Projective tests* are a type of subjective format that uses a highly ambiguous stimulus to elicit an unstructured response from the test taker. Projective stimuli can include pictures and written or spoken words. Test takers might respond verbally or by drawing pictures.
- Some people have *response sets,* patterns of responding that result in false or misleading information. These sets include *social desirability, acquiescence, random responding,* and *faking.*

- Though there is no set of rules that guarantees that items will perform as expected, the test development literature contains a number of suggestions for writing successful items.
- Objective items provide ample sampling of the test universe, but they are more time consuming to develop. Scoring of objective items is easier and likely to be more accurate and reliable.
- Subjective items are easier to construct and revise. Some experts suggest that essay and interview questions are better suited for testing higher-order skills such as creativity and organization. Scoring of subjective items is more difficult, requiring independent scoring by two experts to increase reliability and accuracy.

---

for administering the test help ensure that the test will be administered properly under standardized conditions.

Administrator instructions should address the following:

- Group or individual administration
- Specific requirements for the location, such as privacy, quiet, and comfortable chairs, tables, or desks
- Required equipment, such as No. 2 pencils or a computer with CD-ROM drive
- Time limitations, or approximate time for completion if there are no time limits
- Script for the administrator to read to test takers, including answers to questions that test takers are likely to ask

Instructions for the Test Taker

Instructions for the test taker are usually delivered orally by the test administrator, who often reads a prepared script. Instructions also appear in writing at the beginning of the test or test booklet. Test takers need to know where to respond (for example, on an answer sheet or in the test booklet) and how to respond (for example, blackening the appropriate space on an answer sheet or circling the correct multiple-choice answer.) Each type of item (for example, multiple-choice, essay) should be followed by specific directions for responding.

Test instructions often encourage test takers to provide accurate and honest answers. They might also provide a context for answering, such as *"Think of your current work situation when replying to the following questions."* The test instructions need to be simple and concise. Complicated methods for responding are likely to lead to confused test takers and an increased probability of response errors. For Your Information 10.5 provides an example of instructions for test takers.

GENERAL DIRECTIONS: This final exam contains 20 multiple-choice questions and three essay questions. You have two hours to complete this examination. Read each question carefully. If you have a question or concern, you may ask the test administrator. When you have completed the exam, return it to the test administrator and then leave the testing area.

Please provide the information in the box below. Then proceed to Section I.

NAME:

STUDENT NUMBER:

SECTION:

DIRECTIONS FOR SECTION I: Read each of the following multiple-choice questions carefully and decide which response alternative (a, b, c, d, e) is the *best* answer. Indicate your response by circling the best answer *in this test booklet.* Each question is worth 3 points.

DIRECTIONS FOR SECTION II: Read each question carefully, then write your answer *in this test booklet* in the space provided. Write two or three paragraphs using complete sentences. Each question is worth 10 points.

SUMMARY

This chapter discussed the initial steps for developing psychological tests. The first step in test development is defining the test universe, the target audience, and purpose of the test. This stage provides the foundation for all other development activities. After a review of the literature, the test developer writes a concise definition of the construct, operationalizing the construct in terms of observable and measurable behaviors. The next step is to write out a test plan that specifies the characteristics of the test, including a definition of the construct, the content to be measured (the test universe), the format for the questions, ands how the test will be administered and scored.

The cumulative model of scoring (which assumes that the more the test taker responds in a particular fashion, the more the test taker exhibits the attribute being measured) is probably the most common method for determining an individual's final test score. The categorical model and the ipsative model also provide scoring methods.

After completing the test plan, the test developer begins writing the test questions and instructions. The questions, called "items" by test developers, can be in an objective format (multiple-choice, true/false, forced-choice) or subjective format (essays, interviews). Projective tests, another type of subjective format, use ambiguous stimuli (such as words or pictures) to elicit responses from the test taker.

206

*Section Three
Developing
and Piloting
Psychological Tests
and Surveys*

Some people have response sets, patterns of responding that result in false or misleading information, such as social desirability, acquiescence, random responding, and faking, that cause test scores to contain error. Therefore, test developers need to be aware of these types of responses and guard against them. There is no set of rules that guarantees that items will perform as expected, but the test development literature contains a number of suggestions for writing successful items.

Objective items provide ample sampling of the test universe, but they are more time consuming to develop. Scoring of objective items is easier and likely to be more accurate and reliable. Subjective items are easier to construct and revise. Some experts suggest that essay and interview questions are better suited for testing higher-order skills such as creativity and organization. Scoring of subjective items is more difficult, requiring independent scoring by two experts to increase reliability and accuracy.

After the initial test questions are written, the test developer conducts a pilot test to determine the final form the test will take. The test developer then follows up the pilot test with other studies that provide the necessary data for validation and norming. Conducting the pilot test and analyzing its data are an integral part of the test development process that are addressed in Chapter 11.

KEY CONCEPTS

acquiescence	ipsative model of scoring	subjective test formats
categorical model of scoring	multiple choice	subtle questions
cumulative model of scoring	objective test format	test banks
distracters	projective techniques	test format
essay questions	projective tests	test items
faking	random responding	test plan
forced choice	response sets	testing environment
interview questions	sentence completion	true/false item
	social desirability	
	stem	

LEARNING ACTIVITIES

1. Developing a Test Plan

Test plans in educational settings are based on the material presented for students to learn. Now that you have read and studied this chapter, use it to develop a test plan for a multiple-choice and essay test to measure the information learned from this chapter. Your test plan should include definitions of the constructs being measured (in this case, learning objectives), the content to be measured (the test universe will be the information in this chapter), the format (multiple-choice and essay) and number of questions, the target audience (students), and how the test will be administered and scored.

2. Writing Items

Using the test plan you have developed, write multiple-choice and essay questions for this chapter. Pay close attention to the guidelines for writing items. This exercise not only gives you experience writing items, but it is an excellent way to study for a test!

Piloting and Revising Tests

"Last week I participated in a pilot study of a new self-esteem test. The test administrator asked us not to put our names on our answer sheets, because she said she could not be sure the test was a true measure of our self-esteem. If it's a self-esteem test, why wouldn't our scores be good?"

"I have a copy of a test I took at work on organizational values. I wanted to give it as a demonstration in class. My instructor objected because he said we could not interpret the test scores without the test manual. What's so important about having a test manual?"

"I created a test on math skills for some students I am tutoring. When I showed it to my supervisor, she asked about the 'cut score.' What's a cut score?

"My son's class took a standardized math test. There were a number of questions that were answered correctly by more girls than boys. I suggested to the teacher that the test might be biased against boys. She said that comparing the percentage of each group who answered questions correctly is not a good measure of bias. Why not?"

In Chapter 10 we described the process for designing a test, developing the test's items, and writing the instructions for the test administrator and the test takers. In this chapter, we continue describing the test development process by discussing piloting the test and analyzing the items in terms of their difficulty, their ability to discriminate among respondents, and their likelihood of introducing error into the test results. We also describe the process of revising the test and gathering evidence of reliability and validity. Finally, we discuss briefly the contents of the test manual. You may wish to refer to Figure 10.1 to familiarize yourself with the overall process of test development.

THE PILOT TEST

When developers design a new test, they cannot assume that the test will perform as expected. Just as engineers who have designed a new airplane conduct test flights to find out how well the plane flies, test developers conduct studies to determine how well a new test performs. The **pilot test** is a scientific investigation of the new test's reliability and validity for its specified purpose. It involves administering the test to a sample of the test's target audience. The data obtained from this study are then analyzed, and revisions are made to fix any problems with the test's performance. It would be unsafe to carry passengers on a new airplane that has not been tested for performance and safety. Likewise, it is improper to rely on the results of a psychological test that has not been studied to assure that its data are valid and reliable (that is, that it measures what it says it measures and it does so consistently).

As we saw in Chapter 10, new psychological tests are developed from a test plan, similar to an airplane's blueprints. To the extent that the test matches the test plan, we can say that it has content validity. However, there are a number of important issues beyond content validity that must be tested to ensure that the test scores are accurate and meaningful. For example, are the test items too difficult or too

210

SECTION THREE
*Developing
and Piloting
Psychological Tests
and Surveys*

easy? Do the test items differentiate among individuals—in other words, do the test scores vary, or does everyone get about the same score? Are any of the items more difficult for certain groups of respondents, such as women or minorities? In addition, developers want to know whether the test instructions for the administrator and respondent are clear and easy to follow. Is the length of time allotted for administering the test adequate? Do respondents react to the test favorably and cooperatively? Finally, can the test user rely on the test scores to provide the information described in the test's purpose? Just as engineers rely on test flights to provide evidence of a new plane's safety and performance to specifications, test developers rely on their pilot tests to provide evidence that their new test will produce scores that will be useful for decision making without harming test users or respondents.

Setting Up the Pilot Test

The purpose of the pilot test is to study how well the test performs, so it is important that the test is given in a situation that matches the actual circumstances in which the test will be used. Therefore, developers choose a sample of people to take the test who resemble or are a part of the test's target audience.

For example, if the test is designed to diagnose emotional disabilities in adolescents, the participants for the pilot study should be adolescents. Part of the sample should be adolescents who have been determined to have emotional disabilities. The others should be adolescents who have been determined not to have emotional disabilities. In addition, it would be important to assure that each of those groups contains both males and females from various economic and ethnic backgrounds. The sample should be large enough to provide the power to conduct statistical tests to compare responses of each group. For example, developers need to compare the responses of males with emotional disabilities to those of females with emotional disabilities, and so on.

Likewise the test setting of the pilot test should mirror the planned test setting. If school psychologists will use the test, then the pilot test should be conducted in a school setting using school psychologists as administrators. Conducting the pilot test in more than one school would be preferable, because error introduced by one school's situation can be identified or offset by other schools.

In setting up pilot studies, developers follow the American Psychological Association's codes of ethics (shown in Appendix B). This means that test takers (and their parents or guardians, where appropriate) understand that they are participating in a research study and that the test scores will be used for research purposes only. Developers observe strict rules of confidentiality and publish only aggregate results of the pilot study.

Conducting the Pilot Test

The depth and breadth of the pilot test usually depend on the size and complexity of the target audience. For instance, tests designed for use in a single company or college program require less extensive studies than tests designed for large audiences, such as students applying for graduate school in the United States or adults seeking jobs as managers. In either case, however, it is important that the test administrators adhere strictly to the test procedures outlined in their test instructions.

In addition, pilot studies often require gathering extra data, such as measures of performance and the length of time needed to complete the test. Developers might use questionnaires or interviews that gather information from respondents about the test. For example, developers might ask participants: "Did you readily understand the test instructions?" "Were there any questions you did not understand?" "Did you object to the content of any questions?" "Do you believe the test fairly assessed your skills?" Information on respondents' reactions and thoughts about the test can help developers understand why some questions yielded better data than others. This information makes the process of revising the test easier.

212

Section Three
*Developing
and Piloting
Psychological Tests
and Surveys*

Most pilot tests go well and yield useful data that guide developers in making necessary revisions. But some pilot tests simply do not work. For instance, administrators might ignore test instructions, respondents might complete answer sheets incorrectly, or respondents might exhibit hostility toward the test or the test administrator. In such cases, it is important to recognize the problems with the test, make all necessary revisions before continuing, and conduct a new pilot test that yields appropriate results.

The pilot test provides an opportunity to gather both quantitative and qualitative data about the test. The developers use statistical procedures to analyze the test responses for information regarding each item's difficulty, ability to discriminate among individuals, and likelihood of introducing bias or error. In addition, developers can estimate internal consistency. When data on an external criterion, such as performance or diagnosis, have been collected, developers can also gather preliminary information about how well the test scores correlate with the external criterion scores. This quantitative information is then reviewed with the qualitative information, such as test takers' reactions, to make revisions that enhance the performance of the test.

In the next section, we discuss how developers evaluate the performance of each test item, a process called **item analysis.**

Summary Box 11.1
Conducting the Pilot Test

- The pilot test is a scientific investigation of the new test's reliability and validity.
- The test is given in a situation that matches the actual circumstances in which the test will be used.
- Developers choose a sample of people who resemble or are a part of the test's target audience.
- The test is administered and the test procedures outlined are strictly followed.

- Extra measures and a questionnaire about the test are often given with the test.
- The quantitative and qualitative information obtained during the pilot study is then analyzed to find out how well the test performs.

QUANTITATIVE ITEM ANALYSIS

Each item in a test is a building block that contributes to the test's outcome or final score. Therefore, developers examine the performance of each item to identify those items that perform well, to revise those that could perform better, and to eliminate those that do not yield the desired information. The major portion of such a study involves **quantitative item analysis**—statistical analyses of the responses test takers gave to individual items. As you might recall from Chapter 10, developers usually write twice the number of items they expect to use in the final test. This allows them to select the very best items from those they have written.

Item Difficulty

The purpose of norm-referenced tests (described in Chapter 5) is to compare the test scores of various individuals. Therefore, it is important that test takers have a range of test scores. Items that everyone gets right or everyone gets wrong provide no basis for comparison and yield similar test scores for all test takers. Therefore, developers analyze each test item for its difficulty. **Item difficulty** is defined as the percentage of test takers who respond correctly. We calculate each item's difficulty, or p value, by dividing the number of persons who answered correctly by the total number of persons who responded to the question. When test developers are writing items, they can only guess at how difficult each item will be. The pilot test provides real data for judging item difficulty.

Generally speaking, items with difficulty levels, or p values, of .5 yield distributions of test scores with the most variation. Because difficulty levels can be expected to vary, most developers seek a range of difficulty levels that average about .5. They discard or rewrite items with extreme p values, usually defined as 0 to about .2 (too difficult) or .8 to 1.0 (too easy).

The concept of item difficulty makes intuitive sense for knowledge and skills tests where there is one right answer. Difficulty levels can also be calculated, however, for tests of personality and attitudes. In these tests, no one answer is "correct," yet the test developer still needs assurance that items are not likely to be answered in the same direction or with the same answer by everyone. In this case, the answer that indicates the presence of a construct or attitude is labeled as "correct" for the purpose of the item analysis.

The p value (percentage value) of the item difficulty provides an accurate indication of how difficult the item was for the test takers in the pilot study. However, it does not provide information on the usefulness of the item in measuring the test's construct. Usually, those who have more of the attribute being measured are more likely to respond correctly to the item, but this is not always the case. Sometimes an item can be more difficult for those who have a high degree of the test attribute than for those who have little of the test attribute.

Item Discrimination

To obtain a measure of how well each item separates those test takers who demonstrate a high degree of a skill, knowledge, attitude, or personality characteristic from those who demonstrate little of the same skill, knowledge, attitude, or personality characteristic, test developers create a **discrimination index.** This statistic compares the performance of the upper group who made very high test scores *(U)* with the performance of the lower group who made very low test scores *(L)* on each item. Calculating the percentage of test takers in each group who responded correctly and then obtaining the difference *(D)* between the two percentages creates the discrimination index. The formulas look like this:

$$U = \frac{\text{Number in upper group who responded correctly}}{\text{Total number in upper group}}$$

$$L = \frac{\text{Number in lower group who responded correctly}}{\text{Total number in lower group}}$$

$$D = U - L$$

The upper and lower groups are formed by ranking the final test scores from lowest to highest, then taking the upper third and the lower third to use in the analysis. (Murphy and Davidshofer [1994] suggest that any percentage from 25 percent to 35 percent may be used to form the extreme groups with little difference in the resulting discrimination index.)

Once a *D* value has been calculated for each item, test developers look for items that have high positive numbers. Negative numbers indicate that those who scored low on the test overall responded to the item correctly and those who scored high on the test responded incorrectly. Low positive numbers suggest that there were correct answers from almost as many people who had low scores as those who had high scores. Each of these situations indicates the item is not discriminating between high scorers and low scores. Therefore, test developers discard or rewrite items that have low or negative *D* values.

Inter-Item Correlations

Another important step in the item analysis is the construction of an **inter-item correlation matrix.** This matrix displays the correlation of each item with every other item. Usually each item has been coded as a dichotomous variable—correct (1) or incorrect (0). Therefore, the inter-item correlation matrix will be made up of **phi coefficients,** which are the result of correlating two dichotomous (having only two values) variables. These coefficients are interpreted much like Pearson product-moment correlation coefficients. Table 11.1 shows an inter-item correlation matrix displaying the correlation of six items with each other. As you can see, Item 1 correlates with the other five items fairly well. Item 3 correlates less well with other items.

The inter-item correlation matrix provides important information for increasing the test's internal consistency. Ideally, each item should be highly correlated with every other item measuring the same construct and not correlated with items measuring a different construct. As you will recall from Chapter 6, one method for increasing a test's reliability is to increase the number of items measuring the same construct. In revising the test, however, the developer faces another problem: Which items can be *dropped* without reducing the test's reliability?

The answer is that items that are not correlated with other items measuring the same construct can be (and should be) dropped to increase internal consistency. An item that does not correlate with other items (developed to measure the same construct) is probably measuring a different construct than the other items are measuring. This is not always apparent when reading the items, because the item might be interpreted differently by the target audience.

As you will recall from Chapter 6, a test's overall internal consistency is

TABLE 11.1. Inter-Item Correlation Matrix for Pilot Test

Item	1	2	3	4	5	6
1	—	.39	.39	.36	.49	.57
2		—	.11	.55	.14	.08
3			—	−.03	.01	.19
4				—	.32	.43
5					—	.08
6						—

216

SECTION THREE
Developing
and Piloting
Psychological Tests
and Surveys

calculated using the KR-20 formula for dichotomous items (items coded right or wrong) or the coefficient alpha formula for items that have multiple options for answers. The data from the pilot test are used to calculate an overall estimate of internal consistency, then the developers consult the inter-item correlation matrix to see which items should be dropped or revised to increase the test's overall internal consistency.

Item-Criterion Correlations

Some developers also correlate item responses with a criterion measure, such as a measure of job performance for preemployment tests or a diagnostic measure for clinical tests. Because the responses to the item are usually dichotomous (correct or incorrect), the resulting correlation coefficients are likely to be low and unlikely to reach statistical significance. The item-criterion correlation can, however, be used as a guide for determining whether the item contributes to a prediction of the criterion. For instance, items that do not correlate with the criterion would not be helpful in predicting the criterion.

Some tests are designed so that test scores can be used to sort individuals into two or more categories based on their scores on the criterion measure. These tests are referred to as **empirically based tests,** because the decision to place an individual in a category is based solely on the quantitative relationship between the predictor (test score) and the criterion (possible categories). One advantage of an empirically based test is that the test questions are not required to reflect the test's purpose, therefore test takers have difficulty faking responses. As you might recall from Chapter 10, questions that have no apparent relation to the criterion are referred to as *subtle questions.*

The Minnesota Multiphasic Personality Inventory (MMPI), a widely used personality inventory, is an example of an empirically based test. The developers of the MMPI—Starke Hathaway and John McKinley—wanted to develop a paper-and-pencil test that would distinguish between normal individuals and those with a psychological disorder. For Your Information 11.1 describes the development of the MMPI and some research it has stimulated.

Item Characteristic Curves

In recent years, test developers have begun to rely on the concepts of **item response theory (IRT)** for item analysis. This theory relates the performance of each item to a statistical estimate of the test taker's ability on the construct being measured. A fundamental aspect of IRT is the use of **item characteristic curves (ICCs).** An item characteristic curve is the line that results when we graph the probability of answering an item correctly with level of ability on the construct being measured. It provides a picture of both the item's difficulty and discrimination.

Figures 11.2 and 11.3 show item-characteristic curves for two different items that measure verbal ability. IRT assumes that persons who score high on the test have greater ability than those who score low. Figure 11.2 shows that test takers with high ability have a higher probability of answering the item correctly than test takers with low ability. For Figure 11.3, test takers who did well on the test

The MMPI-2 is a personality test designed to measure emotional and personality disorders that is published by the University of Minnesota Press. The original MMPI—the most widely used personality test in the world—was developed in the late 1930s and published in 1943 as a tool for routine clinical assessment. Its purpose was to help clinicians assign appropriate diagnoses to persons who showed signs of mental disorders.

The developers, Hathaway and McKinley, gathered a large number of questions from textbooks, personality inventories, and clinicians. They administered the questions to patients in hospitals and clinics in Minnesota for whom diagnoses were available. Next, they analyzed the responses by grouping them by diagnostic category. They put in the MMPI only those questions that were answered differently by a diagnostic group (for example, schizophrenic patients). They also added validity scales to detect respondents who answered the questions dishonestly.

The test contains 10 clinical scales:

1. *Hypochondriasis*—excessive or exaggerated concerns about physical health
2. *Depression*—issues of discouragement, pessimism, and hopelessness as well as excessive responsibility
3. *Conversion hysteria*—sensory or motor disorders that have no organic basis; denial and lack of social anxiety
4. *Psychopathic deviation*—the degree to which relatively normal individuals have a willingness to acknowledge problems, including a lack of concern for social or moral standards with a tendency for "acting out"
5. *Masculinity/femininity*—attitudes and feelings in which men and women are thought to differ; originally a measure of homoerotic feelings
6. *Paranoia*—interpersonal sensitivities and tendencies to misinterpret the motives and intentions of others, including self-centeredness and insecurity
7. *Psychastenia*—excessive worries, compulsive behaviors, exaggerated fears, generalized anxiety, and distress, including declarations of high moral standards, self-blame, and rigid efforts to control impulses
8. *Schizophrenia*—strange beliefs, unusual experiences, special sensitivities related to schizophrenia
9. *Hypomania*—excessive ambition, elevated energy, extraversion, high aspirations, grandiosity, and impulsive decision making
10. *Social introversion*—social shyness, preference for solitary pursuits, and lack of social assertiveness

Originally, Hathaway and McKinley thought that the MMPI would provide a clear diagnosis by showing an elevated score (outside the normal range) on one scale only. When the test became widely used, however, test users found that individuals often had elevated scores on more than one scale. As a result, Hathaway published a coding system in 1947 that helped test users make diagnoses based on various combinations of test scores called profiles.

The increasing use of the MMPI stimulated a large body of research regarding its validity in various situations. Much of the research was critical. For example, critics noted that the norming sample for the MMPI was drawn from one region and contained mostly people of one race and ethnic background (Colligan, Osborne, Swenson, & Offord, 1983). Definitions of neurotic and psychotic conditions also changed from the time the MMPI was developed. For instance, in 1994 the fourth revision of the Diagnostic and Statistical Manual (DSM-IV) removed homosexuality from its list of mental disorders.

A committee was formed in the 1980s to study and revise the MMPI. They developed the MMPI-2 using a sample of persons randomly chosen from seven regions of the United States. The sample was designed to resemble the 1980 U.S. census in age, gender, minority status, social class, and education. For the MMPI-2 interpretation of the MMPI scores is based on norms. Individuals who score outside parameters based on standard deviations of the norming sample are diagnosed as dysfunctional. Overall interpretations and diagnoses, however, are based on profiles that take the relation of scales into consideration. Figure 11.1 shows a sample profile of the MMPI-2.

The developers of the MMPI and MMPI-2 placed questions on scales based on their ability to distinguish groups with specific diagnoses (rather than grouping questions according to how well they measured the same construct), so the internal consistency of the MMPI-2 is low. Test-retest reliability is higher, indicating that scores remain somewhat consistent over time. Because empirically based tests are developed without regard to content validity, no link can be made between a domain of mental disorders and the MMPI-2.

Although researchers found evidence that the scores and patterns of scores on the original MMPI predicted various diagnoses, few studies have been published so far regarding the criterion-related validity of the MMPI-2. One theorist (Graham, 1990) argues that the revised MMPI-2 correlates well enough with the original MMPI to assume that the MMPI-2 works as well as the MMPI. Others (Archer, 1992; Nichols, 1992) have questioned whether the tests are equivalent. More research is needed on the criterion-related validity of the MMPI-2, including evidence that the MMPI-2 is valid for use in diagnosing mental disorders and personality issues of minorities.

Sources: Adapted from Duckworth (1990), Butcher, Dahlstrom, Graham, Tellegen, & Kaemmer (1989), and Cohen, Swerdlik, & Phillips (1996).

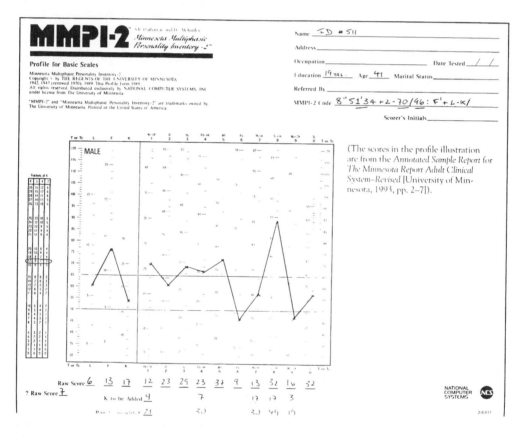

FIGURE 11.1. Sample profile of the MMP1-2

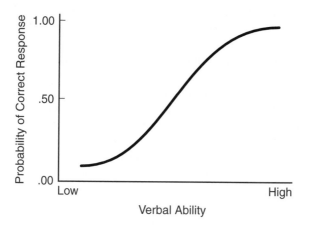

FIGURE 11.2. Test takers with high ability have a higher probability of answering the item correctly than test takers with low ability.

Source: Murphy, K. R. & Davidshofer, C. O. (1994). *Psychological Testing: Principles & Applications. Third edition.* Englewood Cliffs, NJ: Prentice Hall. Figure 9–1. Reprinted with permission.

have only a slightly higher probability of answering the question correctly. We can conclude that Figure 11.2 with the greater slope provides better discrimination between high performers (those presumed to have high reading comprehension) and low performers (those presumed to have low reading comprehension.)

On the ICC, difficulty is determined by the location of the point at which the curve indicates a probability of .5 (a 50–50 chance) for answering correctly. The higher the ability level associated with this point, the more difficult the question.

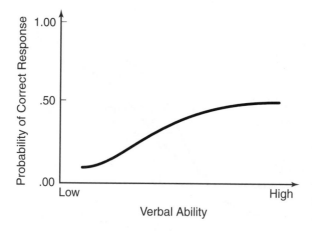

FIGURE 11.3. Test takers with high ability have only a slightly higher probability of answering the item correctly than test takers with low ability.

220

SECTION THREE
Developing
and Piloting
Psychological Tests
and Surveys

Figure 11.4 shows three ICC curves plotted for three different items. Item 1 is easier because less ability is associated with having a 50–50 chance of answering correctly. Items 2 and 3, which have different slopes, intersect at the same point for having a 50–50 chance of answering correctly. These items therefore have the same difficulty level, and both are more difficult than Item 1.

The development of item characteristic curves relies on complex methodology and sophisticated computer programming beyond the scope and objectives of this text. In addition, the amount of research on IRT continues to grow as test developers apply this theory to empirical data. However, students and test purchasers can better understand test development data and documentation if they know how to interpret item characteristic curves.

Item Bias

Test developers are also interested in establishing that differences in responses to test items are not related to differences in culture, gender, or experience of the test taker. For instance, test items should be of equal difficulty for all groups. Researchers have proposed a number of methods for investigating **item bias**—an item's being easier for one group than for another. These methods range from comparing scores or passing rates of various groups to comparing group performance in terms of an external criterion (Murphy & Davidshofer, 1994).

The method preferred by researchers such as Lim and Drasgow (1990) involves the computation of item characteristics by group (for instance, women and men). Plotting the curves on the graph allows differences in difficulty and discrimination to be readily detected. Figure 11.5 shows item characteristic curves for women and men on one test item. As you can see, the item discriminates between high and low performers better for women than for men. The item is also more difficult for men.

For Your Information 11.2 discusses the Golden Rule case to illustrate the advantages of using IRT to detect bias.

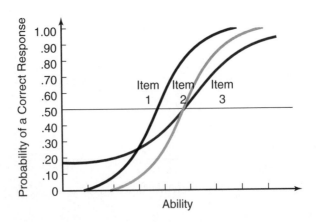

FIGURE 11.4. Hypothetical item characteristic curves for three items

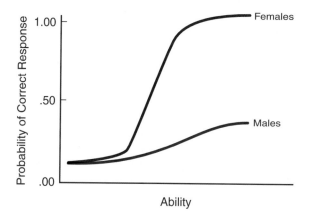

FIGURE 11.5. Item characteristic curves for men and women on one test item

QUALITATIVE ITEM ANALYSIS

In addition to conducting a quantitative analysis of test takers' responses, test developers often ask test takers to complete a questionnaire about how they viewed the test itself and how they answered the questions. Such questionnaires enable developers to conduct a **qualitative analysis.** Test developers might also use individual or group discussions with test takers for understanding how test takers perceive the test and how changes in the test content or administration instructions will improve the accuracy of the test results. Finally, test developers might also ask a panel of experts—people knowledgeable on the test's content or knowledgeable on testing in general—to review the test and provide their opinions on possible sources of error or bias.

Questionnaires for Test Takers

Table 11.2 shows a list of topics and sample questions from Cohen, Swerdlik, and Phillips (1996). Some or all of these topics could be addressed in an open-ended survey, or the test developers might wish to construct Likert scales (see Chapter 12) to make responding easier for the pilot test participants. The open-ended format yields more information, but participants might not have the time to answer a lengthy questionnaire. If Likert scales are used, discussion groups with a sample of participants can focus on portions of the test that are targeted for revision. For instance, test takers might find the test length to be appropriate but express concerns about face validity; then discussion would focus on face validity, not test length.

Expert Panels

Test developers also find the information provided by experts to be helpful in understanding and improving test results. One group of experts would be people who are

In the early 1980s, the Golden Rule Insurance Company sued the Illinois Department of Insurance and the Educational Testing Service (ETS). Their suit asserted that two insurance licensing exams developed by ETS for the state of Illinois were biased against Black test takers. The basis for their claim was that the percentage of correct responses from Whites was greater than the percentage of correct responses from Blacks on a number of items. The statistic the suit referred to was the p value, which indicates level of difficulty. This difference in difficulty level for Whites and Blacks caused a larger number of Whites than Blacks to pass the test and obtain their licenses. The case was settled out of court with the stipulation that ETS would develop subsequent exams using items for which the proportions of correct responses for all test takers were at least .40. Furthermore, the settlement stipulated that items in which the difference between proportions correct for Whites and Blacks exceeded .15 would not be used.

A number of testing experts suggested there was a problem with the Golden Rule settlement. They noted that comparing item difficulty levels in the form of p values failed to take into consideration the level of ability of test takers. In other words, was the failure to give the correct answer because the item was poorly written or simply because the test taker did not know how to answer the question correctly?

As researchers noted in a symposium at an annual American Psychological Association convention (Bond, 1987; Faggen 1987; Linn & Drasgow, 1987) and in an official statement by the American Psychological Association (Committee on Psychological Test and Assessments, 1988) item response theory (IRT) provides a better way to evaluate items for being more difficult for one group than another. As you recall, item characteristic curves associate item difficulty with test takers' ability. Comparing item characteristic curves provides a better way to evaluate item difficulty, because it takes test-taker ability into account. Furthermore, Rodney Lim, in his master's thesis, demonstrated this principle empirically by using both methods to evaluate item responses from a simulated dataset (Lim & Drasgow, 1990). He found that the Golden Rule procedure identified 90 percent of the items as biased and that the IRT method found approximately 25 percent to be biased when ability was taken into account.

knowledgeable about the test's constructs. For example, if the test measures job skills, such as financial planning or systems analysis, then people who perform these jobs well can be recruited to review the test and provide their opinions on the test's content.

Another area of expertise is psychological measurement. Review by another test developer who has not been involved in the development process can provide a fresh look at issues of test length, administration instructions, and other issues not related to test content.

In summary, the pilot test provides a thorough examination of how the new test works and the results that it yields. After the test has been administered to a sample of participants, the test developers review and analyze all data collected. These data—the test takers' responses, their qualitative appraisal of the test, and reviews by experts—then provide the basis for revising the test and arriving at the final version.

REVISING THE TEST

Revision of the test is a major part of the test development process. Test developers write more items than needed. They use the quantitative and qualitative

TABLE 11.2. Potential Areas of Exploration by Means of Qualitative Item Analysis

This table lists sample topics and questions of possible interest to test users. The questions could be raised either orally or in writing shortly after a test's administration. Additionally, depending upon the objectives of the test user, the questions could be placed into other formats, such as true-false or muliple-choice. Depending upon the specific questions to be asked and the number of test-takers being sampled, the test user may wish to guarantee the anonymity of the respondents.

Topic	Sample Question
Cultural Sensitivity	Did you feel that any item or aspect of this test was discriminatory with respect to any group of people? If so, why?
Face Validity	Did the test appear to measure what you expected it would measure? If not, what about this test was contrary to your expectations?
Test Administrator	Did the behavior of the test administrator affect your performance on this test in any way? If so, how?
Test Environment	Did any conditions in the room affect your performance on this test in any way? If so, how?
Test Fairness	Do you think the test was a fair test of what it sought to measure? Why or why not?
Test Language	Were there any instructions or other written aspects of the test that you had difficulty understanding?
Test Length	How did you feel about the length of the test with respect to (a) the time it took to complete, and (b) the number of items?
Testtaker's Guessing	Did you guess on any of the test items? About what percentage of the items would you estimate you guessed on? Did you employ any particular strategy for guessing, or was it basically random guessing?
Testtaker's Integrity	Do you think that there was any cheating during this test? If so, please describe the methods you think may have been used.
Testtaker's Mental/Physical State upon Entry	How would you describe your mental state going into this test? Do you think that your mental state in any way affected the test outcome? If so, how? How would you describe your physical state going into this test? Do you think that your physical state in any way affected the test outcome? If so, how?
Testtaker's Mental/Physical State During the Test	How would you describe your mental state as you took this test? Do you think that your mental state in any way affected the test outcome? If so, how? How would you describe your physical state as you took this test? Do you think that your physical state in any way affected the test outcome? If so, how?
Testtaker's Overall Impressions	How would you describe your overall impression of this test? What suggestions would you offer the test developer for improvement?
Testtaker's Preferences	Was there any part of the test that you found educational, entertaining, or otherwise rewarding? What specifically did you like or dislike about the test? Was there any part of the test that you found anxiety-provoking, condescending, or otherwise upsetting? Why?
Testtaker's Preparation	How did you prepare for this test? If you were going to advise others as to how to prepare for it, what would you tell them?

analyses of the test to choose those items that together provide the most information about the construct being measured. Because the instructions for test takers and test administrators are an essential part of the test, the information provided by test takers and experts provides a basis for revising the instructions in a way that facilitates the process of test administration.

Choosing the Final Items

Choosing the items that make up the final test requires the test developer to weigh each item's evidence of content validity, item difficulty and discrimination, inter-item correlation (a measure of reliability), and bias. Issues such as test length and face validity must also be taken into account.

Many test developers find that constructing a matrix makes it easier to select the best items. The simulated matrix in Table 11.3 lists each item, followed by its performance in terms of content area, item difficulty, discrimination, and bias. The test developer's job is to choose the best performing items taking care that each area of content is represented in the proportion required by the test plan.

As you recall, high inter-item correlation coefficients suggest the item is measuring the same construct as other items—evidence of internal reliability. The best items will have high and positive inter-item correlations. They will also be close to .5 in difficulty with discrimination indices that are positive and high. Items that have evidence of bias are not acceptable unless they can be rewritten to relieve that problem. (Such rewrites might require further testing to assure that bias no longer exists.) It is unusual for all items to meet all the criteria for a "good" item, so the test developer has the complicated job of weighing the merits of each item and choosing a set of final items that work well together to provide accurate test results for all participants.

As you can see from the data in Table 11.3, the items represented have varying merits. Item 1 has appropriate difficulty and discrimination and is not biased; however, it is not correlated with the other items. Although it appears to measure accurately, it might be measuring a different construct than the other items are measuring. Item 2, on the other hand, has a high inter-item correlation and shows no bias, but it is very difficult and its discrimination index is negative (suggesting that poor performers got this item right and good performers got this item wrong.) Item 3 has the best data of the items measuring translation (T). Its inter-item correlation is fairly high, its difficulty level is close to .5, its discrimination index is high and positive, and it shows no evidence of bias. Therefore, Item 3 would be a better choice than Items 1 or 2.

TABLE 11.3. Stimulated Item Statistics Matrix for Items From a Reading Comprehension Test

Item Number	Content Area*	Average Inter-Item Correlation	Difficulty	Discrimination	Bias
1	T	−.02	.50	2	NO
2	T	.50	.20	−1	NO
3	T	.40	.60	3	NO
4	I	.30	.65	4	NO
5	I	.25	.50	1	YES
6	I	.50	.50	−3	NO
7	E	.56	.49	3	NO
8	E	.44	.70	4	NO
9	E	.60	.90	−2	YES

* T = translation; I = interpretation; E = extrapolation

Now you can see why the test developer must write many more items for a test than are required. Each item must be judged acceptable on a number of criteria in order to be chosen for inclusion in the test. Of the remaining items, which would you choose to include in the final test? If you chose items 4, 7 and 8, then you agree with the authors of this text.

When test developers have written an ample number of test items, the task of compiling the final test is simply a matter of choosing the correct number of "good" items that meet the requirements of the test plan. When test items must be rewritten to increase or decrease difficulty or discrimination or to avoid bias, those items should be piloted again to be sure that the changes made produced the desired results. Extensive changes or rewrites signal the need for another pilot test.

Revising the Test Instructions

No matter how well the final items work together, the test cannot produce accurate results unless the instructions for test takers and test administrators are concise and understandable. Clear and comprehensive directions ensure that the test will be administered in the same way for all participants and under circumstances that are advantageous for test taking. Likewise, directions for the test takers help to prevent test takers from giving useless responses. The qualitative information obtained from the test takers and administrators provides a useful guide for revising instructions to promote maximum performance.

Instructions to the test administrator should provide guidance on topics such as choosing the testing room (a quiet place where interruptions are unlikely), answering questions (clarify instructions but do not elaborate or provide help), equipment or supplies needed (No. 2 pencils), and test length (a specified time period or unlimited time). The instructions might include a section on answering frequently asked questions—information obtained during the pilot test.

Instructions to test takers include directions for responding ("Darken the box next to the answer you have chosen with a No. 2 pencil"), instructions on guessing (whether or not guessing is penalized), and special instructions ("Think of how you interact with people at work when answering these questions"). Often tests include sample questions that the test takers complete with the test administrator to be sure that directions for responding are clearly understood.

When the final test has been compiled, it is time to move into the next stage of test development—conducting the validation study. Chapters 7, 8, and 9 described in detail the concepts of content validity, criterion-related validity, and construct validity. Therefore, the next section in this chapter simply provides an overview of designing the validation study.

VALIDATION AND CROSS-VALIDATION

As you will recall, **validation** is the process of obtaining evidence that the test effectively measures what it is supposed to measure. As we said at the beginning of this chapter, it would be unsafe to carry passengers on a new airplane that has not been tested for performance and safety. Likewise, it is improper to rely on the results of a psychological test that has not been evaluated to ensure that its data are

Summary Box 11.2
Item Analysis

- Item analysis uses quantitative methods to examine how well each test item performs.
- The difficulty of each item is calculated by finding the percentage of test takers who responded to the item correctly. Most developers seek a range of difficulty levels that average about .5.
- Test developers also create a discrimination index. This statistic compares the performance on each item of those who made very high test scores with those who made very low test scores.
- An inter-item correlation matrix provides information for increasing the test's internal consistency. Each item should be highly correlated with every other item measuring the same construct.
- In item response theory, the performance of each item is related to the test taker's ability on the construct being measured. The resulting item characteristic curve is a graph of the probability of answering an item correctly given a certain level of ability. It combines item difficulty and discrimination.
- Item bias refers to whether an item is easier for one group than another. There are many ways to investigate item bias, such as comparing group scores or comparing group performance on an external criterion.
- Test developers use questionnaires and expert panels for a qualitative analysis of the test items.
- Test items are then revised or dropped until a final form of the test is reached. The test instructions are also revised based on how well respondents were able to follow directions in the pilot test.

reliable and valid. The validation study provides data on the test's reliability, its correlation with any appropriate outside criteria such as performance evaluations, and its correlation with other measures of the test's construct. In addition, the validation study provides data that can be used for establishing norms and interpreting test scores.

The first part of the validation process—establishing content validity—is carried out as the test is developed. Evidence that the test measures one or more constructs (construct validity) and has the ability to predict an outside criterion such as performance (criterion-related validity) must be gathered in another round of data collection.

Standards for setting up the validation study are similar to those suggested for designing the pilot study. The validation study should take place in one or more situations that match the actual circumstances in which the test will be used. Using more than one test site will provide evidence that the results are **generalizable,** meaning the test can be expected to produce similar results even though it has been administered in different locations. Likewise, developers choose a sample of people to take the test who resemble or are a part of the test's target audience. The sample should be large enough to provide the power to conduct the desired statistical tests. The test developers continue to follow the American Psychological Association's codes of ethics by observing strict rules of confidentiality and by affirming that they will publish only aggregate results of the validation study. Again as in the pilot study, the scores resulting from the administration of the test should not be used for decision making or evaluation of individuals. The sole purpose of the validation study is to affirm the test's ability to yield meaningful results.

Test developers collect data on the test's reliability, its correlation with any appropriate outside criteria such as performance evaluations, and its correlation with other measures of the test's construct. In addition, the developers collect data on the demographic characteristics of the test takers (sex, race, age, and so on). Chapters 6, 7, 8, and 9 provide guidelines for evaluating the test results for acceptable levels of reliability and validity. Test developers also conduct another item analysis similar to that conducted in the pilot study to affirm that each item is performing as expected. Minor changes in the test may be made at this time, such as dropping items that do not contribute to prediction of an outside criterion or further clarifying test instructions.

Cross-Validation

If the final revision yields scores with sufficient evidence of reliability and validity, the test developers conduct a final analysis called **cross-validation.** The process of cross-validation involves a final round of test administration to another sample of test takers representative of the target audience. Because of chance factors that contribute to random error, this second administration can be expected to yield lower correlations with criterion measures. In other words, the criterion-related validity coefficient will be lower than the one found in the original validation study. This decrease in correlation with an outside criterion—referred to as *shrinkage*—is largest when sample size for the initial validation study is low. Also, attention to prediction of the criterion in the pilot study and initial validation study can reduce shrinkage during cross-validation (Cascio, 1991).

This shrinkage is so predictable that researchers have developed formulas to predict the amount of shrinkage that can be expected (Cattin, 1980; Wherry, 1931). When resources are not available to carry out a cross-validation study, statistical estimation of shrinkage is acceptable or even preferred (Cascio, 1991).

Differential Validity

Sometimes tests have different validity coefficients for different groups. For example, a test might be a better predictor for women than for men or a better predictor for Blacks than for Whites. Tests can also produce different slopes or different intercepts for different subgroups. When a test yields significantly different validity coefficients for subgroups, we say it has **differential validity.** When a test is valid for one group but not another (for instance, valid for Whites but not for Blacks), it has **single-group validity.**

The differential validity of standardized college admissions tests for women and minorities (Elliott & Strenta, 1988; Grant & Sleeter, 1986; Linn, 1990; Strenta & Elliott, 1987) is an example of this phenomenon. According to John Young (1994) at Rutgers University, research has consistently yielded higher validity coefficients for women than for men and higher validity coefficients for White students than for minority students. Young decided to verify these findings in a replication study using 3,703 college freshmen who subsequently earned an undergraduate degree within five years.

Young computed prediction equations for the total sample and for women and men as subgroups using multiple regression analysis. (Chapter 8 explains the purpose and interpretation of multiple regression.) Three measures—SAT verbal scores (SATV), SAT mathematical score (SATM), and class rank in high school (HS)—

228

SECTION THREE
*Developing
and Piloting
Psychological Tests
and Surveys*

were the predictors. Cumulative grade point average (GPA) at graduation was the criterion. The resulting equations for men and women are shown in Table 11.4.

As you can see in Table 11.4, the validity coefficients (Multiple *R*s) and the equations themselves are different for men and women. Young reports that his findings are typical of what is reported in institutional studies. In Young's study, men generally scored higher on both sections of the SAT than women who earned higher grades in high school. Women also, in general, scored higher on the criterion measure (college GPA). The predictors also showed differential validity for Whites and minorities, although the sample of Whites was much larger than any of the samples of minorities.

What accounts for this difference in validity for women and men? Young suggests that differences in course selection between men and women may partially account for the underprediction of women's grades by the single validity coefficient. In other words, courses and departments with higher average grades are likely to have a higher proportion of women enrolled.

What is the practical significance of differential validity? If a single validity coefficient and regression line is used to establish cutoff scores to select applicants for admissions, then the equation will overpredict the number of men, and underpredict the number of women, who will be successful in college. On the other hand, as Cascio (1991) points out, establishing different scores for admissions by subgroup is likely to be viewed with suspicion and perceived as unfair.

Defining Unfair Discrimination

When psychological tests are used to compare individuals, their purpose is to discriminate or illuminate the differences among individuals. That discrimination, however, should be the result of individual differences on the trait or characteristic being measured. When group membership changes or contaminates test scores, then test bias exists, and members of some groups might be treated unfairly as a result.

Guion (1966) stated that employment tests discriminate unfairly "when persons with equal probabilities of success on the job have unequal probabilities of being hired for the job" (p. 26). In other words, performance on both the predictor and the criterion must be taken into consideration. Cascio (1991) states,

> a selection measure cannot be said to discriminate unfairly if inferior predictor performance by some group also is associated with inferior job performance by the same group. . . . A selection measure is unfairly discriminatory only when some specified group performs less well than a comparison group on the measure,

TABLE 11.4. Multiple-Regression Equations for Total Sample and Subgroups by Sex, From Young's Differential Validity Study

Group	Multiple Regression Formula	Multiple R
Total	GPA = 1.4856 + .0014 × SATV + .0002 × SATM + .0084 × HS	.41
Women	GPA = 1.4258 + .0015 × SATV + .0003 × SATM + .0075 × HS	.44
Men	GPA = 1.5426 + .0012 × SATV + .0003 × SATM + .0075 × HS	.38

Source: Young (1994).

but performs just as well as the comparison group on the job for which the selection measure is a predictor. (p. 179)

Based on empirical investigations, researchers generally agree that differential validity is not a widespread phenomenon. The only statistic for which there is consistent evidence of difference is the intercept of regression lines when they are calculated separately for Whites and minorities (Cleary, Humphreys, Kendrick, & Wesman, 1975; Bartlett, Bobko, Mosier, and Hannan, 1978; Hartigan & Wigdor, 1989; Gael, Grant, & Richie, 1975; Linn, 1982). When differential prediction takes place, the result is usually a slight overprediction of minority group performance. In other words, tests might predict that minorities will do better on the job than they actually do (Cascio, 1991). Chapter 10 discusses ways to address the problem of bias when developing a test.

In summary, test developers administer the test items a number of times to ensure that the test is effectively measuring the construct as intended. First, test developers pilot test and revise test items and instructions. They compile the test from items that perform effectively and the readminister it to new participants to obtain data on reliability and validity. Finally, they cross-validate the test by administering it again to different test takers or they adjust the validity coefficients obtained in the initial validation study for shrinkage. Validation studies also check for evidence of differential validity.

Validation of a test is an ongoing process. Responsible test developers and publishers continue to monitor the test by continuing to collect information about how it is performing. They also invite others to collect data on the test and publish the results of their analyses. Sometimes over the course of time, a test becomes outdated or flaws are identified. In this case, publishers often choose to revise the test—using the procedures outlined in this chapter—to increase the test's effectiveness. Educational tests, such as the GRE and SAT, have been revised a number of times. Likewise, clinical tests, such as the MMPI have been revised to increase their effectiveness.

DEVELOPING NORMS AND CUT SCORES

Both norms and **cut scores**—decision points for dividing test scores into pass or fail groupings—provide information that assists the test user in interpreting test results. Not all tests have published norms or cut scores. The development of norms and cut scores depends on the purpose of the test and how widely it is used.

Developing Norms

As you saw in Chapter 5, **norms**—distributions of test scores—are one aid for interpreting an individual's test score. Comparing an individual's score to the test norms, such as the mean and standard division, provide information about whether the person's score is high or low. For instance, if Robert scores 70 on the final exam, we would like to know the mean and standard deviation of that exam. If Robert scores 70 on an exam that has a mean of 80 and standard deviation of 10, we can interpret his score as low. If Robert scores 70 on an exam that has a mean of 60 and a standard deviation of 5, then Robert has done very well.

230

SECTION THREE
Developing
and Piloting
Psychological Tests
and Surveys

The purpose of test norms is to provide a reference point or structure for understanding one person's score. Ideally, the test norms would contain a test score for each person in the target audience or the population for which the test has been developed. Such a case, however, is rarely possible. Instead, test developers must rely on constructing norms from a sample of the target audience.

The next-best situation would be for test developers to obtain a random sample of the target audience. As you know, the larger and more representative the sample is of the population, the less error is associated with its measurement. Again, obtaining a truly random sample is rarely possible. Random sampling requires that each member of the population have an equal chance of being selected. To obtain a true random sample, researchers must have a list of each member of the population—an unlikely circumstance for tests with large target audiences.

Therefore, test developers rely on administering the test to people in the target audience in various locations—usually constructing a large database from which various statistics can be computed to be used as norms. Test developers might start with data obtained during the validation process and supplement those scores with new data as the test begins to be used. Although it is not appropriate to use test scores obtained during the validation process for making decisions about individuals, it is appropriate to use these scores as a basis for calculating norms. Likewise, scores from tests administered for use by individuals can be added to the database used for calculating norms. As the size of the database grows, the statistics used for norms will become more stable or unchanging. At this point, test developers can publish the norms with confidence that the sample in the database is representative of the test's target audience.

Larger databases also allow **subgroup norms**—statistics that describe subgroups of the target audience—to be developed. Subgroup norms might be developed for demographic characteristics (such as race, sex, or age) or for locations (such as regions or states). Again, a large enough sample is needed for each subgroup so that the statistics they yield will be stable or unchanging as new scores are added.

The test norms—means, standard deviations, percentile rankings, etc.—are published in the test manual. When there are indications that norms are changing due to changes in the target audience or the test environment, publishers should publish new norms. This has been the case with the SAT test published by the Educational Testing Service (ETS).

Identifying Cut Scores

When tests are used for making decisions (such as whether to hire an individual or recommend a person for clinical treatment), test developers and test users often identify cut scores—the score at which the decision changes. For example, an employer might decide that the minimum score needed for hiring is 60 on a test that yields possible scores of 0 to 100. Those who score 60 and above will be eligible for hire, and those who score below 60 will be ineligible for hire. Therefore, we would refer to 60 on this particular test as the cut score. Not all tests have cut scores, and sometimes it is appropriate that the cut score be set by the test user, such as an employer, rather than the test developer.

Setting cut scores is a difficult process that has legal, professional, and psychometric implications beyond the scope of this text (Cascio, Alexander, & Barrett, 1988). Generally speaking, however, there are two approaches to setting cut scores. One approach used for employment tests employs a panel of expert judges who provide an opinion or rating about the number of test items that a barely qualified person is likely to answer correctly. Test developers use this information to arrive at a cut score that represents the minimum score acceptable for hiring.

The other general approach is more empirical and uses the correlation between the test and an outside criterion to predict the test score that a person who performs at a minimum level of acceptability is likely to make. For example, if the validation study correlated test scores with supervisor ratings (5 = excellent, 4 = very good, 3 = good, 2 = fair, 1 = unacceptable), we can use a regression formula to predict the score that persons rated 2 (fair) were likely to make. This score then becomes the cut score.

Often the expert panel approach and the empirical approach are combined. Experts identify a minimum level of test and criterion performance, then the consequences of using the cut score are tested empirically. Cut scores on employment tests are also affected by external variables such as the labor market. When numerous qualified job applicants are available for hiring, cut scores can be set higher than when the number of qualified applicants is low.

Cut scores are also used with some educational and clinical tests. For example, most graduate programs set a minimum admissions score on the Graduate Record Exam (GRE) of 1,000. Clinical tests suggest diagnoses based on cut scores.

A major problem with setting cut scores is allowing for test error. As you will recall from Chapter 6, the standard error of measurement (SEM) is an indicator of how much error exists in an individual's test score. It is quite possible that a person who scores only a few points below the cut score might score above the cut score upon retaking the test. The difference in the two scores would be due to test error, not to the person's performance. For this reason, Anastasi and Urbina (1997) suggest that the cut score be a band of scores rather than a single score. Using this method, the cut score of 60 proposed in our first example might be expanded to a four-point band, 58 to 62. The standard error of measurement provides the information necessary for establishing the width of that band.

DEVELOPING THE TEST MANUAL

As we have pointed out in previous chapters, the test manual is an important part of the test itself. The manual provides the rationale for constructing the test, a history of the development process, and the results of the validation studies. In addition, the manual describes the appropriate target audience and instructions for administering and scoring the test. Finally, the manual contains norms and information on interpreting individual scores.

For Your Information 11.3 shows the table of contents for the test manual for the Wisconsin Card Sorting Test (WCST) (Heaton, Chelune, Talley, Kay, & Curtiss, 1993), which we discussed in Chapter 6. As you can see, the manual provides important information for administering the test and interpreting the results. A review of the manual provides the test user with information about the test's reliability and validity, as well as the limitations of its use and measurement accuracy.

TABLE OF CONTENTS

234

SECTION THREE
Developing
and Piloting
Psychological Tests
and Surveys

Although we have left the discussion of the test manual until the end of our discussion of test development, we must emphasize that writing the test manual is an ongoing process that begins with the conception of the test. It continues throughout the development process as a source of documentation for each phase of test development. After the processes of piloting, revising, and validating the test are complete, test developers compile the information they have accumulated into a readable format. This compilation of information then is published as the test manual.

SUMMARY

The pilot test is a scientific investigation of the new test's reliability and validity for its specified purpose. The purpose of the pilot test is to study how well the test performs, so it is important that the test is given in a situation that matches the actual circumstances in which the test will be used. Therefore, developers choose a sample of people to take the test who resemble or are a part of the test's target audience. When the test is given, it is important that the test administrators adhere strictly to the test procedures outlined in their test instructions. In addition, test developers might use questionnaires or interviews that gather extra information about the respondents or the test.

Each item in a test is a building block that contributes to the test's outcome or final score. Therefore, developers examine the performance of each item to identify those items that perform well, revising those that could perform better, and eliminating those that do not yield the desired information. Developers analyze each item for its difficulty (the percentage of test takers who respond correctly), discrimination (how well it separates those who show a high degree of the construct from those who show little), correlation with other items (for reliability) and with an outside criterion (for criterion-related validity), and bias (whether it is easier for one group than another). Item characteristic curves provide pictures of each item's difficulty and discrimination. They also can provide information about whether an item is biased against a subgroup of test takers. Test developers might also use individual or group discussions with test takers or experts to gather qualitative information about how to revise the test to improve the its accuracy.

After the test has been revised, developers conduct the validation study by administering the test to another sample of people. Standards for the validation study are similar to those for designing the pilot study. The validation study provides data on the test's reliability, its correlation with any appropriate outside criteria such as performance evaluations (evidence of criterion-related validity), and its correlation with other measures of the test's construct (evidence of construct validity). If the validation study provides sufficient evidence of reliability and validity, the test developers conduct a final analysis called cross-validation, a final round of test administration to yet another sample of test takers. This second administration can be expected to yield lower validity coefficients. When resources are not available to carry out a cross-validation study, statistical estimation of the decrease in the validity coefficients is acceptable.

After validation is complete, test developers can develop norms (distributions of test scores used for interpreting an individual's test score) and cut scores (decision points for dividing test scores into pass or fail groupings). Their development depends on the purpose of the test and how widely it is used.

At the end of the validation process, the test manual is assembled and finalized. Contents of the manual include the rationale for constructing the test, a history of the development process, the results of the validation studies, a description of the appropriate target audience, instructions for administering and scoring the test, and information on interpreting individual scores.

KEY CONCEPTS

cross-validation
cut scores
differential validity
discrimination index
empirically based tests
generalizable
inter-item correlation
   matrix

item analysis
item bias
item characteristic curves
   (ICC)
item difficulty
item response theory
   (IRT)
norms

phi coefficients
pilot test
qualitative analysis
quantitative item analysis
single-group validity
subgroup norms
validation

LEARNING ACTIVITIES

1. Setting Up a Pilot Test

Following are descriptions of three situations in which a test has been developed. Read each situation, then design a pilot test. Answer the following questions about the pilot test:

1. Who will take the test?
2. Will you gather other information? If so, what information is needed and how will you gather it?
3. What should the testing environment be like?
4. Who should administer the test?
5. Do you foresee any problems that need to be investigated during the pilot test?

Situation 1: The admissions office at your college has developed a test for incoming students. The purpose of the test is to identify students who might have difficulty adapting to campus life at your college. The college accepts students of both traditional and nontraditional age with varying cultural and socioeconomic backgrounds. The 50-item test has a multiple-choice format that can be scored using an electronic scan system. The admissions office plans to include the test in its application package. They will ask prospective students to return the test with their applications.

Situation 2: Dr. Query has a local clinical practice for persons who are depressed. She has noticed that some of her clients do better when they participate in group interventions, whereas others make more progress when she sees them individually. She has developed a 20-minute intake interview that can be conducted by a graduate assistant or caseworker in her office. The purpose of the interview is to

236

SECTION THREE
*Developing
and Piloting
Psychological Tests
and Surveys*

identify the type of treatment (group or individual) that is likely to work best for each client.

Situation 3: AAAA Accounting prepares individual and corporate tax returns. They have developed a test to measure knowledge of federal income tax law, which they want to use to hire tax preparers. The test they have developed has 400 items, 100 of which require calculations. The test will be administered in their offices when prospective employees apply to be tax preparers.

2. Which Statistic Should I Use?

This chapter describes a number of kinds of statistics that are used for quantitative item analysis. In the table below, the first column lists research questions. In the second column, write in the appropriate kind of statistic(s) that answers the research question. Note: More than one kind of statistic might be appropriate for answering some questions.

Research Question	Appropriate Kind of Statistic
1. Does this item measure the same construct as other items?	
2. Is this item easier for men than for women?	
3. Does this item provide information that helps predict a criterion?	
4. How difficult is this item?	
5. If I drop this item from the test, will it increase or decrease the test's internal reliability?	
6. How did the people who did well on this test overall do on this item?	
7. Is this item of sufficient difficulty, and does it discriminate between high and low performers on the test?	
8. Is this test biased against a minority group?	

3. What's the Difference?

This chapter describes three data collection studies—the pilot test, the validation study, and the cross-validation study. What are the differences between these studies? What are the similarities? Address issues such as these: (1) Who are the test takers? (2) What is done with the data? (3) What decisions might be made using the data?

Constructing, Administering, and Using Survey Data

238

SECTION THREE
*Developing
and Piloting
Psychological Tests
and Surveys*

"I am taking a survey research methods class. The instructor told us we needed a foundation in the scientific method before we studied surveys. She said that survey construction is both a science and an art. I wanted to learn how to construct a survey, not what science is all about. What is the deal?"

"Our human resources department was interested in finding out how employees feel about our company benefits program. They wanted to know whether employees are aware of the medical, retirement, and flexible spending plans that are available to them—and, if so, whether they are valuable to them. They wanted this information to find out whether the existing benefits program needs to be modified to fit employees' needs. It took the human resources staff about two months to design this survey. Why did it take so long?"

"I had to complete a course evaluation survey for my research methods class. One of the questions on the survey was, 'Was the teacher available and responsive to your needs?' Another questions was, 'How much time did you spend studying for this class?' My teacher said that these were not very good survey questions. Why?"

In Chapter 1 we said that surveys, like psychological tests, are used to collect information from individuals. Surveys, however, differ from psychological tests in two ways. First, psychological tests focus on individual outcomes, whereas surveys focus on group outcomes. Second, the results of psychological tests are usually reported as overall derived scores or scaled scores, and the results of surveys are often reported at the item level.

Although this definition seems to clearly distinguish between psychological tests and surveys, students often ask why they find psychological tests in magazines that report at the question level and why there are instruments that report in terms of scales or an overall derived score but have the word *survey* in their title. There are several explanations. First, it is possible that an instrument has been inappropriately labeled as a psychological test or a survey. Second, some instruments do not have all of the characteristics of either a psychological test or a survey, so they are considered one or the other. Third, like other areas in psychology, things do not always neatly fit into a category.

So what exactly is a survey? Broadly defined, **surveys** are research tools that collect information to describe and compare people's attitudes *(how they feel),* knowledge *(what they know),* and behaviors *(what they do)* (Fink, 1995a). For example, elementary schools use surveys to determine how parents feel about implementing a new policy *(how they feel),* how much parents know about the school's curriculum *(what they know),* or what parents do with their children to facilitate the learning process *(what they do).* Every four years, television news stations use surveys (or what they call political polls) to predict who the next president of the United Sates will be. The federal government conducts the Current Population Survey to determine our unemployment rate; the Consumer Expenditure Survey to determine how people spend their money; the National Health Interview Survey to collect information about people's health conditions, use of health services, and behaviors that affect the risk of illness; and the National Crime Survey to determine the crime rate (Fowler, 1993).

Surveys are popular research tools (Babbie, 1973), and according to Bradburn and Sudman (1988), millions of surveys are conducted each year in the United

States. As a result of their popularity, in the late 1980s there were nearly 2,000 **survey research firms**—companies that specialize in the construction, administration, and analysis of survey data (Stanton, 1989). Unfortunately, though surveys are popular and valuable research tools, they are also often misunderstood (Rosenfeld, Edwards, & Thomas, 1993) or misinterpreted.

As with psychological tests, we use the data collected from surveys to make important decisions. For example, an elementary school might require children to wear uniforms to school if the results of a survey indicate that parents feel this would be a positive move. A school might implement programs to increase parents' knowledge of the school's curriculum if a survey indicates that parents do not know much about the curriculum.

Because the data collected from surveys are used to make important decisions, one must pay careful attention to the design, administration, and analysis of survey data. Surveys, like psychological tests, are not error free, and how one approaches these steps can affect how well the survey data describe what they are intended to describe (Fowler, 1993).

The purpose of this chapter is to increase your understanding of how to properly design and administer a survey and analyze survey data. Though this chapter provides an excellent overview of surveys, we encourage those interested in constructing and administering surveys and analyzing survey data to consult the additional sources mentioned throughout the chapter.

How we collect information affects the quality of the data, so we begin with an overview of the different ways we collect and acquire knowledge. We focus on one approach, the scientific method, which is the very essence of collecting accurate survey data. After briefly reviewing the scientific method, we focus on a five-phase scientific approach to constructing, administering, and analyzing surveys.

KNOWLEDGE ACQUISITION, SCIENCE, AND RESEARCH METHODS

Everyday we are bombarded with information. We might read at the breakfast table a newspaper article that describes a miracle cure for AIDS, an article that claims the unemployment rate has decreased, or an article suggesting that companies are no longer downsizing. Later that day we might watch a television commentary that suggests that television viewing increases teenage violence and attending preschool improves children's intelligence. At the drug store, a pharmacist might tell us that a certain brand of aspirin more effectively alleviates headaches than another brand.

Often we believe this information, and we use it to make decisions about ourselves and others. For example, we might decide that our children will watch very little television, or we might change the brand of aspirin we use. Unfortunately, some of the information we hear and learn about is misleading (Christensen, 1997) and, if taken as fact, could result in poorly informed decisions.

How Do We Acquire Knowledge?

Before making decisions that are based on what we hear or see, we must verify that the information is accurate. To do this, we must look at how the information

240

*SECTION THREE
Developing
and Piloting
Psychological Tests
and Surveys*

was obtained. How did the pharmacist come to the conclusion that one brand of aspirin is more effective than another? How did the radio talk show host come to the conclusion that watching television increases teenage violence?

According to Helmstadter (1970), we obtain knowledge in at least six different ways—through **tenacity, intuition, authority, rationalism, empiricism,** and the **scientific method.** Table 12.1 summarizes and defines these methods.

What Is the Scientific Method?

Though Helmstatdter's (1970) first five methods help us gather information, they are not the best means for gathering *accurate* information (Christensen, 1997). The other method, the **scientific method**—a process for generating a body of knowledge (Christensen, 1997)—often allows us to obtain more accurate information through systematic and objective observations. There are five steps associated with the scientific method:

1. *Identifying a problem or issue and forming a hypothesis.*
2. *Designing a study to explore the problem or issue and test the hypothesis.*
3. *Conducting the study.*
4. *Analyzing and interpreting the data (testing the hypothesis).*
5. *Communicating the research results.*

The scientific method involves several methods for collecting information. These can be categorized as experimental research techniques and descriptive re-

TABLE 12.1. Helmstadter's (1970) Six Methods for Acquiring Knowledge

Method	Definition
Tenacity	We acquire information based on superstition or habit, which leads us to continue believing something we have always believed. For example, we come to believe that walking under a ladder will cause us bad luck.
Intuition	We acquire information, based on a hunch, without any reasoning or inferring. For example, we come to believe that one brand of aspirin is more effective than another just because we believe it is so.
Authority	We acquire information from a highly respected source. For example, we come to believe that one brand of aspirin is better than another because a pharmacist tells us so.
Rationalism	We acquire information through reasoning. For example, we come to believe that one brand of aspirin more effectively reduces headaches than another brand because the first brand includes ingredients that are similar to another medicine that we use that really helps us.
Empiricism	We acquire information through personal experience. For example, we come to believe that one brand of aspirin more effectively reduces headaches because we have used it and it works for us.
Scientific Method	We acquire information by testing ideas and beliefs according to a specific testing procedure that can be objectively observed. This method is without personal beliefs, perceptions, biases, values, attitudes, and emotions. For example, we come to believe that one brand of aspirin is more effective at reducing headaches because systematic research has accumulated evidence of this.

search techniques. In general, **experimental research techniques** help us determine cause and effect. **Descriptive research techniques** help us describe a situation or a phenomenon (Christensen, 1997).

Most surveys are descriptive, used to describe, or even compare, a situation or phenomenon (for example, a class evaluation survey might indicate that your tests and measurements professor was an effective professor or even that your tests and measurements professor appeared to be more effective than your cognitive psychology professor). Surveys are not commonly used for determining cause and effect (for example, survey data cannot establish that having Professor Miller teach your tests and measurements class will cause you to learn more than having Professor McIntire teach your tests and measurements class). A true experiment (in which an independent variable is manipulated) must be set up to establish cause and effect. In some cases, however, surveys can be used as data collection instruments within an experimental technique.

Summary Box 12.1
Knowledge Acquisition, Science, and Research Methods

- To determine whether information is reliable and valid, you must look at how the information was obtained.
- According to Helmstadter (1970), there are at least six methods for obtaining information: tenacity, intuition, authority, rationalism, empiricism, and the scientific method.
- Information obtained using the scientific method is more accurate and reliable than information obtained in other ways.
- The scientific method is a process or method for generating a body of knowledge.
- This process includes identifying a problem or issue and forming a hypothesis; designing a study to explore the problem, issue, or hypothesis; conducting the study; analyzing and interpreting the results; and communicating the research results.
- A variety of research techniques can be used to collect information using the scientific method.
- One such technique is the survey.
- Surveys, like psychological tests, are used to collect important information from individuals.
- Surveys are research tools that collect information to facilitate the description and comparison of people's attitudes, knowledge, and behaviors.

THE SURVEY RESEARCH METHOD

Many people believe that constructing a survey is a simple procedure. In fact, your authors constructed the course evaluation survey in For Your Information 12.1 in five minutes.

The survey in For Your Information 12.1 looks okay, doesn't it? But in fact it is not very good at all. It has several weaknesses. First, we did not take the time to think through the objective(s) or purpose of the survey. Second, we did not take the time to carefully construct the survey questions, and we did not pretest the survey to determine whether students would understand the questions as we intended them to. Third, we did not take the time to carefully format the survey, providing instructions and formatting, to make the survey easy to complete and score.

1. How did you hear about this course?
   ___Another student
   ___College catalogue
   ___Faculty member

2. Did the professor show preferential treatment to certain students?
   ___Yes
   ___ No

3. What preferential treatment did you observe?_____

4. Please give your overall opinion of the course.

	Excellent	*OK*	*Mediocre*	*Poor*
Course organization	___	___	___	___
Course content	___	___	___	___
Clarity of presentation	___	___	___	___
Audiovisual aids	___	___	___	___
Syllabus materials	___	___	___	___

5. Overall, did you enjoy and would you recommend this course to other students?
   ___Yes
   ___ No

This is not a complete list of the weaknesses of this survey, but we have made our point. Though this survey might, at first glance, appear to be a good one, it is probably not very reliable or valid. No one would want to make any decisions (like promotion of a faculty member, or elimination of a course) based on the results of this survey!

Constructing a reliable and valid survey takes time, and it is as much a science as it is an art. Surveys are a science because science is a process—and good surveys follow a scientific process (method). Survey research is an art because knowing how much rigor to put into the design and writing good questions takes years of practice.

For Your Information 12.2 presents a much better course evaluation survey. By the end of this chapter, you should be able to determine what makes this survey better than the survey in For Your Information 12.1.

The Scientific Method of Survey Design

Experienced **survey researchers**—people who design, conduct, and analyze the results of surveys—generally would all tell you the same things about what makes a good survey: First, they would probably tell you that good surveys

- have specific and measureable objectives.
- contain straightforward questions that can be understood similarly by most people.

This survey asks some questions related to the success of this course. Please take a few moments and answer the following questions to the best of your ability. Your comments are essential for the planning of future courses.

1. How did you hear about this course? (Please select one of the following)
   ___Another student
   ___College catalogue
   ___Faculty member
   ___Other (please specify_____)

2. Did the professor show preferential treatment to certain students?
   ___Yes
   ___No (go to question 4)

3. What preferential treatment did you observe?_____

4. Please rate each of the following as being "excellent," "good," "fair," or "poor." (Please make a check mark in the appropriate box.)

	Excellent	Good	Fair	Poor
Course organization	___	___	___	___
Course content	___	___	___	___
Clarity of presentation	___	___	___	___
Audiovisual aids	___	___	___	___
Syllabus materials	___	___	___	___

5. Overall, did you enjoy this course?
   ___Yes
   ___No

6. Would you recommend this course to other students?
   ___Yes
   ___No

- have been pretested to ensure there are no unclear questions or directions.
- have been administered to an adequate population or sample of respondents so that generalizations can be made.
- include the appropriate analysis to obtain the objectives.
- include an accurate reporting of results (verbal and written).
- are reliable and valid.

Second, they would probably tell you that using a scientific approach to survey research will increase the chances that a survey will have the features above. A scientific approach to surveys involves five general phases (Edwards & Thomas, 1993), each corresponding to the steps of the scientific method. Table 12.2 shows the five steps of the scientific method, the corresponding steps of survey design, and the competencies the survey researcher needs in order to be able to perform those steps.

TABLE 12.2. Steps in the Scientific Method

Steps in the Scientific Method	Corresponding Step for Designing Surveys	Competencies of the Survey Researcher
1. Identify a problem and form a hypothesis	Presurvey issues	Know how to conduct a literature review Know how to gather people who are knowledgeable about the survey topic Know how to conduct focus groups
2. Design a study to explore the problem and test the hypothesis	Construct the survey	Know different types of surveys Know the different types of survey questions Know how to write effective survey questions Know how to assemble questions into a survey instrument Know the various methods for pretesting surveys Know how to interpret data to revise and finalize the survey
3. Conduct the study	Administer the survey	Know the methods for sampling respondents Understand the logistics of administering various surveys
4. Analyze the research data	Analyze the survey data	Know how to code survey data Know how to enter survey data in a database Know the methods for analyzing survey data
5. Communicate the research findings	Communicate the findings of the survey	Know how to write a report Know how to prepare presentation materials Know how to present information to a group

Source: Adapted from *The Survey Handbook* (Fink, 1995b).

Third, they would probably tell you to choose a level of detail appropriate for the purpose of the survey project. Regardless of the purpose of a survey, it is important to carefully identify the objectives of the survey, carefully construct the survey, carefully enter and analyze survey data, and clearly present the findings. However, because the scientific approach to survey research requires detailed planning, is complex and time consuming, and can be expensive, the amount of energy and time you spend on each of these phases will depend on the objectives of the survey. For example, designing and administering a class evaluation survey is less complex and therefore requires less planning, time, and money than designing and administering the **decennial census survey**—a survey that is administered by the U.S. Bureau of the Census every 10 years to primarily determine the population of the United States.

Preparing for the Survey

245

CHAPTER 12
*Constructing,
Administering, and
Using Survey Data*

The first phase in developing a survey involves identifying the objectives of the survey, operationally defining the objectives, and constructing a plan for completing the survey.

Identifying the Objectives

The first step in preparing the survey is to define the **survey objectives**—the purpose of the survey and what the survey will measure (Edwards & Thomas, 1993). For example, one survey's objectives might be to determine why there is a high degree of turnover in an organization. Another survey's objective could be to assess whether the general public likes a new product or service. The objective of a third survey might be to determine whether students thought a college course was beneficial.

Where do the objectives come from? The objectives come from a particular need, from literature reviews, and from experts. For example, suppose that your college's administration decides that they need to know whether each of their college courses are fulfilling the needs of students. They might contact the college's institutional research office and ask them to design a course evaluation survey to be administered in each class at the end of the semester. There is an obvious need here, and the exact objectives of the survey would come from discussions with college administrators, faculty, and students.

Survey objectives can also come from **literature reviews** (systematic examinations of published and unpublished reports on a topic) and **experts** (individuals who are knowledgeable about the survey topic or who will be affected by the survey's outcomes). By reviewing the literature on a specific topic, survey researchers find out what is known about the topic. They then use this information to identify important aspects of a topic or gaps in knowledge about the topic. By talking to experts, you can take an idea about a survey (for example, "I just want to design a class evaluation survey") and define exactly what information the survey should collect—its specific objectives (for example, determine whether faculty are treating some students preferentially, whether faculty are meeting the needs of students, whether faculty are presenting information in an organized manner, etc.). For a class evaluation survey, your experts might be faculty, college administrators, or students.

Operationally Defining the Objectives

After identifying the objective(s) of the survey, the next step is to define the objective(s) operationally, and determine how many questions are needed to gather the information to meet the objective(s). For Your Information 12.3 lists the objectives, the operational definitions for each objective, and the number of questions used to measure each objective of a class evaluation survey designed by students in one of the author's research methods courses. The objectives of the survey are listed separately in the left-hand column. The **operational definitions**—specific behaviors or questions that represent the purpose—are listed in the second column for each objective. The number of questions used to measure each objective is listed in the third column. Note how similar this table is to the test specification table for ensuring the content validity of a psychological test (discussed in Chapter 7).

For Your Information   **12.3**

Objectives and Outline for a Class Evaluation Survey

One of your authors instructed students to develop a college-level course evaluation survey. Discussions with subject-matter experts (faculty, administration, and students), reviews of course evaluations used by other colleges, and a literature review, helped students clearly define the survey objectives.

After defining the survey objectives, students operationally defined each objective and determined how many would be developed to measure each objective. The objectives, operational definitions, and number of questions for each objective are shown below.

Objective	Operational Definition	Number of Questions
To measure student opinions of course format and learning materials	Did the course use relevant reading material and contribute to students intellectual growth?	5
	Did exams assess the information presented in class?	
To measure instructor's organization	Was the instructor prepared for class and organized?	5
	Did the instructor make objectives clear?	
To measure instructor's knowledge and enthusiasm of subject matter	Was the instructor knowledgeable about the material?	5
	Did the instructor show enthusiasm for the material?	
To determine the overall effectiveness of course	Was the instructor effective overall?	5
	Was the course a good course?	

Constructing a Plan

The next step is to write a plan for constructing the survey. Such a plan includes a list of all of the phases and steps necessary to complete the survey, an estimate of the costs associated with the survey's development and administration and the analysis of the survey data, and a time line for completing each phase of the survey. For more information on documenting a plan, we suggest a book edited by Rosenfeld, Edwards and Thomas (1993), titled *Improving Organizational Surveys*.

Constructing the Survey

The second phase in developing a survey involves selecting the type of survey to be constructed, writing survey items, preparing the survey instrument, and pretesting the survey.

Types of Surveys

Before starting from scratch, developers find that it is always a good idea to search for an existing survey that meets the survey's objectives. They find existing surveys by conducting literature reviews and speaking with subject-matter experts.

If an appropriate survey does not exist, they must design their own survey, first deciding what type of survey to use. Surveys take many forms. **Self-administered surveys** are surveys that individuals complete themselves. These include **mail surveys** that are mailed to respondents with instructions for respondents to complete and return them and **individually administered surveys** that are disseminated by a facilitator for respondents to complete alone. At one time or another you have probably received a survey in the mail. Likewise, you have probably been stopped in a shopping mall and asked to complete a survey. These are examples of mail and individually administered surveys, respectively.

Personal interviews are surveys that involve direct contact with the respondent in person or by phone. Personal interviews include **face-to-face surveys,** in which an interviewer asks a series of questions in a respondent's home, a public place, or the researcher's office. These also include **telephone surveys** in which an interviewer calls respondents and asks questions over the phone. You have probably been stopped at one time or another and asked a few questions about a product. Likewise, you might have been contacted on the phone and asked to listen to music segments and asked to indicate whether you like, have heard enough of, or dislike each music segment. These are examples of face-to-face and telephone surveys, respectively. For both, interviewers can read survey questions from a paper-and-pencil form or from a laptop computer. We are even beginning to have computers dial and ask survey questions over the telephone by themselves!

Structured record reviews involve forms that guide data collection from existing records, such as personnel files. **Structured observations** involve forms that guide an observer in collecting behavioral information, such as forms used to document the play behaviors of children on the playground. Though these are less common, they are also considered surveys.

Each type of survey has advantages and disadvantages. The type that is appropriate depends on the objectives of the research and the target audience. For further information about the advantages and disadvantages of different types of surveys, read *Developing and Using Questionnaires* by the U.S. General Accounting Office (GAO, 1986).

Developing Survey Questions

After selecting the type of survey, researchers write survey questions that match the survey's objectives. Just as there are different types of surveys, there are also various types of survey questions. These are some of the most popular (GAO, 1986):

- Open-ended questions
- Closed-ended questions
- Yes/no questions
- Fill-in-the blank questions
- Implied no choice
- Single-item choices
- Enfolded formats
- Free choices
- Multiple-choice format
- Ranking questions
- Rating questions

248

SECTION THREE
Developing
and Piloting
Psychological Tests
and Surveys

- Guttman format
- Likert and other intensity scale formats
- Semantic differential format
- Paired comparisons and constant referent comparisons

The type of question chosen depends on the kind of information needed. In Greater Depth 12.1 provides examples of survey questions.

No matter the type of question, writing survey questions (and test questions as you already know) is not an easy task due to the complex cognitive processes one goes through to answer a question. For Your Information 12.4 explains the cognitive aspects of answering questions.

Survey developers must pay careful attention to writing understandable, readable, and appealing survey questions, because there are many chances for error in understanding a question, formulating an answer, and providing a response (Fowler, 1988). To facilitate the question-answering process and increase the likelihood of obtaining accurate information, survey developers make sure their survey questions have the characteristics listed below.

Survey questions should be purposeful and straightforward. The relationship between what the question is asking and the objectives of the survey should be clear. In fact, the survey researcher should begin with an explanation of the purpose of a group of questions. This helps the survey respondent focus on the appropriate issue(s). For example, given the second and third objectives of the class evaluation survey presented in For Your Information 12.3, the following statements and questions would be purposeful:

> We would like your feedback on your instructor's organization and knowledge of subject matter. Please indicate whether you strongly agree (SA), agree (A), disagree (D), or strongly disagree (SD) with each of the following statements. Place a circle around the number that best represents your response.

The instructor . . .	SA	A		D	SD
seemed well prepared for class	5	4	3	2	1
presented material in an organized fashion	5	4	3	2	1
explained assignments clearly	5	4	3	2	1
allowed ample time for completion of assignments	5	4	3	2	1
kept students informed about their progress/grades in course	5	4	3	2	1
had a thorough knowledge of course content	5	4	3	2	1
showed enthusiasm for the subject	5	4	3	2	1

Survey questions should be unambiguous. All survey questions should be concrete and should clearly define the context of the question. Questions should not contain jargon or acronyms, unless all respondents to a particular survey are familiar with the jargon and acronyms.

Unacceptable	*Better alternative*
Do you go out often?	Which of the following best describes how often you have
____Yes	gone out to dinner in the past three months? (Please
____No	select one)

      ____ Not at all   ____ 3–4 times
      ____ 1–2 times   ____ 5 or more times

Examples of Survey Questions

Different types of survey questions serve different purposes, and each has strengths and weaknesses. For a detailed description of the strengths and weaknesses of these formats, consult *Developing and Using Questionnaires* (GAO, 1986).

Open-Ended Questions

Last year you were a member of student government. Please comment on your experience.

_____

_____

Closed-Ended Questions

Yes/no questions

1. Did you attend last week's biology study group?
   _____ Yes
   _____ No

Fill-in-the-Blank

How many brothers and sisters do you have? _____

Row Format

Please indicate how many hours per week you study for each of the following courses.

Course	Hours
Psychology	_____
Biology	_____
Calculus	_____
Art History	_____

Column Format

For each of the courses listed below, identify how many hours you study for the course per week and how many pages you read for the course per week.

Course	Hours per week you study	Pages per week you read
Psychology	_____	_____
Biology	_____	_____
Calculus	_____	_____
Art History	_____	_____

Implied No Choice

Why didn't you pass your psychology exam?

___ I did not study
___ I did not feel well
___ I don't know

Did your professor review the following materials before your exam?

	Yes	No
Test-retest reliability	____	____
Alternate forms reliability	____	____
Split-half reliability	____	____
Content validity	____	____
Criterion-related validity	____	_____
Construct validity	____	_____

Free Choices

If the Psychology Department started a Psychology Club, would you attend the meetings?
___ Yes
___ Probably yes
___ Uncertain
___ Probably no
___ No

Multiple Choice

Which of the following best explains why you decided to transfer to another college/university? (Select one only)
____ I could not afford the tuition
____ I did not like the other students
____ I did not like the faculty
____ Other (describe)_____

Ranking Questions

Students select colleges for various reasons. Consider each of the following items that might influence a student's decision to apply to a specific college. Rank-order each of the items from most important (1) to least important (5).

Cost   ____
Location   ____
Majors   ____
Faculty   ____
Clubs/organizations ____

Rating Questions

How organized was your professor?
____ Very organized
____ Somewhat organized
____ Marginally organized
____ Not organized at all

Likert Format

Being able to approach your professor is a major advantage of attending a small college. The question is, how often do you approach your professor for help?
___ Always
___ Very often
___ Fairly often
___ Sometimes
___ Almost never
___ Never

Semantic Differential

Please circle the number representing the demeanor of your professor.

Happy   1   2   3   4   5   6   7   Grumpy

Answering questions is a complex cognitive task (Cannell, Miller, & Oksenberg, 1981; Groves, 1989; Kahn & Cannell, 1957; Miller, Mullin, & Herrmann, 1990; Tourangeau, 1984). Research suggests that when people answer questions they go through at least four stages. First, they must comprehend the question. Second, they must retrieve the answer to the question. Third, they must judge the appropriate answer to the question. Fourth, they must communicate the answer.

Comprehension
    →

    Retrieval
        →

        Judgment
            →

                Response Communication

COMPREHENSION

When a respondent is asked a question, they must first understand each word in the question and what the entire question is asking. In order to comprehend or understand a question, the respondent must have sufficient attention span to pay attention to the question, adequate language ability to understand the vocabulary and the entire question, and general knowledge that enables them to understand the concepts contained in the question.

RETRIEVAL

Once the respondent understands the meaning of the question, they must search their memory for an answer. If answer choices are presented to the respondent (as in a multiple choice question), the respondent must recognize the most appropriate answer. If answer choices are not presented to the respondent, the respondent must search their memory in a more thorough fashion for the correct answer. If the appropriate cues, or hints, are available, the respondent will probably find the answer. If inappropriate cues are available (for example, something that distracts them), the respondent will take bits and pieces of the information and reconstruct an answer to fit what is most likely to be the answer.

JUDGMENT

After the respondent has identified or constructed an answer to the question, they must judge or decide whether their answer meets the objectives of the question. For example, if the question asks respondents to recall events from a specific time period, the respondent will judge whether the events occurred during the appropriate time frame (for example, if a question asks for one's grocery expenditures over the past week, they will judge whether their answer includes *all* of the grocery expenditures over the past week).

RESPONSE COMMUNICATION

Once the respondent has comprehended the question, found an answer, and judged an answer for its appropriateness, they must communicate the answer to the question. If a question involves response choices, the respondent must match their answer to the available choices. If the question requires that the respondent verbalize or write a response, they must construct an understandable response. However, before they communicate their response, the respondent will evaluate whether the answer to the question meets their own personal motives and objectives. If a respondent believes their answer is threatening or not socially desirable (it is not a typical response or a response that would be expected), they might choose not to provide the correct answer. In other words, they might refuse to answer or might provide a "fake" answer.

252

SECTION THREE
Developing
and Piloting
Psychological Tests
and Surveys

The unacceptable question above does not clearly define what the survey developer is asking (whether I go outside often? to the movies often?). The better alternative makes the exact meaning clearer.

Survey questions should be in correct syntax. That is, all survey questions should be complete sentences.

Unacceptable	*Alternative*
School attended?	Where did you go to graduate school?

Survey questions should use appropriate rating scales and response options. Many questions ask respondents to rate their attitude about something on a rating scale. The rating scale should always match the type of information being asked about. Look at the following question from a local hotel satisfaction survey. Do you see a problem?

How satisfied were you with the overall quality of the services you received?

Excellent	Very Good	Average	Below Average	Poor

The rating scale does not match the type of information the question is seeking. In other words, the rating scale describes "quality of service," but the question asks about the customer's level of satisfaction. A better alternative would be the following:

How satisfied were you with the overall quality of the services you received?

Extremely satisfied	Very satisfied	Somewhat satisfied	Not very satisfied	Not satisfied at all

In Greater Depth 12.2 displays the types of rating scales as identified by Fink (1995a).

Survey questions should include the appropriate categorical alternatives. If you are asking a question for which you have no idea what the possible responses are, you should leave the question open-ended. If you do provide alternatives, the question should include an inclusive list of response alternatives or an "other" category. For example, if you are interested in finding out whether students enjoyed their psychology class, it would not be appropriate to allow them only the responses "Yes, extremely" or "Not at all."

IN GREATER DEPTH 12.2

Rating Scales

According to Fink (1995a), rating questions usually ask for endorsement, frequency, intensity, influence, or comparison. Survey developers consider which of these is appropriate before selecting a rating scale.

- Endorsement (e.g., definitely true, true, don't know, false, definitely false)

  I spend at least two hours a day studying for class (select one of the following):

Definitely true	True	False	Definitely false
1	2	3	4

- Frequency (e.g., always, very often, fairly often, sometimes, almost never, never)

  How often do you study for pop quizzes in your tests and measurements class?

Always	Very often	Fairly often	Sometimes	Almost never	Never
1	2	3	4	5	6

- Intensity (e.g., none, very mild, middle, moderate, severe)

  How would you describe the weather on July 4?

Mild		Moderate		Severe
1	2	3	4	5

- Influence (e.g., big problem, moderate problem, small problem, very small problem, no problem)

  Some people believe that the quality of our health care will decline with managed care. How do you feel about managed care? Is it a . . . (select one of the following)

Big problem	Moderate problem	Small problem	Very small problem	No problem
1	2	3	4	5

- Comparison (e.g., much more than others, somewhat more than others, about the same as others, somewhat less than others, much less than others)

  How often do you study?

Much more than others	Somewhat less than others	About the same as others	Somewhat less than others	Much more than others
1	2	3	4	5

254

SECTION THREE
*Developing
and Piloting
Psychological Tests
and Surveys*

Unacceptable

Did you enjoy your introductory
  psychology course?

_____ Yes, extremely
_____ No, not at all

Alternative

Did you enjoy your introductory
  psychology course?

_____ Yes, extremely
_____ Yes, for the most part
_____ No, for the most part
_____ No, not at all

Survey questions should ask one and only one question. Be careful not to ask a
double-barreled question—a question that is actually asking two or more questions. Here are two examples of double-barreled (actually, triple-barreled) questions your authors recently found in a hotel satisfaction survey.

> Was our staff well informed, knowledgeable, and professional?
> Were we responsive to your needs, solving any problems you may have had
> efficiently and to your satisfaction?

If a survey respondent said "yes" to either of these questions, it is impossible to
tell if they are saying yes to the entire question or only to a part of it. The same is
true if a survey respondent says "no" to either of these questions. It would have
been more appropriate to ask one or more of the following questions:

Was our staff well informed?	___ Yes	___ No
Was our staff knowledgeable?	___ Yes	___ No
Was our staff professional?	___ Yes	___No
Was our staff responsive to your needs?	___ Yes	___No
Did our staff efficiently solve any problems you might have had?	___ Yes	___ No
Did our staff solve to your satisfaction any problems you might have had?	___ Yes	___ No

Survey questions should be at a comfortable reading level. Survey developers try to
write questions that are easy to read (low readability level) so that respondents will
be more likely to understand and interpret questions appropriately.

Preparing the Survey Instrument

Once the survey developers have written the questions, they must put them together into a package. Their goals are to catch the repondent's attention and motivate the respondent to complete the survey in order to reduce the errors associated
with completing the survey (GAO,1986). For Your Information 12.5 displays the
course evaluation survey developed by one of the author's research methods
classes. This survey demonstrates many of the items discussed below.

- *Title and seal.* The front page of the survey should always have a title in large
  font centered on the top of the page so that it stands out from the survey questions. The title should indicate what the questionnaire is about (e.g., Course
  Evaluation Survey). Many times, survey researchers also identify the target
  audience (for example, Survey of Employees Regarding Child Care Arrange-
  ments) (GAO, 1986). When possible, the first page should also include a seal
  or a company logo to lend more credibility.
- *Appeal and instructions.* The survey should include an appeal to the respondent and survey completion instructions. The appeal and instructions concisely

and courteously (1) state the purpose of the survey, (2) explain who is sponsoring or conducting the survey, (3) explain why it is important for everyone to complete the survey to the best of their ability, (4) assure respondents that their name will not be associated with their responses, and (5) thank respondents for their cooperation (GAO, 1986). If the survey is a mail survey, the instructions should also include information about how to return the survey. If a professional administers the survey, she or he should read these instructions to the respondent.

- *Headings and subheadings.* The survey should include headings and subheadings. Headings and subheadings help guide the respondent through the survey. The headings and subheadings should be short phrases that tell survey respondents what each part of the survey is about and should stand out from the survey questions.
- *Transitions.* Survey respondents should be given a transition into each new section and topic. The transition informs the respondent about the next section of the survey. The transition should also include any specific instructions about how to answer the questions in the new section.
- *Response directions.* Developers provide response instructions that tell the respondents how to answer appropriately or that lead them to another part of the questionnaire. Response instructions are short directions, often in parentheses and italics.
- *Bold typeface.* Survey researchers often use bold typeface to emphasize key points in directions or questions.
- *Justification of response spaces.* It is common practice to justify the response spaces (i.e., a line, a check box) to the left of response choices and columns to the right.
- *Shading.* It is also a good idea to use shading to prevent respondents from writing in specific sections, to separate rows of text on a horizontal layout, or to help guide respondents across a page of text.
- *White space.* Survey designers also make sure there is adequate white (blank) space on the survey. A crowded survey does not look inviting and can be difficult to complete. Margins should be at least 1 inch wide, and there should be ample space between questions and sections of the survey.
- *Printing.* Surveys less than or equal to two pages in length are usually printed on two sides of a sheet of paper. If it is necessary for the survey to be longer, pages should be stapled in the upper left corner. Extremely long surveys can be spiral bound or printed in a booklet format.
- *Font type.* Designers should use an attractive, businesslike, and readable font and make sure the overall format is organized and inviting. This makes the survey professional looking and easier to complete, which in turn makes respondents pay more attention to the survey, decreasing survey completion time and the effort required of the respondent.

Pretesting the Survey

The third task in the survey construction phase is to pretest the survey. **Pretesting** (1) identifies sources of **nonsampling measurement errors** (errors associated with the design and administration of the survey); (2) examines how effective the revisions of a question or the entire survey are; (3) indicates the effect

COURSE EVALUATION SURVEY

_____   _____   ____   ____   _____

COURSE NAME   COURSE #   TERM   YEAR   INSTRUCTOR NAME

The Hamilton Holt School of Rollins College administers a course survey to all students. Your evaluation will be used

by the instructor to refine and improve the course, and by Rollins administration to evaluate instructor performance, as

well as make decisions about tenure, promotions, and other personnel issues. Your name will not be associated with

your responses.

Rollins College Hamilton Holt School would like your feedback on the course and the effectiveness of the instructor. **It is very important that you complete the entire survey.**

PART 1—COURSE
First we would like to ask you about the course. Please indicate whether you strongly agree (SA), agree (A), disagree (D), or strongly disagree (SD) with each of the following statements by placing a circle around the number which best represents your response.

The Course . . .	SA	A	N	D	SD
• contributed to my intellectual growth	5	4	3	2	1
• was useful to my work/career	5	4	3	2	1
• used a current text	5	4	3	2	1
• included helpful text readings	5	4	3	2	1
• included exams that tested my understanding of the material	5	4	3	2	1

PART 2—INSTRUCTOR
Now, we would like to ask you about the instructor. Please indicate whether you strongly agree SA), agree (A), disagree (D), or strongly disagree (SD) with each of the following statements by placing a circle around the number which best represents your response.

The Instructor . . .	SA	A	N	D	SD
• presented material in an organized fashion	5	4	3	2	1
• seemed well prepared for class	5	4	3	2	1
• explained assignments clearly	5	4	3	2	1
• allowed ample time for completion of assignments	5	4	3	2	1
• kept students informed about their progress/grades in course	5	4	3	2	1
• was available outside of class time	5	4	3	2	1
• had a thorough knowledge of course content	5	4	3	2	1
• showed enthusiasm for the subject	5	4	3	2	1
• utilized teaching methods that were well suited for the course	5	4	3	2	1

Since the instructors are very interested in identifying ways in which to improve the content of each course and their effectiveness as instructors, please comment below for those statements listed on the previous page which you have circled as a 2 or below.

_____

_____

Next, please comment on each of the following questions. Your opinion counts so please be candid with your response!

1. Overall, why was the instructor effective or ineffective?

_____

_____

2. Overall, why would you classify this as a good course or a poor course?

_____

_____

3. Overall, on a scale of 1 to 10 (with 10 being the highest) I would rate this course: _____

4. Add any other comments.

_____

_____

THANK YOU FOR YOUR FEEDBACK!

---

of alternative versions of a question or the survey; and (4) assesses the final version of a questionnaire for respondent understanding, time to complete, and ease of completion (GAO,1986). There are various methods for pretesting surveys, and the method the survey developer chooses depends on the objectives of the pretest and the available resources, such as time, funds, and staff. Some pretesting methods are more appropriate for the preliminary stages of survey development. For example, the following methods are useful for providing survey designers with knowledge of respondent understanding of survey concepts and wording (qualitative analysis).

- **One-On-One Interviews:**
  - *Concurrent "think aloud" interviews.* During these interviews, respondents describe their thoughts as they think about and answer the survey questions.
  - *Retrospective "think aloud" interviews.* Typically one-on-one interviews, the interviewer asks respondents, after they complete the survey, how they went about generating their answers.
  - *Paraphrasing.* Interviewers ask respondents to repeat questions in their own words.
  - *Confidence ratings.* After answering survey questions, respondents rate how confident they are that their responses are correct.
- **Respondent Focus Groups.** A **focus group** brings people who are similar to

258

SECTION THREE
*Developing
and Piloting
Psychological Tests
and Surveys*

the target respondents together to discuss issues related to the survey. Usually each person in the group completes the survey and then the respondents discuss the survey experience with the test developer or a trained facilitator. Some pretesting methodologies evaluate the drafted survey under conditions that mimic the actual survey process. These methodologies help researchers identify problems (respondent fatigue, distraction, hostility, lack of motivation) that are difficult to identify using other pretesting methods.

- **Behavior Coding of Respondent/Interviewer Interactions.** Behavior coding involves coding the interchange between an interviewer and a survey respondent. Behavior coding helps identify the types and frequencies of interviewer behaviors (e.g., interviewer reads question exactly as written vs. interviewer reads question with major change in meaning) and respondent behaviors (e.g., respondent provides an adequate response vs. respondent asks for clarification) that can affect the reliability and validity of a survey. It is a systematic technique for identifying problems with questions. It is most useful for personal interviews, though it can be modified for other types of surveys. Behavior coding is a popular pretesting technique for government surveys.
- **Interviewer and Respondent Debriefings.** This method involves asking interviewers or respondents questions following a **field test**—an administration of the survey to a large representative group of individuals to determine any problems.
- **Split-Sample Tests.** This method involves field-testing two or more versions of a question, set of questions, or surveys. The objective is to determine which version of the question or survey is "better."
- **Item nonresponse.** This method involves distributing the survey and then calculating the **item nonresponse rate**—how often an item was left blank.

It is very important that a survey be pretested to ensure that the questions are appropriate for the target population. Most survey questions need to be revised multiple times before they are finalized. Before moving on to the survey administration phase, the survey should meet the following criteria:

- The questions reflect the purpose of the survey.
- There is no technical language and jargon (unless you are sure that it will be universally understood).
- There are no long and complex questions that might be difficult to understand.
- The meanings of all key terms are explained.
- There are no double-barreled questions.
- Adequate, explicit, and inclusive alternatives are presented for multiple-choice questions.
- The survey vocabulary is appropriate for all respondents.
- There are no misspelled words or grammatical errors.
- The survey has a title and headings.
- The survey includes instructions.
- The survey layout includes adequate white space.
- The type on the survey is large enough to be comfortably read.
- There are introductory and transition statements between questions.
- The directions for answering are clear.
- The style of the items is not too monotonous.
- The survey format flows well.
- The survey items are numbered correctly.

- The skip patterns are easy to follow.
- The survey is not too long.
- The questionnaire is easy to read and is attractive.

Fink (1995b) suggests that when pretesting surveys, survey researchers ask the questions presented in In Greater Depth 12.3. These questions are categorized by the type of survey being used.

IN GREATER DEPTH 12.3

Questions to Ask When Pretesting Surveys

MAIL AND OTHER SELF-ADMINISTERED QUESTIONNAIRES

- Are instructions for completing the survey clearly written?
- Are the questions easy to understand?
- Do respondents know how to indicate their answers (e.g., circle or mark the response; use a special pencil; use the space bar)?
- Are the response choices mutually exclusive (not double barreled)?
- Are the response choices exhaustive?
- Do respondents understand what to do with completed questionnaires (e.g., return them by mail in a self-addressed envelope; fax them)?
- Do respondents understand when to return the completed survey? If a computer-assisted survey, can respondents correctly use the software commands?
- If a computer-assisted survey, do respondents know how to change (or "correct") their answers?
- If an incentive is given for completing the survey, do respondents understand how to obtain it (e.g., it will automatically be sent on receipt of completed survey; it is included with the questionnaire)?
- Is privacy respected and protected?
- Do respondents have any suggestions regarding the addition or deletion of questions, the clarification of instructions, or improvements in format?

TELEPHONE INTERVIEWS

- Do interviewers understand how to ask questions and present options for responses?
- Do interviewers know how to get in-depth information, when appropriate, by probing respondents' brief answers?
- Do interviewers know how to record information?

- Do interviewers know how to keep the interview to the time limit?
- Do interviewers know how to return completed interviews?
- Are interviewers able to select the sample using the instructions?
- Can interviewers readily use the phone logs to record the number of times and when potential respondents were contacted?
- Do interviewers understand the questions?
- Do interviewees understand how to answer the questions (e.g., pick the top two; rate items according to whether they agree or disagree)?
- Do interviewees agree that privacy has been protected? Respected?

IN-PERSON INTERVIEWS

- Do interviewers understand how to ask questions and present options for responses?
- Do interviewers know how to get in-depth information, when appropriate, by probing respondents' brief answers?
- Do interviewers know how to record information?
- Do interviewers know how to keep the interview to the time limit?
- Do interviewers know how to return completed interviews?
- Do interviewees understand the questions?
- Do interviewees understand how to answer the questions (e.g., pick the top two; rate items according to whether they agree or disagree?)
- Do interviewees agree that privacy has been protected? respected?

Source: Fink (1995b).

260

SECTION THREE
Developing
and Piloting
Psychological Tests
and Surveys

Administering the Survey

The third phase requires administering the survey to the target population. This involves selecting the appropriate respondents, choosing a sample size, and distributing the survey.

Selecting the Appropriate Respondents

The survey might be administered to the entire **population**—all members of the target audience—or the survey users might choose to administer the survey to a subset of the population that represents the entire population, known as a **sample.** This decision often depends on the survey's purpose, the cost of administering the survey, and the availability of respondents.

If you were interested in designing a class evaluation survey to measure the success of a particular class, your population would be all of the members of the class. Because it would be easy to do, you would probably choose to administer the survey to the entire population (all class members). However, if you were interested in designing a survey to determine how high school seniors feel about the usefulness of the Scholastic Assessment Test (SAT) as a college admissions instrument, then your population would be all high school seniors who have completed the SAT and plan on attending college. Because it would be very expensive and infeasible to distribute your survey to all high school seniors who have completed the SAT, you would probably sample all high school seniors who have completed the SAT and who plan to attend college.

A good sample would be a representative group of the population of high school seniors. If the sample is not representative, it is difficult to generalize the survey results to the entire population. That is, it would be difficult to say that the results would be the same if we had given the survey to the entire population. The goal is to find a sampling method that gives everyone, or almost everyone, in your population and equal chance of being selected and to end up with a sample that is truly representative of the population (Fowler, 1993). There are various methods for selecting a sample. Most can be classified into two categories: probability sampling and nonprobability sampling.

Probability Sampling. **Probability sampling** is a type of sampling that uses statistics to ensure that a sample is representative of a population. Probability sampling includes simple random sampling, systematic sampling, stratified random sampling, and cluster sampling.

With **simple random sampling**, every member of a population has an equal chance of being chosen as a member of the sample. To select a random sample, many people use a table of random numbers. Using this technique, a researcher assigns consecutive numbers to each individual in the population. Then, using a table of random numbers (found in the appendices of many statistics books) the researcher reads the numbers in any direction. When the researcher reaches a number that matches one of the assigned numbers, the individual becomes a member of the sample. Of course, researchers could also write the names of individuals on pieces of paper and throw these into a hat to select individuals to be included in their sample!

Because each member of a population has an equal chance of being selected, we often presume that a simple random sample will be representative of the characteristics of a population. Unfortunately, simple random sampling does not ensure that the sample includes adequate proportions of individuals with certain characteristics. For example, if a particular population is three-fourths female and one-fourth male, simple random sampling will not guarantee the same proportion of females to males in your sample.

A variation of simple random sampling is **systematic sampling**—every *Nth* (for example, 5th) person in a population is chosen as a member of the sample. To systematically sample, the researcher assigns consecutive numbers to each individual in the population, then selects every *Nth,* for example *5th,* person to become a member of the sample. This technique has the same weakness as random sampling—it might not have the same proportion of individuals as the population.

Unlike simple random sampling, with **stratified random sampling** a population is divided into subgroups, or what we call strata (for example, gender, age, socioeconomic status). A random sample is selected from each stratum. The strata are based on some evidence that they are related to the issue or problem the survey addresses. For example, if you are interested in exploring how high school seniors feel about the value of the SAT for predicting college success, your population includes all high school seniors. You might wish to stratify by gender because the SAT seems to be a better predictor for females.

Cluster sampling is used when it is not feasible to list all of the individuals who belong to a particular population. This method is often used with surveys with large target populations. With **cluster sampling,** the researcher selects clusters (for example, regions of the country, states, high schools) and then selects participants from each cluster. In Greater Depth 12.4 provides an example of cluster sampling.

Nonprobability Sampling. **Nonprobability sampling** is a type of sampling in which not everyone has an equal chance of being selected from the population. Nonprobability sampling methods are often used because they are convenient and less expensive than probability sampling. One method of nonprobability sampling is convenience sampling. With **convenience sampling,** an available group of participants is used to represent the population. For example, if your population of interest is high school seniors, you might choose to use the high school seniors at a local high school as your participants.

Determining Sample Size

Sample size refers to the number of people needed to accurately represent the target population. What number of people constitutes a good sample size? This is not an easy question, because there are various factors that must be considered. One thing to consider is the homogeneity of the population—how similar the people in your population are to one another. The more similar the population, the smaller the sample necessary. The more dissimilar the members of the population, the larger the sample because it is necessary to have this variation represented in the sample. Remember that the fewer people chosen to participate in a survey (the smaller the sample), the more error the survey results are likely to include. This error is referred to as **sampling error**—a statistic that reflects how much error can be attributed to the lack of representation of the target population by the sample of respondents chosen.

Cluster Sampling

Population

Cluster 1	Cluster 2	Cluster 3	Cluster 4
(North)	(South)	(East)	(West)
(Urban) (Rural)	(Urban) (Rural)	(Urban) (Rural)	(Urban) (Rural)
(HS1)(HS2)(HS1)(HS2)	(HS1)(HS2)(HS1)(HS2)	(HS1)(HS2)(HS1)(HS2)	(HS1)(HS2)(HS1)(HS2)
High school seniors	High school seniors	High school seniors	High school seniors

Let's say you were interested in surveying high school seniors. You could divide the population of high school seniors into four initial clusters by the region of the country where they attend high school (North, South, East, West), then divide the high schools in each of these regions into those that are in urban settings and those that are in rural settings. You could then randomly select two high schools from each rural setting and two high schools from each urban setting and administer your survey to each student in the randomly selected high schools or randomly select students in each of these high schools.

There are various references (e.g., Howell, 1995) that include statistical calculations that researchers use to estimate a sample size.

Distributing the Survey

Finally it is time to distribute the survey. How the survey is prepared and distributed depends on the type of survey (for example, mail survey, face-to-face interview, telephone survey). The survey user who is conducting an individually administered or face-to-face survey must decide when, where, and how people will meet with the survey researcher. The survey user who is conducting a telephone survey must decide who will make the phone calls and when. For mail surveys, it must be decided when and how to mail the surveys. (Dillman, 1978, is an excellent reference for conducting mail and telephone surveys.)

Special materials (special paper to print the survey on, envelopes for mail surveys, pencils for self-administered surveys, telephones for telephone surveys, etc.) might be required. Finally, self-administered surveys must be assembled (papers stapled together, envelopes stuffed and addressed) so that they are ready for respondents.

Coding, Entering, and Analyzing Survey Data

The fourth phase of survey development involves coding and entering the survey data into the computer for analysis. This process includes coding the survey questions, entering the data into a spreadsheet program, verifying that the data are entered correctly, conducting the statistical analysis, and interpreting the results.

Coding Survey Questions

The answers to all survey questions must be coded before they can be entered into a computer program. Coding answers to closed-ended survey questions is relatively simple; coding answers to open-ended questions can be difficult. With closed-ended questions, survey researchers typically assign a code or numerical value to each of the possible response choices. For example, let's say the question is this:

Why didn't you pass your psychology exam?" (Select one of the following)

_____ I did not study
_____ I did not feel well
_____ I don't know
_____ Other

The first response option might be coded "1," the second as "2," the third as "3," and the fourth as "4." Thus, each person's response would get a 1, 2, 3, or 4. Sometimes, researchers use A, B, C, D, etc., instead of numbers, depending on the level of measurement of the question. Note that these are nominal data; statistical analyses are limited to calculating frequency of response and percentage of responses.

If the respondent was allowed to choose more than one answer for a question, (e.g., *please select all that apply*), then you would code the number corresponding to the response options chosen by the respondent. With these types of questions, it is often necessary to record the answers to the question as if it were two. For more information on coding survey items, see Fink (1995b).

Coding is more difficult for open-ended questions. Usually the first step is to take all of the answers to a particular open-ended question and sort them based on a criterion. For example, imagine the following survey item: "Last year you were a member of student government. Please comment on your experience." You might sort by positive and negative experiences (a criterion), or you might sort by the contents of the answers (another criterion) (Edwards & Thomas, 1993). All open-ended questions need to be coded before they can be entered in the computer.

Entering and Verifying Data

Survey researchers usually use statistical software packages, such as SPSS, SAS, Lotus 1-2-3, or Excel, to record and analyze responses. The responses are entered into the computer. In doing so, the researchers construct a **database,** a matrix in the form of a spreadsheet that shows the responses (rows) for each question (column) in the survey. After entering the data and before starting the analysis, the researcher verifies that the data have been entered correctly.

Table 12.3 provides an example of a database with 8 records (8 survey respondents) and 7 variables (7 survey questions).

Conducting the Analysis

Usually survey developers plan the data analysis at the time of the survey's construction. Having a data analysis plan ensures that the data gathered will be appropriate for meeting the survey's objectives. (Recall our discussion of nominal, ordinal, interval, and ratio data in Chapter 5). The actual analysis is usually a matter of a point of the mouse and a click of the button.

One statistic important for all surveys is the **response rate**—the number of individuals who responded to the survey divided by the total number who received the survey. Response rates tend to vary depending on the type of survey. For instance, one-on-one interviews can be expected to have a higher response than a mail survey.

TABLE 12.3. Sample Database

Respondent	Question 1	Question 2	Question 3	Question 4	Question 5	Question 6	Question 7
1	1	2	3	2	1	3	2
2	2	3	2	2	1	3	3
3	4	2	2	2	1	3	1
4	2	2	4	4	3	2	2
5	2	2	3	4	2	1	4
6	2	4	2	3	4	3	4
7	1	3	2	1	3	2	4
8	4	3	2	1	3	4	3

Survey researchers also calculate and report the reliability (internal consistency) of each of the dimensions on the survey. For example, earlier in this chapter we said that one objective of the course evaluation survey was to measure student opinions of course format. The reliability coefficient (KR-20 or coefficient alpha) shows whether the items in the survey that were intended to measure one objective are related to one another as expected (Edwards & Thomas, 1993).

The data analysis also includes calculating the sampling error. Used with means and standard deviations, sampling error tells how accurately the data reflect what the results would have been if the researchers had surveyed the entire population. Many survey researchers believe that if the results of a survey are within 5 percentage points of the entire population, the survey has done a good job. For more information on computing sampling errors for surveys, read Fowler (1988).

Next, the researcher conducts **univariate analyses**—computations of statistics that summarize individual question responses. Univariate analyses include frequency counts, percentages, means, modes, and medians. Frequency counts are tallies of how many people choose each of the response options for a question. Percentages are calculated by taking the number of individuals who chose a particular response and dividing that number by the total number of people who responded to the question. For questions that yield interval-level data, such as ratings from 1 to 10, the researcher might wish to calculate the mean, median, or the mode. We discussed these concepts in detail in Chapter 5.

The survey objectives might require the researcher to compare the responses given by two or more subgroups of respondents or the responses to two or more questions by all respondents. Such an analysis requires bivariate or multivariate analysis. A **bivariate analysis** provides information on two variables or groups; a **multivariate analysis** provides information three or more variables or groups. These analyses can include calculating correlation coefficients, cross tabulations, chi-square comparisons, T tests, or analysis of variance. The techniques chosen depend on the objectives of the survey and the level of measurement provided by the survey.

Presenting the Findings

The fifth and final phase involves reporting the survey to those who commissioned the survey's development and sometimes to the public at large. Whether the report is written or oral, its effectiveness and usefulness depends on how well it is prepared and how well it addresses the questions and general knowledge of its audience (Fink, 1995a). For instance, reports that contain numerous tables and statistical jargon will be useful for statisticians, but the general public needs a simpler version in everyday words.

Outlining a Report

In general, survey reports include a description of the survey's objectives, details about survey construction and administration, and the survey findings (Fink, 1995a). To ensure that each of these areas is covered in the report, the researcher prepares an outline of the information similar to the one below.

1. Survey Objectives—*Class Evaluation Survey*
   - To measure student opinions of course format and learning materials
   - To measure instructor's organization and knowledge of subject matter
   - To determine the overall effectiveness of the course
2. Survey Methods
   - Performed literature review
   - Communicated with subject matter experts (dean of the faculty, faculty)
   - Identified survey objectives
   - Operationally defined survey objectives
   - Wrote survey questions
   - Prepared survey instrument
   - Pilot tested survey
   - Revised and finalized survey
   - Administered survey
3. Survey Findings
   - 80% reported relevant reading material
   - 90% reported that exams assessed information presented in class
   - 90% reported the instructor was prepared for class
   - 85% reported that the instructor was organized
   - 90% reported that the instructor made course objectives clear
   - 100% reported that the instructor was knowledgeable about the material
   - 80% reported that the course was effective
   - 90% reported that this was a good course
4. Implications
   - Students liked the course
   - Students thought the instructor was organized and knowledgeable
   - Students thought the course was effective

Ordering and Determining the Contents of a Presentation

The general headings of the presentation outline provide a summary of the report and can serve as a structure for presenting the survey results. The focus of the presentation and the amount of detail provided should be adjusted to reflect the needs of the audience. For example, if you are presenting to researchers, they might be interested in knowing more about the size of the sample, the response rate, and the methods of analysis. General audiences might be more interested in a more nontechnical presentation.

266

Section Three
Developing
and Piloting
Psychological Tests
and Surveys

Using Transparencies, Slides, and Handouts

Professionals use learning aids, such as transparencies, slides, and handouts, to keep the attention of the audience and to increase the audience's understanding of the results. You can use these learning aids to display your presentation outline, to display major points related to each section of the outline, and to display charts, tables, and graphs. Typically, this information is prepared on a transparency or slide or in a PowerPoint (or some other software) presentation. Copies are then made of the information and provided to the audience in the form of handouts. Handouts help the audience follow the presentation without having to copy down everything that is said.

SURVEY RELIABILITY AND VALIDITY

Only good surveys provide information about attitudes, behaviors, and knowledge that we can feel confident about. Psychometrics (which we discussed in Section Two) allow us to determine whether a survey is good. What is a good survey? Like a good psychological test, a good survey consistently and accurately measures what it says it is measuring. A good survey is reliable and valid. A survey that is not reliable and valid is a survey that does not collect good information. Without good information, we tend to make poor decisions.

An unreliable survey cannot be valid because with inconsistent data you cannot have accurate findings (Fink, 1995b). However, a reliable survey can be invalid—it can give you similar information each time you use it, but not be serving its purpose.

Survey Reliability

In survey research we often speak of two types of errors: **random errors** (errors that are unpredictable) and **measurement errors** (errors that are associated with how a survey performs in a particular population). Recall from Chapter 6 that reliability is a statistical measure that tells you how good an instrument is at obtaining similar results each time it is used. A reliable survey is one that gives you similar information each time you use it. A reliable survey it is free from measurement error that can be caused by poorly worded questions, ambiguous terms, inappropriate reading level, and unclear directions, to name a few.

As with psychological tests, there are various ways to determine the reliability of a survey; these include test-retest, alternate forms, and split half. Test-retest and split half are the most common. These were discussed in detail in Chapter 6. You can increase a survey's reliability by writing multiple items for each dimension, determining whether other organizational members would assign an item to the dimension for which it was written, and grouping all items from a single dimension together.

Survey Validity

Recall from Chapters 7, 8, and 9 that validity tells us how well an instrument measures what it claims to measure. If a survey is designed to measure students' satisfaction with course content, it should measure this—not student's satisfaction with their grade!

As with psychological tests, there are various ways to determine the validity of a survey; these include content, criterion-related, construct, and face validity, which are evaluated using the procedures as described in Chapters 7, 8, and 9.

Summary Box 12.2
The Survey Research Method

- Surveys are one of various research methods you can use to collect information.
- Constructing a reliable and valid survey takes time, and it is as much a science as it is an art.
- Using a scientific approach to survey research will increase the reliability and validity of a survey.
- A scientific approach to surveys involves five generally phases: Identifying survey objectives and forming a hypothesis, constructing the survey, administering the survey, entering and analyzing the data, and presenting the findings.
- During the first phase, researchers identify the survey objectives, operationally define the objectives, and construct a plan for completing the survey.

- During the second phase, researchers select the type of survey, write the survey questions, prepare the survey for distribution, and pretest the survey.
- During the third phase, researchers select the appropriate respondents, determine the sample size, and distribute the survey.
- During the fourth phase, researchers code the survey questions, enter and verify the data, and conduct the analyses.
- During the fifth phase, researchers prepare and present an oral or written report.
- It is important that surveys are reliable and valid.

SUMMARY

Every day we encounter new information in different ways. When we acquire information using the scientific method, we can feel more confident that the information is accurate. The scientific method is a process of collecting information that involves (1) identifying the issues and forming a hypothesis, (2) designing a study, (3) conducting the study, (4) analyzing the results, and (5) communicating the results.

A variety of research techniques can be used when following the scientific method to acquiring knowledge. One such technique is the survey. The survey is a measurement instrument that helps us collect information about people's attitudes, behaviors, and knowledge. The scientific approach to surveys involves five phases: (1) identifying the survey objectives, (2) constructing the survey, (3) administering the survey, (4) entering and analyzing the data, and (5) presenting the findings. During the first phase, you identify the objectives of the survey, operationally define the objectives, and construct a plan for completing the survey. During the second phase, you must select the type of survey you will conduct, write your survey questions, prepare your survey, and pretest your survey. During the third phase, you administer your survey. During the fourth phase, you develop coding schemes for your questions, enter the data into a computer program, verify the data, and analyze the data. During the fifth phase, you present the results orally or in written format. Like psychological tests, it is very important that surveys be reliable and valid.

268

*Section Three
Developing
and Piloting
Psychological Tests
and Surveys*

KEY CONCEPTS

authority
bivariate analysis
cluster sampling
convenience sampling
database
decennial census survey
descriptive research
   techniques
double-barreled question
empiricism
experimental research
   techniques
experts
face-to-face surveys
field test
focus group
homogeneity of the
   population
individually administered
   surveys

intuition
item nonresponse rate
literature reviews
mail surveys
measurement errors
multivariate analysis
nonprobability sampling
nonsampling
   measurement errors
operational definition
personal interviews
population
pretesting
probability sampling
random errors
rationalism
response rate
sample
sample size
sampling bias

sampling error
scientific method
self-administered surveys
simple random sampling
stratified random
   sampling
structured observations
structured record reviews
survey
survey objectives
survey research firm
survey researcher
systematic sampling
telephone surveys
tenacity
univariate analysis

LEARNING ACTIVITIES

1. In your class, break into groups and brainstorm a purpose statement for a survey. Operationalize your purpose statement.
2. Go find an existing survey (e.g., your college's course evaluation survey, a hotel customer satisfaction survey, a survey used by a faculty member as a part of his or her research). What are the survey's strengths? What are the survey's weaknesses?
3. Read each of the following survey items. What is the problem with each, and how could you improve each?

   Did you participate in any athletic activities in high school?
   ___ Yes   ___ No

   Do you go swimming more than four times a week?
   ___ Yes   ___ No

   Was your professor eager for you to learn and receptive to your needs?
   ___ Yes   ___ No

   How much money have you spent in the past three months on groceries?
   _____ (in U.S. dollars)

4. Recall this statement from the beginning of this chapter:

   I had to design a course evaluation survey for my research methods class. One of the questions on my survey was 'Was the teacher available and responsive to your needs?' Another questions was 'How much time did survey developer spend studying for this class?' My teacher said that these were not very good survey questions. Why?"

   What is wrong with the two questions this student mentions?

5. Name the type of sampling used in the following examples:

A. Your psychology professor constructs a survey to measure college student's attitudes toward fraternities and sororities on your college campus. The professor gets a list of all students from the Registrars Office. He divides the students into freshmen, sophomore, juniors, and seniors. He then divides them into males and females. He randomly samples students from each of these groups.

B. Your sociology professor constructs a survey to measure females' attitudes toward all-male schools. The professor administers the survey to all of the students in her classes.

C. The U.S. Bureau of the Census constructs a supplement to the decennial census. The decennial census is a census of all people in the United States. The Bureau of the Census takes all people who responded to the most recent decennial census and has a computer select 5,000 to take the supplemental survey.

Using Tests in Different Settings

The fourth section of this text consists of three chapters that
introduce you to tests in different settings.

- **CHAPTER 13—Using Tests In Educational Settings** In Chapter 13, we focus on psychological testing in educational settings. We begin with an overview of the types of decisions that are made in educational settings based on the results of psychological tests. We then discuss how tests are used in the classroom, and we highlight how tests are used in educational settings to make selection and placement decisions, counseling and guidance decisions, and curriculum/administrative policy decisions. We end with a discussion of norm-referenced, criterion-referenced, and authentic assessment in educational settings.

- **CHAPTER 14—Using Tests In Clinical and Counseling Settings** In Chapter 14, we focus on psychological testing in clinical settings. We begin with the role psychological testing and assessment plays in the fields of clinical psychology and counseling. We discuss three models of assessment in clinical practice. Lastly, we discuss the role of the clinical interview, personality tests, projective techniques, neuropsychological tests, and tests for clinical disorders (e.g., depression, anxiety).

- **CHAPTER 15—Using Tests In Organizational Settings** In Chapter 15 we discuss the use of psychological tests in organizational settings. After discussing the history of psychological assessment in organizations, we examine the different types of tests used by organizations, including interviews, tests of performance, and personality and integrity tests. We end with a discussion of how organizations use psychological assessment to evaluate employee performance.

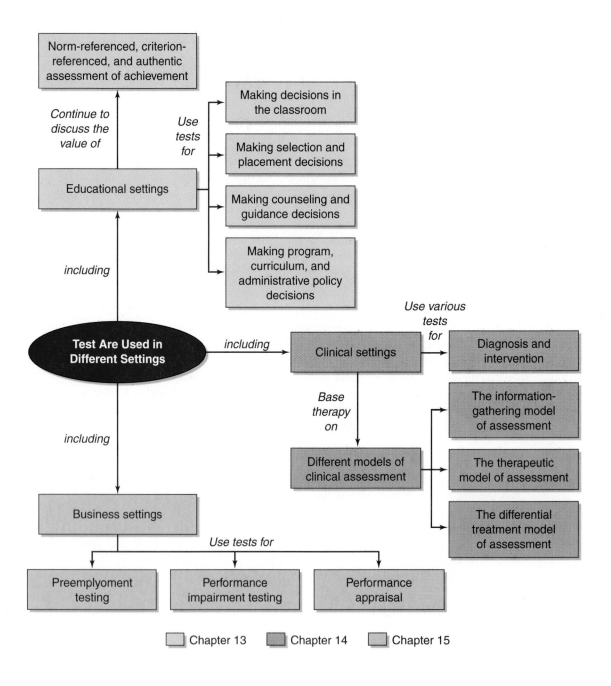

Norm-referenced, criterion-referenced, and authentic assessment of achievement

Continue to discuss the value of

Use tests for

Making decisions in the classroom

Making selection and placement decisions

Making counseling and guidance decisions

Making program, curriculum, and administrative policy decisions

Educational settings

including

Test Are Used in Different Settings

including

Clinical settings

Use various tests for

Diagnosis and intervention

Base therapy on

Different models of clinical assessment

The information-gathering model of assessment

The therapeutic model of assessment

The differential treatment model of assessment

including

Business settings

Use tests for

Preemplyoment testing

Performance impairment testing

Performance appraisal

Chapter 13   Chapter 14   Chapter 15

272

Using Tests in Educational Settings

"I asked my teacher why she always identifies and discusses the objectives of a specific unit of instruction before she begins teaching. She said that she needs the objectives to guide her teaching and to determine what material should be included on classroom exams. I always wondered how teachers determine what should be on the exams."

"I had to take several different kinds of tests this year. Why do teachers make us do this? I thought they only used tests to assign grades."

"As an elementary school teacher, I don't believe that tests by themselves can accurately measure a student's understanding of material. Do I have other options?"

In the first section of this text we covered the basics of psychological measurement and testing. Among other things, we discussed the characteristics of psychological tests, the different ways of classifying tests, where to locate information about tests, why testing is important, and who uses psychological tests. In the second section of this text, we discussed how test users interpret test scores as well as the concepts of reliability and validity. In the third section, we discussed how psychological tests are developed and piloted, and how we construct, administer, and use survey data. In this fourth and last section we discuss how tests are used in three settings: educational, clinical, and organizational.

In this chapter we focus on the use of psychological tests in educational settings. We begin with an overview of the types of decisions that are made in education based on the results of psychological tests. We discuss educators as test users and we provide a few examples of situations where educators did not properly use tests. Following a detailed discussion of exactly how tests are used in the classroom, we highlight how tests are used in educational settings to make selection and placement decisions, counseling and guidance decisions, and curriculum and administrative policy decisions. We end with a discussion of norm-referenced, criterion-referenced, and authentic assessment in educational settings.

DECISION MAKING IN THE EDUCATIONAL SETTING

Every day, educators make important decisions based on the results of psychological tests. Thorndike, Cunningham, Thorndike, and Hagen (1991) classify these into decisions of eight types: (1) **instructional,** (2) **grading,** (3) **diagnostic,** (4) **selection,** (5) **placement,** (6) **counseling and guidance,** (7) **program and curriculum,** and (8) **administrative policy.** Instructional, grading, and diagnostic decisions are made frequently by classroom teachers typically using teacher made tests. Decisions about selection, placement, counseling and guidance, program and curriculum, and administrative policy are made by testing specialists, educational administrators, or committees and are often made on the basis of standardized tests of aptitude or achievement. Table 13.1 lists each of these decisions, who typically makes the decision, what type of test is typically involved, and an example of the decision.

TABLE 13.1. Decisions Made by Educational Institutions Based on Psychological Tests

Type of Decision	Individuals Who Typically Make These Decisions	Tests These Decisions Typically Are Based On	Example of This Kind of Decision
Instructional	Classroom teacher	Teacher-made	Determining the pace of the course (e.g., should they slow down, speed up, or continue their teaching pace or skip a topic altogether)
Grading	Classroom teacher	Teacher-made	Assigning grades to students
Diagnostic	Classroom teacher	Teacher-made	Determining whether a student has a learning difficulty (e.g., a test might reveal that Zachary can write a complete sentence, but only a simple complete sentence)
Selection	Specialists or administrators	Standardized (e.g., SAT)	Admissions decisions; selection for special programs (e.g., gifted and remedial programs)
Placement	Specialists or administrators at the school level	Standardized	Placement of students into the proper level of a course (e.g., colleges and universities might use test scores to determine which math course an individual should be placed in)
Counseling and Guidance	Specialists or administrators at the school or district level	Standardized	Helping students select majors and careers that match the students' strengths and interests
Program and Curriculum	Specialists or administrators at the district level	Standardized	Determining the success of a program or curriculum (e.g., are students who go through the new curriculum learning more than students who go through the old curriculum?); determining which program or curriculum should be implemented or dropped
Administrative Policy	Specialists or administrators at district, state, or national level	Standardized	Determining where money should be spent and what programs should be implemented to improve a school's, a district's, or a nation's achievement scores

Source: Adapted from Thorndike, Cunningham, Thorndike, and Hagen. (1991).

EDUCATORS AS TEST USERS

As you can see, psychological tests are used by a variety of individuals in the educational setting (from classroom teachers to district level administrators) to make a wide range of important decisions. In fact, the role of psychological tests in educational settings is likely to continue to increase (Bowers, 1996; Kubiszyn & Borich, 1996).

Because teachers, specialists, and administrators use psychological tests, they are test users. As test users, each should be properly trained in the appropriate use

of psychological tests. Recall our discussion in Chapter 3 of what it means to be a test user. When educators who use psychological tests are not properly informed and trained, the result can range from embarrassment of the educator to improper grade assignment to improper diagnosis.

Inadequate Testing Knowledge of Classroom Teachers

The following two dialogues reflect inadequate testing knowledge on the part of a classroom teacher. The first dialogue occurs between one of the authors of *Educational Testing and Measurement: Classroom Applications and Practice* (Kubiszyn & Borich, 1996) and a classroom teacher. The second dialogue occurs between Ms. Wilson (a sixth-grade teacher) and some of her colleagues at school. Both dialogues are from Kubiszyn and Borich (1996).

Dialogue One

TEACHER: Hi, I'm Jeff's second-grade teacher. What can I do for you so early in the year?

AUTHOR: Jeff says he's in the low reading group, and I am curious about why he is. Could you explain that to me?

TEACHER: Oh, don't worry—we don't label kids at this school. I think that would be a terrible injustice.

AUTHOR: I see, but could you explain why Jeff is in the "Walkers" instead of the "Runners"?

TEACHER: Oh, those are just names, that's all.

AUTHOR: Are both groups at the same level in reading?

TEACHER: They're both at the first-grade level, yes.

AUTHOR: I'm beginning to catch on. Are they reading in the same-level books in the same reading series?

TEACHER: Of course not! Some children are further along than others—that's all—but the kids don't know.

AUTHOR: Let me guess; the "Runners" are further ahead?

TEACHER: Yes, they're in book 9.

AUTHOR: And the "Walkers" are in . . .

TEACHER: Book 5. But they are grouped for instructional purposes—I have twenty-five students, you know!

AUTHOR: I'm confused. Jeff's reading scores on the California Achievement Test last May were above the ninetieth percentile.

TEACHER: *(chuckles to herself)* I can understand your confusion. Those test scores are so hard to understand. Why, even we professionals can't understand them.

AUTHOR: A score at the ninetieth percentile means the score was higher than the score of 90 percent of the students who took the test all across the country.

TEACHER: Oh, really? It is very complicated. As I said, even professional educators don't understand testing.

AUTHOR: Some do, Mrs. B.

Dialogue Two

MS. WILSON: I know you all feel we've covered a tremendous amount this year. Well, you're right. We have. And now it's time to find out how much you've learned. It's important for you to know how well you're doing in each subject so you can work harder in the areas where you might need improvement. It's also nice to know in what areas you might be smarter than almost everyone else. So, next week, I want you to be ready to take tests over all the material we have covered so far. *(A few students groan in unison.)* Remember, this will be your chance to show me how smart you are. I want you to get plenty of sleep Sunday night so you'll be fresh and alert Monday. *(As the bell rings, Ms. Wilson shouts over the commotion of students leaving the classroom.)* Don't forget, I'll be collecting homework on Monday!

(As Ms. Wilson collapses into her chair, Ms. Palmer, an experienced teacher, walks in.)

MS. PALMER: Glad this grading period is just about over. Next week will be a nice break, don't you think? Just reviewing and giving tests. It'll sure be nice to have this weekend free without any preparations to worry about.

MS. WILSON: You mean you won't be making up tests this weekend?

MS. PALMER: No. I have tests from the last three years which I've been refining and improving. With only a few modifications, they'll do fine.

MS. WILSON: You're awfully lucky. I'm afraid I haven't had a chance to even think about how I'm going to test these kids. All these subjects to make tests for, and then all the scoring and grading to do by next Friday. I think I'm going to have an awful weekend.

MS. PALMER: Will you be giving criterion-referenced or norm-referenced tests?

MS. WILSON: Umm . . . well . . . I don't know. I remember hearing those terms in a tests and measurement class I once took, but I guess I just haven't had time to worry about those things until now. I suppose I'm going to have to get my old textbook out tonight and do some reviewing. Gosh! I hope I can find it.

Ms. PALMER: Well, if you use norm-referenced tests, there are some available in Ms. Cartwright's office. You know, she's the counselor who is always so helpful with discipline problems. In fact, she has a whole file full of tests.

Ms. WILSON: Will you be using norm-referenced tests next week?

Ms. PALMER: Not really. For these mid-semester grades, I like to make my tests very specific to what I've been teaching. At this point in the year it seems to provide better feedback to the kids and parents—especially the parents. Anyway, the parents aren't really interested in where their kid scores in relation to other students until later in the semester, when I've covered more content and the kids have had a chance to get their feet on the ground.

Ms. WILSON: You mean these norm-referenced tests don't cover specially what you've taught?

Ms. PALMER: *(trying to be tactful)* Well, no. Not exactly. I guess you have forgotten a few things since you took that tests and measurements course.

Ms. WILSON: I guess so.

Ms. PALMER: Why don't you make a test blueprint and compare it to some of the items in Ms. Cartwright's test file?

Ms. WILSON: A test *what* print?

Ms. PALMER: A test blueprint. You know, where you take the objectives from your lesson plans and construct a table that shows the content you've been teaching and the level of complexity—knowledge, comprehension, applications—that you're shooting for. Then, see how Ms. Cartwright's tests match the test blueprint.

Ms. WILSON: But what if I didn't write down all my objectives? I had objectives, of course, but I just didn't write them down all the time, or when I did, I usually didn't keep them for long. You know what I mean? *(No comment from Ms. Palmer.)* And I don't think I wrote them so they included levels of complexity according to the taxonomy-of-objectives thing I think you're referring to.

Ms. PALMER: But I'm afraid that without objectives, you won't know if the items on Ms. Cartwright's tests match what you've taught. Would you believe that last year a teacher in this school flunked half his class using a test that didn't match what he taught? Boy, what a stir that caused.

Ms. WILSON: *(looking worried)* I guess I'll have to start from scratch, then. It looks like a very long weekend.

Ms. PALMER: Of course, you might consider giving some essay items.

Ms. WILSON: You mean long-answer, not multiple-choice questions?

Ms. PALMER: Yes, but you'll have to consider the time it will take to develop a scoring guide for each question and the time you'll spend grading all those answers. And, then, of course, only some of your objectives may be suited to an essay format.

Ms. WILSON: *(trying to sort out all of what Ms. Palmer just said without sounding too stupid)* By scoring guide, do you mean the right answer?

Ms. PALMER: Well, not quite, as you know, essay items can have more than one right answer. So, first you will have to identify all the different elements that make an answer right and then decide how to assign points to each of these elements, depending on what percentage of the right answer they represent.

Ms. WILSON: How do you decide that?

Ms. PALMER: *(trying to be polite and being evasive for the sake of politeness)* Well . . . very carefully.

MS. WILSON: I see *(long pause)*. Well, maybe my old tests and measurement book will have something on that.

MS. PALMER: I'm sure it will.

MS. WILSON: Sounds as though I have my work cut out for me. I guess I'll just have to organize my time and start to work as soon as I get home.
(Ms. Palmer and Ms. Wilson leave the classroom and meet Mr. Smith, another teacher).

MR. SMITH: You won't believe the meeting I just had with Johnny Haringer's parents!

MS. PALMER AND MS. WILSON: What happened?

MR. SMITH: Well, they came to see me after Johnny missed an A by two points on one of my weekly math tests. It was the first time that he had missed an A the entire semester.

MS. WILSON: Were they mad?

MR. SMITH: They were at first. But I stayed calm and explained very carefully why two points on the test really should make a difference between and A and a B.

MS. WILSON: What kinds of things did you tell them?

MR. SMITH: Well, luckily I keep student data from past years for all my tests. This allows me to calculate reliability and validity coefficients for my tests using one of the PCs in the math lab. I simply explained to Johnny's parents, in everyday, commonsense language, what reliability and validity of a test meant, and then gave them some statistical data to support my case. I also explained the care and deliberation I put into the construction of my tests—you know, all the steps you go through in writing test items and then checking their content validity and doing qualitative and quantitative item analyses. I think they got the idea of just how much work it takes to construct a good test.

MS. WILSON: And?

MR. SMITH: And after that they calmed down and were very responsive to my explanation. They even commented that they hadn't realized the science of statistics could be so helpful in determining the reliability and validity of a test. They even commended me for being so systematic and careful. Can you believe that?

MS. WILSON: Umm . . . reliability and validity? Do you mean we have to know the reliability and validity for every test we use?

MR. SMITH: Ever since that lawsuit by the parents of some kid over at Central for unfair testing, the school board has made every teacher individually responsible for using reliable and valid tests.
(Looking surprised, Ms. Wilson turns to Ms. Palmer and Ms. Palmer slowly and painfully nods to indicate her agreement with what Mr. Smith has been saying).

MS. WILSON: Boy! I don't think I could explain reliability and validity that well—at least not to parents—and I know I wouldn't have the slightest idea of how to calculate them.

MR. SMITH: Well, I guess we won't have any preparations to worry about this weekend. Nothing but review and testing next week. You have a nice weekend.

MS. PALMER: Well, it may not be all that bad. You've got that tests and measurement text at home, and next quarter, who knows? You may have time to plan for all this ahead of time.

MS. WILSON: *(being purposely negative)* That's if I don't have to explain reliability and validity to some irate kid's parents, construct a test blueprint, learn the difference between norm-reference and criterion-referenced tests, make a scoring key for an essay test, and, of course, compute some test item statistics I probably can't even pronounce!

Source: Dialogues are from T. Kubiszyn & G. Borich, *Educational Testing and Measurement: Classroom Applications and Practice* (5th ed.) (New York: HarperCollins, 1996), pp. 471-475.

The teacher in the first dialogue obviously did not understand how to interpret test scores and therefore made an inappropriate decision about which reading group Jeff should be in. So what? By placing Jeff in a lower-level reading group, the teacher was not appropriately challenging Jeff.

Ms. Palmer, in the second dialogue, did not know very much about psychological testing. Perhaps most importantly, she did not know that a test should be constructed or selected based on the objectives of a specific unit of instruction. Without this knowledge, we can guarantee that Ms. Palmer's tests would not be content valid and thus would not measure how well students learned the material. How would you feel if your classroom grade were based on your performance on tests that did not measure what you had been learning in class?

Summary Box 13.1
Decision Making in the Educational Setting

- Psychological tests play an important role in educational settings, and their role there will likely continue to increase.
- Teachers, testing specialists, and educational administrators use psychological tests to make a variety of important decisions.
- Teachers use psychological tests to make instructional, grading, and diagnostic decisions.
- Testing specialists and educational administrators use psychological tests to make decisions about selection, placement, counseling and guidance, program or curriculum, and administrative policy.
- Teachers, testing specialists, and educational administrators are test users and therefore should be properly trained on the appropriate use of psychological tests.
- Educators without proper testing knowledge can make some improper decisions, which can cause them embarrassment or worse.

PSYCHOLOGICAL TEST USE IN EDUCATIONAL SETTINGS

In this section, we discuss in more detail the specific uses of psychological tests in educational settings. We focus most of our attention on how psychological tests are used by teachers in the classroom to make instructional, grading, and diagnostic decisions. We highlight how specialists and administrators use psychological tests to make selection and placement decisions, how specialists use tests to help students make decisions about their future and career, and how specialists, administrators, and committees use tests to make program, curriculum, and administrative policy decisions. In addition, we reference a variety of psychological tests throughout this section.

Tests Used for Making Decisions in the Classroom

281

CHAPTER 13
Using Tests in
Educational
Settings

Teachers must make a variety of decisions in the classroom. For example, teachers must decide whether students are ready to learn new material, and, if they are, how much of the new material students already know. Teachers must decide what information students are learning and what information they are having difficulty learning. Teachers must also decide what grades to assign students. Teachers often use psychological tests, combined with other assessment methods, to help them make these types of decisions.

Gronlund (1998) sorts the decisions teachers make in the classroom into those that are made at the beginning of instruction, those that are made during instruction, and those that are made at the end of instruction. Table 13.2 lists the questions teachers ask, according to Gronlund, in order to make these decisions.

Decisions Made at the Beginning of Instruction

At the beginning of a course or before a new unit of instruction, teachers will often use psychological tests as **placement assessments.** Placement assessments are used to answer those questions presented in the first column of Table 13.2—to determine whether students have the skills or knowledge necessary to understand new material and to determine how much information students already know about the new material (Gronlund, 1998). For example, as a teacher, I might decide to give each student in my experimental design course a test to measure their understanding of statistics before proceeding to the last section of the course, which covers data analysis techniques. I might use this information to determine whether I need to begin my discussion of data analysis techniques by focusing on basic data analysis skills or whether I can go right into advanced data analysis skills. I might also use this information to break the class into two groups—those who have the appropriate statistical knowledge will be taught more advanced data analysis techniques (analysis of variance, analysis of covariance), and those who lack the statistical knowledge will be taught more basic data analysis techniques (e.g., measures of central tendency, *T*-tests). I might also give my students a test to measure how much they already know about advanced statistical techniques. If they have mastered some of the material, I might modify my teaching plans or place students in different levels of instruction.

TABLE 13.2. Decision Making in the Classroom: The Questions Teachers Ask

Beginning of Instruction	During Instruction	End of Instruction
To what extent do the students possess the skills and abilities that are needed to begin instruction?	*On which learning tasks are the students progressing satisfactorily? On which ones do they need help?*	*Which students have mastered the learning tasks to such a degree that they should proceed to the next course or unit of instruction?*
To what extent have the students already achieved the intended learning outcomes of the planned instruction?	*Which students are having such severe learning problems that they need remedial work?*	*What grade should be assigned to each student?*

Source: Gronlund (1998).

Decisions Made During Instruction

Periodically throughout the year, teachers might use psychological tests as **formative assessments.** Formative assessments help teachers answer those questions presented in the second column of Table 13.2—to determine what information students are and are not learning during the instructional process. Teachers can use this information to adjust the pace of their teaching and the material they are covering (Gronlund, 1998). For example, I might choose to give a test at the end of every unit of instruction to determine what students have and have not learned. If a number of my students do poorly on a particular test item or group of items, I might choose to spend more time reviewing the material. If only a few of my students do poorly on a test item, I might choose to work with those students individually and assign them additional reading or problems.

If a student continues to experience problems with some material, teachers might suggest that the student's learning abilities be evaluated using a more thorough **diagnostic assessment**—an in-depth evaluation of an individual. Diagnostic assessments often include psychological tests that consist of many items that are very similar. For example, if a student is having difficulties adding, then one group of test items might include the addition of two numbers that do not require any carrying (e.g., 3 + 5). Another set might include items that require minimal carrying (e.g., 5 + 6). Another group of test items might require more carrying (e.g., 56 + 84). These slight differences allow a teacher to determine exactly where students are having difficulties (Gronlund, 1998).

Because diagnostic tests can be difficult to design and because some learning difficulties cannot be identified and overcome using the formative and diagnostic tests typically used by teachers, diagnostic testing is typically done by a psychologist. Some psychologists are professionally trained to conduct the evaluation and diagnostic testing necessary to identify specific learning difficulties.

Decisions Made at the End of Instruction

At the end of the year, teachers typically use tests as **summative assessments.** Summative assessments help teachers answer those questions in the third column of Table 13.2—to determine whether students have learned what the teacher intended them to, or what they should know by the end of the grade, and to assign grades (Gronlund, 1998). For example, I might give my introductory psychology class a final exam to determine if they learned the material I intended them to and to assign grades. Or an elementary school teacher might give a standardized test of achievement at the end of the school year to determine whether students learned what they were expected to learn.

One of your author's children was given two achievement tests at the end of third grade in an Orange County, Florida, elementary school. One of these tests was the Stanford Achievement Test, which is often administered to students at the end of the year to determine how their reading and mathematics skills compare to those of other students in the same grade level, across the nation. For Your Information 13.1 discusses the Stanford Achivement Test. For Your Information 13.2 discusses the other test, the Orange Curriculum-Aligned Test (OCAT), which is used by Orange County, Florida, schools to measure how well students perform on various benchmarks, which, according to Orange County, students should know and perform by the end of third grade.

Additional Ways Assessment Can Benefit the Instructional Process

283

CHAPTER 13
*Using Tests in
Educational
Settings*

Psychological tests can benefit the instructional process in other ways. In addition to measuring the skills and abilities of students prior to, during, and after instruction, assessments, and thus tests, can (1) help motivate students, (2) help students retain and transfer what they have learned to new problems, issues, and situations, (3) help students understand their strengths and weaknesses, and (4) help teachers evaluate the effectiveness of their instruction (Gronlund, 1998).

Student Motivation. Tests can motivate students in the classroom. They can help students develop short-term achievement goals, understand what information they need to learn, and understand how well they are learning the information being taught to them (Gronlund, 1998).

For Your Information
The Stanford Achievement Test

13.1

Test Name:	**Stanford Achievement Test Series**
Publisher:	**The Psychological Corporation**
Publication Date:	**1988**
Grade Level:	**K–12**

The Stanford Achievement Test Series is commonly used in educational settings. The series consists of a battery of tests designed to measure the achievement of children in kindergarten through 12th grade. There are three groups of tests in the series. The first group is the Early Stanford School Achievement Test (SESAT). The SESAT is designed for use by kindergartners and students in their first half of first grade. The SESAT measures children's basic reading, comprehension, grammatical, mathematical, and listening skills. It takes ten 25- to 45-minute sittings to administer the entire test.

The second group of tests is the Stanford Achievement Test. The Stanford Achievement Test is designed to be taken by children in their second half of first grade through ninth grade. In addition to what is measured on the SESAT, the Stanford Achievement Test has modules that measure children's knowledge of science and social studies as well as research and study skills. Administering the entire test requires twelve 20- to 55-minute sittings.

The third group of tests is the Stanford Test of Academic Skills (TASK). The TASK is designed for use by 9th- through 12th-graders as well as college students. The TASK measures many of the same skills but also measures children's ability to use information and think critically.

This year, my son Zachary brought home a letter telling me he would be taking the Stanford Achievement Test. Along with the letter was a brochure *(Let's Talk Testing: Parents' Guide to Achievement Testing*; Orange County Public Schools, 1996) that explained all about the Stanford Achievement Test. Needless to say, I read the entire brochure, and I found it to be quite thorough. The brochure very nicely addressed all of those issues parents get nervous about when it comes to testing their child. It contained the following:

- An explanation of what the test was.
- Some sample questions.
- An explanation of how we could help our child prepare for the test.
- An explanation of how the test scores would be reported.
- An explanation of parents' rights.
- A reference for further information.

On the following page are the contents of the brochure.

Zachary took the Stanford Achievement Test in April 1998. The results were helpful to the teacher, the school, and us because they provided all of us with a piece of information regarding how Zachary was doing in reading and mathematics compared to other third-grade students across the nation. A sample score report is shown in Figure 13.1. As you can see, like the brochure produced by Orange County, the report is easy to read.

This spring your child will take the Stanford Achievement Test at school. Testing is one way for you, your child, and the teacher to know how your child is doing in school. In addition to test scores there are other ways to measure success. These include grades, class participation, attitude, and how well the child can use the skills that have been learned. Test scores are a good source of information about how well a child is learning, but test scores can be affected by a number of other things including how the child was feeling on the day of the test and knowledge of the English language.

ABOUT THE STANFORD

The Stanford is a standardized test. This means that each student who takes the test receives the same directions, questions and time limits. Because the tests are standardized, estimates can be made about how Orange County students who took the test compare with students in the nationwide reference group, known as the norm group. This group includes thousands of students from all over the country who took the Stanford in 1988.

All students taking the Stanford will have questions in these areas:

Reading Comprehension
Concepts of Number
Mathematics Computation
Mathematics Applications

TESTING DAYS AND TESTING TIMES

Schools are given a certain period during which they may test. Each school decides the specific days to test based on the school's calendar. Every effort is made to avoid religious holidays and to schedule the test on the days that will be best for students. The following chart shows the amount of time needed for testing:

GRADE	TESTING TIME*
2	1 hour and 50 minutes
3	2 hours and 15 minutes
4	2 hours and 50 minutes
5	2 hours and 50 minutes
6	2 hours and 50 minutes
7	2 hours and 50 minutes
8	2 hours and 50 minutes

*The whole test will not be taken at one time. Students will have breaks between sections.

SAMPLE QUESTIONS

The following is a sample question from the Reading Comprehension section on the 4th grade test:

The Election

"What's taking so long?" Marty asked, "We've been standing outside this office since 3:00."

"There are over eighty students in all the eighth-grade classes." Sally replied. It takes a long time to count all those ballots."

"But we've been waiting for half an hour!" Marty said. Just then Mrs. Daily, the principal, came from her office.

"Sally, Marty, it's a tie. You both received exactly 43 votes. I was so surprised, I recounted the ballots five times! This means you can serve together as president of the class." Sally saw that Marty was frowning. She held out her hand to him.

"Well, " she said, "half a loaf is better than none." Marty smiled and shook her hand. "I guess you're right. Now let's get to work. There's plenty of work for both of us."

What will Marty and Sally probably do next?

—— recount the ballots
—— make plans
—— wait for the principal
—— ask for another election

Which word best describes Sally's attitude at the end of the story?

—— surprised
—— jealous
—— resentful
—— friendly

The following is a sample question from the Mathematics Computation section on the 4th grade test:

18.9+64.3 =
—— 72.2
—— 81.12
—— 82.2
—— 83.2
—— N.H (not here).

The following is a sample question from the Concepts of Number section on the 7th grade test:

What is 264,153 rounded to the nearest thousand?

—260,000
—265,000
—264,000
—300,000

The following is a sample question from the Mathematics Application section on the 7th grade test:

The Millers are going to drive a total of 1000 miles. If they drive 300 miles the first day, what fraction of the total distance will they have driven?

—2/5
—3/10
—7/10
—3/11
—1/100

HOW YOU CAN HELP YOUR CHILD

Since tests provide important information about a child's performance in school, you naturally want your child to do well on them. You as a parent can do some things that will prepare your child for the test:

• Be supportive. Help your child realize that a test is not a threat or something to be afraid of, but a chance to show what has been learned up to this time.

• Understand that studying for the test is not a good idea. These tests cover many skills that have been learned over a long period of time. Studying for the test probably will not help.
• See that your child has a good night's sleep before a test and begins the day with a nutritious breakfast. Test taking requires a lot of physical energy.
• Encourage your child to do his/her best, but do not overly stress the test.
• Help your child understand that students are not expected to know everything on the test, and that all students should simply try their best.

UNDERSTANDING YOUR CHILD'S RESULTS

A standardized test provides information about your child's achievement of the skills and content measured on the test. The results may indicate strengths or weaknesses that you were not aware your child had. Remember that the score is the result of your child's work on one day.

The most commonly reported test score is called a percentile rank. This number will tell you how your child's performance on the test compares to the performance of the children in the norm group. For example, a 4th grade child may have a percentile rank of 65 on Reading Comprehension. This means that the child scored higher that 65% of the 4th graders in the national norm group who took the Reading Comprehension test. For each grade level, a percentile rank of 50 is average. The highest possible percentile is 99; the lowest is 1.

Tests are not perfect and there is some error associated with each test score. A percentile band shows where the child probably would score if he or she took the test on a number of different occasions. In the following chart, the percentile band for a score of 65 ranges from a percentile rank of about 50 to a percentile rank of about 75. Therefore, for a percentile rank of 65 you would know that if the child took the test again you could expect a score anywhere from about 50 to 75.

Reading 1 10 30 50 70 90 99
Comprehension ■■

PARENTS' RIGHTS

With regard to achievement testing, parents have these rights:

1. To know ahead of time the upcoming test activities
2. To know the general content that will be covered on the test (Parents may see any practice materials and sample questions used by the school, if any, but not the actual test.)
3. To know how the test scores will be used
4. To have questions answered to their satisfaction
5. To request a review of the testing situation to decide if their child's scores are accurate and/or valid

FOR FURTHER INFORMATION

If this brochure does not answer all of your questions, there are several people who can help you. Your child's teacher, the school counselor, and the principal can answer questions about the test or your child's scores. They also can suggest ways for you to help your child, if necessary, including modifications of testing conditions if your child is an exceptional education student. In addition, the district testing staff is available at (phone number).

```
STUDENT  : XXXXXX      XXXXXX   STUDENT #: XXXXXXXXXX
*TESTPAK*  ORANGE COUNTY PUBLIC SCHOOLS             FORM : J        PAGE
TEACHER  : XXX                                      LEVEL: P3           1
SCHOOL   : XXXX-XXXXXXXXX                           GRADE:  3  SPR
DISTRICT : Orange County Public Schools             TEST DATE 04/10/98
FILENAME : XXXX                                     RUN  DATE 05/19/98


                                      NATIONAL PERCENTILE
         SUBTEST            PR 1  2   5 10   20 30 40 50 60 70 80    90 95   98 99
                           -----------------------------------------------------
READING COMPREHENSION      83                                  ******
CONCEPTS OF NUMBER         99                                            ******
MATH COMPUTATION           93                                ******
MATH APPLICATIONS          96                                     ******
TOTAL MATHEMATICS          98                                            ******
                           PR 1  2   5 10   20 30 40 50 60 70 80    90 95   98 99
                           -----------------------------------------------------
                            |   LOW   | -AVERAGE | AVG| +AVERAGE |   HIGH    |
```

FIGURE 13.1. Sample Stanford Achievement Test score report

Retention and Transfer of Learning. Tests can measure a student's knowledge of information (e.g., their ability to identify, name, list, and select). In addition, tests can help students retain the information they learn and apply the information they learn to various situations. To aid in the retention and transfer of
learning, tests should measure advanced learning outcomes, such as a student's
ability to understand the information (e.g. explain, summarize, distinguish), apply the information (solve, relate, demonstrate), and interpret the information.
Tests with these more advanced learning outcomes familiarize students with the
importance of these outcomes, allow students to practice these important skills
and abilities, and help students permanently store the information (Gronlund,
1998).

Student Self-Assessment. Tests can help students better understand themselves. Tests can provide students with objective information about what they
know and do not know (i.e., their strengths and weaknesses), and students can use
this information to make decisions about themselves (Gronlund, 1998).

Instructional Effectiveness. Tests can help teachers understand whether their
instructional objectives were realistic and whether their teaching methods were

The Orange Curriculum-Aligned Test (OCAT) is administered in the spring to Orange County, Florida, students in grades 3 to 7. Florida's Sunshine State Standards state that there are certain things students should know and be able to perform in grades 3 to 7, and this test measures what students know and can perform. The results of the OCAT will give information regarding what a child learned well and what a child may need more instruction in. Figure 13.2 shows a letter to parents that explains how to read an OCAT score report, and Figure 13.3 shows an actual OCAT score report.

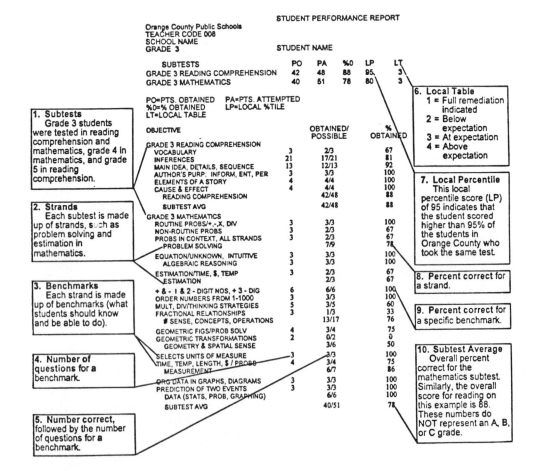

FIGURE 13.2. Letter to parents accompanying an OCAT score report

```
                    STUDENT PERFORMANCE REPORT                    GRADE 3 RDG & MATH
ORANGE                                                            GRADE 3 MATH
XXX
XXXXXXXXX                XXXXXX        XXXXXX
GRADE  3

   SUBTESTS                        PO  PA  %O LP  LT

GRADE 3 READING COMPREHENSION     41  48  85 92   3
GRADE 3 MATHEMATICS               48  51  94 99   4

PO=PTS. OBTAINED     PA=PTS. ATTEMPTED
%O=% OBTAINED        LP=LOCAL %TILE
LT=LOCAL TABLE

   OBJECTIVE                       OBTAINED/   %
                                   POSSIBLE OBTAINED

GRADE 3 READING COMPREHENSION
   VOCABULARY                3       3/3      100
   INFERENCES               21      18/21      86
   MAIN IDEA,DETAILS,SEQUENCE 13    11/13      85
   AUTHOR'S PURP:INFORM,ENT,PER 3   1/3       33
   ELEMENTS OF A STORY      4        4/4      100
   CAUSE & EFFECT           4        4/4      100
   READING COMPREHENSION           41/48      85

   SUBTEST AVG                     41/48      85

GRADE 3 MATHEMATICS
   ROUTINE PROBS/+,-,X,DIV  3        3/3      100
   NON-ROUTINE PROBS        3        2/3       67
   PROBS IN CONTEXT,ALL STRANDS 3   3/3      100
   PROBLEM SOLVING                  8/9       89

   EQUATION/UNKNOWN, INTUITIVE 3    3/3      100
   ALGEBRAIC REASONING              3/3      100

   ESTIMATION/TIME, $, TEMP   3      3/3      100
   ESTIMATION                       3/3      100

   + & - 1&2-DIGIT NOS, + 3-DIG 6   6/6      100
   ORDER NUMBERS FROM 1-1000 3      3/3      100
   MULT,DIV/THINKING STRATEGIES 5   5/5      100
   FRACTIONAL RELATIONSHIPS  3       2/3       67
   # SENSE,CONCEPTS,OPERATIONS      16/17      94

   GEOMETRIC FIGS/PROB SOLV   4      4/4      100
   GEOMETRIC TRANSFORMATIONS  2      1/2       50
   GEOMETRY & SPATIAL SENSE         5/6       83

   SELECTS UNITS OF MEASURE   3      3/3      100
   TIME,TEMP,LENGTH,$/PROBS   4      4/4      100
   MEASUREMENT                      7/7      100

   ORG DATA IN GRAPHS,DIAGRAMS 3    3/3      100
   PREDICTION OF TWO EVENTS   3      3/3      100
   DATA (STATS,PROB,GRAPHING)       6/6      100

   SUBTEST AVG                     48/51      94

              BATCH XXXXXX-XXXX        ID NUMBER   XXXXXXXXX
              TEST DATE: 04/10/98      CODED INFO 1.........
              RUN DATE:  05/26/98      XXXX  XXX
```

FIGURE 13.3. Sample OCAT score report

effective. If a number of students perform poorly on a test, or on a particular section of a test, it could be that the teacher tried to teach material that the students were not yet ready to learn. Or the teacher might have used ineffective teaching methods. Teachers can use this information to modify their learning outcomes and their instructional methods (Gronlund, 1998).

Tests Used for Selection and Placement Decisions

Some educational institutions offer admission only to select individuals (e.g., magnet schools, some private secondary schools, colleges and universities, graduate and professional schools). Likewise, some educational institutions offer special programs for students once they attend that institution (e.g., gifted learning programs, English as a Second Language programs, honors degree programs). Some institutions even offer students the opportunity to place into different levels of a course (e.g., Math 101 instead of Math 100; German 200 instead of German 100). Administrators and testing specialists are often responsible for deciding who will be selected for admittance to educational institutions and who will be selected for and benefit from specific programs or classes within educational institutions.

Although teachers often use teacher-made tests to make decisions in the classroom, administrators and testing specialists often use standardized tests of achievement, aptitude, and intelligence to make such selection and placement decisions.

Tests Used for Selection Decisions

As part of the admissions application process, some educational institutions (i.e., some private secondary schools, most colleges and universities, and most graduate and professional schools) require students to submit standardized test scores along with an application for admission. Although admissions testing is sometimes controversial, many institutions use these test scores to predict how successful a student will be at the institution. Most colleges and universities require students to submit their scores on an aptitude test. In addition to this, some colleges and universities require students to submit their scores on one or more achievement tests.

At the very least, undergraduate colleges and universities typically require undergraduate applicants to submit their scores for these tests:

- The Scholastic Assessment Test (SAT I) or the American College Test (ACT)

Graduate schools often require students to submit their scores for this test:

- The Graduate Record Exam (GRE)

Professional schools typically require students to submit their scores for one of these tests:

- The Medical School Admission Test (MCAT) (for application to medical school)
- The Law School Admission Test (LSAT) (for application to law school)
- The Dental Admission Test (DAT) (for application to dental school)
- The Graduate Management Admission Test (GMAT) (for application to a master's in Business Administration)
- The Optometry Admission Test (OAT) (for application to schools of optometry)
- The Pharmacy College Admission Test (PCAT) (for admission to schools of pharmacy)
- The Veterinary Admission Test (VAT) (for admission to schools of veterinary medicine)

For Your Information 13.3 highlights the Scholastic Assessment Test (SAT). For Your Information 13.4 discusses the differences between the SAT and the

DESCRIPTIVE INFORMATION

Title: Scholastic Assessment Test (SAT)
Author: Educational Testing Service (ETS)
Publisher: College Board
Publication date: Updated in 1994

PURPOSE AND NATURE OF TEST

The Scholastic Assessment Test (SAT) has several purposes, but it is most widely known for its use in the college admissions process. Because SAT scores are thought to predict who will perform well in college, many colleges and universities require applicants to submit their SAT scores as a part of their admissions application. Colleges use this information, along with other information, such as high school curriculum, high school grade point average, extracurricular activities, counselor recommendations, and writing samples, to make admissions decisions. The SAT is taken by approximately 2 million college-bound high school students each year during the spring of their junior year.

The Scholastic Assessment Test used to be called the Scholastic Aptitude Test. Its name was changed in the early 1990s to reflect the fact that it now measures a wider range of skills and knowledge than previously and because it was thought to be valuable for more than predicting success in college courses. For instance, the SAT is now sometimes used by job counselors to help students plan their future after graduation from high school and to help professionals advise students about an appropriate course of study in college.

HISTORICAL ANTECEDENTS

The Original SAT

The SAT was first introduced in 1926. For approximately 90 years, the SAT was a three-hour test divided into a Verbal section and a Mathematics section. The Verbal section consisted of an Analogies part and an Antonyms part (both of which measured a student's vocabulary knowledge), a Reading Comprehension part (involving reading passages containing subject material from a variety of academic areas, such as science, social studies, and the humanities), and a Sentence Completion part (involving single sentences or paragraphs in which one or two words had been replaced with blanks, the examinee's task being to select the choice that best completes the written thought).

The Mathematics section of the SAT assessed the understanding and application of mathematical principles, as well as numerical reasoning ability. The subject matter of the test questions on this section assumed knowledge of basic arithmetic operations such as addition, subtraction, multiplication, division, averages, percentages, odd/even integers, and geometric and algebraic concepts, including linear and quadratic equations, exponents, and factoring.

The Revised SAT

In March 1994 the ETS introduced an updated SAT that was thought to better asses the academic skills, knowledge, and abilities (KSAs) students need in the college classroom. The test now consists of what is referred to as the SAT I: Reasoning Tests and the SAT II: Subject Tests. The SAT I: Reasoning Tests consist of a mathematics section and a verbal section. Both sections are aptitude tests that measure general verbal and mathematical abilities students have developed over many years.

In addition to a change in name, the 1994 revision introduced a number of major changes to the content of the SAT I and SAT II.

The SAT 1: Reasoning Test

Verbal section. There were various changes to the verbal section. The antonym sections were dropped, and more emphasis was placed on having students read and answer more questions from more challenging and longer reading passages. In the verbal section, students are now given 75 minutes to answer 19 sentence-completion questions, 19 analogy questions, and 40 questions from four reading passages.

Math section. There were also various changes to the math section. More open-ended mathematics questions were added. These questions now require students to create their own answers instead of choosing from multiple-choice answers. There is now more emphasis on students' ability to apply mathematical concepts and interpret data. Students can now use calculators. For the mathematics section, students are given 75 minutes to solve 15 quantitative comparison problems, to answer 35 multiple-choice problems, and to create their own answers to 10 additional questions.

Overall, the number of questions on the SAT I decreased, but the overall time to answer questions increased. On the verbal section and the math section, possible scores range from 200 to 800 points. The standardized sample (norm group) has a mean of 500 and a standard deviation of 100.

In addition to its standard questions, the SAT I test typically contains a separate experimental section, either verbal or mathematics. Student performance on the experimental section is not used to calculate a student's score. Rather, the experimental section is used to refine questions to be added to future versions of the SAT.

The SAT II Subject Tests

The SAT II Subject Specific Tests, previously called achievement tests, were renamed the SAT II Subject Tests. Many undergraduate institutions require applicants to sumbit SAT II Subject Test scores along with their SAT I scores as a part of their admissions application. There are approximately 17 subject tests. Each is designed to measure a students' knowledge of a particular subject (e.g. English, psychology). The SAT II Subject Tests now include a writing test that requires students to produce an impromptu draft of an essay. Not all students take one or more of the achievement tests.

PSYCHOMETRIC PROPERTIES

Historically, women have scored higher on the verbal section of the SAT and men have scored higher on the math section. Now, men are outscoring women on both sections and the gap between men's and women's scores on the math section continues to widen. Because men are now outscoring women on both sections, people have begun questioning the validity of the SAT in general. Many are also questioning the validity of the SAT for predicting success in college, because even though women tend to score lower on both sections, they have better high school and college freshmen grades.

The National Center for Fair and Open Testing, as well as others, says that the SAT discriminates against women and that this is the reason for this discrepancy in scores (Bracey, 1993). If the SAT does discriminate against women, then it is unfair to use the SAT to make important college admissions decisions and to determine eligibility for scholarships. Fewer qualified women would be admitted to college, and fewer qualified women would be eligible for scholarships.

Several studies have attempted to learn more about SAT scores and performance in college. Wainer and Steinberg (1992) explored the SAT math scores and college grades of 47,000 men and women who were taking similar college courses. They found that women and men had very similar grades in math courses, but women tended to have lower SAT math scores (27 to 67 points lower). This study suggests that the mathematics section of the SAT is less predictive of college success for women than for men.

Although many believe that the SAT discriminates against women, some people believe that the SAT does predict success in college and that women have higher college freshmen grades because women tend to take college courses that award higher grades. Others say that women do better in college because it is easier for them to win the affection of course instructors (Bracey, 1993).

Unfortunately, we don't really know exactly why women are scoring lower on the SAT but receiving higher grades in college. If the SAT does not predict college success to begin with, then its use is overemphasized and its misuse in college admissions and scholarship awarding is detrimental to women because the test underpredicts women's academic performance.

The potential bias of the SAT raises several questions. First, is the SAT worth the millions of dollars families collectively spend on it each year? Can the use of the SAT be justified in the college admissions process and scholarship awarding? We don't yet know the answer to this question. What we do know is that psychological tests are not perfect, but they are one of the best available means (when used with other assessment methods) for measuring a person's achievement and ability.

Nonetheless, because of its questionable use, some colleges are choosing to rely less on the SAT and some have even abandoned its use. Rollins College, a small liberal arts college located in Winter Park, Florida, now provides students with the option of submitting a "portfolio" instead of SAT scores.

It used to be that colleges and universities stipulated which college admissions test they would accept (the SAT or the ACT). Colleges and universities on the West and East Coasts as well as those in the Northeast typically required the SAT. Colleges and universities in the Midwest typically required the ACT. Today, most colleges and universities will accept either test (Stafford, 1998). Given this information, it makes sense that college-bound high schools students should take both the SAT and ACT and submit the test that they score best on. However, for various reasons not all college-bound students are able to take both tests. At the least, college-bound students should realize that the test they choose can dramatically affect their chances for admission to a college or university, because the SAT and ACT measure different skills. Depending on their skills, a student might perform better on the SAT than on the ACT, or vice versa.

According to Kaplan Educational Centers (1998) and Stafford (1998) the ACT and SAT reward different attributes, so what test a high school student takes should depend on what type of test taker they are.

THE ACT

- Measures academic achievement
- Includes four sections: reading, writing, math, and science
- Includes trigonometry
- Measures vocabulary
- Is entirely multiple choice
- Does not have a guessing penalty
- Measures English grammar

THE SAT

- Measures ability or intelligence
- Includes two sections: verbal and mathematical reasoning
- Does not include trigonometry
- Measures more vocabulary
- Is not entirely multiple choice
- Has a guessing penalty
- Does not measure English grammar

ACT. For Your Information 13.5 highlights the GRE, a test most graduate school applicants take as a part of the graduate school admissions process.

Tests Used for Placement Decisions

Before placing students into special programs, such as a gifted program, a remedial program, or an English as a Second Language program, most educational institutions require the students to take standardized tests. In many cases, the results of these achievement, aptitude, or intelligence tests are used along with other evaluative information to determine if an individual would benefit from the program. For example, educators might use the results of achievement tests along with general classroom performance to place a student in a gifted or honors program.

Before placing students in some courses (e.g., Math 101 instead of Math 100), some educational institutions require that the students take placement tests. For example, college educators might use the results of a standardized test of math achievement along with a student's performance in high school math courses to place a student in the appropriate college-level math course.

Tests Used for Counseling and Guidance Decisions

At one time or another, most of us have asked ourselves one more of the following questions: "Should I go to college?" "What should I major in?" "What career

DESCRIPTIVE
INFORMATION

Title: Graduate Record
               Exam
Author: Educational Testing
               Service (ETS)
Publisher: Educational Testing
               Service

PURPOSE AND NATURE
OF TEST

The Graduate Record Exam
(GRE) is a group of standardized
multiple-choice tests used by many graduate schools
as part of the admissions process. The GRE General
Test is available in pencil-and-paper form as well as
on the computer. The GRE General test currently
measures verbal, quantitative (math), and analytical
skills. Beginning in 1999, the Educational Testing
Service has plans to make this three part test a five
part test which will include, (1) verbal reasoning, (2)
quantitative reasoning, (3) analytical reasoning, (4)
mathematical reasoning, and (5) writing. There are
also various subject tests that measure achievement
in 16 different fields of study. All tests are scored on
a scale from 200 to 800 points.

Prior to 1993, the GRE was only available in
paper-and-pencil form. In 1993, the ETS became
the first national testing organization to offer computerized admissions tests. The computerized ver-

sion of the GRE General Test was
one of the first offered by the ETS.
During the 1994–1995 year, 67,581
people took the computerized version of the GRE General Test.

The more traditional paper-
and-pencil GRE General Test is administered only five times a year.
The computerized version can be
administered more frequently at local test centers. The computerized
version is adaptive and quickly assesses a test-taker's abilities by tai-
loring each question to previous re-
sponses. Test takers receive their scores immediately,
and academic institutions receive scores within 10
days. At this time, the Subject Matter tests are not
available on computer.

The Educational Testing Service anticipates
that the paper-and-pencil version of the GRE General Test will be discontinued by the year 1999.
They anticipate expanding the computer version of
the General Test to five modules: Analytical Reasoning, Mathematical Reasoning, Quantitative
Reasoning, Verbal Reasoning, and Writing. They
believe that this expansion will allow graduate programs to pick and choose scores from a mix of the
modules that most closely match the evaluation criteria and the abilities they require. In the next few
years, many other standardized tests will also become available on the computer.

---

should I pursue?" Psychological tests can play a major role in helping us answer
these questions. Used along with other evaluative information, career counselors
use the results of psychological tests to help individuals understand their interests,
strengths, abilities, and preferences, and translate this information into career
guidance decisions.

For many years people have been using psychological tests to understand vocational interests and make career guidance decisions. The use of tests for this purpose probably began in 1915 when James Miner developed a questionnaire to help
students make vocational choices. However, the first real vocational test was de-

veloped 12 years later by E. K. Strong. In 1927 E. K. Strong developed the first version of his Vocational Interest Blank (SVIB) (Strong, 1927). After another 12 years, in 1939, Kuder developed his first version of the Kuder Preference Record (KPR). As we approach the 21st century, there is a variety of measures of vocational interest available—yet the Strong and Kuder inventories remain two of the most popular.

These are some of the more popular tests for measuring vocational interests:

- Strong Interest Inventory
- Kuder Occupational Interest Survey
- The Career Assessment Inventory
- The Campbell Interest and Skill Survey
- The Jackson Vocational Interest Survey
- The Minnesota Vocational Interest Inventory
- The Self-Directed Search

Tests Used for Program, Curriculum, and Administrative Policy Decisions

Educational administrators are responsible for doing all they can to maintain and improve the quality of our educational system. Of course, administrators must have a way of assessing the quality of the existing system and a way of assessing what would improve the quality of the system. As you would expect, educational administrators use the results of psychological tests, along with other evaluative information, to evaluate and modify educational systems. For example, two schools might use two different math curriculums, and school district administrators might want to know which curriculum fosters greater student learning. At the end of the school year, the district administrators might decide to administer math achievement tests to the students in each curriculum to determine which curriculum is benefiting students the most. The administrators might use the results of the test, along with other information, to determine which program or curriculum should be implemented or dropped. Likewise, district, state, or national educational administrators might use the results of psychological tests and other information to determine where money should be spent (e.g., they might decide to give money to a school to buy more books because their reading scores are low) or what programs should be implemented (e.g., they might decide to start a gifted program because there are a number of students who are scoring in the 99th percentile on the intelligence tests).

NORM-REFERENCED, CRITERION-REFERENCED, AND AUTHENTIC ASSESSMENT OF ACHIEVEMENT

Throughout this chapter we have been discussing how tests are used in the educational setting. All of the tests that are used can be classified as either norm-referenced or criterion-referenced.

- Teachers use psychological tests as placement assessments, formative assessments, and summative assessments.
- When teachers use tests as placement assessments, the tests help them determine if students have the skills or knowledge necessary to understand new material and to determine how much information students already know about new material.
- When teachers use tests as formative assessments, the tests help them determine what information students are and are not learning.
- When teachers use tests as summative assessments, the tests help them determine whether students have achieved what they intended them to and to assign grades.
- Tests can also help motivate students, help students retain and apply information, and help students understand themsleves.
- Tests can also help teachers evaluate the effectiveness of their teaching methods.
- Administrators and testing specialists are often responsible for deciding who will be selected for admittance to educational institutions and who will be selected for and benefit from specific programs or classes within educational institutions.

- Administrators and testing specialists often use standardized tests of achievement, aptitude, and intelligence to help make these selection and placement decisions.
- The most common tests required for undergraduate admission are the SAT and ACT. The most common tests required for graduate and professional school admission are the GRE, MCAT, LSAT, DAT, GMAT, OAT, PCAT, and VAT.
- Career counselors and other testing professionals use psychological tests, along with other information, to help students understand their interests, strengths, abilities, and preferences and translate this information into career guidance decisions.
- The most common tests used by career counselors include the Strong Interest Inventory, Kuder Occupational Interest Survey, Career Assessment Inventory, Campbell Interest and Skill Survey, Jackson Vocational Interest Survey, Minnesota Vocational Interest Inventory, and the Self-Directed Search.
- Educational administrators use psychological tests to make program, curriculum, and administrative policy decisions.

Norm-Referenced Tests

The most common tests are **norm-referenced tests**—standardized tests that have been given to a large representative group of test-takers, whose scores have been used to create norms (recall our discussion of norms in Chapter 5). Educators use norm-referenced tests so they can compare their students' performance to the performance of other students. With norm-referenced tests we can compare a student's performance to the performance of his or her classmates or to students in general. We can compare the performance of students at one school to the performance of students at other schools. We can make statements such as "Mike scored better than 60% of his third-grade classmates on the math achievement test" and "Students at XYZ High School performed better than 70% of schools in the South on the SAT." The Stanford Achievement Test is an example of a norm-referenced test.

Some educators believe that using norm-referenced tests to measure student achievement can be harmful to the educational process. They state that teachers and other educators know what material the norm-referenced tests will measure and that, instead of teaching the subject matter that they should, they will do whatever it takes to improve their students' chances of scoring well—like "teaching to the test" and teaching test-taking skills (Charlesworth, Fleege, & Weitman, 1994).

Criterion-Referenced Tests

295

*CHAPTER 13
Using Tests in
Educational
Settings*

Criterion-referenced tests involve comparing an individual's test scores to an objective standard of achievement, such as being able to multiply numbers. Criterion-referenced tests allow us to measure a student's level of knowledge and identify what area needs more attention.

Criterion-referenced tests allow us to make statements such as "Michelle has learned 50% of the material she needs to know to demonstrate proficiency in third-grade mathematics," and "Michelle still needs to work on her multiplication." Many teacher-made classroom tests are criterion-referenced tests.

Many educators believe that criterion-referenced tests are more useful to students and teachers than norm-referenced tests because, instead of comparing a student's performance to that of other students, criterion-referenced tests help identify how much material a student has learned and what the student must still learn.

Authentic Assessment

Despite their efficiency and ease of scoring, norm- and criterion-referenced tests are criticized as being too structured and often containing only true/false or multiple-choice questions. Elliot (1991) says that we need to measure what is important, not what we can measure using multiple-choice questions. Others contend that we should focus on assessing students' abilities to perform "real-life" tasks such as solving problems (Gronlund, 1998).

According to some educators, authentic assessment does just this. **Authentic assessment** focuses on a student's ability to apply what he or she has learned in real-world settings. Authentic assessment is now becoming more popular in educational settings (Wiggins, 1993). Proponents of authentic assessment believe that students acquire their knowledge in order to produce a product and their performance should be evaluated as such. Authentic assessment relies on more than one measure of performance, is criterion-referenced, and relies on human judgment. One authentic assessment method would be to have students perform tasks. For example, to measure a student's knowledge of validity, a teacher might require the student to give an oral report on the validity of a particular test or ask the student to design some tests of validity. To measure a student's level of mathematics knowledge, a teacher might require the student to keep a notebook with the solutions to math problems or to answer open-ended math problems. Another authentic assessment method would be to have students create portfolios.

A **portfolio** is a selection of an individual's work that is completed over time (Kubiszyn & Borich, 1996). Portfolios have been used for years by artists, photographers, writers, models, as well as others to display samples of their work; the use of portfolios in the educational setting is relatively new. A growing number of educators believe that a single test is not a good measure of an individual's ability or knowledge, so portfolios are now being used by college admissions offices as a method of making admissions decisions.

Because portfolios include a collection of work, they can tell a story about an individual (Paulson & Paulson, 1991). Portfolios might include observations of a student's behavior (e.g., observing a student forming a sculpture), the results of specific projects (e.g., research reports, scrapbooks), or other items selected by the individual that reflect what the individual has learned (e.g., photographs, sculptures, videotapes, reports, models, narratives, musical scores), as well as other information.

The use of portfolios in college admissions is reforming how admissions offices evaluate candidates. For example, Rollins College recognizes that not all students perform well on standardized tests and recognizes that students have other "intelligences" than those assessed on standardized tests of aptitude and achievement. Therefore, Rollins does not require students to submit standardized test scores in order to be considered for admission (approximately 6% of Rollins's applicants choose this option). Instead, students may submit a personal portfolio and a graded writing sample. Some portfolios consist of theatrical performances and musical scores, some consist of slides of photography and sculptures, some consist of scrapbooks of community service involvement. However, although Rollins, like other institutions of higher education, allows students to submit portfolios in lieu of standardized test scores for admission consideration, they do not yet award academic merit scholarships unless standardized test scores are submitted.

Despite their numerous advantages, portfolios are time consuming to maintain and to evaluate. As with any evaluation (e.g., a teacher-made test, a standardized test), we must have established criteria for evaluating portfolios. The criteria should address what type of performance educators are willing to accept as evidence that the students are displaying the intended learning outcomes and that the students are displaying work that truly shows their ability. These criteria can then be used to prepare rating scales or scoring rules to be used in evaluating the portfolio.

Some educators claim that authentic testing is fairer and a better measure of student achievement. Other educators do not support authentic assessments because the reliability and validity of authentic assessment is unknown (Terwilliger, 1996) and because the large-scale testing typically done by school systems is impractical with authentic assessment. More research is necessary to determine which type of testing is best for measuring student achievement and ability.

Gronlund (1998) agrees that if you want to know whether a student can write, have the student write something. This will help you determine whether the student can perform the task. Gronlund argues that an emphasis on such types of as-

---

Summary Box 13.3
Norm-Referenced, Criterion-Referenced, and Authentic Assessment of Achievement

- Most of the psychological tests used in educational settings can be classified as either norm-referenced or criterion-referenced.
- The most common tests are norm-referenced.
- Educators use norm-referenced tests so they can compare their students' performance to the performance of other students.
- Educators use criterion-referenced tests so that they can compare their students' performance to an objective standard of achievement, such as being able to multiply numbers.
- Many educators believe that criterion-referenced tests are more useful to students and teachers than

norm-referenced tests because, instead of comparing a student's performance to that of other students, criterion-referenced tests help identify how much material a student has learned and what the student must still learn.
- Some people believe that norm- and criterion-referenced tests are too structured and that instead authentic assessment should be used.
- Authentic assessment focuses on a student's ability to apply what she or he has learned in real-world settings and involves looking at an assortment of a student's products.

sessment would improve the assessment of learning outcomes, but that other types of tests should not be forgotten because they too play an important role. According to Gronlund (1998), there is a knowledge component to most of what we do. To be a good writer, we must have a good knowledge of vocabulary, grammar, and spelling. A writing task does not always sample these knowledges well because it is easy for us to hide our inabilities. When we write, it is easy for us to use only those words we know, write only those sentences that are easy for us to punctuate, and use only the words we are sure how to spell. Gronlund (1998) recommends we measure achievement using paper-and-pencil tests and performance assessments.

SUMMARY

Teachers, specialists, and administrators use psychological tests to help them make decisions about instruction, selection and placement, counseling and guidance, and program, curriculum, and administrative policy. The decisions they make range from deciding what information students already know to deciding what new programs should be implemented in the school system.

During the instructional process, teachers use psychological tests as placement assessments (to determine if student's are ready to learn new material and to determine how much of the material they already know); formative assessments (to determine what information students are and are not learning); diagnostic assessments (to more thoroughly determine a student's learning difficulty); and summative asessment (to determine what students have learned and to assign grades). In the classroom, psychological tests can also help motivate students, help students retain and transfer what they have learned, help students understand their strengths and weaknesss, and provide teachers with information regarding the effect of their teaching methods.

Administrators and testing specialists use psychological tests to make selection and placement decisions. Selection and placement decisions are typically made using standardized tests of achievement, aptitude, and intelligence. Some private secondary schools and most undergraduate and graduate colleges and universities require applicants to submit standardized test scores as a part of the admissions application. Specialists and administrators use these scores, along with other information, to make admissions decisions.

Many of these same institutions use standardized test scores to place students into programs once they are at the institution. For example, a school might use the results of an intelligence test along with general classroom performance to place a student in a gifted or honors program.

Career counselors use the results of psychological tests, along with other information, to help individuals understand their interests, abilities, and preferences and determine what college majors and careers they should consider.

Educational administrators also use psychological tests to maintain and improve the quality of the educational system. They might use the results of tests to select the best curriculum for a school and to determine where funds should be directed.

Many different psychological tests are used in the educational setting. Most are either norm-referenced or criterion-referenced. Norm-referenced tests are the most common. These standardized tests have been normed on a large representative group of test-takers, whose scores are used to establish the norms to which individual scores are compared. Sometimes individual scores are compared to the scores of classmates, to other students in the same county, or to students in general. Criterion-referenced tests involve comparing an individual's score to an objectively stated standard of achievement.

There are positives and negatives associated with both norm-referenced and criterion-referenced tests. Some educators believe that norm- and criterion-referenced tests do not measure what is important in real life. Many believe that authentic assessment does just this. Authentic assessment involves evaluating a student's ability to apply information to real-world settings. Authentic assessment often requires students to perform tasks and create portfolios. Not everyone agrees with authentic assessment. Some believe that the reliability and validity is unknown and it is impractical to do large-scale authentic testing in the school systems.

KEY CONCEPTS

administrative policy
   decisions
authentic assessment
counseling and guidance
   decisions
criterion-referenced tests
diagnostic assessment

diagnostic decisions
formative assessment
grading decisions
instructional decisions
norm-referenced tests
placement assessment
placement decisions

portfolio
program and curriculum
   decisions
selection decisions
summative assessment

LEARNING ACTIVITIES

1. Interview two college professors (perhaps one psychology professor and one physics professor). Ask them how many tests they typically administer per year. Find out how they construct their tests. Also find out if they feel it is important to know about the principles of testing—and why or why not.
2. Interview an elementary school teacher and find out what tests they typically administer during the school year. What do they use the results of these tests for? Identify whether these tests are being used for placement, formative, diagnostic, or summative assessments.
3. Go to your career services office and tell them you would like to know more about the methods they use to help college students explore potential career opportunities. Perhaps they will go through the process with you.
4. Call the Department of Education and see if you can find out how they have used the results of tests administered in the school systems in your county to make program, curriculum, or administrative policy decisions.

Using Tests in Clinical and Counseling Settings

"What is the difference between a clinical psychologist and a counselor? Don't they both do the same thing?"

"My cousin was in a car accident and later she was examined by a neuropsychologist. Does that mean she has brain damage?"

"How do psychologists evaluate infants and children?"

"My professor says that neuropsychological testing is an up-and-coming specialty in the field of psychology. What type of tests do neuropsychologists use?"

"The school psychologist tested my son by asking him to draw a house, a tree, and a person. He concluded that my son has emotional problems. Is this an appropriate way to diagnose children?"

In this chapter, we discuss the role of psychological testing and assessment in the fields of clinical psychology and counseling. We describe the use of assessment in clinical practice in terms of three models: the information-gathering model, the therapeutic model, and differential treatment model. We also discuss the clinical interview, tests for personality, projective techniques, neuropsychological tests, and tests for clinical disorders, such as depression and anxiety.

CLINICAL ASSESSMENT AND PSYCHOLOGICAL TESTING

In Chapter 1 we discussed the difference between psychological testing and assessment: Both are methods for collecting information, but assessment is broader than psychological testing—psychological tests are only one tool in the assessment process. Psychological testing has to do with the instrumentation part of assessment—using psychometric tools for information gathering. For example, a clinical psychologist might conduct a psychological assessment of a client and as a part of this assessment might administer a psychological test (for example, the MMPI).

More specifically defined, **clinical assessment** includes a broad set of information-gathering and interpretive skills used by the professional counselor-therapist. According to one clinical practitioner, "without clinical assessment, the counselor-therapist is . . . reduced to being no more (and no less) than a social helper" (Woody, 1972, p. 1). Clinical assessment, according to Woody (1972), includes the therapist's initial reaction to the client, the decision to accept the client, the services and techniques offered, the decision to end the intervention, an assessment of the effectiveness of the intervention, and its relevance to serving future clients.

In this chapter, we focus on the types of assessment that involve psychometric instruments for diagnosing and intervening with clients. These tests fall into four basic categories: interviews, observation, objective tests, and projective tests (Dana, 1986). We begin, however, with three models of how psychological assessment is used by clinicians and counselors.

Major changes are taking place in the field of mental health and psychological assessment. Managed care is playing a larger role in shaping the diagnosis and treatment of individuals than ever before in the history of clinical psychology and counseling. One of the basic tenets of managed care is the demand for greater accountability. Another influence of managed care is the reluctance to provide long-term psychological interventions or counseling. According to this outlook, clients during a short intervention should develop a new perspective and acquire behaviors or coping skills that enable effective problem solving during a short-term program. Unfortunately, such interventions are not always successful (Butcher, 1997).

There is also disagreement between practitioners and managed care providers about the role of psychological assessment. Practitioners have noted a decrease in the clinical use of psychological testing, because managed care organizations are reluctant to pay for extensive assessment (Finn & Tonsager, 1997). On the other hand, Butcher (1997) suggests that the primary tool the clinician or counselor can use to prevent or counterbalance problems in short-term interventions is the use of psychological assessment to obtain a clear picture of the client's diagnosis, personal attributes, and amenity to treatment.

Psychological assessment has a long history in the field of mental health. Its roles have varied as approaches to the treatment and prevention of mental disorders have altered and evolved. Finn and Tonsager (1997) define the use of assessment in clinical practice in terms of three models: the information-gathering model, the therapeutic model, and differential treatment model.

The Information-Gathering Model of Assessment

When assessment is used primarily as a way to gather information to make a diagnosis and facilitate communication, the practitioner is using the **information-gathering model** of assessment. In this model, tests provide standardized comparison with others and allow the assessor to make predictions about the client's behavior outside the assessment setting. In addition, test results provide a baseline that the clinician or counselor can use to identify disorders and design an individualized treatment program. For Your Information 14.1 provides an example of the information-gathering model using the case study for Mrs. M (Haynes, Leisen, & Blaine, 1997), who suffered from recurrent headaches and sleep problems.

The Therapeutic Model of Assessment

Another model is the **therapeutic model** of assessment. In this model, the goal of the therapeutic assessment is to provide a new experience and new information that clients can use to make changes in their lives. The practitioner uses the assessment information to encourage self-discovery and growth. The process of assessment and the resulting dialogue it guides become an intervention for positive change. This model evolved during the humanistic movement of the 1950s and 1960s. Although some humanists strongly objected to testing and considered psychological assessment dehumanizing, others believed that assessment, when properly used, provides a valuable tool for facilitating growth and insight.

Treatment programs that involve behavioral interventions, such as desensitization or establishing schedules of reinforcement, usually differ among clients even though the clients have the same behavior problems. Psychological assessment provides an important tool for designing such behavioral interventions. The case of Mrs. M shows how clinical tests provide diagnostic information for the practitioner. Using assessment for diagnosis is an example of the information-gathering model of assessment.

Mrs. M was 35 years old, married, and the mother of a 12-year-old son. A neurologist referred Mrs. M to a behavioral practitioner because she was experiencing frequent headaches and problems sleeping. The neurologist referred Mrs. M for behavioral therapy instead of medication because Mrs. M was 28 weeks pregnant.

The practitioner gathered information regarding Mrs. M's problem in two assessment sessions. In the first session, Mrs. M was given an unstructured interview to determine the range of her concerns. In that interview, Mrs. M reported that she and her husband were having frequent arguments, usually about the discipline of their son. Mrs. M was interviewed regarding her headaches and sleep problems. She reported that over the last 3 years her headaches had become more frequent and severe. At the time of her first session, she was experiencing severe headaches daily that lasted 2 to 4 hours. She also reported that her husband was more helpful and attentive when she had a headache and she feared his helpfulness would lessen if her headaches improved. She recalled that her sleep problems started about the same time as her headaches. Her symptoms included taking about an hour to fall asleep and her sleep was fragmented and shallow with frequent awakenings.

Between the first and second assessment sessions, Mrs. M was asked to quantify her behavior problems by rating her headaches each hour on a 5-point scale (0 = *no headache;* 5 = *very severe headache*). She also kept a sleep diary in which she recorded time taken to fall asleep, number of nightly wakings, amount of sleep lost, and time of waking in the morning. Mr. and Mrs. M also completed the Dyadic Adjustment Scale (Spanier, 1976) to assess marital adjustment, the Spouse Verbal Problem Checklist (Carter & Thomas, 1973) to assess satisfaction with communications, and a martial attitudes questionnaire.

Based on information gathered in the first assessment session, Mrs. M's marital relationship was identified as an important concern and possibly linked to her headaches and sleep problems. Therefore, both Mr. and Mrs. M completed assessments in the second session.

The data gathered by Mrs. M on her headaches and sleep agreed with what she reported in her interview. She had experienced no headache-free hours during the previous week and her sleep was interrupted 2 to 5 times nightly. Scores on the Marital Satisfaction Questionnaire placed Mr. M within the satisfied range. Mrs. M indicated dissatisfaction with the marital relationship. Scores on the Spouse Verbal Problem Checklist indicated that both perceived communication problems, although their explanations of the problems were different.

Since depression is often associated with chronic pain and sleep disturbance, Mr. and Mrs. M completed the Beck Depression Inventory (Beck, Steer, & Garbin, 1988). Mr. M's score was well within the nondepressed range. Mrs. M's score indicated mild depression, but her responses showed her depression to be related to pain rather than mood or cognitive concerns.

In this session, Mr. M was also given an unstructured interview to determine his perceptions of marital difficulties, and both were given a semistructured interview regarding behaviors and methods to improve the relationship. The couple was also asked to discuss for 10 minutes a topic that caused arguments at home. This discussion was audiotaped and two assessors independently rated the couple's interactions using the Marital Interaction Coding System (Weiss & Heyman, 1990). This behavioral assessment indicated high rates of positive and negative statements by Mrs. M, mostly negative statements by Mr. M, and low rates of problem solving by both.

Based on the data gathered in the two assessment sessions and at home by Mrs. M, the practitioner concluded that Mrs. M's headaches and sleep disturbance were probably caused by distress with her marital relationship. Furthermore, the data indicated that general communication problems, rather than child management issues, were contributing to her marital distress.

In cases like those of Mrs. M, psychological assessment in the form of interviews and objective tests provides important information, such as underlying problems and contextual issues. This informa-

tion allows the practitioner to design an intervention or treatment program that addresses the root causes of behavioral problems instead of symptomatic issues.

Source: Adapted from Haynes, Leisen, & Blaine (1997).

For Your Information 14.2 shows how test results can be used as part of an intervention, an example of the therapeutic model. It relates the case study of Mrs. P (Shore, 1972) who was suffering from postpartum depression.

The Differential Treatment Model of Assessment

Finally, psychological tests can be used to conduct research or to evaluate program outcomes. Tests can provide definitive answers about whether clients as a group have responded positively to a particular therapy or intervention. Using assessment for research purposes is called the **differential treatment model** of assessment. This research model requires tests that have evidence of high reliability and validity related to the research purpose.

One example of the differential treatment model is a study by Negy and Snyder (1997) that compared the marriage satisfaction of 75 Mexican American couples and 66 non-Hispanic White American Couples. All couples lived in the same geographic region of the southwestern United States. The researchers' analyses suggested somewhat higher levels of relationship distress for the Mexican-American couples when compared to the non-Hispanic couples. These group differences disappeared, however, when demographic variables, such as education, were controlled. This comparison allowed researchers to draw conclusions about the effects of acculturation on the marriage satisfaction of Mexican American couples.

The differential treatment model also applies to pre- and posttest research designs. In these diagrams, a group of clients is given a psychological test before and after an intervention to determine whether the intervention was successful in changing behavior or attitudes. For instance, Boy Scouts and Girls Scouts completed the Personal Attribute Inventory for Children (Parish & Taylor, 1978a, 1978b), a measure of attitudes toward handicaps and handicapped persons. The scouts were then assigned to five experimental groups and a control group. The scouts in the experimental groups interacted socially with a handicapped child one-hour per week. The control group had no contact with handicapped children. At the end of six weeks, all scouts again completed the Personal Attribute Inventory. Five out of the six experimental groups showed an increase in favorable attitudes toward the handicapped when compared to the control group (Newberry & Parish, 1987).

Mrs. P was 32 years old and hospitalized for post-partum depression following the birth of her second child. She had many fears and phobias, particularly of dirt and contamination that she could not control. She acted helpless and inadequate. For instance, she often burned food when she cooked.

Mrs. P's history revealed she was born premature and there was a question of whether she would survive. Psychological tests at the time of her admission showed clear signs of organic brain damage that had not been detected before. During her lifetime, Mrs. P had developed an attitude of helplessness and inadequacy, and she required the support of others for most tasks.

When the test results were given to Mrs. P, she was told that she had a number of strengths as well as certain limitations. In other words, it was clear that she had the ability to do certain things she was not doing. Her therapist told her she would be expected to begin doing the things she could do.

Mrs. P resisted the therapist's interpretation, and she maintained that the tests were inaccurate. The therapist, however, constantly pointed out what she was doing and using the test results supported her efforts to become more self-sufficient.

A remarkable change took place. Mrs. P began entertaining friends and accepting responsibility she would have formerly avoided.

Source: Adapted from Shore (1972).

Roles of the Clinician and the Counselor

Traditionally, clinical psychologists and counselors have approached the assessment of clients from different perspectives. According to Hohenshil (1996), many counselors believe that the primary difference between counseling and clinical psychology or psychiatry is that counselors provide services for those with normal developmental problems, such as marital, career, or school adjustment problems, whereas clinical psychologists and psychiatrists (medical doctors who specialize in mental illness) treat those who exhibit abnormal behavior, mental disorders, or emotional disabilities. In practice, however, these roles are often blurred or overlapping.

For both counselors and clinicians, psychological testing provides important information for providing services to clients. In terms of Finn and Tonsager's (1997) three models, counselors are more apt to subscribe to the therapeutic model. Campbell (1990) states that the "major focus of test use in counseling is the test taker, who 'is viewed as the primary user of the test results.' " (p. 1). In contrast, clinical psychologists might be predisposed to use the information-gathering model. In this model, the clinician is the primary user of the test results, which provide the basis for identifying a diagnosis and designing an intervention.

The next section describes how clinical psychologist and counselors use psychological tests to make diagnoses and carry out interventions.

TESTS USED FOR DIAGNOSIS AND INTERVENTION

Diagnosis is the meaning or interpretation that the assessor derives from the information-gathering process of assessment (Hohenshil, 1996). In other words, diagnosis is the identification of the client's problem or disorder. The process of arriving at a diagnosis is often called **screening.** As you can see from the case of Mrs. M, diagnosis can result in identifying a group of symptoms and relating them to a classification system such as the *Diagnostic and Statistical Manual of Mental Disorders,* fourth edition *(DSM-IV)* (American Psychiatric Association, 1994). For Your Information 14.3 introduces the *DSM-IV* and provides a brief overview of its use by health care professionals. Alternatively, a diagnosis might be an informal statement of a client's needs. For instance, a career counselor might conclude from assessment information that a client is having difficulty making career decisions because she has little knowledge of her own aptitudes and values.

Whether the assessor's goal is to treat a mental disorder or to improve the client's quality of life, the diagnosis leads to the design or selection of an intervention technique or treatment plan to alleviate unwanted behaviors or symptoms or solve the client's problem.

The Clinical Interview

Most practitioners use the **clinical interview** as a primary tool for gathering information about the client. The clinical interview involves a discussion between the client and the assessor—often a clinical psychologist or counselor—in which the assessor observes the client and gathers information about the client's symptoms or problems. A **structured clinical interview** has a predetermined set of questions for the client to answer. The assessor might then assign numbers or scores to the answers based on their content. The assessor uses these scores to arrive at a diagnosis. An unstructured or **nondirective clinical interview,** on the other hand, has few predetermined questions. Instead, the assessor's questions are more likely to be determined by the client's responses. Most clinical interviews are nondirective and unstructured (Murphy & Davidshofer, 1994).

The **semistructured interview** provides a compromise between the structured interview and the nondirective interview. The semistructured interview contains a list of predetermined questions based on the construct being measured. However, the format also allows the assessor to ask some open-ended questions and to ask follow-up questions to clarify the interviewee's responses.

According to Geertsma (1972), the strength of the nondirective interview is its flexibility, which permits the interviewer to respond to the client's responses and behavior. The assumption in using the traditional interview is that the client will

Have you ever heard terms such as *mental retardation, learning disorder, delirium* or *dementia* and wondered exactly what they mean? What does it mean when a clinician diagnoses a person as schizophrenic or depressed? Is there really such a thing as a sexual identity disorder or a personality disorder?

Cataloging and classifying the numerous mental disorders that clinicians and researchers have documented is a necessary and perhaps overwhelming task. In fact, ever since physicians began to diagnose disorders of the psyche or mind, there have been schemes to catalog and define them.

A first attempt in recent times to identify and track mental disorders was in the U.S. census of 1840, which recorded the frequency of "idiocy/insanity." In the 1880 census, mental illness was distinguished by seven classifications—mania, melancholia, monomania, paresis, dementia, dipsomania, and epilepsy. In the following years, the U.S. Bureau of the Census and the U.S. Army in collaboration with the organization now known as the American Psychiatric Association made several attempts to construct a classification system for identifying mental disorders. These classification systems were used mainly for diagnosing patients in mental hospitals.

In 1952, the American Psychiatric Association Committee on Nomenclature and Statistics published the first comprehensive manual of mental disorders—the *Diagnostic and Statistical Manual: Mental Disorders (DSM-I)*—designed to provide explicit definitions for clinical diagnoses. Since then, this manual has undergone three complete revisions. It now provides definitions based on the most recent research in the field of clinical psychology and psychiatry. The current *DSM-IV,* published in 1994, is the result of extensive research by 13 work groups sponsored by the American Psychiatric

Association. The work groups used a three-stage process to identify and classify mental disorders. First, they researched published literature. Next, they reanalyzed already collected sets of data. Finally, they conducted field trials sponsored by organizations such as the National Institute of Mental Health and the National Institute on Drug Abuse.

The *DSM-IV* classifies mental disorders into 17 aggregate categories, each of which has a number of subcategories. These subcategories list specific disorders that are defined by diagnostic features or symptoms as well as behavioral criteria for identifying the disorder. For instance, depression is listed under the aggregate heading of Mood Disorders. The subcategory Depressive Disorders includes Major Depressive Disorder (Single Episode and Recurrent), Dysthymic Disorder (Early Onset/Late Onset and With Atypical Features), and Depressive Disorder Not Otherwise Specified. The manual provides specific information on symptoms, associated features, specific gender, age, and culture features, and specific diagnostic criteria for each disorder. The manual also gives each disorder a unique classification or code number.

The *DSM-IV* was developed for use by persons trained and experienced in clinical diagnosis. These persons might work in clinical, educational, or research settings. The manual's introduction clearly states that the classification system is meant to serve as guidelines for informed clinical judgment. Its diagnostic system is not to be applied in mechanical or strict fashion by untrained persons. The manual and its classification system provide significant resources for professionals who diagnose and develop treatment plans for individuals. It also serves as a basis for constructing criterion measures that can be used to establish validity for psychological tests used in clinical settings.

directly or indirectly present the information that is relevant or necessary for diagnosis. The risk to this approach, pointed out by Murphy and Davidshofer (1994) and others, is that the interviewer could have preconceived notions that influence the direction or outcome of the interview. For instance, **hypothesis confirmation bias** (Darley & Fazio, 1980) suggests that decision-makers form hypotheses about the behavior of others, such as the client, then they search for and elicit information to confirm their hypotheses. Another source of bias is **self-fulfilling prophecy,** a well-documented phenomenon in which the researcher's or interviewer's expectations influence the behavior of respondents and lead them to meet the interviewer's expectations.

307

CHAPTER 14
Using Tests in
Clinical and
Counseling
Settings

The nondirective interview can be divided into three parts: initial, middle, and termination phases (Houck & Hansen, 1972). In the initial phase, the interviewer greets the client and establishes rapport. Next, the interviewer focuses on the client's perception of his or her problem and the set of attitudes and emotions the client advocates and displays. The interviewer gathers observational data by noting facial expressions, eye contact, posture, activity (for example, nervous mannerisms), grooming, and level of responsiveness. Finally, the initial stage includes establishing expectations and goals for the interview, other assessment activities, and the eventual course of treatment.

The middle phase of the nondirective interview focuses on gathering a detailed social and medical history that includes demographic data (occupation, marital status, and so on). The client's coping behaviors (for example, changes in voice tone or posture) can also be observed, because the interview itself is likely to cause some stress and anxiety. In this phase, the interviewer might begin to formulate a hypothesis regarding a diagnosis and make observations and gather information to support or refute the hypothesis. Finally, the interviewer makes a prognosis, an estimation of the length of treatment and the likelihood of a successful outcome. The hypothesis and prognosis are for the assessor's use and are not necessarily shared with the client.

In the termination phase, the interviewer might inquire whether the client has any questions, then after answering all questions, the interviewer briefly summarizes the interview. It is important that the interviewer and client maintain rapport and that the interviewer convey concern and understanding. Further assessment or treatment activities, where appropriate, should be briefly explained and scheduled before ending the interview.

Research on the validity of the nondirective clinical interview (Murphy & Davidshofer, 1994; Wiggins, 1973) suggests that the interview might be more useful in a therapeutic sense than for assessment. For over 50 years, researchers have debated the accuracy of making diagnoses using the unstructured interview (called the clinical method) compared to using structured psychological tests (called the statistical method). In 1954, Meehl published results of his examination of 20 studies that compared clinical and statistical predictions. His conclusion was that statistical methods were as accurate as, and often more accurate than, clinical methods. Subsequent research (Dawes & Corrigan, 1974; Goldberg, 1970; Wiggins, 1973) continues to support Meehl's conclusions.

Structured Personality Tests

Over the years, psychologists have developed many self-report, paper-and-pencil tests to provide a more objective assessment of general personality characteristics. Perhaps the most widely used instrument of this kind is the Minnesota Multiphasic Personality Inventory, described in detail in Chapter 11. Originally published by Hathaway and McKinley in 1943, the test underwent revisions in the 1980s. The revised version—the MMPI-2—was published in 1989. The MMPI-2 contains 10 basic clinical scales (see Chapter 11) that cover a range of personality traits or pre-dispositions. A large number of content scales that measure specific disorders and dispositions have also been published. Interpreting the MMPI requires specialized training and knowledge. Many practitioners use computerized scoring systems that construct profiles and provide basic interpretations by comparing the individual's score to the test norms. Currently, the MMPI-2 is used as a screening and diagnostic tool in most hospitals and mental health settings. It has also been widely used in research on normal and abnormal personality.

Another personality test that is closely related to the MMPI is the California Psychological Inventory (CPI). Gough, the original developer of the CPI, studied with Hathaway at the University of Minnesota. Gough, however, developed the CPI to assess normal individuals. The revised CPI assesses 20 dimensions of interpersonal behavior. The results of a number of studies suggest that the dimensions of the CPI relate closely to the five-factor model of personality (discussed in more detail in Chapter 15) dimensions and can be interpreted in terms of that theory (Bolton, 1992). The CPI is a popular instrument for research on personality. Trained clinicians and counselors also use the CPI for therapeutic and diagnostic purposes.

The NEO Personality Inventory was specifically designed to measure the five-factor model dimensions: neuroticism, extraversion, openness to experience, agreeableness, and conscientiousness. NEO is an acronymn for the three factors that were developed first. Like the CPI, the NEO (discussed in Chapter 1) assesses normal personality traits and, as such, provides an excellent tool for research on personality and behavior. In addition, this test can be appropriate for use by trained clinicians for therapeutic and diagnostic purposes.

Finally, the 16 Personality Factor Questionnaire (16PF) is another test that measures normal personality. This test was designed by Raymond B. Cattell in the 1940s as part of his attempt to identify and measure the fundamental building blocks of personality. The test is widely used today for research and counseling.

Summary Box 14.2
Diagnosing Using the Interview and Structured Personality Tests

- A diagnosis is the definition of a client's problem or disorder, and screening is the process of conducting a psychological assessment to arrive at a diagnosis.
- The clinical interview, in which the practitioner observes and gathers information about the client, is a primary tool for gathering information about the client.
- There are three types of interviews: the structured clinical interview, which has a predetermined set of questions; the nondirective clinical interview, in which the practitioner's questions follow up on the client's responses; and the semistructured interview, in which some questions are predetermined

- but the practitioner also asks follow-up questions based on the client's responses.
- The practitioner who uses the nondirective approach risks two major sources of bias: the hypothesis confirmation bias and self-fulfilling prophecy.
- The nondirective interview might be more useful as an intervention (the therapeutic model) than for diagnosis.
- Practitioners also use standardized personality tests, such as the MMPI-2, the NEO Personality Inventory, and the 16 Personality Questionnaire, to make diagnoses.

Projective Techniques

309

CHAPTER 14
Using Tests in
Clinical and
Counseling
Settings

As we said in Chapters 1 and 9, projective tests require test takers to respond to unstructured or ambiguous stimuli such as incomplete sentences, inkblots, or abstract pictures. In a more general sense, **projective techniques** ask test takers to give meaning to ambiguous stimuli. Often the response requirements are relatively unclear to encourage test takers to create responses that describe the thoughts and emotions they are experiencing. This section presents three types of projective techniques: projective storytelling, projective drawing, and sentence completion.

The idea of projective testing is based on a concept from early Freudian theory. According to psychoanalytic theory, **projection** is a defense mechanism that relieves anxiety by allowing a person to attribute thoughts or emotions to external events or individuals. Later theorists (Rabin, 1986) have suggested that projection is a normal cognitive operation rather than a defense mechanism. In either case, the theoretical concept underlying projective testing assumes that individuals attribute their own thoughts and emotions to others in their environment.

Projective Storytelling

The Rorschach Inkblot Technique and the Thematic Apperception Test (TAT) (discussed in Chapters 1 and 9) are two common examples of **projective storytelling,** tests that require respondents to tell a story. The Swiss psychiatrist Hermann Rorschach (1921) developed the Rorschach in the four years prior to 1921. The test requires test takers to view inkblots and describe to the test examiner objects or people they think the inkblots resemble. For Your Information 14.4 describes the Rorschach Inkblot Technique in more detail.

American psychologists, Henry A. Murray (1943) and C. D. Morgan, developed the Thematic Apperception Test (TAT). This personality test requires test takers to look at pictures and tell stories about each picture. The TAT was originally developed as a tool for therapy (the therapeutic model of assessment) rather than for diagnosis. Although a number of scoring schemes are available for the TAT, none appears to be psychometrically sound enough to warrant the test's use for diagnosis (Worchel & Dupree, 1990). Nonetheless, the TAT remains a popular instrument for training and clinical practice. Figure 14.2 shows a stimulus card from the TAT.

Projective Drawing

Another projective technique is **projective drawing,** in which the assessor directs the test takers to draw their own pictures. Projective drawing is one of the oldest methods of assessment. Florence Goodenough (1926) first used this approach to evaluate children's intelligence. Later theorists and practitioners recognized that emotional factors were also represented in clients' drawings (Hammer, 1958).

Two well-known projective drawing methods are the House-Tree-Person and Draw-A-Person Techniques. These methods, as their names imply, require the test taker to draw houses, trees, or persons. In this case, the "tests" are the stimuli or instructions and the methods and scoring schemes for interpreting the drawings. For Your Information 14.5 describes in more detail the administration and interpretation of the Draw-A-Person technique.

The Rorschach Inkblot Test is a projective personality test that involves showing ambiguous stimuli (inkblots) to an individual and having the individual respond with what he or she sees. Figure 14.1 shows a typical inkblot from the Rorschach Test. Clinical psychologists learn to administer and interpret this test in their doctoral training programs to diagnose personality disorders. The inkblots are sold without a test manual, meaning that the purchaser of the test does not get administration, scoring, or interpretation directions with the test. Instead, there are numerous manuals and handbooks that can be purchased (for example, Exner, 1993; Exner & Weiner, 1982; Piotrowski, 1957). Each contains different systems for administering, scoring, and interpreting the Rorschach Test.

The Rorschach was designed based on the **projective hypothesis**—the hypothesis that when people attempt to understand ambiguous stimuli, their interpretation of the stimulus reflects their personal qualities or characteristics: their needs, feelings, anxieties, inner conflicts, experience, and thought processes. Kaplan and Succuzzo (1997) provide a good example of this rationale. When a scared little boy looks into a dark room and sees a huge shadow and he interprets the shadow as a monster, he is projecting his fear on the shadow. The shadow is neither good nor bad. What the child sees is a reflection of the inner workings of his mind. The Rorschach is thought to tap into deep layers of personality and bring out (through projection) what is not conscious to the test taker. The

FIGURE 14.1. An inkblot from the Rorschach test
Reprinted with permission.

Rorschach can be used for anyone over the age of 3 regardless of their mental ability.

Inkblots were used to understand individuals long before the development of the Rorschach Test. In the late 19th century, when Rorschach was only 10 years old, Alfred Binet suggested that inkblots might be useful in assessing personality. Not much later, in 1910, Whipple published the first set of inkblots. Nonetheless, Herman Rorschach is widely known for developing and publicizing the of use inkblots for identifying psychological disorders.

In 1921, after 10 years of research, Herman Rorschach published his book *Pschodiagnostik,* which provided the rationale for the Rorschach. Rorschach had a number of critics. American psychologists did not readily accept either the test or David Levy, who is known for introducing Rorschach's test to the United States. They believed that the test was scientifically unsound and found little use for it. Nevertheless, the Rorschach Test has become quite popular over the years since its arrival.

This increase in popularity is often attributed to the writings and research of individuals such as Samuel J. Beck, Marguerite Hertz, Bruno Klopfer, and Zygmunt Piotrawski (Exner, 1976). Each developed a different system for administering, scoring, and interpreting the results of the Rorschach. Each administration, scoring, and interpretation system gained its own followers.

The Rorschach consists of 10 cards with symmetrical inkblots. Five are black; two are gray; two contain black, gray, and red; and three are pastel colors of various shades. Rorschach created each inkblot by dripping ink onto a white piece of paper and then folding the paper. This resulted in a totally unique, bilaterally symmetrical picture on a white background. Although Rorschach experimented with thousands of inkblots, he eventually narrowed the set to 10.

The Rorschach is administered to one individual at a time. Each inkblot is shown to the test taker two times, once during a free-association phase and once during an inquiry phase. After providing information about the purpose of the test, the test administrator begins the free-association phase by presenting the test taker with the first of the 10 cards and asking "What might this be?" If the test taker asks for clarification, the administrator gives as little information as possible. If the test taker says that he or she does not see anything, the administrator says something like, "Most people see something here. Just take your time." If the test taker provides only one response, the administrator says something like, "Some people see more than one thing here." The examiner records every word and sound made by the test taker, how long it takes the test taker to respond to the card, and the position of the card when the test taker responds with her or his answer (for example, sideways, right side up, upside down). Either following the free association or in a second round, the administrator will ask questions to identify where the test taker saw the perception.

Although the Rorschach is easy to administer, it has a complex system for scoring and interpreting the results. In most cases the test taker's responses are scored on at least the five following dimensions:

1. *Location:* The location on the blot where the perception was seen (whether the test taker responded to the whole blot, a common or well-defined part of the blot used, or an unusual or poorly defined part of the blot)
2. *Determinants:* What feature of the inkblot determined the response (the shape or outline of the blot, perceived movement, color, texture, shading)
3. *Form quality:* The extent to which the perception matched the stimulus properties of the inkblot (well, poorly)
4. *Content:* What was perceived (human, animal, nature)
5. *Frequency of occurrence:* To what extent the response was original or similar to that given by others.

The scoring of these dimensions provides quantitative information about the test taker's responses. This quantitative information provides data on the individual's personality as well as information for developing norms for particular groups. If the test taker deviates from typical performance, then the administrator must decide why the test taker responded differently from most people. The Rorschach also gathers qualitative information about test takers. As you can see, scoring becomes difficult and complex. Today, there is a variety of computer software available to help score and interpret the Rorschach. Interpretation of the test results, however, requires advanced graduate training and supervision. Exner (1993) and Exner and Weiner (1982) provide more detailed information on scoring.

The Rorschach is a popular psychological test even though its psychometric properties have been criticized for years. A perception of low reliability and low validity can be attributed to the lack of a universally accepted method for administering and scoring the Rorschach. There is a variety of different "test manuals" available, some of which include directions for lengthy introductions and explanations about how to respond to the stimuli, others which include very few explanations. Some manuals have very lenient scoring rules, others have more stringent rules. This means that practitioners are not using the test in a standardized fashion. Lack of standardization makes it difficult to determine the reliability and the validity of the test. If people score the same answers differently, it is nearly impossible to get the same results.

With the advent of statistical techniques such as meta-analysis—a way of analyzing the results of multiple studies at once—the psychometric characteristics of the Rorschach have improved. For example, Parker (1983) analyzed 530 statistics from nine papers published in the 1970s and found an overall internal reliability coefficient of .83.

Overall, more research is needed to determine the reliability and validity of the Rorschach. In order for this research to provide us with valuable information, practitioners must agree on a standard method of administering and scoring. As a step in this direction, Exner (1993) proposed a comprehensive system that provides standard administration and scoring procedures developed and refined by empirical analysis. This system was developed by combining the best elements of the various Rorschach administration and scoring systems.

FIGURE 14.2. A picture from the Thematic Apperception Test

Source: Picture from the TAT. Henry A. Murray, Cambridge, Harvard University Press, ©1943, by the President and Fellows of Harvard College, ©1971 Henry A. Murray.

Sentence Completion

A third type of projective assessment is **sentence completion.** Like projective drawing, sentence completion techniques date back to the 1920s. This technique, however, grew out of another psychoanalytic concept, word association. In sentence completion tests, the assessor administers partial sentences, verbally or on paper, and asks the test taker to respond by completing each sentence.

Research suggests that sentence completion tests are one of the main techniques used by school psychologists to assess children's personalities (Goh & Fuller, 1983). Haak (1990) describes how sentence completion tests can be used to evaluate school-age children for problems such as intellectual difficulties, attention deficit disorder, stress, depression, anxiety, thought disturbance, and defensiveness. She admits, however, that there is little research to support their psychometric soundness.

The Controversy About Projective Techniques

Most proponents of projective techniques concede that a major weakness of most projective tests is a lack of evidence of traditional psychometric soundness, such as reliability and validity. Numerous scoring schemes have been devised to overcome these psychometric deficiencies, but many psychologists still doubt the

The Draw-A-Person technique is a traditional projective test whose antecedents date back to the psychoanalytic schools of Freud and Jung. It is more often used by psychoanalysts and child psychologists than by counselors.

The assessor gives the test taker a blank piece of paper, usually 8-1/2 by 11 inches, and a soft pencil. The assessor asks the participant, "Will you please draw a person?" In response to questions about which person or what kind of person or drawing, the assessor says, "Draw whatever you like in any way you like." The assessor also assures the participant that artistic talent is not important and not part of the exercise. After the first drawing is completed, the assessor then asks the participant to draw a person whose sex is opposite of the first person. For instance, the assessor might say, "This is a male figure [or man]; now please draw a female [or woman]." Figure 14.3 shows an example of the sorts of drawings that might be produced by the participant.

There are various methods for interpreting and scoring the resulting drawing. These focus on aspects such as these:

- The completeness of the drawing.
- Did the participant draw a person of his own sex first? Usually the first picture is a person of the participant's own sex.
- The size of the two figures in relation to each other and in relation to the page.
- The amount of movement or ability to move of the figures in the drawing.
- Distortions or omissions, such as an enlarged head, the attention to detail in drawing the hair, and the positions of arms and hands.

Proponents of the use of projective drawing techniques point out that unusual drawings or aspects of drawings do not constitute a diagnosis of a mental disorder. Instead, the drawings guide the psychotherapist or test user in eliciting information that will have diagnostic usefulness. Critics of projective techniques point out, however, that therapists

FIGURE 14.3. The "Draw-A-Person" projective technique

From Hammer, *The Clinical Application of Projective Drawings*, 4/e, © 1975. Courtesy of Charles C Thomas, Publisher, Ltd., Springfield, Illinois.

who use drawings to guide diagnosis can be in danger of hypothesis confirmation bias. In this regard, projective techniques, such as the Draw-A-Person technique, might lend themselves more to the therapeutic model of assessment rather than the diagnostic model of assessment.

Hammer (1958), a proponent of projective techniques, suggests that adults and adolescents who have training or skill as an artist might have an enhanced capacity for self-expression. Rather than contaminating the drawing with outside influences, artistic skill allows participants to clearly express aspects of their personality, such as self-concept and ego ideal.

validity of projective techniques. Practitioners who use projective techniques contend that they provide richer and more personal data than structured personality tests. The value of projective tests might therefore be in their usefulness as an intervention rather than as diagnostic or research instruments.

Sometimes the results of a routine administration of a battery of psychological tests, such as intelligence or personality tests, can signal that abnormal responses might be related to physiological dysfunction. In that case, the clinician conducts a more in-depth neuropsychological assessment.

Neuropsychological Tests

Neuropsychology is a special branch of psychology that concentrates on the relation between how the brain functions and the behavior it produces. This field is of growing importance in assessing and treating clients with abnormal behavior as well as those with neurological or brain damage. Neuropsychological assessment requires specialized training and is usually conducted by psychologists or psychiatrists rather than counselors or mental health workers. For Your Information 14.6 provides an overview of the problems and disorders that can be explored using neuropsychological tests.

Neuropsychologists use electrophysiological techniques, such as electroencephalography, and neuroimaging methods, such as positron emission tomography (PET) and magnetic resonance imaging (MRI). Two major electrophysiological methods for investigating brain function are the **electroencephalogram (EEG),** a continuous written record of brain-wave activity, and **event-related potential**

For Your Information   14.6
Areas of Neuropsychological Assessment

The field of neuropsychology developed from research conducted in the early 1940s on brain damage in adults. Although many people still associate the use of neuropsychological tests with brain dysfunction, the scope of neuropsychological assessment has widened to include identification of a variety of disorders and abnormalities. Following is a list of applications for neuropsychological testing taken from the *Handbook of Neuropsychological Assessment* (Goldstein, 1992):

• Identification and localization of brain lesions and related behaviors.
• Assessment of the development or decline of brain function across the life span.
• Assessment of competence and evaluation for disability in forensic settings.

• Evaluation of students for learning disabilities and related academic problems.
• Assessment for schizophrenia and mood disorders.
• Health status assessment for persons with numerous general medical disorder or exposure to toxic substances.
• Research on basic brain-behavior relationships.
• Monitoring the effects of drugs or experimental treatment procedures during clinical trails.
• Investigation of the neurobiological roots of genetic disorders.
• Assessment of the influence of medication, fatigue, or toxic substances on employee performance in industrial settings.
• Supplement to traditional aptitude and achievement tests in educational settings.

(ERP), a record of the brain's electrical response to the occurrence of a specific event. Researchers have used individual differences in EEG and ERP indexes to predict psychological traits, cognitive function and dysfunction, and psychopathology (Boomsma, Anokhin, & de Geus, 1997). Neuroimaging involves making pictures of brain functions, such as blood flow (PET records changes in brain blood flow) or magnetic fields (MRI provides a three-dimensional picture of brain tissue). Researchers have also shown a relation between neuroimaging techniques and behavior.

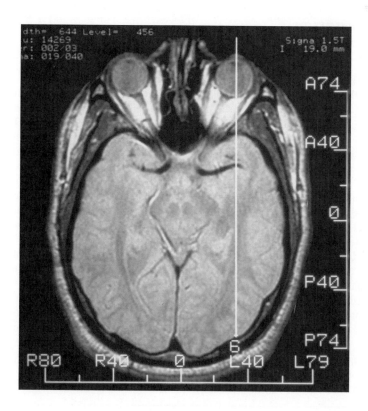

For Your Information 14.7 discusses research using electrophysiological assessment to investigate the possibility that conditions such as alcoholism are inherited.

Most neuropsychological testing falls into two categories: developmental and psychopathological, related to mental dysfunction or mental disorders.

Developmental Applications

When assessing brain and neurological functioning, it is important for the assessor to consider the clients' behavior in the context of their developmental period. In other words, the brain and nervous system of a child are different from the brain and nervous system of an adult. Although neuropsychologists should possess a strong knowledge of development issues and tests appropriate for children, approximately two-thirds routinely assess children and adolescents without acquiring the necessary expertise. Until recently, many inaccurate assumptions have been made about brain–behavior relationships in children based on research conducted on adults. Fortunately, research on brain–behavior relationships in children has begun to dispel some of these assumptions (Cohen, Branch, Willis, Weyandt, & Hynd, 1992).

For Your Information   14.7
Genetic Components of Electrophysiological Behavior

Investigation of a relationship between electrical activity in the brain and underlying inherited traits date back to the 1930s. Recent advances in mapping human chromosomes and genes, however, have provided evidence that behavioral potentials, such as increased risk for alcoholism, can be traced to specific genes and transmitted in families much like eye color or blood groups.

For example, individual EEG differences caused by alcohol appear to be controlled at the genetic level. Results of several studies suggest that genes located on chromosomes 2 and 6 influence brain activity in the frontal, executive, and the sensory-processing areas. These genes in turn have been shown to influence brain activity (low P300 amplitude) that has been linked to increased risk for alcoholism. These studies concur with pharmacological studies that suggest an association with dopamine, a neurotransmitter.

In addition, twin and family studies have provided evidence of greater consistency of spontaneous electrical activity in the brain for conditions, such as sleep, resting wakefulness, sensory stimulation, and performance of various tasks, for those sharing the same genes. Studies by some researchers (Bouchard, Lykken, McGue, Segal, & Tellegen, 1990; Stassen, Lykken, Propping, & Bomben, 1988) suggest that differences in EEG activity among individuals are mostly determined by genetic factors.

Researchers have also linked ERPs to individuals' genetic makeup, although to a lesser degree than that for EEGs. Some of this variability could be due to the variety of tasks used to evoke ERPs. For instance, elementary stimuli, such as light flashes, evoke more consistent responses attributable to a genetic influence than ERP responses to tasks requiring language skills.

These studies represent only the start of programs of research designed to understand how genes influence electric activity in the brain. Future plans for research include linking specific genes to the brain areas where they are expressed.

Source: Adapted from Boomsma, Anokhin, & deGeus (1997).

Neonatal and Early Childhood. Neurological disorders that can occur prior to birth include spina bifida (abnormal development of neural tube), intrauterine growth retardation often caused by a small or insufficient placenta, anoxia (total reduction of oxygen), and hypoxia (partial reduction of oxygen). Assessment of neurological deficits for neonates and young children can be divided into four functional areas: (1) biochemical, (2) electrophysiological, (3) neurobehavioral, and (4) social-emotional functioning (Emory, Savoie, Ballard, Eppler, & O'Dell, 1992).

Biochemical assessment refers to analysis of blood gases to determine the concentration of oxygen and carbon dioxide at the tissue level. **Electrophysiological assessment** is the monitoring of vital signs, such as heart rate and spontaneous electrical activity of the brain. Many hospitals monitor fetal heart rate during delivery to determine fetal well-being. The clinical neuropsychologist usually does not conduct these tests. When a medical practitioner provides this information to the clinical psychologist, it is valuable information for making a psychological diagnosis.

Most neuropsychologists use diagnostic methods in the area of **neurobehavioral assessment.** Traditionally, practitioners elicit various reflexes, such as the Moro reflex, Babinski reflex, and tonic-neck reflex, to assess the functioning and maturity of the infant's central nervous system. In addition to reflexive screening exams, psychologists rely heavily on observations of infants and children's behaviors to assess developmental progress. Well-known batteries include developmental screening tests, such as the Gesell Developmental Schedules (Knobloch, Stevens, & Malone, 1980), the Bayley Scales (Bayley, 1993), and the Denver Developmental Screening Test (Frankenburg & Dodds, 1967). For Your Information 14.8 describes these instruments and how they are used.

Social-emotional functioning, the fourth area of assessment, includes tests that measure temperament or personality. In addition, practitioners use intelligence tests, academic achievement tests, language assessment, visual and tactile perception evaluations, and assessment of sustained attention (ability to remain aroused and vigilant over time) and selective attention (ability to focus on key aspects of the environment) (Cohen, Branch, Willis, Weyandt, & Hynd, 1992). Cohen and colleagues (1992) point out that the child neuropsychologist must be proficient in qualitative analysis of observational data as well as in test administration and interpretation.

Adulthood and Aging. Neuropsychologists must take into account the normal changes in brain function that result from aging. In addition, aging can exaggerate the psychological impact of medical conditions. A number of physiological changes in the brain that result from aging have been documented. These include decreased weight and volume of the brain, decreases in certain neurotransmitters, decreases in dominant EEG frequency, and changes in brain metabolism. Therefore, practitioners need to pay close attention to the characteristics of the norm group when comparing individual scores to test norms. Research comparing test results for older adults compared to younger adults report larger standard deviations (more variation) in scores for older adults than in scores for younger adults (La Rue, 1992).

317

CHAPTER 14
Using Tests in
Clinical and
Counseling
Settings

GESELL DEVELOPMENTAL SCHEDULES

The Gesell Developmental Schedules (Knobloch, Stevens, & Malone, 1980) are a refinement of early attempts to construct a taxonomy of normal development. The first Gesell schedules were published in 1940 and represented the results of longitudinal studies conducted by Gesell and his colleagues at Yale (Ames, 1989). The assessor using the Gesell schedules observes and records a child's responses to predetermined toys and other stimuli. Information provided by a parent or caregiver supplements the observational data to determine neurological defects or behavioral abnormalities (Anastasia & Urbina, 1997).

BAYLEY SCALES OF INFANT DEVELOPMENT

The Bayley Scales of Infant Development (Bayley, 1993) use a methodology similar to that of the Gesell schedules. However, the Bayley Scales are generally considered to be better constructed and to have more evidence of reliability and validity. The battery is composed of three scales: The Mental Scale (perception, memory, problem solving, verbal communication, and abstract thinking), the Motor Scale (gross motor ability), and the Behavior Rating Scale (emotional and social behavior, attention span, persistence, and goal orientation). Like the Gesell schedules, the Behavior Rating Scale relies on information provided by the child's caregiver. Norms for this battery are based on 1,700 children representing ages 1 to 42 months and representative of the U.S. population in terms of race or ethnicity, geographic regions, and parental education level. Bayley designed the battery to assess developmental status rather than to predict subsequent ability levels. Although more research is needed, the battery is helpful in early detection of sensory or neurological defects, emotional disturbances, and environmental deficits (Anastasi & Urbina, 1997). Chapter 6 contains more information on the Bayley Scales and their psychometric properties.

DENVER DEVELOPMENTAL SCREENING TEST

The Denver Developmental Screening Test (Frankenburg, Dodds, Fandal, Kazuk, & Cohrs, 1976) is another norm-referenced battery specifically designed for early identification of developmental or behavioral problems. The target audience for this battery is children from birth to 6 years of age. Unlike the Bayley Scales, the Denver Developmental Screening Test requires no special training for the administrator and takes a short interval—approximately 20 minutes—to administer. This test measures four developmental areas: personal-social development, fine motor development, language development, and gross motor development. The test contains 105 items that are administered according to the child's chronological age. The authors report evidence of test-retest reliability, content validity, and construct validity.

Two disorders that increase with aging are Alzheimer's disease and depression. Confirmation that an individual is suffering from Alzheimer's disease cannot be made prior to death. Clients are, however, diagnosed as having dementia of the Alzheimer type (DAT) based on specified behaviors and laboratory results. Likewise, depression often cannot be clearly identified until the condition passes. Scores on depression rating scales are often higher for older individuals because respondents endorse more physical symptoms. Older clients can also experience cognitive deficits that are due to aging rather than to depression.

Psychopathological Applications

According to Puente and McCaffrey (1992), three major areas of psychopathological disorders—anxiety, depression, and schizophrenia—have been researched extensively by neuropsychologists.

319

CHAPTER 14
*Using Tests in
Clinical and
Counseling
Settings*

Anxiety. There are a number of mental health conditions that can be grouped under the general classification of anxiety disorders. The *Diagnostic and Statistical Manual of Mental Disorders* (American Psychiatric Association, 1994) lists a number of conditions characterized by unrealistic or excessive anxiety and worry, such as generalized anxiety disorder, obsessive-compulsive disorder, panic disorder, and posttraumatic stress disorder. The research on the neurological basis for anxiety can serve as a model of assessment of other mental health disorders (Orsillo & McCaffrey, 1992). Researchers have identified specific associations between the emotion of anxiety and particular brain structures and neurotransmitter systems (Charney, Heninger, & Breier, 1984; Horel, Keating, & Misatone, 1975; LeDoux, Thompson, Iadelcola, Tucker, and Reis, 1983). Orsillo and McCaffrey (1992) conclude that involvement of the temporal lobe area is consistently reported. Neurological assessment procedures used by researchers include electrophysiological recordings, such as PET, computerized transaxial tomography (CT) (a three-dimensional depiction of the brain), ERP, and the EEG (Orsillo & McCaffrey, 1992). These measures can be supplemented by psychological tests, such as those for intelligence, auditory learning, temporal orientation, memory, and visual retention.

Depression. Recent research suggests that depression, which usually affects neurologically impaired individuals at some time during their illness, can have a significant impact on neuropsychological test performance (Miller, 1975; Newman and Sweet, 1992). Newman and Sweet (1992) suggest that the effects on test performance can be extreme or subtle and cluster into three major areas of impairment: (1) psychomotor speed, (2) motivation and attention, and (3) memory and learning. Failure to consider the effects of depression on neuropsychological tests can lead to misdiagnosis of a client's condition, resulting in inappropriate treatment.

Schizophrenia. Although once classified as a disorder without an identifiable neurological basis, schizophrenia has now been linked by researchers to evidence of abnormal brain functioning (Walker, Lucas, & Lewine, 1992). A number of studies have compared individuals diagnosed as schizophrenic with individuals with known brain damage. Two neuropsychological test batteries used to study the performance of schizophrenics are the Halstead-Reitan Neurological Battery and the Luria-Nebraska Neurological Battery.

Researchers have also used PET and regional cerebral blood flow (RCBF) analysis to search for an organic basis for schizophrenia. One finding has been a reduction in frontal lobe activity in the brain in clients diagnosed as schizophrenic (Weinberger, Berman, & Zec, 1986; Weinberger & Berman, 1988).

Specialized Tests for Clinical Disorders

Psychologists also use traditional paper-and-pencil tests to identify mental disorders such as anger, anxiety, and depression. Such tests should be developed and validated using the procedures described in Chapters 10 and 11. Because thousands of specialized tests are available from publishers, a comprehensive discussion of clinical tests is beyond the scope of this text. Several of the most commonly used tests are discussed below to illustrate the role that paper-and-pencil tests play in clinical diagnosis. These tests differ from general personality inventories, such as the MMPI and the NEO Personality Inventory, because they focus on a narrow band of traits or behaviors.

Single-Construct Tests

The Beck Depression Inventory (Beck & Steer, 1987) (revised in 1996) is one of the best examples of a widely used self-report test that measures a single construct. Beck and his associates developed the original inventory in 1961. Since that time, the test has been revised and has been cited in over 3,000 studies (Waller, 1995b). The Beck Depression Inventory is used to assess the severity of depression in adults and adolescents as well as to screen normal populations.

A number of studies have found a high correlation (.40 to .70) between depression and anxiety (Waller, 1995a), so the development of the Beck Anxiety Inventory was a logical extension of Beck's research. The test is designed to measure characteristics of anxiety that might or might not occur with those of depression. Both tests are the products of extensive research and careful psychometric development.

Identification of Construct Duration

Charles Spielberger (1985) and his associates at the University of South Florida added another dimension to the measurement of mental constructs. Their long-term research on anxiety, anger, and curiosity included the concept of trait duration. They asked the question, "Is the attribute a temporary **state** or an ongoing part of a person's personality and therefore a **trait?**" Two well-known tests that came out of this research are the State-Trait Anger Expression Inventory (STAXI) and State-Trait Anxiety Inventory (STAI). For instance, the STAI attempts to distinguish between a temporary condition of anxiety (perhaps brought on by situational circumstances) and a long-standing quality of anxiety that has become a part of the person's personality. Likewise, the STAXI assesses temporary anger (state anger) and angry temperament and angry reaction (trait anger).

321

CHAPTER 14
Using Tests in
Clinical and
Counseling
Settings

Observational Scales

Some clients, such as children, are not able to complete self-report measures about themselves. Trained professionals or family members using observational scales then carry out the assessment. Typically, the assessor observes predetermined behaviors and then rates the behaviors on a Likert-type scale.

The Attention Deficit Disorders Evaluation Scale (ADDES) is a good example of a test that relies on observation of the client. The ADDES is used to assess children for attention deficit disorder as defined in the *DSM-IV.* The test measures three constructs: inattention, impulsiveness, and hyperactivity. Any person who has extended contact with the child may complete the scale by rating how often each behavior occurs. Scores are interpreted by comparing them to norms obtained by assessing thousands of children from 4 to 20 years of age.

The tests cited in this section were developed over a period of years using the rigorous methodology for test development described in Chapters 10 and 11. Each has demonstrated high levels of reliability and construct validity. Not all clinical tests available from test publishers or scholarly journals demonstrate psychometric soundness. It is important that the clinical practitioner or counselor use caution to select tests that meet accepted standards of psychometric soundness.

In summary, psychological tests and assessments are important tools used by clinical psychologists, counselors, and others. Their primary role is one of information gathering to facilitate diagnosis, but they are also used as part of the intervention process and for research. Psychologists, counselors, and others who use tests for these purposes should receive specialized training in the general principles of psychological testing as well as specific training for interpreting each instrument.

Summary Box 14.5
Specialized Tests for Clinical Disorders

- Psychologists also use traditional paper-and-pencil tests to identify mental disorders such as anger, anxiety, and depression.
- The Beck Depression Inventory and the Beck Anxiety Inventory are examples of tests that assess single constructs or disorders.

- Another dimension of measurement is the assessment of whether an attribute is temporary (state) or an ongoing part of the personality (trait).
- When clients, such as children, cannot complete self-report measures, trained professionals use observational scales to rate observed behaviors.

Clinical assessment includes a broad set of information-gathering and interpretive skills used by the professional counselor-therapist. There are three models of clinical assessment. The information-gathering model uses standardized tests to make diagnoses. The therapeutic model uses tests as an intervention that provide new information for the client to use for self-discovery and growth. The differential treatment model uses tests for conducting research or evaluating program outcomes. Counselors primarily provide services for those with normal developmental problems, and clinical psychologists and psychiatrists generally treat those with abnormal behavior, mental disorders, or emotional disabilities.

Diagnosis is the identification of the client's problem or disorder. The process of arriving at a diagnosis is called screening. Diagnosis leads to the design or selection of an intervention to alleviate unwanted behaviors or symptoms or to solve the client's problem.

Most practitioners use the clinical interview as a primary tool for gathering information about the client. The clinical interview involves a discussion between the client and the assessor in which the assessor observes the client and gathers information. A structured clinical interview has a predetermined set of questions. An unstructured or nondirective clinical interview, on the other hand, has few predetermined questions. Instead, the assessor's questions are more likely to be determined by the client's responses. The semistructured interview provides a compromise between the structured interview and the nondirective interview.

Research on the validity of the nondirective clinical interview suggests the nondirective interview might be more useful in a therapeutic sense than for assessment. The practitioner who uses the nondirective approach risks two major sources of bias: hypothesis confirmation bias and self-fulfilling prophecy. Practitioners also use standardized personality tests, such as the MMPI-2, the NEO Personality Inventory, and the 16 Personality Questionnaire, to make diagnoses.

Projective techniques ask test takers to give meaning to ambiguous stimuli. Projective storytelling requires test takers to tell a story about some visual stimuli, such as pictures. In projective drawing, test takers draw and interpret their own pictures. In sentence completion tests, the assessor administers partial sentences, verbally or on paper, and asks the test taker to respond by completing each sentence. A major weakness of most projective tests is a lack of evidence of traditional psychometric soundness, such as reliability and validity. The value of projective tests might therefore be in their usefulness as an intervention rather than as diagnostic or research instruments.

Neuropsychology is a special branch of psychology that concentrates on the relation between how the brain functions and the behavior it produces. Neuropsychologists use electrophysiological techniques, such as the electroencephalogram (EEG), a continuous written record of brain-wave activity, and the event-related potential (ERP), a record of the brain's electrical response to the occurrence of a specific event.

Most neuropsychological testing falls into two categories: developmental and psychopathological. Two developmental tests for infants are biochemical assessment, the analysis of blood gases to determine the concentration of oxygen and carbon dioxide at the tissue level, and electrophysiological assessment, the moni-

323

CHAPTER 14
Using Tests in
Clinical and
Counseling
Settings

toring vital signs, such as heart rate and spontaneous electrical activity of the brain. Neuropsychologists also conduct neurobehavioral assessments, such as eliciting various reflexes to assess the functioning and maturity of the infant's central nervous system. Finally, neuropsychologists also use tests that measure temperament or personality as well as tests of intelligence, academic achievement, language, perception and attention to assess social-emotional functioning in children. When treating the elderly, neuropsychologists must take into account the normal changes in brain function that result from aging, including the fact that aging can exaggerate the psychological impact of medical conditions.

Psychologists also use traditional paper-and-pencil tests to identify mental disorders such as anger, anxiety, and depression. These tests differ from general personality inventories, such as the MMPI and the NEO Personality Inventory, because they focus on a narrow band of traits or behaviors. The Beck Depression Inventory and the Beck Anxiety Inventory are examples of tests that assess single constructs or disorders. Another dimension of measurement is the assessment of whether an attribute is temporary (state) or an ongoing part of the personality (trait). When clients, such as children, cannot complete self-report measures, family members use observational scales to rate observed behaviors.

KEY CONCEPTS

biochemical assessment
clinical assessment
clinical interview
diagnosis
differential treatment
   model
electroencephalogram
   (EEG)
electrophysiological
   assessment
event-related potential
   (ERP)

hypothesis confirmation
   bias
information-gathering
   model
neurobehavioral
   assessment
neuropsychology
nondirective clinical
   interview
projection
projective drawing
projective hypothesis

projective storytelling
projective techniques
screening
self-fulfilling prophecy
semistructured interview
sentence completion
social-emotional
   functioning
state
structured clinical
   interview
therapeutic model
trait

LEARNING ACTIVITIES

1. Models of Clinical Assessment

Define and describe each of the models of assessment. What are the strengths and weaknesses of each? Can more than one model be used at the same time? If so, describe how that can be done. Which model do you think is most often used? Why?

2. The Clinical Interview

Describe three kinds of clinical interviews. What are the strengths and weaknesses of each? How does each contribute to arriving at a clinical diagnosis?

3. *Clinical Tests*

Choose one of the tests that has been referred to in this chapter. Go to your college library or use the Internet to research the test. Be prepared to present a critique of the test orally or in writing. Be sure to include the following: (1) history of the test's development; (2) evidence of reliability and validity; (3) appropriate target audience; (3) test purpose; and (4) construct(s) the test measures.

Using Tests in Organizational Settings

"The company I interviewed with also asked me to complete a personality test. What was that for?"

"When I applied for a job, the company had two people interview me. The interviewers asked very similar questions about the same topics. Isn't one interview enough?"

"Where I work, they do random drug tests. One time I tested positive because I took some cough syrup the night before. I really resent being treated like a criminal!"

"It's performance appraisal time again. My future depends on these ratings, and I'm not convinced they really show what a good worker I am."

Businesses and government have a long history of using psychological tests for hiring, performance evaluation, and research. We start this chapter with a brief history of the role psychological assessment has played in organizations. We then examine various types of tests that are used for hiring employees—such as interviews and tests of performance, personality, and integrity tests. We consider legal constraints on employment testing legislated by Congress and interpreted by the executive branch and the federal court system. We discuss performance impairment tests—similar to video games—which can be used instead of drug testing to determine whether employees can perform their jobs safely. Finally, we describe how organizations use psychological assessment to evaluate employee performance.

A SHORT HISTORY OF EMPLOYMENT TESTING

As the United States moved into the 20th century, the idea that businesses could use scientific principles to increase productivity became popular. Psychologists such as Walter Dill Scott, Hugo Müensterberg, and Walter Bingham began studying and applying psychological principles to the world of work. Both Scott and Müensterberg proposed methods for validating employment tests prior to World War I (Katzell & Austin, 1992).

The Scientific Selection of Salesmen

In 1915, Scott published an article entitled "The Scientific Selection of Salesmen" in which he proposed that employers use group tests for personnel selection. These tests evaluated constructs such as "native intellectual ability" and were part of a scientific selection system to assess "character" and "manner." Scott's evaluation system inspired interest and debate among academic psychologists, who questioned the scientific legitimacy of such systems, but this controversy did not deter Scott from continuing to pursue his goal of developing tests for business use.

Scott's influence among applied psychologists increased as America moved into World War I. He proposed to both the military and the academic community that it was possible to design tests to determine fitness for military jobs such as artillery man or pilot. Political infighting among psychologists who were advising the military, however, resulted in Scott's withdrawal from the group that developed the Army's "alpha" test (Von Mayrhauser, 1987). Scott's influence in the field of employment testing had a lasting effect. For instance, his salesman selection system provided the basis years later for a system for selecting life insurance salespeople developed by the Life Insurance Agency Management Association (Katzell & Austin, 1992).

The Legacy of World War I

Various proposals from psychologists led to the development of the Army's "alpha" and "beta" tests in World War I. As you will recall from Chapter 2, the misuse of these intelligence tests began a controversy about intelligence tests that survives today.

Following World War I, psychologists continued investigating the advantages of employment testing. They also began studying methods for measuring job performance, and they proposed methods for placing workers in various industrial jobs based on their skills and qualifications. For example, Millicent Pond (1927) studied the selection and placement of apprentice metal workers. Others attempted to use interest inventories (questionnaires that assess a worker's attitudes and interests) to differentiate among occupational groups (Katzell & Austin, 1992). The Strong-Campbell Interest Inventory (first published as the Strong Vocational Interest Blank) originated from this early work is in current use today.

Two consulting firms that specialized in using tests in organizations emerged during this time. Walter Scott and his colleagues, who developed a number of instruments that included mental ability tests and performance tests for various trades, founded one. The other was The Psychological Corporation organized by J. McKeen Cattell. This organization continues today as a unit of Harcourt Brace Jovanovich, a major publisher of psychological tests.

Testing From World War II to the Present

Psychologists and psychological testing again played a key role in the U.S. war effort in World War II. Bingham, who served as chief psychologist of the War Department, supervised the development of the Army General Classification Test used to place Army recruits. The Office of Strategic Services explored the assessment center method (featured in Chapter 7). Psychologists also developed new methods for rating personnel and measuring morale and attitudes (Katzell & Austin, 1992).

The use of tests by organizations expanded greatly during the last half of the 20th century. Large companies and organizations, including the federal government, began using psychological tests for selection, placement, attitude assessment, performance appraisal, and consumer surveys. In addition, the beginning of the U.S. civil rights movement drew attention to issues of test validity and fairness. Title VII of the 1964 Civil Rights Act stimulated great interest in fair employment practices, and psychological testing experts eventually played a strong role in developing the federal government's *Uniform Guidelines for Employee Selection* (1978).

Today, organizations use psychological tests in a variety of areas. Organizations use various methods of assessment to make hiring decisions. They use various types of rating scales to evaluate employees' performance. Organizational surveys are a major source of information about employee attitudes, skills, and motivation. Marketing research involves surveying consumers' attitudes and assessing their behavior. In addition, individuals often use interest inventories to choose or change their career goals.

Summary Box 15.1
History of Employment Testing

- In 1915, Scott published "The Scientific Selection of Salesmen" in which he proposed that employers use group tests for personnel selection.
- Proposals from psychologists led to the development of the Army's "alpha" and "beta" tests in World War I.
- Following World War I, psychologists continued investigating employment testing and began studying measuring job performance and placing workers in jobs based on their skills and qualifications.

- Two consulting firms that specialized in using tests in organizations emerged. One was founded by Scott. The other was The Psychological Corporation organized by Cattell.
- Use of tests by organizations expanded greatly during the last half of the 20th century.
- Title VII of the 1964 Civil Rights Act stimulated interest in fair employment practices, and psychologists played a strong role in the developing the federal government's *Uniform Guidelines for Employee Selection* (1978).

PREEMPLOYMENT TESTING

Psychological assessment provides the basis for hiring employees in most organizations. The most popular method of assessment is the employment interview. Organizations supplement interviewing with a variety of tests that measure performance and personality characteristics. In the last decade, drug and integrity testing have also become accepted as methods for screening out candidates who might have undesirable behaviors or attitudes.

The Employment Interview

The **employment interview** is the most pervasive method of preemployment assessment used by organizations. Types of interviews vary from the **traditional interview,** in which the interviewer pursues different areas of inquiry with each job candidate, to highly **structured interviews,** which are standardized with the same questions asked of each job candidate. We will focus on the ends of this continuum, keeping in mind that employers often use interviews that have varying amounts of flexibility and structure.

Traditional Interview

Few managers are willing to risk hiring an employee they have not met. The traditional interview serves the "getting to know you function." However, research shows that it falls very short of being a reliable or valid predictor of job performance. The interview's shortcomings were apparent in 1915 to Scott, who reported disagreement among managers interviewing potential salesmen (Cascio, 1991). More current research provides little evidence that the traditional interview is either reliable or valid. For instance, a meta-analysis of interviews used to predict supervisory ratings yielded a validity coefficient of .14 (Hunter & Hunter, 1984).

Researchers have found traditional interviews to be plagued with bias associated with sex, age, race, and physical attractiveness of the interviewee (Arvey, 1979). Some researchers have argued that such bias is associated more with the competence of the interviewer than the method itself (Dreher, Ash, & Hancock, 1988). Increasing interviewers' awareness of their own perceptual bias might increase the validity of the interview. Cascio (1991) suggests that interviewer training include role-playing, training with minorities, and a planned feedback system to inform interviewers about which candidates succeed and which candidates fail.

Structured Interview

Many shortcomings of the traditional interview, including its low reliability and low validity, can be overcome by structuring the interview and the interviewing procedure. In the structured interview, the interviewer has a planned interview and a quantitative scoring scheme. Each candidate receives the same questions in the same order. The interviewer rates the candidate's answers on an anchored rating scale. Interviewers undergo training on question delivery, note taking, and rating. Such training standardizes the treatment candidates receive as well as the ratings and resulting interview scores. Such standardization increases inter-rater reliability, internal consistency, and concurrent validity.

Interviews that focus on behaviors rather than attitudes or opinions also provide better predictions of job performance. Questions that ask candidates to provide specific accounts of the behaviors they used in the past (for example, planning a project or accomplishing a goal) provide more accurate information for interviewers to rate.

Content validity for the structured interview is established by developing questions using a **job analysis** or detailed job description. In Greater Depth 15.1 describes the process of job analysis. Using a content strategy, the interview is valid to the extent that it covers important job functions and duties without obtaining information about individual characteristics that are unrelated to job performance. As we will discuss later in this chapter, evidence that the interview is job-related (content valid) is especially important when an employer is sued for adverse impact of a selection system.

Recent research suggests that the interview will continue as a primary method of assessing job candidates. Unfortunately, more companies use traditional interviews than structured interviews (Bureau of National Affairs, 1988). Hopefully, this trend will change, as more companies become aware of the benefits of structured interviews and interviewing processes.

Interviews do serve useful purposes other than prediction of job performance. For instance, interviewers can provide candidates with useful information regarding the organization and set expectations about what the job will entail. When candidates have realistic expectations, they are likely to remain on the job longer than candidates who did not receive legitimate information about the job (Jones & Youngblood, 1993; Meglino, DeNisi, Youngblood, & Williams, 1988). In addition, the interview provides an opportunity to begin building positive relationships that

Job Analysis

"What do you do?" is a common question often asked at parties or social gatherings. For organizations, it is an important question that has many implications for managing people. Even if you know a person well, you might have only a general idea of what her or his job requires. Organizations require specific information about the activities of employees in order to make important decisions about hiring, training, and evaluating employees.

Job analysis is a systematic assessment method for answering the "What do you do?" question in organizations. There are a number of ways to conduct job analysis. All methods provide a systematic and detailed procedure for documenting the activities of the job. A typical job analysis provides information on the following job factors:

- *Functions:* A group of activities that allow the incumbent to accomplish one of the primary objectives of the job. Examples: analyzing financial data, coordinating interdepartmental communications, supervising employees.
- *Tasks:* Actions taken by the job incumbent that accomplish job functions. Examples: Estimate sales revenue to prepare budget; monitor customer service representatives to assure high standards of courtesy.
- *Knowledge:* A body of related information that the worker needs in order to perform job tasks. Examples: Knowledge of company policies regarding budget procedures; knowledge of company's products and services.
- *Skills:* Observable and measurable behaviors acquired through training that the worker needs in order to perform a variety of job tasks. Examples: Skill in planning and prioritizing work activities; skill in listening to others.

- *Abilities:* A physical or mental competency based on innate characteristics (generally not trained) that the worker needs to perform job tasks. Examples: Ability to stand for extended periods of time; ability to lift up to 50 pounds.
- *Other characteristics:* Interests or personality traits the worker needs in order to perform or cope with the job environment. Examples: Willingness to work night shifts; conscientiousness; honesty.

Most job analysis methods involve interviewing persons currently in the job and their supervisors and verifying that information by administering a job analysis questionnaire. The questionnaire asks incumbents and supervisors to rate job tasks on their importance and how often they are performed. All tasks that are identified as important and frequently performed are then analyzed to determine the knowledge, skills, abilities, and other characteristics the job incumbent needs to be successful in the job.

Job analysis is an important prerequisite for employment testing, because psychologists and the court system recognize it as a method for providing evidence of content validity. For example, a job analysis for "real estate salesperson" might specify a need for knowledge of local zoning laws, interpersonal skills, ability to climb several flights of stairs, and willingness to work on Sundays. Therefore, when assessing job applicants for real estate salesperson, the organization should choose assessment methods that yield information on those factors. Other factors—such as a college degree—may seem appealing, but unless specified in the job analysis, would not be appropriate job requirements.

Source: Adapted from McIntire, Bucklan, & Scott (1995).

will help new employees adjust and prevent negative perceptions for those who are not selected for hire.

Performance Tests

This category of tests includes a broad range of assessments that require the test taker to perform one or more job tasks. For instance, **assessment centers** (described in detail in Chapter 7) are large-scale replications of the job that require candidates to solve typical job problems by role playing or to demonstrate proficiency at job functions such as making presentations or fulfilling administrative duties. **Work samples** are smaller-scale assessments in which candidates complete a job-related task, such as building a sawhorse or designing a doghouse. A driving test is a performance test that organizations often use to assess people applying for jobs as heavy equipment operators or bus drivers.

Performance tests are often categorized as either high or low fidelity. **High-fidelity tests** are designed to replicate the job setting as realistically as possible. In a high-fidelity assessment, test takers use the same equipment that is used on the job and they complete actual job tasks. For instance, pilots are often trained and assessed on sophisticated flight simulators that not only simulate flight but recreate typical emergency situations. Such high-fidelity tests allow job candidates to perform in realistic situations; however, they remove the risk of unsafe or poor performance. In other words, if the job applicant doesn't fly the plane well, the resulting crash is simulated, not real!

Low-fidelity tests, on the other hand, simulate the task using a written, verbal, or visual description. The test taker might respond by answering open-ended or multiple-choice questions. Video tests are a good example of low-fidelity performance tests. In a video test, the test taker is shown typical job situations and asked to choose her or his response from a multiple-choice format. Such tests have been used to select bank tellers and customer service representatives.

Performance tests generally yield high validity coefficients, because they are designed as miniature reproductions of the job itself. A meta-analysis by Hunter and Hunter (1984) found an average validity of .54 of performance tests predicting job performance criteria. Validation studies of assessment centers have shown comparable results (Gaugler, Rosenthal, Thornton & Bentson, 1987). Because performance tests are developed using actual job tasks and activities, they also have a high degree of content validity.

Personality Inventories

Personality inventories measure ongoing cognitive constructs usually referred to as **personality traits.** Traits, such as conscientiousness, extraversion, agreeableness, are seen by personality theorists as constructs that predispose persons to perform certain behaviors. Personality theorists also suggest that the strength of various traits varies from person to person. Therefore, we might expect a person who has a high degree of extraversion to be more outgoing and energetic in a social situation than a person with a low degree of extraversion.

One of the early developers of a personality inventory was Raymond B. Cattell, who in the 1940s began conducting studies on personality assessment that culminated in the publication of the 16PF personality test in 1949. Cattell's test, which stimulated the development of a number of tests and has itself undergone revision, defines the adult personality in terms of 16 normal personality factors. Researchers have found relationships with some factors on the 16PF with absenteeism and turnover. The 16PF has also been used to predict tenure, safety, and job performance (Krug & Johns, 1990).

The psychological literature contains numerous personality theories and as many or more personality tests. One widely accepted personality theory is the **five-factor model,** which proposes that there are five central personality dimensions: surgency, emotional stability, agreeableness, conscientiousness, and intellect or openness to experience. In Greater Depth 15.2 provides a brief description of this theory and its five core dimensions.

For Your Information 15.1 describes the Hogan Personality Inventory, which is partially derived from the five-factor model and is widely used for preemployment testing and decision making.

Traditionally, personnel psychologists have discouraged the use of personality tests as employment tests, because researchers had shown the relationship between personality and job performance to be minimal at best and often nonexistent. For instance, Hunter and Hunter's (1984) meta-analysis suggested that personality tests were among the poorest predictors of job performance. Recently, however, personnel psychologists have begun to look more favorably on personality tests that reflect the five-factor model (Gatewood & Feild, 1997; Heneman, Heneman, & Judge, 1997). One meta-analysis by Barrick and Mount (1991) suggests that *conscientiousness* serves as a valid predictor of job performance for all occupational groups studied using three types of criteria. *Extraversion* and *emotional stability* appeared to be valid predictors of job performance for some, but not all, occupations. Gatewood and Feild (1997, p. 601) posit that "specific personality dimensions appear to be related to specific jobs and criteria." Although the meta-analysis provided positive information for personality tests, the validity coefficients were low (.20 to .31) when compared to other assessments, such as performance tests.

Most personality tests like the HPI use a self-report, paper and pencil format. Personality can be measured using a projective or interview format. These subjective

---

IN GREATER DEPTH 15.2

The Five-Factor Model of Personality

The five-factor model of personality arose from the work of Warren Norman, who obtained a large number of personality ratings and used factor analysis to determine the underlying constructs of personality (Liekert & Spiegler, 1994). (Chapter 9 provides an overview of the statistical procedure of factor analysis.) From the personality ratings, Norman extracted five factors, which he named surgency, agreeableness, conscientiousness, emotional stability, and culture. Subsequent research has generally confirmed Norman's early findings of five factors, including evidence that the same factors exist in German, Portuguese, Hebrew, Chinese, Korean, and Japanese cultures.

Robert McCrae and Paul Costa (1997) later made significant contributions to the five factor

theory by demonstrating a variety of applications and developing three personality inventories—the original NEO Personality Inventory (NEO-PI), the current NEO Personality Inventory Revised (NEO-PI-R), and the shorter NEO Five Factor Inventory (NEO-FFI)—that assess the personality using the five-factor model. McCrae and Costa defined the five factors as continuums:

- Neuroticism/stability
- Extraversion/introversion
- Openness
- Agreeableness/antagonism
- Conscientiousness/undirectedness

Robert and Joyce Hogan, a husband-and-wife team at the University of Oklahoma, developed the Hogan Personality Inventory (HPI). They originally published it in 1986, then revised it in 1992 (Hogan & Hogan, 1992).

The HPI is a measure of normal personality designed primarily for use as an employment test. It provides information about what the Hogans describe as the "bright side of personality"—individual characteristics that influence social interactions and the ability to get along with others and achieve educational or job-related goals. The HPI is also used for research in organizations to study the relation between personality and factors such as leadership, creativity, and performance.

The HPI has seven primary scales:

1. *Adjustment:* Calm and self-accepting or self-critical and tense
2. *Ambition:* Socially self-confident, leaderlike, competitive, and energetic
3. *Sociability:* Need for or enjoyment of interacting with others
4. *Likeability:* Perceptive, tactful, and socially sensitive
5. *Prudence:* Conscientious, conforming, and dependable
6. *Intellectance:* Perceived as bright, creative, and interested in intellectual matters
7. *School success:* Enjoyment of academic activities and valuing education for its own sake

The HPI also has a scale, referred to as a "validity key," designed to detect careless or random responding. The test contains 206 statements (average sentence length of 7.5 words) to which test takers respond "true" or "false" on an electronic scan sheet. Hogan Assessment Systems provides scoring and interpretation for all tests.

The Hogans began developing the HPI in the late 1970s using the California Psychological Inventory (CPI) (Gough, 1975) as their original model and the five-factor theory of personality as a theoretical basis for construct validity. After developing 420 questions, they tested over 1,700 people, including students, hospital workers, U.S. Navy enlisted personnel, clerical workers, truck drivers, sales representatives, and school administrators. Analyses of these data led to a shortened inventory of 310 questions that made up the original HPI.

Between 1984 and 1992, the HPI was administered to over 11,000 people, most of whom were employed by organizations in the United States. The Hogans and others conducted over 50 validity studies to assess criterion-related and construct validity. On the basis of these studies and factor analyses of the database of tests administered, the Hogans made revisions that yielded the revised edition currently in use.

Reliability: The test manual for the HPI reports internal consistencies for the seven primary scales and subscales obtained by testing 960 employed adults that range from .29 to .89. Test-retest reliability coefficients obtained by testing 140 university students over an interval of four weeks or more range from .34 to .86. In general, subscale reliabilities are within acceptable range and indicate substantial stability over time.

Validity: The HPI test manual presents three types of evidence for the validity of the primary scales: correlations of scale scores with other tests, with peer ratings, and with measures of organizational performance. In general, predictions for correlation with measures of related constructs and no correlation with unrelated or opposing measures were borne out.

Because the HPI was designed to predict how the test taker will be described by others, 128 student volunteers completed the HPI and asked two persons who had known them at least for two years to complete a peer rating form. In general, correlations between HPI scores and peer ratings were positively and significantly correlated as predicted.

Organizational performance measures were also correlated with the HPI to provide evidence of criterion-related validity. Criteria included supervisor ratings, training performance, and job satisfaction. Reported correlations with job performance criteria include a correlation of Sociability scores and sales revenue ($r = .51$, $p < .01$), Prudence scores with supervisors' ratings of conscientiousness ($r = .22$, $p = .02$), and School Success with training performance ($r = .55$ and $.34$, $p < .01$) (Hogan & Hogan, 1992).

formats, however, pose problems in reliability and validity that are not likely to enhance or perhaps detect the slight relationship that appears to exist between personality and job performance.

Integrity Testing

Economic pressures for businesses to become more efficient and competitive have contributed to a growing concern with employee theft and other issues related to the honesty and integrity of workers. One source suggests that employee theft grew from $1 billion in 1968 to $40 to $60 billion in 1991 (Gatewood & Feild, 1997). Assessments for integrity fall into two general categories: physiological measures and paper-and-pencil tests.

Polygraph Testing

The **polygraph,** or lie detector test, is the best-known physiological measure associated with evaluating how truthfully an individual responds to questioning. It was invented by William Marston, who also created "Wonder Woman," an early comic-book character who elicited the truth from criminals with her magic lasso (Lilienfeld, 1993). A trained polygraph administrator interprets physiological data recorded by a polygraph machine. The machine generates a number of graphs of physiological responses, such as skin resistance, pulse or heart rate, and respiration.

The theory behind the use of the polygraph is that when an individual gives an untruthful response, he or she exhibits increases in skin resistance, heart rate, and respiration. To evaluate honesty, the administrator asks a set of predetermined questions that establishes a physiological base line for truthful responses. Then the administrator asks other questions regarding topics such as employee theft. When an individual's physiological response increases above the base line, the administrator might judge that the test taker did not answer the questions truthfully.

One problem with this theory is that an individual's physiological responses can increase for a number of reasons, such as general discomfort and nervousness, and some individuals can control their physiological responses better than others. Lilienfeld (1993) concludes there is no scientific evidence that a specific "lie response" exists and suggests that polygraph users are making the "Othello error"— taking signs of distress as proof of unfaithfulness or dishonesty.

Gatewood and Feild (1997) states that the major drawback to using polygraphs for selection is that they generate a high rate of **false positives,** mistakenly classifying innocent test takers as guilty. In addition, polygraphs might also misclassify a large number of guilty individuals as innocent (Lilienfeld, 1993). The Employee Polygraph Protection Act of 1988, which forbids the use of the polygraph as an employment test, was passed by Congress in recognition of the stigma associated with incorrectly labeling applicants as untruthful and causing them to be rejected for employment. Although some employers (such as those who provide security services and government agencies) are exempted from the 1988 federal law, the poor predictive validity of polygraphs makes their usefulness for any situation highly suspect.

Paper-and-Pencil Integrity Tests

335

CHAPTER 15
Using Tests in
Organizational
Settings

As an alternative to physiological tests for integrity, a number of publishers now offer questionnaires that measure applicants' attitudes regarding employee theft. These tests ask the test takers to provide information about their past behavior (for example, "How many times have you borrowed cash from an employer without permission?") or respond to hypothetical situations (for example, "Is it okay to make personal phone calls from work?").

As you recall from Chapter 1, this type of integrity test has been the subject of much research and debate among psychologists. A meta-analysis of validation studies of integrity tests yielded encouraging results (Ones, Viswesvaran, & Schmidt, 1993). First, although prediction of documented thefts was low (.13), integrity tests predicted counterproductive behaviors much better (.29 to .39). Second, there was evidence these validities generalized across situations. Finally, in addition to predicting counterproductive behaviors, the meta-analysis showed that integrity tests correlated with supervisory ratings of job performance at .41.

Critics (Camara & Schneider, 1994, 1995; Lilienfeld, 1993) rightly point out, however, that studies available for the meta-analysis were conducted by the test publishers themselves, not by independent researchers, and that such studies often contained serious methodological flaws. Other researchers (Lilienfeld, Alliger, & Mitchell, 1995) have expressed concerns that integrity tests might systematically misclassify some honest individuals as dishonest and that most paper-and-pencil integrity tests are highly susceptible to faking.

An interesting study reported by Lilienfeld (1993) tested 41 monks and nuns—people who are assumed to excel in the trait of honesty—using a well-known honesty test. The monks and nuns scored lower (more dishonest) than a group of college students and a group of incarcerated criminals! Lilienfeld concludes that honesty tests, designed as an alternative to the polygraph, suffer from the same deficiencies as the lie detector.

Legal Constraints

When Congress passed the Civil Rights Act of 1964, one of the specific areas addressed was hiring by organizations. Title VII of the Civil Rights Act covered employment practices, including psychological testing, that resulted in discrimination against minorities and women. Following passage of the Civil Rights Act, various federal agencies in the executive branch as well as the federal courts began to issue guidelines and case law that sought to define the steps organizations should take to comply with the requirements of Title VII. The proliferation of guidelines and case law resulted in the federal government's publication of the *Uniform Guidelines for Employee Selection* (1978). It is important to note that Congress did not pass the *Uniform Guidelines* and therefore they are *not* federal law. They do, however, suggest procedures for organizations to follow that enhance the fairness and legal defensibility of their employment practices. The *Uniform Guidelines* were compiled with the help of psychologists and present what can be referred to as "best practices" when using psychological tests in organizations.

According to federal case law, any process that is used to make a hiring decision is defined as a "test." Therefore, all employment screening devices, including application blanks (forms), reference checks, and letters of reference, as well as psychological tests such as interviews and other tests discussed in this chapter are "tests" to which federal law applies.

To summarize briefly, the *Uniform Guidelines* and federal case law suggest that all employment tests should be job-related and based on a job analysis, a systematic examination of the job and the context in which it is performed. Employers should use only tests for which there is evidence of content or criterion-related validity. Organizations should maintain records regarding the race, sex, and ethnic group membership of the applicant pool and the final group of persons who are hired for each job. When a test results in adverse impact, exclusion of a disproportionate number of persons in a group protected by federal law—referred to as a **protected class**—then the employer should find an alternative method for assessing job candidates.

Summary Box 15.2
Preemployment Testing

- Psychological assessment provides the basis for hiring employees in most organizations.
- The most popular method of assessment is the employment interview.
- Types of interviews vary from the traditional interview in which the interviewer pursues different areas of inquiry, with each job candidate to highly structured interviews that are standardized with the same questions asked of each job candidate.
- Many shortcomings of the traditional interview, including its low reliability and low validity, can be overcome by structuring the interview and the interviewing procedure.
- Performance tests require the test taker to perform one or more job tasks.

- Personality inventories measure ongoing cognitive constructs, such as conscientiousness, extraversion, and agreeableness, that might influence persons to perform certain behaviors.
- One widely accepted personality theory is the five-factor model, which proposes that there are five central personality dimensions.
- Integrity tests that predict an employee's predisposal to be dishonest fall into two general categories, physiological measures and paper-and-pencil tests.
- The *Uniform Guidelines* suggest procedures for organizations to follow that enhance the fairness and legal defensibility of their employment practices.

PERFORMANCE IMPAIRMENT TESTS

Many organizations use medical tests that analyze samples of blood, urine, saliva, or hair to determine whether an employee or job candidate has used an illegal substance, such as marijuana or cocaine, in the recent past. These measures do not fit our definition of psychological testing, because they involve a chemical analysis for the presence of drugs that have been metabolized by the body. Psychological tests, as you recall, involve inferences made on the basis of a behavior.

As an alternative to chemical analysis, some researchers have developed **performance impairment tests** that resemble video games. These simulations detect impairment in motor skills or hand-eye coordination that indicate that the test taker might not be prepared to perform a job, such as operating a motor vehicle, safely. Proponents point out that impairment testing provides information on the employer's most significant question—Does the employee have the ability to work on a given day?—without intruding on the test taker's privacy or revealing unnecessary personal information (Maltby, 1990). In addition, impairment tests, which take about a minute, can be administered on a regular, even daily, basis. Random drug testing is likely to occur infrequently and take the worker off the job for a longer period of time. Performance tests give no indication of cause of performance impairment, nor are they subject to the type of errors inherent in medical testing, such as confusing metabolites generated by prescribed and illegal drugs.

Software for impairment tests establishes a baseline of performance for each individual and then monitors that individual's performance over time. Developers claim that test takers cannot establish an unreasonably low baseline. It takes about 40 trials to establish a baseline, and the test taker is expected to improve on each trail. If there is no improvement over a number of consecutive trials, the software signals a potential problem with faking. Because individuals are evaluated on the basis of past performance, these tests are appropriate for evaluating current employees only. They are not appropriate for preemployment tests, nor would it be appropriate to compare individuals' performance (Fine, 1992).

A survey conducted by the American Management Association in 1990 (Greenberg, 1990) indicated that about half of the 1,021 responding firms used chemical drug tests. Although few firms currently conduct performance impairment tests, those numbers might increase due to the job-related, nonintrusive, ongoing nature of impairment testing.

PERFORMANCE APPRAISAL

Most organizations carry out formal evaluations of employees' job performance. This process is call **performance appraisal.** Usually an employee's supervisor or manager completes a performance appraisal that requires assigning numeric values to the employees' performance. These performance appraisals qualify legally as "tests" and they fulfill our criteria for calling them psychological tests. The major types of performance appraisal systems are described below.

Ranking Employees

When supervisors rank people, they compare the performance of one employee to the performance of other employees. (As you recall from Chapter 5, rankings are ordinal measures.) To rank employees, the supervisor must decide who is the "best" employee, the "next best," and so on, based on predetermined dimensions or criteria. Some ranking methods, such as **forced distribution,** require the supervisor to assign a certain number of employees to each performance category, such as "poor," "below average," "average," "above average," and "outstanding." Assigning people to categories prevents the ranker from assigning all people to one category. However, it also can result in workers who are performing satisfactorily being identified as "poor" when compared to their peers.

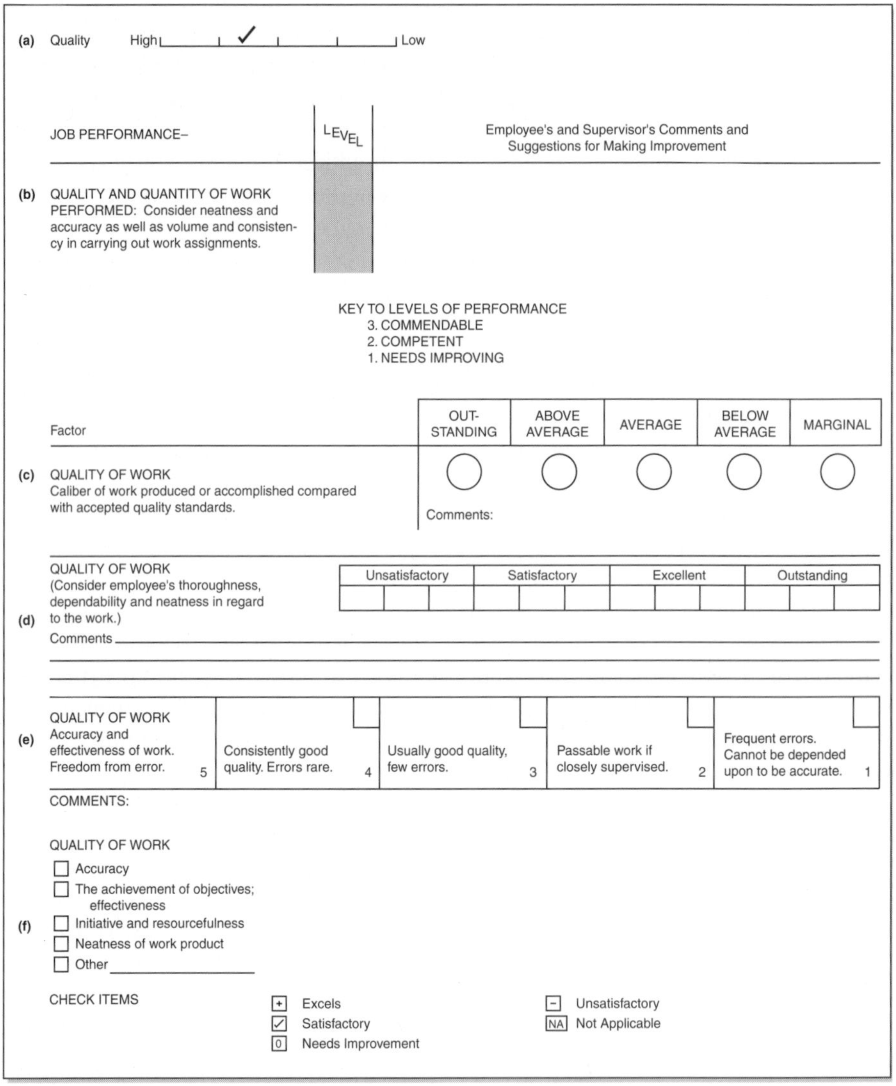

FIGURE 15.1. Examples of graphic rating scales

Source: Applied Psychology in Personnel Management, 4/e., by Cascio © 1991. Figure 5–4, p. 89. Reprinted by permission of Prentice-Hall, Inc., Upper Saddle River, NJ. Copyright © by the American Psychological Association Corporation.

Rating Employees

Most organizations prefer to rate employee performance using a scale that specifies job dimensions or job behaviors. The most popular method of rating employee performance is based on a **graphic rating scale** (Cascio, 1991). Figure 15.1 shows examples of graphic rating scales. As you can see, each of the scales represents a dimension, such as quality or quantity of work, on which the employee is rated. The scale is divided into categories defined by numbers, words, or both. Guided

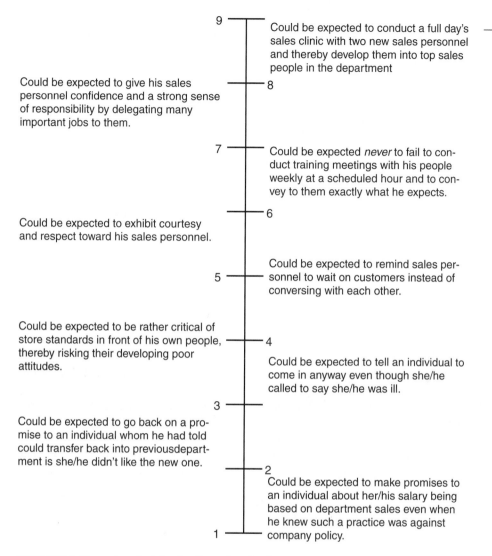

Could be expected to give his sales personnel confidence and a strong sense of responsibility by delegating many important jobs to them.

Could be expected to exhibit courtesy and respect toward his sales personnel.

Could be expected to be rather critical of store standards in front of his own people, thereby risking their developing poor attitudes.

Could be expected to go back on a promise to an individual whom he had told could transfer back into previous department is she/he didn't like the new one.

9 — Could be expected to conduct a full day's sales clinic with two new sales personnel and thereby develop them into top sales people in the department

8

7 — Could be expected *never* to fail to conduct training meetings with his people weekly at a scheduled hour and to convey to them exactly what he expects.

6

Could be expected to remind sales personnel to wait on customers instead of conversing with each other.

5

4

Could be expected to tell an individual to come in anyway even though she/he called to say she/he was ill.

3

2
Could be expected to make promises to an individual about her/his salary being based on department sales even when he knew such a practice was against company policy.

1

FIGURE 15.2. Examples of a behaviorally anchored rating scale (BARS) Reprinted by permission

by these numbers or words—called **anchors**—the rater chooses the category that best represents the employee's performance on the specified dimension.

Behaviorally anchored rating scales (BARS) are another method that uses on-the-job behaviors as anchors for the rating scale. In a BARS scale, the rater chooses the rating category by choosing the behavior that is most representative of the employee's performance on that dimension (see Figure 15.2). Raters can also evaluate performance by rating the frequency of important behaviors required by the job. This method, known as the **behavioral checklist,** is illustrated in For Your Information 15.2.

Rating Errors

Ratings of job performance involve making subjective decisions about how to quantify job performance. As you recall, measurement that involves making subjective judgments often contains error. Industrial psychologists have identified a number of rating errors that occur when raters make systematic errors in judging employee performance. **Leniency errors** result when raters give all employees ratings better than they deserve, and **severity errors** result when raters give all employees worse ratings than they deserve. **Central-tendency errorr** results when the rater uses only the middle of the rating scale and ignores the highest and lowest scale categories. **Halo effect** occurs when raters let their judgment on one dimension influence judgments on other dimensions. For instance, an employee who receives a low rating on "quality of work" might also be rated low on "quantity of work" even though the employee meets the performance standards for quantity output.

To avoid inaccurate ratings, organizations should provide rater training for all persons conducting performance appraisals. Research on rater training (Fay & Latham, 1982) suggests that such training programs usually have only short-term effects, so it is a good idea for organizations to provide "brush-up" courses for training raters. Training objectives should include mastery of observing behavior, avoiding making rating errors, and maintaining consistent standards across employees (intra-rater reliability).

Who Should Rate?

Traditionally, organizations have given the job of rating employee performance to the employee's supervisor or manager. In recent years, however, many companies have begun to use a method of performance appraisal called **360° feedback.** In this method, employees receive ratings from their supervisors, peers, subordinates, or customers. (Peer, subordinate, and customer ratings are provided anonymously.) In addition, employees rate themselves. These ratings are compiled usually by computer to provide the employee with information on every dimension by every rater. This method provides rich feedback for the person being rated and might be perceived by some as fairer because misperceptions or rating errors by one person can be balanced by the opinion of others. Again, careful attention should be paid to training all raters to rate honestly the performance of others.

TOPIC (APPROPRIATE, INFORMATIVE)

Behavior Shown	Almost Never	A Few Times	Sometimes	Many Times	Almost Always
Gave examples from organizations					
Referred to sources when making assertions					
Wandered from the topic					
Demonstrated enthusiasm for topic					
Provided information in a clear and logical order					
Demonstrated knowledge and understanding of the topic					
Defined terms and jargon					

PUBLIC SPEAKING SKILLS

Behavior Shown	Almost Never	A Few Times	Sometimes	Many Times	Almost Always
Spoke clearly and audibly					
Connected sentences with "uh," "um," etc.					
Spoke too rapidly for audience understanding					
Spoke in a monotone voice					
Read from notes					
Used distracting gestures					
Used vulgar or politically incorrect language or phrases					

HANDOUTS AND AUDIOVISUAL AIDS

Behavior Shown	Almost Never	A Few Times	Sometimes	Many Times	Almost Always
Visual Aids were easy to read or understand					
Visual Aids were attractive					
Visual Aids demonstrated important points					

CLASS DISCUSSION

Behavior Shown	Almost Never	A Few Times	Sometimes	Many Times	Almost Always
Interacted with audience					
Gave audience tasks to do					
Elicited questions from audience					
Answered audience questions appropriately and to their satisfaction					

TIMING (ON TIME, ETC.)

Behavior Shown	Almost Never	A Few Times	Sometimes	Many Times	Almost Always
Became bogged down on certain points					
Repeated information					

SUMMARY

In the early 20th century, psychologists such as Walter Dill Scott, Hugo Müensterberg, and Walter Bingham began studying and applying psychological principles to the world of work. Both Scott and Müensterberg proposed methods for validating employment tests prior to World War I. Following the war, psychologists designed tests for hiring individuals and interest inventories for predicting occupational success. Psychological tests also played a key role in World War II, providing an impetus for development of the assessment centers. Since World War

Summary Box 15.3
Performance Impairment and Performance Appraisal

- Performance impairment tests are simulations that resemble video games and indicate when the test taker is not able to safely perform a job.
- Most organizations carry out formal evaluations of employees' job performance called performance appraisals.
- The major types of performance appraisal systems are ranking employees or rating employees on various types of scales.
- The most popular method of rating employee performance uses the graphic rating scale.

- Two other methods are the behaviorally anchored rating scale (BARS) and the behavioral checklist.
- Raters need to be trained so they do not make rating errors, such as leniency, severity, central-tendency, or halo-effect errors.
- Supervisors and managers usually rate their subordinates.
- In 360° feedback, an individual is rated by her or his manager, peers, subordinates, or customers, and the individual rates herself or himself.

II, organizations have used psychological tests for selection and placement of new employees, evaluation of current employees, and surveying consumers.

The employment interview is the most widely used method for employment testing. Most companies use the traditional interview, although structured interviews have been shown to have greater reliability and validity. Organizations also use performance tests, such as assessment centers and work samples, to assess how well job candidates can perform job tasks. High-fidelity performance tests replicate the job setting in great detail. Low-fidelity performance tests simulate job tasks using written, verbal, or visual descriptions.

Personality inventories measure ongoing cognitive constructs, usually referred to as personality traits, such as conscientiousness, extraversion, and agreeableness, that predispose people to perform certain behaviors. The most popular theory today among personality theorists is the five-factor model. Traditionally, personnel psychologists discouraged the use of personality tests as employment tests, because researchers had shown little relation between personality and job performance. Recently, personnel psychologists have begun to look more favorably on personality tests that reflect the five-factor model.

Organizations also use paper-and-pencil tests to assess job candidates' behavior that relates to abuse of alcohol or use of illegal drugs. Organizations interested in assessing job candidates' integrity may use paper-and-pencil tests, but Congress has forbidden the polygraph or lie detector for employment testing.

When Congress passed the Civil Rights Act of 1964, one of the specific areas addressed was hiring by organizations. The *Uniform Guidelines* and federal case law suggest that all employment tests should be job-related and have evidence of content validity or criterion-related validity. Organizations should maintain records regarding protected classes applying for jobs. If a test results in adverse impact, then the employer should find an alternative method for assessing job candidates.

Most employers conduct performance appraisals to evaluate the performance of their employees. Most organizations ask supervisors to evaluate employee performance by either ranking or rating employees on a number of predetermined dimensions, traits, or behaviors. The most popular method of rating employee performance is based on a graphic rating scale. Two other scales based on observing and rating behaviors are the behaviorally anchored rating scale (BARS) and the behavioral checklist. Persons who rate performance should be trained to avoid ratings errors, such as lenience, severity, central tendency, and the halo effect. In recent years, many companies have starting using 360° feedback, in which employees compare self-ratings to ratings received from their supervisors, peers, subordinates, or customers.

KEY CONCEPTS

360° feedback	forced distribution	personality traits
anchors	graphic rating scale	polygraph
assessment center	halo effect	protected class
behavioral checklist	high-fidelity test	severity error
behaviorally anchored	job analysis	structured interview
rating scale (BARS)	leniency error	traditional interview
central-tendency error	low-fidelity test	work sample
employment interview	performance appraisal	
false positive	performance impairment	
five-factor model	test	

LEARNING ACTIVITIES

1. What's Happening in the "Real World"?

Researchers have spent a great deal of time identifying the best ways to assess job candidates to fill positions in organizations. But what happens in the "real world"? In this activity, your assignment is to interview a person who is responsible for hiring employees in an organization in your community. In large companies, you will find this person in the human resources or personnel department. Managers, however, also are often given these responsibilities—particularly in decentralized companies such as food service, banking or retail—so you might wish to interview a store manager. You may choose a personal acquaintance for the interview, or choose an organization that you would like to know more about.

PART I: Thinking about what you would like to learn from your interview, write 8 to 10 questions that you plan to ask. Have your instructor review your questions. When you schedule your interview, explain that you are carrying out a class assignment and ask for 30 minutes of your interviewee's time. You will need to be flexible in order to inconvenience your interviewee as little as possible.

PART II: After your instructor has reviewed your questions, you may carry out your interview. Be sure to take notes. (It is okay to tape the interview, if your interviewee agrees.) Remember to follow up on questions and keep your interviewee talking. During the interview, it will be your job to gather information, *not* give advice. After the interview, send a thank-you note acknowledging the time and interest that were given to you. Don't forget to dress professionally—this might be an organization you would like to work for some day!

PART III: Write a paper based on your interview that describes the organization's hiring program. Include some background on the company. Your paper should contain your critique of the company's program based on what you have learned about assessment.

2. The Customer Service Problem: A Role-Play

The following exercise allows you to observe a role-play and then rate the performance of the service representative using one of three performance appraisal forms. Each form represents a type of assessment discussed in this chapter. When you have observed the role-play and completed your performance appraisal form, fill out and discuss the Evaluation of Performance Appraisal Form. Share your experience with other class members and determine which type of assessment provided the most accurate information.

ROLE-PLAY INSTRUCTIONS

Service Representative

You are the customer service representative for an office machine repair company based in Orlando. Your company services all major brands of office machines, and your parts department stocks parts for the major manufacturers. You are now at the XYZ Industries main office. It is 5 P.M. on Friday evening, and you have been at XYZ for about half an hour. During that time you have examined the copy machine that has a broken part in the collator. (The machine will make copies, but it will not sort and collate them.) You now have to inform the customer that

- The collater has a broken part
- The part is in stock
- The parts department closes at 5 P.M.
- You will be back Monday morning to fix the machine

After you inform the customer of the circumstances, react in whatever way you think appropriate to the customer. Your objectives are to keep the customer's business, but remain cost effective. Your company will support any solutions to the customer's problems that you generate.

Manager, XYZ Industries

It is Friday afternoon at 5 P.M. You have promised your customer that he will receive 20 copies of a large report by Federal Express on Monday morning. Just as your copy clerk was beginning to copy and collate the report, the copy machine broke down. The clerk has informed you that the copy machine is still working, but the reports (200 pages each) must be collated by hand. The report must be shipped on Saturday morning to make the deadline. You are tired and frustrated. You cannot think of any way to solve this problem, so feel free to take your frustrations out on the service representative when he or she gives you the bad news that the machine cannot be fixed until Monday.

Performance Appraisal 1
Service Representatiave

Rate the employee on the following:

	1	2	3	4	5
Technical service skills	LOW				HIGH
Interpersonal skills	1 LOW	2	3	4	5 HIGH
Flexibility	1 LOW	2	3	4	5 HIGH
Creativity	1 LOW	2	3	4	5 HIGH
Cost awareness	1 LOW	2	3	4	5 HIGH
Problem solving	1 LOW	2	3	4	5 HIGH
Time management	1 LOW	2	3	4	5 HIGH

Performance Appraisal 2
Service Representatiave

Rate the frequency of observed behaviors by checking the appropriate box after each statement. (For the purpose of this exercise, assume that you have witnessed a number of instances such as this one.)

	1 NEVER	2 RARELY	3 SOMETIMES	4 USUALLY	5 ALWAYS
Interacts cordially with customers					
Presents alternative solutions to customers					
Listens attentively to customers' problems					
Proposes the most cost-effective method of meeting customer needs					
Describes company policies to customer in detail					
Minimizes the time spent at customer site					
Repeats customer concerns in conversation to ensure understanding					
Rearranges schedule to meet customer needs					
Works overtime when required to meet customer needs					
Maintains calm temperament when dealing with angry customers					
Defends company policies to customer					

Rate the following by checking the appropriate box for each skill.

	1	2	3	4	5
Technical service skills	Rarely fixes machine	Often has return calls for same problem	Usually fixes machines	Always fixes machines	Frequently prevents machine breakdown
Interpersonal skills	Always discourteous to customers	Often discourteous to customers	Sometimes lacks courtesy with customers	Usually friendly and courteous	Always friendly and courteous to customers
Flexibility	Never changes approach	Usually uses one approach	Relies on several approaches	Often tries new approaches	Generates new approaches often
Cost awareness	Never considers costs to company	Sometimes considers costs to company	Generally chooses cost effective approaches	Often generates cost savings	Usually generates cost savings
Problem solving	Often seeks help unnecessarily	Consistently seeks and needs help	Seeks help only when needed	Generally solves own problems	Generates good solutions for self and others

Evaluation of Performance Appraisal Form

1. What kind of rating form did you use?

2. Did this form assist you in making the ratings? If so, how?

3. Did this form hinder you in making ratings? If so, how?

4. Did you generate information that will be useful to the employee? Will it assist you in giving the employee feedback?

5. Do you think you gave accurate ratings using this form? Explain why or why not.

Appendix A: Guidelines for Critiquing a Psychological Test

To make informed decisions about tests, you need to know how to properly critique a test. A critique of a test is an analysis of the test. A good critique answers many of the questions below. Your instructor might have additional ideas about what constitutes a good critique.

General Descriptive Information

- What is the title of the test?
- Who is the author of the test?
- Who publishes the test and when was it published (include dates of manuals, norms, and supplementary materials)?
- How long does it take to administer the test?
- How much does it cost to purchase the test (include the cost of the test, answer sheets, manual, scoring services, etc.)?

Purpose and Nature of the Test

- What does the test measure (include scales)?
- What does the test predict?
- What behavior does the test require the test taker to perform?
- What population was the test designed for (age, type of person)?
- What is the nature of the test (e.g., maximal performance, behavior observation, or self-report; standardized or nonstandardized; objective or subjective)?
- What is format of the test (e.g., paper-and-pencil or computer-based, multiple-choice or true/false)?

Practical Evaluation

- Is the test manual comprehensive (e.g., does it include information on how the test was constructed, its reliability and validity, composition of norm groups, is it easy to read, etc.)?
- Is the test easy or difficult to administer?
- How clear are the administration directions?
- How clear are the scoring procedures?
- What qualifications and training does a test administrator need to have?
- Does the test have face validity?

Technical Evaluation

- Is there a norm group?
- Who is the norm group?
- What type of norms are there (e.g., percentiles, standard scores)?
- How was the norm group selected?
- Are there subgroup norms (e.g., by age, gender, region, occupation, etc.)?
- What is the test's reliability?
- How was reliability determined?
- What is the test's validity?
- How was validity determined?

Test Reviews

- What do reviewers say are the strengths and weaknesses of the test?

Summary

- Overall, what do you see as being the strengths and weaknesses of the test?

Appendix B:
Excerpts from the Ethical Principles of Psychologists and Code of Conduct

INTRODUCTION

The American Psychological Association's (APA's) Ethical Principles of Psychologists and Code of Conduct (hereinafter referred to as the Ethics Code) consists of an Introduction, a Preamble, six General Principles (A–F), and specific Ethical Standards.[1] The Introduction discusses the intent, organization, procedural considerations, and scope of application of the Ethics Code. The Preamble and General Principles are *aspirational* goals to guide psychologists toward the highest ideals of psychology. Although the Preamble and General Principles are not themselves enforceable rules, they should be considered by psychologists in arriving at an ethical course of action and may be considered by ethics bodies in interpreting the Ethical Standards. The Ethical Standards set forth *enforceable* rules for conduct as psychologists. Most of the Ethical Standards are written broadly, in order to apply to psychologists in varied roles, although the application of an Ethical Standard may vary depending on the context. The Ethical Standards are not exhaustive. The fact that a given conduct is not specifically addressed by the Ethics Code does not mean that it is necessarily either ethical or unethical.

Membership in the APA commits members to adhere to the APA Ethics Code and to the rules and procedures used to implement it. Psychologists and students, whether or not they are APA members, should be aware that the Ethics Code may be applied to them by state psychology boards, courts, or other public bodies.

This Ethics Code applies only to psychologists' work-related activities, that is, activities that are part of the psychologists' scientific and professional functions or that are psychological in nature. It includes the clinical or counseling practice of psychology, research, teaching, supervision of trainees, development of assessment instruments, conducting assessments, educational counseling, organizational consulting, social intervention, administration, and other activities as well. These work-related activities can be distinguished from the purely private conduct of a psychologist, which ordinarily is not within the purview of the Ethics Code.

The Ethics Code is intended to provide standards of professional conduct that can be applied by the APA and by other bodies that choose to adopt them. Whether or not a psychologist has violated the Ethics Code does not by itself determine whether he or she is legally liable in a court action, whether a contract is enforceable, or whether other legal consequences occur. These results are based on legal rather than ethical rules. However, compliance with or violation of the Ethics Code may be admissible as evidence in some legal proceedings, depending on the circumstances.

In the process of making decisions regarding their professional behavior, psychologists must consider this Ethics Code, in addition to applicable laws and psychology board

[1]Only a portion of the Ethical Standards are reprinted in this appendix.

Source: "Ethical Principles of Psychologists and Code of Conduct" (from *American Psychologist,* 1992, 47, pp. 1597–1611). Copyright © 1992 by the American Psychological Association. Reprinted with permission.

352

*APPENDIX B:
Excerpts from the
Ethical Principles
of Psychologists
and Code of
Conduct*

regulations. If the Ethics Code establishes a higher standard of conduct than is required by law, psychologists must meet the higher ethical standard. If the Ethics Code standard appears to conflict with the requirements of law, then psychologists make known their commitment to the Ethics Code and take steps to resolve the conflict in a responsible manner. If neither law nor the Ethics Code resolves an issue, psychologists should consider other professional materials[2] and the dictates of their own conscience, as well as seek consultation with others within the field when this is practical.

The procedures for filing, investigating, and resolving complaints of unethical conduct are described in the current Rules and Procedures of the APA Ethics Committee. The actions that APA may take for violations of the Ethics Code include actions such as reprimand, censure, termination of APA membership, and referral of the matter to other bodies. Complainants who seek remedies such as monetary damages in alleging ethical violations by a psychologist must resort to private negotiation, administrative bodies, or the courts. Actions that violate the Ethics Code may lead to the imposition of sanctions on a psychologist by bodies other than APA, including state psychological associations, other professional groups, psychology boards, other state or federal agencies, and payors for health services. In addition to actions for violation of the Ethics Code, the APA Bylaws provide that APA may take action against a member after his or her conviction of a felony, expulsion or suspension from an affiliated state psychological association, or suspension or loss of licensure.

PREAMBLE

Psychologists work to develop a valid and reliable body of scientific knowledge based on research. They may apply that knowledge to human behavior in a variety of contexts. In doing so, they perform many roles, such as researcher, educator, diagnostician, therapist, supervisor, consultant, administrator, social interventionist, and expert witness. Their goal is to broaden knowledge of behavior and, where appropriate, to apply it pragmatically to improve the condition of both the individual and society. Psychologists respect the central importance of freedom of inquiry and expression in research, teaching, and publication. They also strive to help the public in developing informed judgments and choices concerning human behavior. This Ethics Code provides a common set of values upon which psychologists build their professional and scientific work.

This Code is intended to provide both the general principles and the decision rules to cover most situations encountered by psychologists. It has as its primary goal the welfare and protection of the individuals and groups with whom psychologists work. It is the individual responsibility of each psychologist to aspire to the highest possible standards of conduct. Psychologists respect and protect human and civil rights, and do not knowingly participate in or condone unfair discriminatory practices.

[2]Professional materials that are most helpful in this regard are guidelines and standards that have been adopted or endorsed by professional psychological organizations. Such guidelines and standards, whether adopted by the American Psychological Association (APA) or its Divisions, are not enforceable as such by this Ethics Code, but are of educative value to psychologists, courts, and professional bodies. Such materials include, but are not limited to, the APA's General Guidelines for Providers of Psychological Services (1987), Specialty Guidelines for the Delivery of Services by Clinical Psychologists, Counseling Psychologists, Industrial/Organizational Psychologists, and School Psychologists (1981), Guidelines for Computer Based Tests and Interpretations (1987), Standards for Educational and Psychological Testing (1985), Ethical Principles in the Conduct of Research With Human Participants (1982), Guidelines for Ethical Conduct in the Care and Use of Animals (1986), Guidelines for Providers of Psychological Services to Ethnic, Linguistic, and Culturally Diverse Populations (1990), and Publication Manual of the American Psychological Association (3rd ed., 1983). Materials not adopted by APA as a whole include the APA Division 41 (Forensic Psychology)/American Psychology-Law Society's Specialty Guidelines for Forensic Psychologists (1991).

The development of a dynamic set of ethical standards for a psychologist's work-related conduct requires a personal commitment to a lifelong effort to act ethically; to encourage ethical behavior by students, supervisees, employees, and colleagues, as appropriate; and to consult with others, as needed, concerning ethical problems. Each psychologist supplements, but does not violate, the Ethics Code's values and rules on the basis of guidance drawn from personal values, culture, and experience.

353

APPENDIX B:
Excerpts from the
Ethical Principles
of Psychologists
and Code of
Conduct

GENERAL PRINCIPLES

Principle A: Competence

Psychologists strive to maintain high standards of competence in their work. They recognize the boundaries of their particular competencies and the limitations of their expertise. They provide only those services and use only those techniques for which they are qualified by education, training, or experience. Psychologists are cognizant of the fact that the competencies required in serving, teaching, and/or studying groups of people vary with the distinctive characteristics of those groups. In those areas in which recognized professional standards do not yet exist, psychologists exercise careful judgment and take appropriate precautions to protect the welfare of those with whom they work. They maintain knowledge of relevant scientific and professional information related to the services they render, and they recognize the need for ongoing education. Psychologists make appropriate use of scientific, professional, technical, and administrative resources.

Principle B: Integrity

Psychologists seek to promote integrity in the science, teaching, and practice of psychology. In these activities psychologists are honest, fair, and respectful of others. In describing or reporting their qualifications, services, products, fees, research, or teaching, they do not make statements that are false, misleading, or deceptive. Psychologists strive to be aware of their own belief systems, values, needs, and limitations and the effect of these on their work. To the extent feasible, they attempt to clarify for relevant parties the roles they are performing and to function appropriately in accordance with those roles. Psychologists avoid improper and potentially harmful dual relationships.

Principle C: Professional and Scientific Responsibility

Psychologists uphold professional standards of conduct, clarify their professional roles and obligations, accept appropriate responsibility for their behavior, and adapt their methods to the needs of different populations. Psychologists consult with, refer to, or cooperate with other professionals and institutions to the extent needed to serve the best interests of their patients, clients, or other recipients of their services. Psychologists' moral standards and conduct are personal matters to the same degree as is true for any other person, except as psychologists' conduct may compromise their professional responsibilities or reduce the public's trust in psychology and psychologists. Psychologists are concerned about the ethical compliance of their colleagues' scientific and professional conduct. When appropriate, they consult with colleagues in order to prevent or avoid unethical conduct.

Principle D: Respect for People's Rights and Dignity

Psychologists accord appropriate respect to the fundamental rights, dignity, and worth of all people. They respect the rights of individuals to privacy, confidentiality, self-determina-

354

APPENDIX B:
Excerpts from the
Ethical Principles
of Psychologists
and Code of
Conduct

tion, and autonomy, mindful that legal and other obligations may lead to inconsistency and conflict with the exercise of these rights. Psychologists are aware of cultural, individual, and role differences, including those due to age, gender, race, ethnicity, national origin, religion, sexual orientation, disability, language, and socioeconomic status. Psychologists try to eliminate the effect on their work of biases based on those factors, and they do not knowingly participate in or condone unfair discriminatory practices.

Principle E: Concern for Others' Welfare

Psychologists seek to contribute to the welfare of those with whom they interact professionally. In their professional actions, psychologists weigh the welfare and rights of their patients or clients, students, supervisees, human research participants, and other affected persons, and the welfare of animal subjects of research. When conflicts occur among psychologists' obligations or concerns, they attempt to resolve these conflicts and to perform their roles in a responsible fashion that avoids or minimizes harm. Psychologists are sensitive to real and ascribed differences in power between themselves and others, and they do not exploit or mislead other people during or after professional relationships.

Principle F: Social Responsibility

Psychologists are aware of their professional and scientific responsibilities to the community and the society in which they work and live. They apply and make public their knowledge of psychology in order to contribute to human welfare. Psychologists are concerned about and work to mitigate the causes of human suffering. When undertaking research, they strive to advance human welfare and the science of psychology. Psychologists try to avoid misuse of their work. Psychologists comply with the law and encourage the development of law and social policy that serve the interests of their patients and clients and the public. They are encouraged to contribute a portion of their professional time for little or no personal advantage.

Evaluation, Assessment, or Intervention

2.01 Evaluation, Diagnosis, and Interventions in Professional Context.

(a) Psychologists perform evaluations, diagnostic services, or interventions only within the context of a defined professional relationship. (See also Standards 1.03, Professional and Scientific Relationship.)

(b) Psychologists' assessments, recommendations, reports, and psychological diagnostic or evaluative statements are based on information and techniques (including personal interviews of the individual when appropriate) sufficient to provide appropriate substantiation for their findings. (See also Standard 7.02, Forensic Assessments.)

2.02 Competence and Appropriate Use of Assessments and Interventions.

(a) Psychologists who develop, administer, score, interpret, or use psychological assessment techniques, interviews, tests, or instruments do so in a manner and for purposes that are appropriate in light of the research on or evidence of the usefulness and proper application of the techniques.

(b) Psychologists refrain from misuse of assessment techniques, interventions, results, and interpretations and take reasonable steps to prevent others from misusing the information these techniques provide. This includes refraining from releasing raw test results or raw data to persons, other than to patients or clients as appropriate, who are not qualified to use such information. (See also Standards 1.02, Relationship of Ethics and Law, and 1.04, Boundaries of Competence.)

2.03 Test Construction.

Psychologists who develop and conduct research with tests and other assessment techniques use scientific procedures and current professional knowledge for test design, standardization, validation, reduction or elimination of bias, and recommendations for use.

2.04 Use of Assessment in General and With Special Populations.

(a) Psychologists who perform interventions or administer, score, interpret, or use assessment techniques are familiar with the reliability, validation, and related standardization or outcome studies of, and proper applications and uses of, the techniques they use.

(b) Psychologists recognize limits to the certainty with which diagnoses, judgments, or predictions can be made about individuals.

(c) Psychologists attempt to identify situations in which particular interventions or assessment techniques or norms may not be applicable or may require adjustment in administration or interpretation because of factors such as individuals' gender, age, race, ethnicity, national origin, religion, sexual orientation, disability, language, or socioeconomic status.

2.05 Interpreting Assessment Results.

When interpreting assessment results, including automated interpretations, psychologists take into account the various test factors and characteristics of the person being assessed that might affect psychologists' judgments or reduce the accuracy of their interpretations. They indicate any significant reservations they have about the accuracy or limitations of their interpretations.

2.06 Unqualified Persons.

Psychologists do not promote the use of psychological assessment techniques by unqualified persons. (See also Standard 1.22, Delegation to and Supervision of Subordinates.)

2.07 Obsolete Tests and Outdated Test Results.

(a) Psychologists do not base their assessment or intervention decisions or recommendations on data or test results that are outdated for the current purpose.

(b) Similarly, psychologists do not base such decisions or recommendations on tests and measures that are obsolete and not useful for the current purpose.

2.08 Test Scoring and Interpretation Services.

(a) Psychologists who offer assessment or scoring procedures to other professionals accurately describe the purpose, norms, validity, reliability, and applications of the procedures and any special qualifications applicable to their use.

(b) Psychologists select scoring and interpretation services (including automated services) on the basis of evidence of the validity of the program and procedures as well as on other appropriate considerations.

(c) Psychologists retain appropriate responsibility for the appropriate application, interpretation, and use of assessment instruments, whether they score and interpret such tests themselves or use automated or other services.

2.09 Explaining Assessment Results.

Unless the nature of the relationship is clearly explained to the person being assessed in advance and precludes provision of an explanation of results (such as in some organizational consulting, pre-employment or security screenings, and forensic evaluations), psychologists ensure that an explanation of the results is provided using language that is reasonably understandable to the person assessed or to another legally authorized person on behalf of the client. Regardless of whether the scoring and interpretation are done by the psychologist, by assistants, or by automated or other outside services, psychologists take reasonable steps to ensure that appropriate explanations of results are given.

355

APPENDIX B:
Excerpts from the
Ethical Principles
of Psychologists
and Code of
Conduct

356

*APPENDIX B:
Excerpts from the
Ethical Principles
of Psychologists
and Code of
Conduct*

2.10 Maintaining Test Security.

Psychologists make reasonable efforts to maintain the integrity and security of tests and other assessment techniques consistent with law, contractual obligations, and in a manner that permits compliance with the requirements of this Ethics Code. (See also Standard 1.02, Relationship of Ethics and Law.)

Privacy and Confidentiality

These Standards are potentially applicable to the professional and scientific activities of all psychologists.

5.01 Discussing the Limits of Confidentiality.

(a) Psychologists discuss with persons and organizations with whom they establish a scientific or professional relationship (including, to the extent feasible, minors and their legal representatives) (1) the relevant limitations on confidentiality, including limitations where applicable in group, marital, and family therapy or in organizational consulting, and (2) the foreseeable uses of the information generated through their services.

(b) Unless it is not feasible or is contraindicated, the discussion of confidentiality occurs at the outset of the relationship and thereafter as new circumstances may warrant.

(c) Permission for electronic recording of interviews is secured from clients and patients.

5.02 Maintaining Confidentiality.

Psychologists have a primary obligation and take reasonable precautions to respect the confidentiality rights of those with whom they work or consult, recognizing that confidentiality may be established by law, institutional rules, or professional or scientific relationships. (See also Standard 6.26, Professional Reviewers.)

5.03 Minimizing Intrusions on Privacy.

(a) In order to minimize intrusions on privacy, psychologists include in written and oral reports, consultations, and the like, only information germane to the purpose for which the communication is made.

(b) Psychologists discuss confidential information obtained in clinical or consulting relationships, or evaluative data concerning patients, individual or organizational clients, students, research participants, supervisees, and employees, only for appropriate scientific or professional purposes and only with persons clearly concerned with such matters.

5.04 Maintenance of Records.

Psychologists maintain appropriate confidentiality in creating, storing, accessing, transferring, and disposing of records under their control, whether these are written, automated, or in any other medium. Psychologists maintain and dispose of records in accordance with law and in a manner that permits compliance with the requirements of this Ethics Code.

5.05 Disclosures.

(a) Psychologists disclose confidential information without the consent of the individual only as mandated by law, or where permitted by law for a valid purpose, such as (1) to provide needed professional services to the patient or the individual or organizational client, (2) to obtain appropriate professional consultations, (3) to protect the patient or client or others from harm, or (4) to obtain payment for services, in which instance disclosure is limited to the minimum that is necessary to achieve the purpose.

357

APPENDIX B:
Excerpts from the
Ethical Principles
of Psychologists
and Code of
Conduct

(b) Psychologists also may disclose confidential information with the appropriate consent of the patient or the individual or organizational client (or of another legally authorized person on behalf of the patient or client), unless prohibited by law.

5.06 Consultations.

When consulting with colleagues, (1) psychologists do not share confidential information that reasonably could lead to the identification of a patient, client, research participant, or other person or organization with whom they have a confidential relationship unless they have obtained the prior consent of the person or organization or the disclosure cannot be avoided, and (2) they share information only to the extent necessary to achieve the purposes of the consultation. (See also Standard 5.02, Maintaining Confidentiality.)

5.07 Confidential Information in Databases.

(a) If confidential information concerning recipients of psychological services is to be entered into databases or systems of records available to persons whose access has not been consented to by the recipient, then psychologists use coding or other techniques to avoid the inclusion of personal identifiers.

(b) If a research protocol approved by an institutional review board or similar body requires the inclusion of personal identifiers, such identifiers are deleted before the information is made accessible to persons other than those of whom the subject was advised.

(c) If such deletion is not feasible, then before psychologists transfer such data to others or review such data collected by others, they take reasonable steps to determine that appropriate consent of personally identifiable individuals has been obtained.

5.08 Use of Confidential Information for Didactic or Other Purposes.

(a) Psychologists do not disclose in their writings, lectures, or other public media, confidential, personally identifiable information concerning their patients, individual or organizational clients, students, research participants, or other recipients of their services that they obtained during the course of their work, unless the person or organization has consented in writing or unless there is other ethical or legal authorization for doing so.

(b) Ordinarily, in such scientific and professional presentations, psychologists disguise confidential information concerning such persons or organizations so that they are not individually identifiable to others and so that discussions do not cause harm to subjects who might identify themselves.

5.09 Preserving Records and Data.

A psychologist makes plans in advance so that confidentiality of records and data is protected in the event of the psychologist's death, incapacity, or withdrawal from the position or practice.

5.10 Ownership of Records and Data.

Recognizing that ownership of records and data is governed by legal principles, psychologists take reasonable and lawful steps so that records and data remain available to the extent needed to serve the best interests of patients, individual or organizational clients, research participants, or appropriate others.

5.11 Withholding Records for Nonpayment.

Psychologists may not withhold records under their control that are requested and imminently needed for a patient's or client's treatment solely because payment has not been received, except as otherwise provided by law.

Forensic Activities

APPENDIX B:
*Excerpts from the
Ethical Principles
of Psychologists
and Code of
Conduct*

7.01 Professionalism.

Psychologists who perform forensic functions, such as assessments, interviews, consultations, reports, or expert testimony, must comply with all other provisions of this Ethics Code to the extent that they apply to such activities. In addition, psychologists base their forensic work on appropriate knowledge of and competence in the areas underlying such work, including specialized knowledge concerning special populations. (See also Standards 1.06, Basis for Scientific and Professional Judgments; 1.08, Human Differences; 1.15, Misuse of Psychologists' Influence; and 1.23, Documentation of Professional and Scientific Work.)

Appendix C:
Code of Fair Testing
Practices in Education

PREPARED BY THE JOINT COMMITTEE
ON TESTING

The Code of Fair Testing Practices in Education states the major obligations to test takers of professionals who develop or use educational tests. The Code is meant to apply broadly to the use of tests in education (admissions, educational assessment, educational diagnosis, and student placement). The Code is not designed to cover employment testing, licensure or certification testing, or other types of testing. Although the Code has relevance to many types of educational tests, it is directed primarily at professionally developed tests such as those sold by commercial test publishers or used in formally administered testing programs. The Code is not intended to cover tests made by individual teachers for use in their own classrooms.

The Code addresses the roles of test developers and test users separately. Test users are people who select tests, commission test development services, or make decisions on the basis of test scores. Test developers are people who actually construct tests as well as those who set policies for particular testing programs. The rules may, of course, overlap as when a state education agency commissions test development services, sets policies that control the test development process, and makes decisions on the basis of the test scores.

The Code presents standards for educational test developers and users in four areas:

A. Developing/Selecting Tests
B. Interpreting Scores
C. Striving for Fairness
D. Informing Test Takers

Organizations, institutions, and individual professionals who endorse the Code commit themselves to safeguarding the rights of test takers by following the principles listed. The Code is intended to be consistent with the relevant parts of the *Standards for Educational and Psychological Testing* (AERA, APA, NCME, 1985). However, the Code differs from the Standards in both audience and purpose. The Code is meant to be understood by the general public; it is limited to educational tests; and the primary focus is on those issues that affect the proper use of tests. The Code is not meant to add new principles over and above those in the Standards or to change the meaning of the Standards. The goal is rather to represent the spirit of a selected portion of the Standards in a way that is meaningful to test takers and/or their parents or guardians. It is the hope of the Joint Committee that the Code will also be judged to be consistent with existing codes of conduct and standards of other professional groups who use educational tests.

Source: American Psychologist, 1992, 47, pp. 1597–1611; Copyright © 1992 by The American Psychological Association. Reprinted with permission.

360

APPENDIX C:
Code of Fair
Testing
Practices in
Education

The Code has been developed by the Joint Committee on Testing Practices, a cooperative effort of several professional organizations, that has as its aim the advancement, in the public interest, of the quality of testing practices. The Joint Committee was initiated by the American Educational Research Association, the American Psychological Association, and the National Council on Measurement in Education. In addition to these three groups, the American Association for Counseling and Development/Association for Measurement and Evaluation in Counseling and Development, and the American Speech-Language-Hearing Association are now also sponsors of the Joint Committee.

This is not copyrighted material. Reproduction and dissemination are encouraged. Please cite this document as follows:

Code of Fair Testing Practices in Education. (1988) Washington, D.C.: Joint Committee on Testing Practices. (Mailing Address: Joint Committee on Testing Practices, American Psychological Association, 1200 17th Street, NW, Washington, D.C. 20036.)

A. DEVELOPING/SELECTING APPROPRIATE TESTS

Test Developers Should:

1. Define what each test measures and what the test should be used for. Describe the population(s) for which the test is appropriate.
2. Accurately represent the characteristics, usefulness, and limitations of tests for their intended purposes.
3. Explain relevant measurement concepts as necessary for clarity at the level of detail that is appropriate for the intended audience(s).
4. Describe the process of test development. Explain how the content and skills to be tested were selected.
5. Provide evidence that the test meets its intended purpose(s).
6. Provide either representative samples or complete copies of test questions, directions, answer sheets, manuals, and score reports to qualified users.
7. Indicate the nature of the evidence obtained concerning the appropriateness of each test for groups of different racial, ethnic, or linguistic backgrounds who are likely to be tested.
8. Identify and publish any specialized skills needed to administer each test and to interpret scores correctly.

Test Users Should:

1. First define the purpose for testing and the population to be tested. Then, select a test for that purpose and that population based on a thorough review of the available information.
2. Investigate potentially useful scores of information, in addition to test scores, to corroborate the information provided by tests.
3. Read the materials provided by test developers and avoid using tests for which unclear or incomplete information is provided.
4. Become familiar with how and when the test was developed and tried out.
5. Read independent evaluations of a test and of possible alternative measures. Look for evidence required to support the claims of test developers.
6. Examine specimen sets, disclosed tests or samples of questions, directions, answer sheets, manuals, and score reports before selecting a test.
7. Ascertain whether the test content and norms group(s) or comparison group(s) are appropriate for the intended test takers.
8. Select and use only those tests for which the skills needed to administer the test and interpret scores correctly are available.

Test Developers Should:

9. Provide timely and easily understood score reports that describe test performance clearly and accurately. Also explain the meaning and limitations of reported scores.
10. Describe the population(s) represented by any norms or comparison group(s), the dates the data were gathered, and the process used to select the samples of test takers.
11. Warn users to avoid specific, reasonably anticipated misuses of test scores.
12. Provide information that will help users follow reasonable procedures for setting passing scores when it is appropriate to use such scores with the test.
13. Provide information that will help users gather evidence to show that the test is meeting its intended purpose(s).

Test Users Should:

9. Obtain information about the scale used for reporting scores, the characteristics of any norms or comparison group(s), and the limitations of the scores.
10. Interpret scores taking into account any major differences between the norms or comparison groups and the actual test takers. Also take into account any differences in test administration practices or familiarity with the specific questions in the test.
11. Avoid using tests for purposes not specifically recommended by the test developer unless evidence is obtained to support the intended use.
12. Explain how passing scores were set and gather evidence to support the appropriateness of the scores.
13. Obtain evidence to help show that the test is meeting its intended purpose(s).

C. STRIVING FOR FAIRNESS

Test Developers Should:

14. Review and revise test questions and related materials to avoid potentially insensitive content or language.
15. Investigate the performance of test takers of different races, gender, and ethnic backgrounds when samples of sufficient size are available. Enact procedures that help to ensure that differences in performance are related primarily to the skills under assessment rather than to irrelevant factors.
16. When feasible, make appropriately modified forms of tests or administration procedures available for test takers with handicapping conditions. Warn test users of potential problems in using standard norms with modified tests or administration procedures that result in non-comparable scores.

Test Users Should:

14. Evaluate the procedures used by test developers to avoid potentially insensitive content or language.
15. Review the performance of test takers of different races, gender, and ethnic backgrounds when samples of sufficient size are available. Evaluate the extent to which performance differences may have been caused by inappropriate characteristics of the test.
16. When necessary and feasible, use appropriately modified forms of tests or administration procedures for test takers with handicapping conditions. Interpret standard norms with care in the light of the modifications that were made.

D. INFORMING TEST TAKERS

Test Developers or Test Users Should:

17. When a test is optional, provide test takers or their parents/guardians with information to help them judge whether the test should be taken, or if an available alternative to the test should be used.

18. Provide test takers the information they need to be familiar with the coverage of the test, the types of question formats, the directions, and appropriate test-taking strategies. Strive to make such information equally available to all test takers.

19. Provide test takers or their parents/guardians with information about rights test takers may have to obtain copies of tests and completed answer sheets, retake tests, have tests rescored, or cancel scores.

20. Tell test takers or their parents/guardians how long scores will be kept on file and indicate to whom and under what circumstances test scores will or will not be released.

21. Describe the procedures that test takers or their parents/guardians may use to register complaints and have problems resolved.

Appendix D:
Table of Critical Values for Pearson Product-Moment Correlation Coefficients

Critical values for Pearson product-moment correlation coefficients, r*

| df | α Levels (two-tailed test) | | | | |
	.10	.05	.02	.01	.001
(df = N − 2)	α Levels (one-tailed test)				
	.05	.025	.01	.005	.0005
1	.98769	.99692	.999507	.999877	.9999988
2	.900000	.95000	.98000	.990000	.99900
3	.8054	.8783	.93433	.95873	.99116
4	.7293	.8114	.8822	.91720	.97406
5	.6694	.7545	.8329	.8745	.95074
6	.6215	.7067	.7887	.8343	.92493
7	.5822	.6664	.7498	.7977	.8982
8	.5494	.6319	.7155	.7646	.8721
9	.5214	.6021	.6851	.7348	.8371
10	.4973	.5760	.6581	.7079	.8233
11	.4762	.5529	.6339	.6835	.8010
12	.4575	.5324	.6120	.6614	.7800
13	.4409	.5139	.5923	.6411	.7603
14	.4259	.4973	.5742	.6226	.7420
15	.4124	.4821	.5577	.6055	.7246
16	.4000	.4683	.5425	.5897	.7084
17	.3887	.4555	.5285	.5751	.6932
18	.3783	.4438	.5155	.5614	.6787
19	.3687	.4329	.5034	.5487	.6652
20	.3598	.4227	.4921	.5368	.6524
25	.3233	.3809	.4451	.4869	.5974
30	.2960	.3494	.4093	.4487	.5541
35	.2746	.3246	.3810	.4182	.5189
40	.2573	.3044	.3578	.3932	.4896
45	.2428	.2875	.3384	.3721	.4648
50	.2306	.2732	.3218	.3541	.4433
60	.2108	.2500	.2948	.3248	.4078
70	.1954	.2319	.2737	.3017	.3799
80	.1829	.2172	.2565	.2830	.3568
90	.1726	.2050	.2422	.2673	.3375
100	.1638	.1946	.2301	.2540	.3211

* To be significant the r obtained from the data must be equal to or larger than the value shown in the table.

Source: Table VII from Fisher & Yates, *Statistical Tables for Biological, Agricultural, and Medical Research.* Copyright © 1963 by Addison Wesley Longman Ltd., Pearson Education Limited, Edinburgh Gate, Harlow Essex CM20. Reprinted with permission.

Glossary

360° feedback A method of performance appraisal in which managers receive ratings from their supervisors, peers, subordinates, or customers, and also rate themselves.

absolute decisions Decisions that are made by seeing who has the minimum score needed to qualify.

abstract attributes Attributes that are more difficult to describe in terms of behaviors, such as personality, intelligence, creativity, and aggressiveness, because people disagree on which behaviors represent the attribute.

achievement tests Tests designed to measure a person's previous learning in a specific academic area.

acquiescence The tendency of some test takers to agree with any ideas or behaviors presented.

adaptive tests Tests made up of questions chosen from a large test bank to match the skill and ability level of the test taker.

administrative policy decisions Decisions that are typically made by testing specialists, educational administrators, or committees.

alternate forms Two forms of the test that alike in every way except questions. Used to overcome problems such as practice effects. Also referred to as parallel forms.

anchors Numbers or words on a rating scale that the rater chooses to indicate the category that best represents the employee's performance on the specified dimension.

anonymity The practice of administering tests or obtaining information without knowing the identity of the participant.

aptitude tests Tests that are designed to assess test takers' potential for learning or ability to perform in an area in which they have not been specifically trained.

area transformations A method for changing scores for interpretation purposes that changes the unit of measurement and the unit of reference, such as percentile ranks.

assessment center Large-scale replications of a job that require test takers to solve typical job problems by role playing or to demonstrate proficiency at job functions such as making presentations or fulfilling administrative duties. Used for assessing job-related dimensions, such as leadership, decision making, planning, and organizing.

attention deficit hyperactivity disorder (ADHD) A disorder characterized by excessive daydreaming and distraction, not considered a learning disability.

authentic assessment Assessment that measures a student's ability to apply what she or he has learned in real world settings.

365

behavior   An observable and measurable action.

behavior observation tests   Tests that involve observing persons' behavior to learn how they typically respond in a particular context.

behavioral checklist   A checklist that helps raters evaluate performance by recording the frequency of important behaviors required by the job.

behaviorally anchored rating scales (BARS)   A type of performance appraisal that uses behaviors as anchors. The rater rates by choosing the behavior that is most representative of the employee's performance.

biochemical assessment   An analysis of blood gases to determine the concentration of oxygen and carbon dioxide at the tissue level.

bivariate analysis   An analysis that provides information on two variables or groups.

categorical model of scoring   A model for scoring tests that places test takers in a particular group or class.

central-tendency error   A rating error that results when the rater uses only the middle of the rating scale and ignores the highest and lowest scale categories.

class intervals   A way to group adjacent scores for the purpose of displaying them in a table or graph.

clinical assessment   A broad set of information gathering and interpretive skills used by the professional counselor-therapist to make a diagnosis.

clinical interview   A primary tool for gathering information about the client that involves a discussion between the client and the assessor—often a clinical psychologist or counselor—in which the assessor observes the client and gathers information about the client's symptoms or problems.

cluster sampling   A type of sampling that involves selecting clusters of respondents and then selecting respondents from each cluster.

coefficient of determination   The amount of variance shared by two variables being correlated, such as a test and criterion, obtained by squaring the validity coefficient.

cognitive impairments   Mental disorders that include mental retardation, learning disabilities, and traumatic brain injuries.

comparative decisions   Decisions that are made by comparing test scores to see who has the best score.

computer phobia   Fear of computers.

concrete attributes   Attributes that can be described in terms of specific behaviors, like the ability to play the piano.

concurrent validity   An alternative form of criterion-related validity in which test administration and criterion measurement happen at approximately the same time.

confidence interval   A range of scores that we are confident includes the true score.

confidentiality   The assurance that all personal information will be kept private and not disclosed without explicit permission.

confirmatory factor analysis   A procedure in which researchers, using factor analysis, consider the theory associated with a test and propose a set of underlying factors they expect the test to contain, then conduct a factor analysis to see whether the factors they proposed do indeed exist.

construct   An attribute that exists in theory, but is not directly observable or measurable.

construct explication   Defining or explaining a psychological construct.

construct validity   Evidence that the test relates to other tests and behaviors as predicted by a theory.

content areas   The topics that are covered in the test.

content validity   The extent to which the questions on a test are representative of the material that should be covered by the test.

convenience sampling   A type of sampling in which an available group of participants are used to represent the population.

convergent validity   Evidence that the scores on a test correlate strongly with scores on other tests that measure the same construct.

correlation   Statistical procedure that provides an index of the strength and direction of the linear relationship between two variables.

correlation coefficient   A statistic that describes the relationship between two distributions of scores.

correlation matrix   A table in which the same tests and measures are listed in the horizontal and vertical headings and correlations of the tests are shown in the body of the table.

counseling and guidance decisions   Decisions that are typically made by testing specialists, educational administrators, or committees.

criterion   The measure of performance that is correlated with test scores.

criterion contamination   When the criterion in a validation study measures more dimensions than those measured by the test.

criterion-referenced tests   Tests that involve comparing an individual's test scores to an objectively stated standard of achievement, such as being able to multiple numbers.

criterion-related validity   The extent to which the scores on a test correlate with scores on a measure of performance or behavior.

cross-validation   Following the validation study, administering the test another time to confirm the results of the validation study.

cumulative model of scoring   A scoring model that assumes that the more the test taker responds in a particular fashion, the more the test taker exhibits the attribute being measured. The test taker receives one point for each "correct" answer, and the total number of "correct answers" becomes the raw score.

cut scores   Decision points for dividing test scores into pass or fail groupings.

database   A matrix in the form of a spreadsheet that shows the responses for each survey (rows) for each question in the survey (column).

decennial census survey   A survey administered by the U.S. Bureau of the Census every 10 years, primarily to determine the population of the United States.

descriptive research techniques   Techniques that researchers use to help us describe a situation or a phenomena.

descriptive statistics   Numbers calculated from a distribution that describe or summarize the properties of the distribution of test scores, such as the mean, median, mode, and standard deviation.

diagnosis   The identification of the client's problem or disorder; also called screening.

diagnostic assessment   Assessments that involve an in-depth evaluation of an individual to identify characteristics for treatment or enhancement.

diagnostic decisions   Decisions that are made concerning a disorder.

differential treatment model   The model of assessment in which psychological tests provide definitive answers about whether clients as a group have responded positively to a particular therapy or intervention.

differential validity   When a test yields significantly different validity coefficients for subgroups.

discriminant validity   Evidence that test scores are not correlated with unrelated constructs.

discrimination index   A statistic that compares the performance of those who made very high test scores with those who made very low test scores on each item.

distracters   The incorrect responses in a multiple-choice question.

double-barreled question   A question that is actually asking two or more questions in one.

electroencephalogram (EEG)   A continuous written record of brain-wave activity.

electrophysiological assessment   The monitoring of vital signs, such as heart rate and spontaneous electrical activity of the brain.

emotional intelligence   One's ability to understand one's own feelings and the feelings of others and to manage one's emotions.

employment interview   The most pervasive method of pre-employment assessment used by organizations in which the interviewer asks the job candidate open-ended questions.

equal-interval scales   The level of measurement in which numbers are assigned with the assumption that each number represents a point that is an equal distance from the points adjacent to it.

essay questions   Popular subjective test items in educational settings that are usually general in scope and require lengthy written responses by test takers.

ethical dilemmas   Problems for which there are no clear or agreed-on moral solutions.

ethical standards   A set of guidelines or codes for professional practice.

ethics   Issues or practices that influence the decision-making process in terms of "doing the right thing."

event-related potential (ERP)   A record of the brain's electrical response to the occurrence of a specific event.

experimental research techniques   Research designs that provide evidence for cause and effect.

experts   Individuals who are knowledgeable about a specific topic.

face-to-face surveys   Surveys in which an interviewer asks a series of questions in person—for instance, in the respondent's home, a public place, or the researcher's office.

face validity   The perception of the test taker that the test measures what it is supposed to measure.

factor analysis   An advanced statistical procedure based on the concept of correlation that helps investigators identify the underlying constructs or factors being measured.

faking   The inclination of some test takers to try to answer items in a way that will cause a desired outcome or diagnosis.

false positive   A score that mistakenly classifies innocent test takers as guilty.

field test   An administration of a survey or test to a large representative group of individuals to identify problems with administration, item interpretation, etc.

five-factor model   A widely accepted personality theory that proposes that there are five central personality dimensions.

focus group   A method that involves bringing together people who are similar to the target respondents to discuss issues related to the survey or test.

forced choice   A test format that requires the test taker to choose one of two or more words or phrases that appear unrelated but equally acceptable.

forced distribution   A method of ranking employees that requires the supervisor to assign a certain number of employees to each performance category.

formative assessments   Assessments that help teachers determine what information students are or are not learning during the instructional process.

frequency distribution   An orderly arrangement of a group of numbers (or test scores) showing the number of times each score occurred in a distribution.

generalizable   A test's being likely to produce similar results even though it has been administered in different locations.

goodness-of-fit test   A statistical test of significance that provides evidence that the factors obtained empirically in a confirmatory factor analysis are similar to those proposed theoretically.

grade norms   Norms that allow test users to compare a student's test score to the scores of other students in the same grade.

grading decisions   Decisions made by teachers when they are awarding grades.

graphic rating scale   A graph for rating employees' performance that represents a dimension, such as quality or quantity of work, divided into categories defined by numbers, words, or both.

halo effect   A rating error that occurs when raters let their judgment on one dimension influence their judgments on other dimensions.

heterogeneous   Measuring more than one trait or characteristic.

high-fidelity tests   Tests that are designed to replicate the job tasks and setting as realistically as possible.

homogeneity of the population   A population in which the people are similar to one another.

homogeneous   Measuring only one trait or characteristic.

hypotheses   Educated guesses or predictions based on a theory.

hypothesis confirmation bias   A tendency of decision-makers to form hypotheses about the behavior of others, then search for and elicit information to confirm their hypotheses.

individual decisions   Decisions made by the person who takes the test.

individually administered surveys   Surveys that are given by a facilitator to individual respondents to complete alone.

information-gathering model   The model of assessment in which psychological tests provide standardized comparisons and allow the assessor to make predictions about the client's behavior outside the assessment setting in order identify disorders and design an individualized treatment program.

informed consent   Individuals' right of self-determination. This concept means that individuals are entitled to full explanations of why they are being tested, how the test data will be used, and what the test results mean.

institutional decisions   Decisions that are made by an institution that administers a test or uses test results.

instructional decisions   Decisions made by classroom teachers.

instructional objectives   A list of what one should be able to do as a result of taking a course of instruction.

integrity test   A test that purports to measure the honesty of the test taker.

intelligence tests   Tests that assess the test taker's ability to cope with the environment, but at a broader level than aptitude tests.

inter-item correlation matrix   A matrix that displays the correlation of each item with every other item.

internal consistency   Measure of reliability obtained by giving the test once to one group of people.

intercept   The place where the regression line crosses the Y axis.

interest inventories   Tests that are designed to assess a person's interests in educational programs for job settings and thereby provide information for making career decisions.

internal reliability   Internal consistency of a measurement instrument. For example, the first foot on the yardstick is the same length as the second and third feet, and the length of every inch is uniform.

inter-rater reliability   An estimate of reliability of the scorers calculated by correlating the judgments of two or more raters; also referred to as scorer reliability.

interview questions   The traditional subjective test questions in an organizational setting that make up the employment interview.

intrascorer consistency   Measure of reliability that tells whether the test scorer assigned scores from test to test in a uniform manner.

ipsative model of scoring   A model for scoring tests that compares the test taker's scores on various scales within the inventory to yield a profile.

item analysis   The process of evaluating the performance of each item on a test.

item bias   The tendency for differences in responses to test questions to be related to differences in culture, gender, or experience in the test takers.

item characteristic curve (ICC)   The line that results when we graph the probability of answering an item correctly with level of ability on the construct being measured. The resulting graph provides a picture of both the item's difficulty and discrimination.

item difficulty   The percentage of test takers who answer a question correctly.

item nonresponse rate   How often an item or question was not answered.

item response theory (IRT)   A theory that relates the performance of each item to a statistical estimate of the test taker's ability on the construct being measured.

job analysis   A systematic assessment method for identifying the knowledge, skills, abilities, and other characteristics required to perform a job.

learning disability   A hidden handicap that hinders learning and does not have visible signs.

leniency error   A systematic rating error that occurs when raters give all employees ratings better than they deserve.

levels of measurement   The properties of the numbers used in a test—nominal, ordinal, equal interval, or ratio.

linear regression   The statistical process used to predict one set of test scores from one set of criterion scores.

linear transformations   Methods for changing raw scores for interpretation purposes that do not change the characteristics of the raw data in any way, such as Z scores and T scores.

literature reviews   Systematic examinations of published and unpublished reports on a topic.

low-fidelity test   A test that simulates the job and its tasks using a written, verbal, or visual description.

mail surveys   Surveys that are mailed to respondents with instructions for respondents to complete and return them.

mean   The average score in a distribution.

measurement   Broadly defined, the assignment of numbers according to rules.

measurement error   Variations or inconsistencies in the measurements yielded by a test or survey.

measures of central tendency   Statistics that describe the center of a distribution of scores.

measures of relationship   Statistics, e.g., correlation coefficient, that describe the association between two distributions of scores.

measures of variability   Numbers that represent the spread of the scores in the distribution, such as the range, variance, and the standard deviation.

median   The middle score in a distribution.

mode   The most frequently occurring score in a distribution.

motor impairments   Disabilities that hinder physical movement, such as paralysis or missing limbs.

multiple choice   An objective test format that consists of a question or partial sentence called a stem followed by a number of responses of which only one is correct.

multiple regression   The process in which more than one set of test scores is used to predict one set of criterion scores.

multitrait-multimethod design   A design for test validation that gathers evidence of reliability, convergent validity, and discriminant validity in one study.

multivariate analyses   Analyses that provide information on three or more variables or groups.

nature-vs.-nurture controversy   The debate that focuses on whether intelligence is determined by heredity or develops after birth based on environmental factors.

neurobehavioral assessment   Diagnostic methods in which practitioners elicit reflexes, such as the Moro, Babinski, and tonic-neck reflexes, to assess the functioning and maturity of the infant's central nervous system.

neuropsychology   A branch of psychology that concentrates on the relation between how the brain functions and the behavior it produces.

nominal scale   The most basic level of measurement, in which numbers are assigned to groups or categories of information.

nomological network   A method for defining a construct by illustrating its relation to as many other constructs and behaviors as possible.

nondirective clinical interview   A clinical interview that has few predetermined questions. Instead, the assessor's questions are more likely to be determined by the client's responses.

nonprobability sampling   A type of sampling in which everyone in the population has an equal chance of being selected.

nonsampling measurement errors   Errors associated with the design and administration of a survey.

nonstandardized tests   Tests that do not have standardization samples; these are more common than standardized tests.

norm-based interpretation   The process of comparing an individual's score to the scores of another group of people who took the same test.

norm group   A previously tested group of individuals to which an individual's score can be compared for interpretation.

normal curve   A symmetrical distribution of scores that when graphed shows a distribution that is bell-shaped.

normal probability distribution   A theoretical distribution that exists in our imagination as a perfect and symmetrical distribution; also referred to as the normal curve or bell curve.

norm-referenced tests   Standardized tests that have been given to a large representative group of test takers, whose scores have been used to create norms.

norms   A group of scores that indicate the average performance of a group and the distribution of scores above and below this average.

objective criterion   A criterion that is observable and measurable, such as the number of accidents on the job.

objective test format   A test format that has one response that is designated as "correct" or that provides evidence of a specific construct, such as multiple-choice questions.

objective tests   Tests that are structured and require test takers to respond to structured questions, such as multiple-choice questions.

operational definition   A definition of a construct in terms of specific observable behaviors.

order effects   Changes in test scores resulting from the order in which tests or questions on tests were administered.

ordinal scale   The second level of measurement, in which numbers are assigned to order or rank individuals or objects from greatest to least (or vice versa) on the attribute being measured.

outliers   Scores that are exceptionally higher or lower than other scores in a distribution.

parallel forms   Two equivalent forms of a test, developed to overcome problems such as practice effects; also referred to as alternate forms.

peers   An individual's colleagues or equals, such as other employees at a work site or other students in a class.

percentages   A linear transformation of raw scores obtain by dividing the number of correctly answered items by the total number of items.

percentile rank   An area transformation that indicates the percentage of people who scored above and below the transformed score.

performance appraisal   A formal evaluation of an employee's job performance.

performance impairment tests   Simulations that resemble video games and detect impairment in motor skills or hand-eye coordination, indicating that the test taker might not be prepared to perform a job safely or effectively.

personal interviews   Surveys that involve direct contact with the respondent in person or by phone.

personality tests   Tests designed to measure human character or disposition.

personality traits   Facets of the personality that endure over time.

phi coefficients   Statistic that describes the relationship between two dichotomous variables.

physical and mental challenges   Sensory, motor, or cognitive impairments.

pilot test   A scientific investigation of the new test's reliability and validity for its specified purpose.

placement assessments   Assessments that are used to determine whether students have the skills or knowledge necessary to understand new material and to determine how much information students already know about the new material.

placement decisions   Decisions that are typically made by testing specialists, educational administrators, or committees to determine the appropriate program or job for the test taker.

polygraph   A physiological measure associated with evaluating how truthfully an individual responds to questioning; also known as a lie detector test.

population   All members of the target audience.

power test   A test for which respondents have ample time to respond to all questions.

practice effects   Benefits test takers derive from already having taken a test, enabling them to solve problems more quickly or correctly the second time they take the same test.

predictive validity   A type of criterion-related validity that shows a relationship between test scores and a future behavior.

pretesting   A method for identifying sources of nonsampling measurement errors and examining the effectiveness of revisions of a question or entire survey or test.

probability sampling   A type of sampling that uses a statistical procedure to ensure that a sample is representative of its population.

product-moment coefficient   The most common form of a correlation coefficient used to describe the relationship between two distributions.

program and curriculum decisions   Decisions that are typically made by testing specialists, educational administrators, or committees regarding the content of a program or curriculum.

projection   A defense mechanism that relieves anxiety by allowing a person to attribute thoughts or emotions to external events or individuals.

projective drawing   Psychological tests in which the assessor directs the test takers to draw pictures.

projective hypothesis   The assumption that when people attempt to understand ambiguous stimuli, their interpretation of the stimulus reflects their own personal qualities or characteristics.

projective storytelling   Psychological tests that require respondents to tell a story in response to some ambiguous stimulus.

projective techniques   A type of psychological test in which the response requirements are intentionally made unclear in order to encourage test takers to create responses that describe the thoughts and emotions they are experiencing. Three projective techniques are projective storytelling, projective drawing, and sentence completion.

projective tests   Tests that are unstructured and require test takers to respond to ambiguous stimuli.

protected class   Persons in a group, such as ethnic class or gender, protected by federal law from discrimination.

psychological assessment   A tool for understanding and predicting behavior that involves multiple methods, such as personal history interviews, behavioral observations, and psychological tests, for gathering information about an individual.

psychological tests   Instruments that require the test taker to perform some behavior. The behavior performed is the used to measure some personal attribute, trait, or characteristic that is thought to be important in describing or understanding behavior, like intelligence.

psychometrics   The quantitative and technical aspects of mental measurement.

qualitative analysis   A posttest analysis in which test developers ask test takers to complete a questionnaire about how they viewed the test and how they answered the questions.

quantitative item analysis   The statistical analyses of the responses test takers gave to individual test questions.

random error   The *unexplained* difference between a test taker's true score and the obtained score; errors that are nonsystematic and unpredictable, resulting from an unknown cause.

range   A measure of variability calculated by subtracting the lowest number in a distribution from the highest number in a distribution.

ratio scale   The level of measurement in which numbers are assigned to points with the assumptions that each point is an equal distance from the numbers adjacent to it and that there is a point that represents an absolute absence of the property being measured, called "zero."

raw scores   Basic scores calculated from a psychological test.

reliability   The consistency with which an instrument yields measurements.

response rate   The number of individuals who responded to a survey divided by the total number who received the survey.

response sets   Patterns of responding to a test or survey that result in false or misleading information.

restriction of range   A reduction in the range of scores that causes the validity coefficient to be lower than if all persons were included in the study, usually arising when some people are dropped from a validity study, such as when low performers are not hired or participants drop out.

sample   A subset of a population used to represent the entire population.

sample size   The number of people in a sample.

sampling error   A statistic that reflects how much error can be attributed to the lack of representation of the target population due to the characteristics of the sample of respondents.

scale   See *levels of measurements.*

scientific method   A process for generating a body of knowledge that involves testing ideas and beliefs according to a specific testing procedure that can be objectively observed.

scorer reliability   The degree of agreement between persons scoring a test or rating an individual.

screening   The identification of the client's problem or disorder, also called diagnosis.

selection decisions   Decisions typically made by testing specialists, educational administrators, or committees regarding admission to a program or hiring for a job.

self-administered surveys   Surveys that individuals complete themselves without the presence of an administrator.

self-fulfilling prophecy   A phenomenon in which the interviewer's expectations influence the behavior of respondents and lead them to meet the interviewer's expectations.

self-report tests   Tests that rely on test takers' reports or descriptions of their feelings, beliefs, opinions, or mental states.

semistructured interview   An interview with predetermined questions; the interviewer might also ask some open-ended questions and follow-up questions to clarify the interviewee's responses.

sensory impairments   Disabilities that hinder the function of the five senses, such as deafness and blindness.

sentence completion   Psychological test items in which the assessor administers partial sentences, verbally or on paper, and asks the test taker to respond by completing each sentence.

severity error   A systematic rating error that occurs when raters give all employees worse ratings than they deserve.

simple random sampling   A type of sampling in which every member of a population has an equal chance of being chosen as a member of the sample.

single-group validity   A test's being valid for one group but not another (for instance, valid for Whites but not for Blacks).

slope   The expected change in one unit of Y for every change in X on the regression line.

social desirability   The tendency of some test takers to provide or choose answers that are socially acceptable or that present them in a favorable light.

social-emotional functioning   An area of assessment that includes temperament, personality, intelligence tests, academic achievement, language development, visual and tactile perception, and sustained and selective attention.

speed test   A test that is scored according to the number of correct answers supplied by the test taker in a specified amount of time.

split-half method   A method of estimating the internal consistency or reliability of a test by giving the test once to one group of people, then to make a comparison of scores, dividing the test into halves, and correlating the set of scores on the first half with the set of scores on the second half.

standard deviation   A measure of variability that represents the degree to which scores vary from the mean.

standard deviation units   A number that represents how many standard deviations an individual score is located away from the mean.

standard error of measurement (SEM)   An index of the amount of inconsistency or error expected in an individual's test score.

standard scores   Universally understood units in testing that allow the test user to evaluate a person's performance in reference to other persons who took the same or a similar test, such as Z or T scores.

standardization sample   A group of people who are tested to obtain data to establish a frame of reference for interpreting individual test scores.

standardized tests   Tests that have been administered to a large group of individuals who are similar to the group for whom the test has been designed, in order to develop norms; also implies a standardized procedure for administration.

state   A temporary mood or characteristic.

stem   A statement, question, or partial sentence that is the stimulus in a multiple-choice question.

stratified random sampling   A type of sampling in which a population is divided into subgroups or strata.

structured clinical interview   See *structured interview.*

structured interview   A predetermined set of questions the assessor asks the respondent. The assessor then scores the answers based on their content to arrive at a diagnosis; also referred to as a structured clinical interview, in clinical settings.

structured observations   Observations that are guided by forms or instructions that instruct an observer in how to collect behavioral information (for example, using a form to document the play behaviors of children on the playground).

structured record reviews Forms that guide data collection from existing records (for example, using a form to collect information from personnel files).

subgroup norms Statistics that describe subgroups of the target audience, such as race, sex, or age.

subjective criterion A measurement that is based on judgment, such as supervisor and peer ratings.

subjective test format A test format that does not have a response designated as "correct." Interpretation of responses as "correct" or providing evidence of a specific construct is left to the judgment of the person who administers, scores, or interprets the test.

subtle questions Questions that have no apparent relation to the test purpose or criterion.

summative assessment An assessment that involves determining whether students have learned what the teacher intended them to learn by the end of the program.

survey objectives The purposes of a survey, including a definition of what the survey measures.

survey research firms Companies that specialize in the construction, administration, and analysis of survey data.

survey researcher A person who designs and conducts surveys and analyzes their results.

surveys Research tools that collect information to describe and compare people's attitudes *(how they feel)*, knowledge *(what they know)*, and behaviors *(what they do)*.

systematic error A single source of error that can be identified as constant across all measurements.

systematic sampling A type of sampling in which every *Nth* (for example, 5th) person in a population is chosen as a member of the sample.

T scores Standard scores, which have a mean of 50 and a standard deviation of 10, that are used to compare scores from two tests that have different characteristics.

technostress Increased levels of frustration due to the use computers or other technologically advanced systems.

telephone surveys Surveys in which an interviewer phones respondents and asks questions over the phone.

test bank A large number of multiple-choice, true/false, and short-answer questions that assess knowledge on a subject or group of subjects.

test format The type of questions on a test.

test items Stimuli or test questions.

test of significance A process of determining what the probability is that the study would have yielded the validity coefficient calculated by chance.

test plan A plan for developing a new test that specifies the characteristics of the test, including a definition of the construct, the content to be measured (the test domain), the format for the questions, and how the test will be administered and scored.

test-retest method A method of estimating test reliability in which a test developer gives the same test to the same group of test takers on two different occasions and correlates the scores from the first and second administrations.

test security Steps taken to ensure that the content of a psychological test does not become public knowledge.

test specifications The plan prepared before test development that documents the written test or practical exam.

test taker The person who responds to test questions or whose behavior is measured.

test user   Anyone who participates in purchasing, administering, interpreting, or using the results of a psychological test.

testing environment   The circumstances under which the test is administered.

testing universe   The body of knowledge or behaviors that the test represents.

tests of maximal performance   Tests that require test takers to perform a particular task on which their performance is measured.

therapeutic model   The model of assessment that uses tests as an intervention to provide new information for the client to use for self-discovery and growth.

traditional interview   A preemployment interview in which the interviewer pursues different areas of inquiry with each job applicant.

trait   An ongoing part of a person's personality.

true/false item   A test item that asks the test taker to declare whether a statement is true or false.

univariate analysis   A computation of statistics that summarizes individual question responses.

valid test   A test that measures what it claims to measure.

validation   The process of obtaining evidence that the test effectively measures what it is supposed to measure.

validity   Evidence that a test is being used appropriately and measures what it is supposed to measure.

validity coefficient   The correlation coefficient obtained when test scores are correlated with a performance criterion that represents the amount or strength of criterion-related validity that can be attributed to a test.

variance   A measure of variability that indicates whether individual scores in a distribution tend to be similar to or substantially different from the mean of the distribution.

work samples   Small-scale assessments in which test takers complete a job-related task, such as building a sawhorse or designing a doghouse.

Z scores   Standard scores, which have a mean of 0 and a standard deviation of 1, that are used to compare test scores from two tests that have different characteristics.

References

American Psychiatric Association. (1987). *Diagnostic and statistical manual of mental disorders (3rd ed. rev.).* Washington, DC: Author.

American Psychiatric Association. (1994). *Diagnostic and statistical manual of mental disorders* (4th ed.). Washington, DC: Author.

American Psychological Association. (1953). *Ethical standards of psychologists.* Washington, DC: Author.

American Psychological Association. (1954). *Technical recommendations for psychological tests and diagnostic techniques.* Washington, DC: Author.

American Psychological Association. (1966a). Automated test scoring and interpretation practices. *American Psychologist, 21,* 1141.

American Psychological Association. (1966b). *Standards for educational and psychological tests and manuals.* Washington, DC: Author.

American Psychological Association. (1974a). *Standards for educational and psychological tests and manuals.* Washington, DC: Author.

American Psychological Association. (1974b). Standards for providers of psychological services. *American Psychologist, 32,* 495–505.

American Psychological Association. (1981) *Ethical principles of psychologists.* Washington, DC: Author.

American Psychological Association. (1982). Guidelines for providers of psychological services. *American Psychologist, 42,* 712–723.

American Psychological Association. (1985). *Standards for educational and psychological testing.* Washington, DC: Author.

American Psychological Association. (1986). *Guidelines for computer-based tests and interpretations.* Washington, DC: Author.

American Psychological Association. (1987a). *Casebook on ethical principles of psychologists.* Washington, DC: Author.

American Psychological Association. (1987b). General guidelines for providers of psychological services. *American Psychologist, 42,* 712–723.

American Psychological Association. (1992). Ethical principles of psychologists and code of conduct. *American Psychologist, 47,* 1597–1611.

American Psychological Association, Committee on Professional Standards. (1981a). Special guidelines for the delivery of services by clinical psychologists. *American Psychologist, 36,* 640–651.

American Psychological Association, Committee on Professional Standards. (1981b). Specialty guidelines for the delivery of services by counseling psychologists. *American Psychologist, 36,* 652–663.

American Psychological Association, Committee on Professional Standards. (1981c). Specialty guidelines for the delivery of services by industrial/organizational psychologists. *American Psychologist, 36,* 664–669.

American Psychological Association, Committee on Professional Standards. (1981d). Specialty guidelines for the delivery of services by school psychologists. *American Psychologist, 36,* 670–681.

American Psychological Association, Committee on Professional Standards and Committee on Psychological Tests and Assessment. (1986). *Guidelines for computer-based tests and interpretations.* Washington, DC: American Psychological Association.

American Psychological Association, Division of Industrial and Organizational Psychology. (1980). *Principles for the validation and use of personnel selection procedures* (2nd ed.). Washington, DC: American Psychological Association.

American Psychological Association, Ethics Committee. (1994). Report of the Ethics Committee. *American Psychologist, 49,* 659–666.

American Psychological Association, Science Directorate. (1991). *Questions used in the prediction of trustworthiness in pre-employment selection decisions: An APA task force report.* Washington, DC: American Psychological Association.

American Psychological Association. (1992). Ethical principles of psychologists and code of conduct. *American Psychologist, 47,* 1597–1611.

Ames, L. B. (1989). *Arnold Gesell—Themes of his work.* New York: Human Sciences Press.

Anastasi, A. (1988). *Psychological testing* (6th ed.). New York: Macmillan.

Anastasi, A., & Urbina, S. (1994). *Psychological testing. (6th edition).* Upper Saddle River, NJ: Prentice Hall.

Anastasi, A., & Urbina, S. (1997). *Psychological testing* (7th ed.). Upper Saddle River, NJ: Prentice Hall.

Anton, W. D., & Reed, J. R. (1991). *CAS: College Adjustment Scales professional manual.* Odessa, FL: Psychological Assessment Resources.

Archer, R. P. (1992). Review of the Minnesota Multiphasic Personality Inventory–2. In J. J. Kramer & J. C. Conoley (Eds.), *Eleventh mental measurement yearbook.* Lincoln: University of Nebraska, Buros Institute of Mental Measurements.

Arvey, R. D. (1979). Unfair discrimination in the employment interview: Legal and psychological aspects. *Psychological Bulletin, 86,* 736–765.

Association on Handicapped Student Service Programs in Postsecondary Education. (1991). *College students with learning disabilities.* (2nd ed). [Brochure].

Axelrod, B. N., Goldman, B. S., & Woodard, J. L. (1992). Interrater reliability in scoring the Wisconsin Card Sorting Test. *Clinical Neuropsychologist, 6,* 143–155.

Babbie, E. (1973). *Survey research methods.* Belmont, CA: Wadsworth.

Ballance, C. T., & Ballance, V. V. (1996). Psychology of computer use: 27. Computer-related stress and amount of computer experience. *Psychological Reports, 78,* 968–970.

Bandura, A. (1977). Self-efficacy: Toward a unifying theory of behavioral change. *Psychological Review, 84,* 191–215.

Bandura, A., Barbaranelli, C., Caprara, G. V., & Pastorelli, C. (1996). Multifaceted impact of self-efficacy beliefs on academic functioning. *Child Development, 67,* 1206–1222.

Barrett, G. V., Phillips, J. S., & Alexander, R. A. (1981). Concurrent and predictive validity designs: A critical reanalysis. *Journal of Applied Psychology, 66,* 1–6.

Barrick, M. R., & Mount, M. K. (1991). The big five personality dimensions and job performance: A meta-analysis. *Personnel Psychology, 44,* 1–26.

Bartlett, C. J., Bobko, P., Mosier, S. B., & Hannan, R. (1978). Testing for fairness with a moderated multiple regression strategy: An alternative to differential analysis. *Personnel Psychology, 31,* 233–241.

Bartram, D. (1995). The predictive validity of the EPI and 16PF for military flying training. *Journal of Occupational and Organizational Psychology, 68,* 219–236.

Bayley, N. (1993). *Bayley scales of infant development* (2nd ed.). San Antonio: Psychological Corporation.

Beck, A. T., & Steer, R. A. (1987). *Beck Depression Inventory manual.* San Antonio: Psychological Corporation.

Beck, A. T., Steer, R. A., & Garbin, M. G. (1988). Psychometric properties of the Beck Depression Inventory: Twenty-five years of evaluation. *Clinical Psychology Review, 8,* 77–100.

Berman, A. L., & Jobes, D. A. (1991). *Adolescent suicide: Assessment and intervention.* Washington, DC: American Psychological Association.

Betz, N. E., & Hackett, G. (1986). Applications of self-efficacy theory to understanding career choice behavior. *Journal of Social and Clinical Psychology, 4,* 279–289.

Binet, A., & Simon, T. (1905). Methodes nouvelles pour le diagnostic du niveau intellectuel des anormaux. *Annee Psychologique, 11,* 191–244.

Blouin, A. (1987). *Computerized Diagnostic Interview Schedule (C-DIS).* Ottawa: Ottawa Civic Hospital.

Bolton, B. (1992). California Psychological Inventory–Revised Edition. In J. J. Kramer and J. C. Conoley (eds.). *The eleventh mental measurements yearbook.* Lincoln, NE: The Buros Institute of Mental Measurements.

Bond, L. (1987). The Golden Rule settlement: A minority perspective, *Educational Measurement: Issues and Practice, 6,* 18–20.

Boomsma, D., Anokhin, A., & de Geus, E. (1997, August). Genetics of electrophysiology: Linking genes, brain, and behavior. *Current Directions in Psychological Science, 6* (4), 106–110.

Boone, D. (1995, June). Differential validity of the MMPI-2 subtle and obvious scales with psychiatric inpatients: Scale 2. *Journal of Clinical Psychology, 51,* 526–531.

Booth, A., Johnson, D., & Edwards, J. N. (1983). Measuring marital instability. *Journal of Marriage and the Family, 44,* 387–393.

Bouchard, T. M., Lykken, D. T., McGue, M., Segal, N. L., & Tellegen, A. (1990). Sources of human psychological differences: The Minnesota Study of Twins Reared Apart. *Science, 250,* 223–228.

Bowers, M. (1996, October 10). Educators to decide who'll write state tests. *Virginian-Pilot,* B3.

Bowman, M. L. (1989, March). Testing individual differences in ancient China. *American Psychologist, 44,* 576–578.

Bracey, G. W. (1993). Sex, math, and SATs. *Phi Delta Kappan 74* (5), 415–416.

Bradburn, N. M., and Sudman, S. (1988). Polls and Surveys: Understanding what they tell us. San Francisco: Jossey-Bass.

Bradburn, N. M., & Sudman, S. (1992). The current status of questionnaire design. In P. N. Biemer, R. M. Groves, L. E. Lyberg, N. A. Mathiowetz, & S. Sudman (Eds.), *Measurement errors in surveys.* New York: Wiley.

Brems, C., & Harris, K. (1996). Faking the MMPI-2: Utility of the subtle-obvious scales. *Journal of Clinical Psychology, 52,* 525–533.

Brostoff, M., & Meyer, H. H. (1984). The effects of coaching on in-basket performance. *Journal of Assessment Center Technology, 7(2),* 17–21.

Buros, O. K. (1938). *The 1938 mental measurements yearbook.* New Brunswick, NJ: Rutgers University Press.

Bureau of National Affairs (BNA Report no. 72). Washington, DC: Author.

Butcher, J. N. (1997). Introduction to the special section on assessment in psychological treatment: A necessary step for effective intervention. *Psychological Assessment, 9* (4), 331–333.

Butcher, J. N., Dahlstrom, W. G., Graham, J. R., Tellegen, A., & Kaemmer, B. (1989). *Minnesota Multiphasic Personality Inventory–2 (MMPI-2): Manual for administration and scoring.* Minneapolis: University of Minnesota Press.

Butcher, J. N., Graham, J. R., Williams, C. L., & Ben-Porath, Y. S. (1990). *Development and use of the MMPI-2 content scales.* Minneapolis: University of Minnesota Press.

Camara, W. J., & Schneider, D. L. (1994). Integrity tests: Facts and unresolved issues. *American Psychologist, 49,* 112–119.

Camara, W. J., & Schneider, D. L. (1995). Questions of construct breadth and openness of research in integrity testing. *American Psychologist, 50,* 459–460.

Campbell, D. P. (1971). *Handbook for the Strong Vocational Interest Blank.* Palo Alto, CA: Stanford University Press.

Campbell, D. T., & Fiske, D. W. (1959). Convergent and discriminant validity by the multitrait-multimethod matrix. *Psychological Bulletin, 56,* 81–105.

Campbell, V. L. (1990). A model for using tests in counseling. In C. E. Watkins, Jr., & V. L. Campbell (Eds.), *Testing in counseling practice.* Hillsdale, NJ: Erlbaum.

Cannell, C. F., Lawson, S. A., & Hausser, D. L. (1975). *A technique for evaluating interviewer performance.* Ann Arbor: University of Michigan, Institute for Social Research.

Cannell, C. F., Miller, P. V., & Oksenberg, L. (1981). Research on interviewing techniques, ISR, The University of Michigan.

Cannell, C. F., & Oksenberg, L. (1985). New strategies for pretesting survey questions. *Journal of Official Statistics, 7,* 249–365.

Canter, A. S. (1997). The future of intelligence testing in the schools. *School Psychology Review, 26* (2), 255–261.

Carter, R. D., & Thomas, E. J. (1973). Modification of problematic marital communication using corrective feedback and instruction. *Behavior Therapy, 4,* 100–109.

Cascio, W. F. (1991). *Applied psychology in personnel management* (4th ed.). Englewood Cliffs, NJ: Prentice Hall.

Cascio, W. F., Alexander, R. A., & Barrett, G. V. (1988). Setting cutoff scores: Legal, psychometric, and professional issues and guidelines. *Personnel Psychology, 41,* 1–24.

Cattin, P. (1980). Estimation of the predictive power of a regression model. *Journal of Applied Psychology, 65,* 407–414.

Charlesworth, R., Fleege, P. O., & Weitman, C. J. (1994). Research on the effects of group standardized testing on instrumentation, pupils, and teachers: New directions for policy. *Early Education and Development, 5,* 195–212.

Charney, D. S., Heninger, G. R., & Breier, P. I. (1984). Noradrenergic function in panic anxiety: Effects of yohimbine in healthy subjects and patients with agoraphobia and panic disorder. *Archives of General Psychiatry, 41,* 751–763.

Child denied IQ test because of her race. (1994, April 18), *Jet, 85,* 22.

Christensen L. B. (1997). *Experimental methodology* (7th ed.). Boston: Allyn & Bacon.

Cleary, T., Humphreys, L., Kendrick, S., & Wesman, A. (1975). Educational use of tests with disadvantaged students. *American Psychologist, 30,* 15–41.

Code of Fair Testing Practices in Education (1988). Washington, DC: Joint Committee on Testing Practices.

Cohen, M. J., Branch, W. B., Willis, W. G., Weyandt, L. L., & Hynd, G. W. (1992). Childhood. In A. E. Puente & R. J. McCaffrey (Eds.), *Handbook of neuropsychological assessment: A biopsychosocial perspective.* New York: Plenum Press.

Cohen, R. J., Swerdlik, M. E., & Phillips, S. M. (1996). *Psychological testing and assessment: An introduction to tests and measurements.* (3rd ed.). Mountain View, CA: Mayfield.

Cohen, S. L. (1978). Letter from the editor. *Journal of Assessment Center Technology, 1*(1), 1.

Colligan, R. C., Osborne, D., Swenson, W. M., & Offord, K. P. (1983). *The MMPI: A contemporary normative study.* New York: Praeger.

Committee on Psychological Tests and Assessment. (1988). *Implications for test fairness of the "Golden Rule" company settlement.* Washington, DC: American Psychological Association.

Conoley, J. C., & Impara, J. C. (Eds.). (1995). *The twelfth mental measurements yearbook.* Lincoln: University of Nebraska Press.

Conte, J. M., Landy, F. J., & Mathieu, J. E. (1995). Time urgency: Conceptual and construct development. *Journal of Applied Psychology, 80* (1), 178–185.

Cook, T. D., & Campbell, D. T. (1979). Quasi-experimentation: Design and analysis issues for field settings. Chicago: Rand McNally.

Crawford v. Honig. (1994). 9th Cir. 37 F.3d 485.

Crocker, L., Llabre, M., & Miller, M. D. (1988). The generalizability of content validity ratings. *Journal of Educational Measurement, 25,* 287–299.

Cronbach, L J. (1951). Coefficient alpha and the internal structure of tests. *Psychometrika, 16,* 197–334.

Cronbach, L. J. (1988). Five perspectives on the validity argument. In H. Wainer & H. Brown (Eds.), *Test validity.* Hillsdale, NJ: Erlbaum.

Cronbach, L. J. (1989). Construct validation after thirty years. In R. Linn (Ed.), *Intelligence: Measurement, theory, and public policy.* Urbana: University of Illinois Press.

Cronbach, L. J., & Meehl, P. E. (1955). Construct validity in psychological tests. *Psychological Bulletin, 52,* 281–302.

Dahlstrom, W. G., Welsh, G. S., & Dahlstrom, L. E. (1972). *An MMPI handbook: Vol. 1. Clinical interpretation.* Minneapolis: University of Minnesota Press.

Dana, R. H. (1986). Clinical assessment. In G. S. Tryon (Ed.), *The professional practice of psychology.* Norwood, NJ: Ablex.

Darley, J., & Fazio, R. (1980). Expectancy confirmation processes arising in the social interaction sequence. *American Psychologist, 35,* 867–881.

Dawes, R., & Corrigan, B. (1974). Linear models in decision making. *Psychological Bulletin, 81,* 95–106.

Debra P. v. Turlington, 644F. 2d 397 (5th Cir. (Fla.), May 4, 1981) (No. 79–3074).

Dillman, D. A. (1978). *Mail and telephone surveys: The total design method.* New York: Wiley.

Distefano, M. K., Pryer, M. W., & Erffmeyer, R. C. (1983). Application of content validity methods to the development of a job-related performance rating criterion. *Personnel Psychology, 36,* 621–631.

Dreher, G. F., Ash, R. A., & Hancock, P. A. (1988). The role of the traditional research design in underestimating the validity of the employment interview. *Personnel Psychology, 41,* 315–327.

DuBois, P. H. (1970). *The history of psychological testing.* Boston: Allyn & Bacon.

Duckworth, J. C. (1990). The Minnesota Multiphasic Personality Inventory. In C. E. Watkins, Jr., & V. L. Campbell (Eds.), *Testing in counseling practice.* Hillsdale, NJ: Erlbaum.

Eberhard, W. (1977). *A history of China.* Berkeley: University of California Press.

Eckert, L. H., Goernert, P., Harris, W., & Nelson, K. (1997). *Computer-assisted test administration: Establishing equivalency of two mood measures.* Paper presented at the annual conference of the Human Factors and Ergonomics Society, Albuquerque, NM.

Educational Testing Service. (1993). *Computer based tests: Can they be fair for everyone?* Princeton, NJ: Author.

Educational Testing Service. (1995). *1995 annual report.* New Jersey: Author.

Educational Testing Service. (1996). *ETS publications catalog.* Princeton, NJ: Author.

Edwards, J. E., & Thomas, M. D. (1993). The organizational survey process: General steps and practical considerations. In P. Rosenfeld, J. E. Edwards, & M. D. Thomas (Eds), *Improving Organizational Surveys.* Newbury Park, CA: Sage.

Eells, K., Davis, A., Havighurst, R. J., Herrick, V. E., & Tyler, R. (1951). *Intelligence and cultural differences: A study of cultural learning and problem solving.* Chicago: University of Chicago Press.

Elliott, R., & Strenta, A. C. (1988). Effects of improving the reliability of the GPA on prediction generally and on comparative predictions for gender and race particularly. *Journal of Educational Measurement, 25,* 333–347.

Elliot, S. M. (1991). Authentic assessment: An introduction to a neobehavioral approach to classroom assessment. *School Psychology Quarterly,* 6:273–278.

Elmore, C. (1988, April). An IQ test almost ruined my son's life. *Redbook,* 50–52.

Embretson, S. E. (1996). The new rules of measurement. *Psychological Assessment, 8*(4), 341–349.

Emory, E. K., Savoie, T. M., Ballard, J., Eppler, M., & O'Dell, C. (1992). Perinatal. In A. E. Puente & R. J. McCaffrey (Eds.). *Handbook of neuropsychological assessment: A biopsychosocial perspective.* New York: Plenum Press.

Evan, W. M., & Miller, J. R. (1969). Differential effects of response bias of computer vs. conventional administration of a social science questionnaire. *Behavioral Science, 14,* 216–227.

Exner, J. E. (1976). Projective techniques. In I. B. Weiner (Ed.), *Clinical methods in psychology.* New York: Wiley.

Exner, J. E. (1993). *The Rorschach: A comprehensive supplement: Vol. 1. Basic foundations* (3rd ed.). New York: Wiley.

Exner, J. E., & Weiner, I. B. (1982). *The Rorschach: A comprehensive system: Vol. 3. Assessment of children and adolescents.* New York: Wiley.

Eyde, L., Robertson, G., Krug, S., Moreland, K., Robertson, A., Shewan., C., Harrison, P., Porch, B., Hammer, A., and Primoff, E. (1993). *Responsible Test Use: Case Studies for Assessing Human Behavior.* Washington, DC: American Psychological Association.

Faggen, J. (1987). Golden Rule revisited: Introduction. *Educational Measurement: Issues and Practice, 6,* 5–8.

Fay, C. H., & Latham, G. P. (1982). Effects of training and rating scales on rating errors. *Personnel Psychology, 35,* 105–116.

Fine, C. R. (1992, June). Video tests are the new frontier in drug detection. *Personnel Journal, 71,* 148–161.

Fink, A. (1995a). *How to report on surveys.* Thousand Oaks, CA: Sage.

Fink, A. (1995b). *The survey handbook.* Thousand Oaks, CA: Sage.

Finn, S. E., & Tonsager, M. E. (1997). Information-gathering and therapeutic models of assessment: Complementary paradigms. *Psychological Assessment, 9* (4), 374–386.

Fisher, R. A., & Yates, F. (1963). Statistical tables for biological, agricultural, and medical research (6th ed.). Edinburgh: Oliver and Boyd.

Ford, J. K., & Wroten, S. P. (1984). Introducing new methods for conducting training evaluation and for linking training evaluation to program design. *Personnel Psychology, 37,* 651–665.

Fowler, F. J., Jr. (1988). *Survey research methods.* Newbury Park, CA: Sage.

Fowler, F. J., Jr. (1993). *Survey research methods.* (2nd ed.) Newbury Park, CA: Sage.

Franke, W. (1960). *The reform and abolition of the traditional Chinese examination system.* Cambridge, MA: Harvard Center for East Asian Studies.

Frankenburg, W. K., & Dodds, J. B. (1967). The Denver Developmental Screening Test. *Journal of Pediatrics, 71,* 181–191.

Frankenburg, W. K., Dodds, J. B., Fandal, A., Kazuk, E., & Cohrs, M. (1976). *Denver Developmental Screening Test: Reference manual* (rev. ed.). Denver: LA-DOCA Project & Publishing Foundation.

French, C. C., & Beaumont, J. G. (1991). The differential aptitude test (language usage and spelling): A clinical study of a computerized form. *Current Psychology: Research and Reviews, 10,* 31–48.

Fritzsche, B. A., & McIntire, S. A. (1997). *Constructing a psychological test as an undergraduate class project: Yes, it can be done!* Poster presented at the 19th annual National Institute on the Teaching of Psychology, St. Petersburg, FL.

Gael, S., Grant, D., & Richie, R. (1975). Employment test validation for minority and nonminority clerks and work sample criteria. *Journal of Applied Psychology, 60,* 420–426.

Gatewood, R. D., & Feild, H. S. (1997). *Human resource selection* (4th ed.). Fort Worth: Dryden Press.

Gaugler, B. B., Rosenthal, D. B., Thornton III, G. C., & Bentson, C. (1987). Meta-analysis of assessment center validity. *Journal of Applied Psychology, 72,* 493–511.

Gavzer, B. (1990, May 27). Should you tell all? *Parade Magazine,* 4–7.

Geertsma, R. H. (1972). Observational methods. In R. H. Woody & J. D. Woody (Eds.), *Clinical assessment in counseling and psychotherapy.* Englewood Cliffs, NJ: Prentice Hall.

Ghiselli, E. E. (1955). *The measurement of occupational aptitude.* Berkeley: University of California Press.

Gibbs, N. (1995, October 2). The EQ factor. *Time,* 60–68.

Gilberstadt, H., & Duker, J. (1965). *A handbook for clinical and actuarial MMPI interpretation.* Philadelphia: Saunders.

Goh, D., & Fuller, G. B. (1983). Current practices in the assessment of personality and behavior by school psychologists. *School Psychology Review, 12,* 240–243.

Goldberg, L. R. (1970). Man versus model of man: A rational plus evidence for a method of improving clinical inference. *Psychological Bulletin, 73,* 422–432.

Goldstein, G. (1992). Historical perspectives. In A. E. Puente & R. J. McCaffrey (Eds.), *Handbook of neuropsychological assessment: A biopsychosocial perspective.* New York: Plenum Press.

Goldstein, I. L. (1993). *Training in organizations* (3rd ed.). Pacific Grove, CA: Brooks/Cole.

Goodenough F. (1926). *Measurement of Intelligence by Drawing.* New York: World Book Co.

Gottfredson, L. S. (1991). When job-testing "fairness" is nothing but a quota. *Industrial-Organizational Psychologist, 28*(3), 65–67.

Gottfredson, M. R., & Hirschi, T. (1990). *A general theory of crime.* Stanford, CA: Stanford University Press.

Gough, H. G. (1975). *Manual for the California Psychology Inventory.* Palo Alto, CA: Consulting Psychologists Press.

Graham, J. R. (1990). *MMPI-2: Assessing personality and psychopathology.* New York: Oxford University Press.

Grant, C. A., & Sleeter, C. E. (1986). Race, class and gender in education research: An argument for integrative analysis. *Review of Educational Research, 56,* 195–211.

Grasmick, H. G., Tittle, C. R., Bursek, R. J., & Arneklev, B. J. (1993). Testing the core empirical implications of Gottfredson and Hirschi's general theory of crime. *Journal of Research in Crime and Delinquency, 30,* 5–29.

GRE Board Newsletter. (1994, Winter). Vol. 9, issue 1.

Greaud, V. A., & Green, B. F. (1986). Equivalence of conventional and computer presentation of speed tests. *Applied Psychological Measurement, 10,* 23–34.

Greenberg, E. R. (July 1990). Workplace testing: The 1990 AMA survey, part 2. *Personnel, 67,* 26–29.

Gribbons, B. C., Tobey, P. E., & Michael, W. B. (1995). Internal-consistency reliability and construct and criterion-related validity of an academic self-concept scale. *Educational and Psychological Measurement, 55,* 858–867.

Griggs v. Duke Power Co. (1971). 401 US 424.

Gronlund, N. E. (1998). *Assessment of student achievement* (6th ed.). Boston: Allyn & Bacon.

Groth-Marnat, G. (1990). *Handbook of psychological assessment* (2nd ed.). New York: Wiley.

Groth-Marnat, G. (1997). *Handbook of psychological assessment* (3rd ed.). New York: Wiley.

Groth-Marnat, G., & Schumaker, J. (1989, April). Computer-based psychological testing: Issues and guidelines. *American Journal of Orthopsychiatry, 59* (2), 257–263.

Groves, R. M. (1989). *Survey errors and survey costs.* New York: Wiley.

Guion, R. M. (1965). *Personnel testing.* New York: McGraw-Hill.

Guion, R. M. (1966). Employment tests and discriminatory hiring. *Industrial Relations, 5,* 20–37.

Haak, R. A. (1990). Using the sentence completion to assess emotional disturbance. In C. R. Reynolds & R. W. Kamphaus (Eds.), *Handbook of psychological and educational assessment of children: Personality, behavior, and context.* New York: Guilford Press.

Hammer, E. F. (1958). Projection in the clinical setting. In E. F. Hammer (Ed.), *The clinical application of projective drawings.* Springfield, IL: Charles C. Thomas.

Haney, W. (October 1981). Validity, vaudeville, and values. *American Psychologist, 36,* 1021–1034.

Harrington, G. M. (1975). Intelligence tests may favor the majority groups in a population. *Nature, 258,* 708–709.

Harrington, G. M. (1976). *Minority test bias as a psychometric artifact: The experimental evidence.* Paper presented to the annual meeting of the American Psychological Association, Washington, DC.

Hart, R. R., & Goldstein, M. A. (1985). Computer-assisted psychological assessment. *Computers in Human Services, 1,* 69–75.

Hartigan, J. A., & Wigdor, A. K. (1989) *Fairness in employment testing: Validity generalization, minority issues, and the General Aptitude Test Battery.* Washington: National Academy Press.

Hartnett, R. T., & Willingham, W. W. (1980). The criterion problem: What measure of success in graduate education? *Applied Psychological Measurement, 4,* 281–291.

Hathaway, S. R. (1947). A coding system for MMPI profile classification. *Journal of Consulting Psychology, 11,* 334–337.

Haymaker, J. D., & Grant, D. L. (1982). Development of a model for content validation. *Journal of Assessment Center Technology, 5*(2), 1–8.

Haynes, S. N., Leisen, M. B., & Blaine, D. D. (1997). Design of individualized behavioral treatment programs using functional analytic clinical case models. *Psychological Assessment, 9* (4), 334–348.

Haynes, S. N., Richard, D. C. S., & Kubany, E. S. (1995). Content validity in psychological assessment: A functional approach to concepts and methods. *Psychological Assessment, 7,* 238–247.

Heaton, R. K. (1981). *A manual for the Wisconsin Card Sorting Test.* Odessa, FL: Psychological Assessment Resources.

Heaton, R. K., Chelune, G. J., Talley, J. L., Kay, G. G., & Curtiss, G. (1993). *Wisconsin Card Sorting Test Manual: Revised and expanded.* Odessa, FL: Psychological Assessment Resources.

Helmstadter, G. C. (1970). *Research concepts in human behavior.* New York: Appleton-Century-Crofts.

Heneman, H. G., III, Heneman, R. L., & Judge, T. A. (1997). *Staffing organizations.* Middleton, WI: Mendota House.

Herlhy, B., & Remley, T. P., Jr. (1995). Unified ethical standards: A challenge for professionalism. *Journal of Counseling and Development, 74,* 130–133.

Herrnstein, R. J., & Murray, C. (1994). *The bell curve.* New York: Free Press.

Hilliard, A. (1984). Historical perspectives on Black families. Presented at the National Urban League/National Association for the Advancement of Colored People Summit Conference on the Black family. (Nashville, TN, 1984).

Hobson v. Hobson, 248 N.W. 2d 137 (Iowa, Dec. 15, 1976) (No. 3–59410)

Hoffman, K. I., & Lundberg, G. D. (1976). A comparison of computer monitored group tests and paper-and-pencil tests. *Educational and Psychological Measurement, 36,* 791–809.

Hogan, R., & Hogan, J. (1992). *Hogan personality inventory manual.* Tulsa, OK: Hogan Assessment Systems.

Hohenshil, T. H. (1996, September/October). Assessment and diagnosis in counseling. *Journal of Counseling and Development, 75,* 64–76.

Holman, T. B., Busby, D. M., & Larson, J. H. (1989). *Preparation for Marriage (PREP-M).* Provo, UT: Marriage Study Consortium.

Holman, T. B., Larson, J. H., & Harmer, S. L. (January 1994). The development of predictive validity of a premarital assessment instrument: The PREParation for marriage questionnaire. *Family Relations, 43,* 46–52.

Honaker, L. M. (1990, August). Recommended guidelines for computer equivalency research (or everything you should know about computer administration but will be disappointed if you ask). Paper presented at the annual convention of the American Psychological Association, Boston.

Hopkins, C. D., & Antes, R. L. (1979). *Classroom testing: Construction.* Itasca, IL: Peacock.

Horel, J. A., Keating, E. G., & Misantone, L. J. (1975). Partial Kluver-Bucy syndrome produced by destroying emporal neocortical amygdala. *Brain Research, 94,* 349–359.

Houck, J. E., & Hansen, J. C. (1972). Diagnostic interviewing. In R. H. Woody & J. D. Woody (Eds.). *Clinical assessment in counseling and psychotherapy.* Englewood Cliffs, NJ: Prentice Hall.

Howell, D. C. (1995). *Fundamental statistics for the behavioral sciences* (3rd ed.). Belmont, CA: Duxbury Press.

Hucker, C. O. (1978). *China to 1850: A short history.* Stanford, CA: Stanford University Press.

Hudiburg, R. A. (1990). Relating computer-associated stress to computerphobia. *Psychological Reports, 67,* 311–314.

Hudiburg, R. A. (1991). Relationship of computer hassles, somatic complaints, and daily hassles. *Psychological Reports, 69,* 1119–1122.

Hudiburg, R. A., & Jones, T. (1991). Psychology of computer use: 22. Validating a measure of computer-related stress. *Psychological Reports, 69,* 179–182.

Hudiburg, R. A., & Necessary, J. R., (1996). Psychology of computer use: 35. Differences in computer users' stress and self-concept in college personnel and students. *Psychological Reports, 78,* 931–937.

Hunt, M. (1993). *The story of psychology.* New York: Doubleday.

Hunter, J. E., & Hunter, R. F. (1984). Validity and utility of alternative predictors of job performance. *Psychological Bulletin, 96,* 72–98.

Igbaria, M., & Parasuraman, S. (1989). A path analytic study of individual characteristics, computer anxiety, and attitudes toward microcomputers. *Journal of Management, 15,* 373–388.

Jackson, D. N. (1986). *Computer-based personality testing.* Washington, DC: American Psychological Association, Scientific Affairs Office.

Jacobson, R. L. (1994, August 3). Computerized testing runs into trouble. *Chronicle of Higher Education,* A16–A17.

Jensen, A. R. (1969). How much can we boost IQ and scholastic achievement? *Harvard Educational Review, 39,* 1–123.

Johnson, B., *Performance Assessment Handbook: Volume 1, Portfolios and Socratic Seminars* (Princeton, NJ: Eye on Education, 1996).

Johnson, J. H., & Mihal, W. L. (1973). The performance of blacks and whites in computerized versus manual testing environments. *American Psychologist, 28,* 694–699.

Jones, J. W., & Youngblood, K. L. (1993). *Effect of a video-based test on the performance and retention of bank employees.* Paper presented at the eighth annual conference of the Society for Industrial and Organizational Psychology, San Francisco.

Journal of Assessment Center Technology. (July 1980). Supplement 1.

Kahn, R. L., and Cannell, C. F. (1957). *The dynamics of interviewing.* New York: John Wiley & Sons.

Kamin, L. J. (1995, February). Book review: Behind the curve. *Scientific American,* 99–103.

Kaplan Educational Centers. (1998). ACT or SAT: Which Gives You The Edge? [On-line]. Available on the World Wide Web: http://www.kaplan.com/view/article/0,1275,600,00.html.

Kaplan, R. M., & Saccuzzo, D. P. (1997). *Psychological testing: Principles, applications, and issues* (4th ed.). New York: Brooks/Cole.

Katzell, R. A., & Austin, J. T. (1992). From then to now: The development of industrial-organizational psychology in the United States. *Journal of Applied Psychology, 77,* 803–835.

Keith-Spiegel, P., Wittig, A. R., Perkins, D. V., Balogh, D. W., & Whitley, B. E., Jr. (1994). *The ethics of teaching: A casebook.* Muncie, IN: Ball State University.

Knobloch, H., Stevens, F., & Malone, A. F. (1980). *Manual of developmental diagnosis: The administration and interpretation of revised Gesell and Amatruda Developmental and Neurologic Examination.* Philadelphia: Harper & Row.

Knowles, E. F., & Bean, D. (1981). St. Louis fire captain selection: Litigation and defense of the selection procedures. *Journal of Assessment Center Technology, 4*(1), 9–22.

Kobak, K. A., Reynolds, W. M., & Greist, J. H. (1993). Development and validation of a computer-administered version of the Hamilton Anxiety Scale. *Psychological Assessment, 4,* 487–492.

Kosen D., Kitchen, C., Kochen, M., & Stodolsky, D. (1970). Psychological testing by computer: Effect on response bias. *Educational and Psychological Measurement, 30,* 803–810.

Kracke, E. A. (1963). Region, family, and individual in the examination system. In J. M. Menzel (Ed.), *The Chinese civil service: Career open to talent?* (pp. 67–75). Boston: D.S. Heath.

Krall, V. (1986). Projective play techniques. In A. I. Rabin (Ed.), *Projective techniques for adolescents and children* (pp. 264–278). New York: Springer.

Krug, S. E. & Johns, E. F. (eds). (1990). *Testing in counseling practice.* Hillsdale, NJ: Laurence Erlbaum Associates, Inc.

Kryspin, W. J., & Feldhusen, J. F. (1974). *Developing classroom tests: A guide for writing and evaluating test items.* Minneapolis: Burgess.

Kubiszyn, T., & Borich, G. (1996). *Educational testing and measurement: Classroom application and practice* (5th ed.). New York: HarperCollins.

Kuder, G. F., & Richardson, M. W. (1937). The theory of estimation of test reliability. *Psychometrika, 2,* 151–160.

Kuder, G. F., & Richardson, M. W. (1939). The calculation of test reliability coefficients based on the method of rational equivalence. *Journal of Educational Psychology, 30,* 681–687.

Lachar, D. (1974). *The MMPI: Clinical assessment and automated interpretation.* Los Angeles: Western Psychological Services.

Lankford, J. S., Bell, R. W., & Elias, J. W. (1994). Computerized versus standard personality measures: Equivalency, computer anxiety, and gender differences. *Computers in Human Behavior, 10*(4), 497–510.

Larry P v. Riles, 495 F. Supp. 926 (N. D. Cal. Oct 16, 1979) (No. C-71-2270 RFP).

La Rue, A. (1992). Adult development and aging. In A. E. Puente & R. J. McCaffrey (Eds.), *Handbook of neuropsychological assessment: A biopsychosocial perspective.* New York: Plenum Press.

Larzelere, R. E., Smith, G. L., Batenhorts, L. M., & Kelly, D. B. (1996, February). *Journal of the American Academy of Child and Adolescent Psychiatry, 35,* 166–172.

Lawshe, C. H. (1975). A quantitative approach to content validity. *Personnel Psychology, 28,* 563–575.

LeDoux, J. E., Thompson, M. E., Iadelcola, C., Tucker, L. W., & Reis, D. J. (1983). Local cerebral blood flow increases during auditory and emotional processing in the conscious rat. *Science, 221,* 576–578.

Lee, C., & Bobko, P. (1994). Self-efficacy beliefs: Comparison of five measures. *Journal of Applied Psychology, 79*(4), 364–369.

Liebert, R. M., & Spiegler, M. D. (1994). *Personality strategies and issues* (7th ed.). Pacific Grove, CA: Brooks/Cole.

Lilienfeld, S. O. (1993). Do "honesty" tests really measure honesty? *Skeptical Inquirer, 18,* 32–41.

Lilienfeld, S. O., Alliger, G., & Mitchell, K. (1995). Why integrity testing remains controversial. *American Psychologist, 50,* 457–458.

Lim, R. G., & Drasgow, F. (1990). Evaluation of two methods for estimating item response theory parameters when assessing differential item functioning. *Journal of Applied Psychology, 75,* 164–174.

Linn, R. (1982). Ability testing: Individual differences, prediction, and differential prediction.

Linn, R. L. (1990). Admissions testing: Recommended uses, validity, differential prediction, and coaching. *Applied Measurement in Education, 3,* 297–318.

Linn, R. L., & Drasgow, F. (1987). Implications of the Golden Rule settlement for test construction. *Educational Measurement: Issues & Practice, 6,* 13–17.

Lippmann, W. (1922a). A future for tests. *New Republic, 33,* 9–11.

Lippmann, W. (1922b). The mental age of Americans. *New Republic, 32,* 213–215.

Lippmann, W. (1922c). The mystery of the "A" men. *New Republic, 32,* 246–248.

Lippmann, W. (1922d). The reliability of intelligence tests. *New Republic, 32,* 275–277.

Lippmann, W. (1922e). Tests of hereditary intelligence. *New Republic, 32,* 328–330.

Longshore, D., Turner, S., & Stein, J. A. (1996). Self-control in a criminal sample: An examination of construct validity. *Criminology, 34*(2), 209–228.

Lyman, H. B. (1998). *Test scores: And what they mean* (6th ed.). Boston: Allyn & Bacon.

Maloney, M. P., & Ward, M. P. (1976). *Psychological assessment: A conceptual approach.* New York: Oxford University Press.

Maltby, L. L. (July 1990). Put performance to the test. *Personnel, 67,* 30–31.

Marks, P. A., & Seeman, W. (1963). *The actuarial description of abnormal personality.* Baltimore: Williams & Wilkins.

Marks, P. A., Seeman, W., & Haller, D. (1974). *The actuarial use of the MMPI with adolescents and adults.* Baltimore: Williams & Wilkins.

Martin, W. A. P. (1870). Competitive examinations in China. *North Atlantic Review, 111,* 62–77.

Matarazzo, J. D. (1986). Computerized clinical psychological test interpretations: Unvalidated plus all mean and no sigma. *American Psychologist, 41*(1), 14–24.

Matarazzo, J. D. (1990). Psychological assessment versus psychological testing: validation from Binet to the school, clinic, and courtroom. *American Psychologist, 45,* 999–1017.

McCrae, R. R., & Costa, P. T., Jr. (1997, May). Personality trait structure as a human universal. *American Psychologist, 52,* 509–516.

McIntire, S. A., Bucklan, M. A, & Scott, D. R. (1995). *The job analysis kit.* Odessa, FL: Psychological Assessment Resources.

Meehl, P. E. (1954) Clinical versus statistical prediction: A theoretical analysis and review of the evidence. Minneapolis: University of Minnesota Press.

Meglino, B. M., DeNisi, A. S., Youngblood, S. A., & Williams, K. J. (1988). Effects of realistic job previews: A comparison using an enhancement and a reduction preview. *Journal of Applied Psychology, 72,* 259–266.

Melchert, T. P., Hays, V. A., Wiljanen, L. M., & Kolocek, A. K. (1996, July/August). Testing models of counselor development with a measure of counseling self-efficacy. *Journal of Counseling and Development, 74,* 640–644.

Meyer, J. H., Woodard, P. G., & Suddick, D. E. (Spring 1994). The descriptive tests of mathematics skills: Predictive validity for an elementary mathematics concepts and structures course. *Educational and Psychological Measurement, 54,* 115–117.

Michael, W. B., & Smith, R. A. (1976). The development and preliminary validation of three forms of a self-concept measure emphasizing school-related activities. *Educational and Psychological Measurement, 38,* 527–535.

Michael, W. B., Smith, R. A., & Michael, J. J. (1989). *Dimensions of Self-Concept (DOSC): A technical manual* (rev.). San Diego: EDITS.

Miller, L. A., Mullin, P. A., & Herrmann, D. J. (1990). Memory processes in answering retrospective survey questions. *Proceedings of the International Symposium, MNEMO '90 on Human Memory Modelling and Simulation.* Varna, Bulgaria.

Miller, W. (1975). Psychological deficit in depression. *Psychological Bulletin, 82,* 238–260.

Millon, T. (1994). *Manual for the MCMI-III.* Minneapolis: National Computer Systems.

Morey, L. C. (1991). *Personalty Assessment Inventory.* Odessa FL: Psychological Assessment Resources.

Murphy, C. A., Coover, D., & Owen, S. V. (1989). Development and validation of the computer self-efficacy scale. *Educational and Psychological Measurement, 49,* 893–899.

Murphy, K. R., & Davidshofer, C. O. (1994). *Psychological testing: Principles and applications* (3rd ed.). Englewood Cliffs, NJ: Prentice Hall.

Murray, H. A. (1943). *Thematic apperception test.* Cambridge, MA: Harvard University Press.

National Association of School Psychologists. (1984). *Principles for professional ethics.* Washington, DC: Author.

National Association of School Psychologists. (1992). Principles for professional ethics. *Professional conduct manual,* pp. 1–23. Washington, DC: Author.

National Institute of Mental Health. (1993). *Learning disabilities* (No. 369-181/90240). Washington, DC: U.S. Government Printing Office.

Negy, C. & Synder, D. K. (1997). Ethnicity and acculturation: Assessing Mexican American Couples' Relationships using the Marital Satisfaction Inventory–Revised. *Psychological Assessment, 9* (4), 414-421.

Nevo, B. (1985). Face validity revisited. *Journal of Educational Measurement, 22,* 287–293.

Nevo, B. (1993). Face validity revisited. In B. Nevo & R. S. Jager (Eds.), *Educational and psychological testing: The test takers outlook* (p. 17–28). Gottingen (Germany): Hogrefe & Huber.

Nevo, B., & Sfez, J. (1985). Examinees' feedback questionnaires. *Assessment and Evaluation in Higher Education, 10,* 236–249.

Newberry, M. K., & Parish, T. S. (1987). Enhancement of attitudes toward handicapped children through social interactions. *The Journal of Social Psychology, 127*(1), 59–62.

Newman, P., & Sweet, J. (1986). The effects of clinical depression on the Luria-Nebraska Neuropsychological Battery. *International Journal of Clinical Neuropsychology, 7*(3), 109–114.

Nichols, D. S. (1992). Review of the Minnesota Multiphasic Personality Inventory–2. In J. J. Kramer & J. C. Conoley (Eds.), *The eleventh mental measurements yearbook.* Lincoln: University of Nebraska, Buros Institute of Mental Measurements.

Nunnally, J. (1978). *Psychometric theory.* New York: McGraw-Hill.

Ones, D. S., Viswesvaran, C., & Schmidt, F. L. (1993). Comprehensive meta-analysis of integrity test validities: Findings and implications for personnel selection and theories of job performance. *Journal of Applied Psychology, 78,* 679–703.

Orange County Public Schools, Educational Improvement Department, Assessment Office. (1997). *Let's Talk Testing* [Brochure]. Orlando, FL: Author.

Orsillo, S. M., & McCaffrey, R. J. (1992). In A. E. Puente & R. J. McCaffrey, (Eds.)., *Handbook of neuropsychological assessment: A biopsychosocial perspective.* New York: Plenum Press.

Osman, A., Barrios, F. X., Longnecker, J., & Osman, J. R. (1994, November). Validation of the inventory of college students' recent life experiences in an American college sample. *Journal of Clinical Psychology, 50,* 856–863.

Pajares, F., & Miller, M. D. (1995). Mathematics self-efficacy and mathematics performances: The need for specificity of assessment. *Journal of Counseling Psychology, 42,* 190–198.

Parish, T., & Taylor, J. (1978a). The Personal Attribute Inventory for Children: A report on its validity and reliability as a self-concept scale. *Educational and Psychological Measurement, 38,* 565–569.

Parish, T., & Taylor, J. (1978b). A further report on the validity and reliability of the Personal Attribute Inventory for Children. *Educational and Psychological Measurement, 38,* 1225–1228.

Parker, K. (1983). A meta-analysis of the reliability and validity of the Rorschach. *Journal of Personality Assessment, 42,* 227–231.

Paulson, P., and Paulson, F. (1991) Portfolios: Stories of knowing. In P. H. Dryer (Ed.). Claremont Reading Conference 55th Yearbook.

Piotrowski, Z. (1957). *Perceptanalysis.* New York: Macmillan.

Pirazzoli-t'Serstevens, M. (1982). *The Han Civilization of China.* Oxford: Phaidon.

Pond, M. (1927). Selective placement of metalworkers. *Journal of Personnel Research, 5,* 345–368, 405–417, 452–466.

Pope-Davis, D. B., & Twing, J. S. (1991). The effects of age, gender, and experience on measures of attitude regarding computers. *Computers in Human Behavior, 7,* 333–339.

Puente, A. E., & McCaffrey, R. J. (Eds.) (1992). *Handbook of neuropsychological assessment: A biopsychosocial perspective.* New York: Plenum Press.

Rabin, A. I. (1986). Concerning projective techniques. In A. I. Rabin & M. Haworth (Eds.), *Projective techniques for adolescents and children* (pp. 3–11). New York: Springer.

Ray, N. M., & Minch, R. P. (1990). Computer anxiety and alienation: Toward a definitive and parsimonious measure. *Human Factors, 32*(4), 477–491.

Rezmovic, V. (1977). The effects of computerized experimentation on response variance. *Behavior Research Methods and Instrumentation, 9,* 144–147.

Rodzinski, W. (1979). *A history of china.* Oxford: Pergamon Press.

Rogers, T. B. (1995). *The psychological testing enterprise: An introduction.* Pacific Grove, CA: Brooks/Cole.

Rorschach, H. (1921). *Psychodiagnostik.* Bern: Bircher.

Rosen, L. D., Sears, D. C., & Weil, M. M. (1987). Computerphobia. *Behavior Research Methods, Instruments, and Computers, 19*(2), 167–179.

Rosenfeld, P., Edwards, J. E., & Thomas, M. D. (Eds.). (1993). *Improving organizational surveys.* Newbury Park: Sage.

Rotter, J. B. (1966). Generalized expectancies for internal versus external control of reinforcement. *Psychological Monographs, 80,* 1–28.

Sabatelli, R. M. (1984). The marital comparison level index: A measure for assessing outcomes relative to expectations. *Journal of Marriage and the Family, 46,* 651–662.

Sacher, J., & Fletcher, J. D. (1978). Administering paper-and-pencil test by computer, or the medium is not always the message. In D. J. Weiss (Ed.), *Proceedings of the 1977 Computerized Adaptive Testing Conference.* Minneapolis: University of Minnesota, Department of Psychology.

Schmitt, N. (1996). Uses and abuses of coefficient alpha. *Psychological Assessment, 8*(4), 350–353.

Scott, W. D. (1915). The scientific selection of salesmen. *Advertising and Selling, 5,* 5–7.

Sharpley, C. F., & Ridgway, I. R. (1993). An evaluation of the effectiveness of self-efficacy as a predictor of trainees' counseling skills performance. *British Journal of Guidance and Counseling, 21,* 73–81.

Sherer, M., Maddux, J. E., Mercandante, B., Prentice-Dunn, S., Jacobs, B., & Rogers, R. W. (1982). The self-efficacy scale: Construction and validation. *Psychological Reports, 51,* 663–671.

Shore, M. F. (1972). Psychological testing. In R. H. Woody & J. D. Woody (Eds.), *Clinical assessment in counseling and psychotherapy.* Englewood Cliffs, NJ: Prentice Hall.

Sillup, S. (1992, May). Applicant screening cuts turnover costs. *Personnel Journal,* 115.

Skinner, H. A., & Allen, V. A. (1983). Does the computer make a difference? Computerized versus face-to-face versus self-report assessment of alcohol, drug, and tobacco use. *Journal of Consulting and Clinical Psychology, 51,* 267–275.

Smith, J. E., & Merchant, S. (1990). Using competency exams for evaluating training. *Training and Development Journal, 44,* 65–71.

Smither, R. D. (1994). *The psychology of work and human performance* (2nd ed.). New York: HarperCollins.

Society for Industrial and Organizational Psychology. (1987). *Principles for the validation and use of personnel selection procedures.* College Park, MD: Author.

Spanier, G. (1976). Measuring dyadic adjustment: New scales for assessing the quality of marriage and similar dyads. *Journal of Marriage and the Family, 38,* 15–28.

Spielberger, C. D. (1985). Assessment of state and trait anxiety: Conceptual and methodological issues. *Southern Psychologist, 2,* 6–16.

Stafford, J. E. (1998, Spring). ACT/SAT college survey. *Journal of College Admission,* No. 159, 8–13.

Stanton, M. (1989). Reporting what we think: The pollsters. *Occupational Outlook Quarterly, 33,* 12–19.

Stassen, H. H., Lykken, D. T., Propping, P., & Bomben, G. (1988). Genetic determination of the human EEG. *Human Genetics, 80,* 165–176.

Stevens, S. S. (1946). On the theory of scales of measurement. *Science, 103,* 677–680.

Stevens, S. S. (1951). Mathematics, measurement, and psychophysics. In S. S. Stevens (Ed.), *Handbook of experimental psychology.* New York: Wiley.

Stevens, S. S. (1961). The psychophysics of sensory function. In W. A. Rosenblith (Ed.), *Sensory communication.* New York: Wiley.

Strenta, A. C., & Elliott, R. (1987). Differential grading standards revisited. *Journal of Educational Measurement, 24,* 281–291.

Sudman, S., & Bradburn, N. M. (1982). *Asking questions.* San Francisco: Jossey-Bass.

Strong, E. K. (1927). *Vocational Interest Blank.* Sanford, CA: Stanford University Press.

Szajna, B. (1994, Winter). *Educational and Psychological Measurement, 54,* 926–934.

Tam, S. (1996). Self-efficacy as a predictor of computer skills learning outcomes of individuals with physical disabilities. *Journal of Psychology.* 130(1), 51–58.

Terwilliger, J. S. (1996). *Semantics, psychometrics, and assessment reform: A close look at authentic tests.* (Eric Document Reproduction Service No. ED 397123.).

Thorndike, R. M., Cunningham, G., Thorndike, R. L., & Hagen, E. (1991). *Measurement and evaluation in psychology and education.* New York: Macmillan.

Tipton, R. M., & Worthington, E. L., Jr. (1984). The measurement of generalized self-efficacy: A study of construct validity. *Journal of Personality Assessment, 48,* 545–548.

Tourangeau, R. (1984). Cognitive science and survey methods. In Jabine, T., Straf, M., Tanur, J., and Tourangeau, R. (Eds.). *Cognitive aspects of survey methodology: Building a bridge between disciplines* (pp. 73–199). Washington, DC: National Academy Press.

Turnage, J., & Greenis, J. (1994). *Individual differences in technology's users.* Unpublished manuscript.

Uniform guidelines on employee selection. (1978). *Federal Register, 43,* 38290–38315.

U.S. Congress, Office of Technology Assessment. (1990). *The use of integrity tests for preemployment screening.* OTA-SET-442. Washington, DC: U.S. Government Printing Office.

U.S. General Accounting Office, Program Evaluation and Methodology Division. (1986, July). *Developing and using questionnaires.* Transfer Paper 7. Washington, D.C.: Author.

Von Mayrhauser, R. T. (1987). The manager, the medic, and the mediator: The clash of professional psychological styles and the wartime origins of group mental testing. In M. M. Sokal (Ed.), *Psychological testing and American society.* New Brunswick, NJ: Rutgers University Press.

Wainer, H., & Steinberg, L. S. (1992 Fall). Sex differences in performance on the mathematics section of the Scholastic Aptitude Test: A bidirectional validity study. *Harvard Educational Review, 62*(3), 323–336.

Walker, E., Lucas, M., & Lewine, R. (1992). Schizophrenic disorders. In A. E. Puente & R. J. McCaffrey (Eds.), *Handbook of neuropsychological assessment: A biopsychosocial perspective.* New York: Plenum Press.

Walker, N. L. W., & Myrick, C. C. (1985). Ethical considerations in the use of computers in psychological testing and assessment. *Journal of School Psychology, 23,* 51–57.

Waller, N. G. (1995a). Review of the Beck Anxiety Inventory. In J. C. Conoley & J. H. C. Impara (Eds.), *The twelfth mental measurements yearbook.* Lincoln, NE: Buros Institute of Mental Measurements.

Waller, N. G. (1995b). Review of the Beck Depression Inventory (1993 revised). In J. C. Conoley & J. H. C. Impara, (Eds.), *The twelfth mental measurements yearbook.* Lincoln, NE: Buros Institute of Mental Measurements.

Watson, C. G., Detra, E., Kurt, L. F., Ewing, J. W., Gearhart, L. P., & DeMotts, J. R. (1996, September). *Journal of Clinical Psychology, 51,* (5), 676–684.

Watson, C. G., Thomas, D., & Anderson, P. E. D. (1992). Do computer-administered Minnesota Multiphasic Personality Inventories underestimate booklet-based scores? *Journal of Clinical Psychology, 48,* 744–748.

Weinberg, R., Gould, D., & Jackson, A. (1980). Effect of public and private efficacy expectations on competitive performance. *Journal of Sport Psychology, 2,* 340–349.

Weinberger, D. R., & Berman, K. E. (1988). Speculation on the meaning of cerebral metabolic hypofrontality in schizophrenia. *Schizophrenia Bulletin, 14,* 157–168.

Weinberger, D. R., Berman, K. E., & Zec, R. W. (1986). Physiologic dysfunction of lateral prefrontal cortex in schizophrenia. *Archives of General Psychiatry, 43,* 144–125.

Weiss, D. J. (1985). Adaptive testing by computer. *Journal of Consulting and Clinical Psychology, 53,* 774–789.

Weiss, R. I. L., & Heyman, R. E. (1990). Observation of marital interaction. In F. D. Fincham & T. N. Bradurty (Eds.), *The psychology of marriage: Basic issues and applications* (pp. 87–117). New York: Guilford Press.

Wertheimer, L. (1996, September 29). Mentors test: Can trips, treats boost scores? *Orlando Sentinel,* K3.

Wheeler, V. A., & Ladd, G. W. (1982). Assessment of children's self-efficacy for social interactions with peers. *Developmental Psychology, 18,* 795–805.

Wherry, R. J. (1931). A new formula for predicting shrinkage of the coefficient of multiple correlation. *Annuals of Mathematical Statistics, 2,* 440–457.

Whipple, G. M. (1910). *Manual of mental and physical tests.* Baltimore: Warwick & York.

Wigdor, A. K., (1990, Spring). Fairness in employment testing. *Issues in Science and Technology, 6*(3), 54.

Wiggins, G. P. (1993). *Assessing student performance: Exploring the purpose and limits of testing.* San Fransciso: Jossey-Bass.

Wiggins, J. S. (1973). *Personality and prediction: Principles of personality assessment.* Reading, MA: Addison-Wesley.

Wood, T. D. (1919). Report of committee on health problems in the schools. *National Education Association Proceedings and Addresses, 159*–160.

Woody, R. H. (1972). The counselor-therapist and clinical assessment. In R. H. Woody & J. D. Woody (Eds.), *Clinical assessment in counseling and psychotherapy.* Englewood Cliffs, NJ: Prentice Hall.

Worchel, F. F. & Dupree, J. L. (1990). Projective storytelling techniques. In C. R. Reynolds & R. W. Kamphaus (eds.), *Handbook of psychological and educational assessment of children: Personality, behavior, & context* (pp. 70–88). New York: Guilford Press.

Yerkes, R. M. (1921). Psychological examining in the United States Army. *Memoirs of the National Academy of Sciences, 15,* 91–144.

Young, J. W. (1994, Winter). Differential prediction of college grades by gender and by ethnicity: A replication study. *Educational and Psychological Measurement, 54,* 1022–1029.

Zimmerman, D. W., Zumbo, B. D. & Lalonde, C. (1993). Coefficient alpha as an estimate of test reliability under violation of two assumptions. *Educational and Psychological Measurement, 53,* 33–49.

Credits

In Greater Depth 12.2, p. 253

Fink, Arlene, *The Survey Handbook,* © 1995 by Arlene Fink. Reprinted by Permission of Sage Publications, Inc.

Inadequate testing knowledge; p. 276–280

Inadequate Testing Knowledge of Classroom Teachers, Examples of Dialogues; from T. Kubiszyn and G. Borich, "Educational Testing and Measurement: Classroom Application and Practice," 1996. *Educational Testing and Measurement: Classroom Application and Practice,* 5/e. Copyright © 1996 by HarperCollins Publishers. All rights reserved.

Figure 13.1 Sample Stanford Achievement Test, p. 285

The normative information used to prepare this report is from the *Stanford Achievement Test, Eighth Edition.* Copyright © 1989 by the Psychological Corporation. Used with permission. The test scoring package is TestPak, purchased and licensed from the Psychological Corporation and used under licensed agreement by Orange County Public Schools. Score report reprinted here with permission.

Figure 13.2 Letter to parents accompanying OCAT score report, p. 286

The Orange Curriculum–Aligned Test (OCAT). "Let's Talk Testing" produced by Orange County Public Schools, Orlando, Florida. All rights reserved.

Figure 13.3 Student performance report, p. 287

The OCAT reports are produced by Orange County Public Schools using TestMate™ a registered trademark of the McGraw-Hill Companies, Inc.

Figure 14.3, p. 314

Photo Credits

Page 29, 34, 59, 69, 109, 210, 212, 276, 292: © PhotoDisc, Inc.

Page 142. Reprinted by permission of Wilson Learning Corporation

Page 79: © Dean Hybl, Sports Information Director, Department of Physical Education and Athletics, Rollins College

Figure 14.2: Picture from the TAT, Henry A. Murray, Cambridge, Harvard University Press, © 1943, by the President and Fellows of Harvard College, © 1971 Henry A. Murray.

Page 315: © David Fraser Photo Library

Author Index

Subject Index